When Success
betrays Happiness

a journey into the human mind

Pierre van der Spuy

When Success *betrays* Happiness:
A Journey into the Human Mind
Pierre van der Spuy

www.behindthemaskofsuccess.com

ISBN: 9781615843756
Registration number: TXU001591337
Service Request: 1-123009441
Copyright © 2009 Pierre van der Spuy

Illustration, Cover design, and layout:
Christina Antonakos-Wallace

To Dr. James Masterson,
for being the Guardian of my Real Self.

With special thanks to all the van der Spuys, especially Andre.

Contents

Section IV: Becoming a Success Addict

Section V: On Becoming Humane and Happy

Epilogue: No Hollywood Ending *403*

Prologue

How Success Betrayed Me

One afternoon while I was living in London, my brother Andre and I took some friends for a Sunday-afternoon stroll down Oxford Street. We chatted companionably until I heard Andre ask, "Why do you always need to be a shoulder ahead of us?"

I turned around. "Are you speaking to me?"

Andre explained that every time the group walked faster, I would increase my pace to ensure that I stayed a shoulder ahead of everyone else. When the group slowed down, I would too, but I would still maintain my lead. I realized that Andre was right. I had a relentless drive to lead at all times, and at all costs, even on a leisurely walk. Within minutes of his observation, I was back to impressing, pleasing and charming the group. My non-conscious drive to be number one trumped my conscious knowledge.

The next year, I decided to spend my vacation on a kibbutz in Israel. The only thing I had to do to earn my keep was to take a large coil of wire, feed it through a machine and then make small bundles ready for shipment. Whether I made one or a thousand bundles was of no consequence—there would be no rewards or punishment. But within hours of beginning my task, I had set up a new process to maximize the efficiency of the machine. The moment I achieved my goal, I became bored with the job.

I started to wonder: Why do I always run around as if someone will punish me if I don't perform my best? Why can't I enjoy a relaxed cup of coffee in the morning? Why does my brain shout, "Perform, perform, perform!" from the moment I open my eyes?

For as long as I can remember, I have been obsessed with success. At every school and university I attended in South Africa, I was elected student president. I excelled athletically and twice played state-level rugby. I even experienced a few moments of fame on national television as a student leader involved in national politics. I graduated medical school first in my class. Later, I practiced medicine in Canada and England, before earning an MBA from Yale and becoming a strategic management consultant in Manhattan. I made a lot of money and dated young, gorgeous women.

Before long, I fell in love with the woman of my dreams. I maintained my status as the perfect son and an A-list people pleaser. But every time I achieved a new goal, I felt anxious and empty until I had established yet another extraordinary objective. Never did my success bring me lasting self-esteem, love or peace of mind. Never did I feel as if my life had meaning or passion. Success betrayed me.

So I began to study every self-help book I could find. I tried trendy methods of meditation and visualization. I even tried old-fashioned positive thinking. When this failed, I turned to psychiatry and clinical psychology textbooks. Ultimately, nothing I studied helped me in the moments when I needed it most.

Filled with despair, I realized I needed professional help.

Through many serendipitous events, I found Dr. James Masterson, a world-renowned psychiatrist who has devoted his career to people who sacrifice their personal happiness for success and forfeit their humanity for power—people like me.

For nearly ten years, I lived like a hermit amongst the wealth, beauty and excesses of Manhattan as I faced my non-conscious inner demons for the first time in my life. With Dr. Masterson's help, I explored new career interests and studied the science behind what drives those of us who are so obsessed with success.

My interest in human behavior led me to become an executive recruiter, a career that allowed me to meet and assess many senior executives in corporate America. Later, I became an executive coach and trained other success-addicted business leaders to improve their interpersonal skills.

I also began to develop my creativity. I took poetry, creative writing, painting, photography and opera appreciation classes. One night, on a whim, I decided to see a Broadway play. As I left, a little voice whispered, "You are a playwright." I laughed, but knowing that I had nothing to lose, I decided to give it a try. My writing teachers told me that my plays had plot, but no character development. So I decided to take acting classes to improve my writing. After three years of telling acting teachers and students that I was a playwright trying to improve my writing, I finally reached a moment when it dawned on me: "I am both playwright and an actor." In January 2005, I produced, directed and starred in *Anton*, a play I wrote on the life of the doctor-turned-playwright Anton Chekhov. Now, when people ask me who I am, I say, "I am an actor, writer and director."

My journey from a perfectionist, success-addicted boy to a man who struggles to love and engage authentically has significantly shifted the course of my life. My hours in therapy and the years that I spent studying the latest research in neuroscience, child development theories, positive psychology and clinical psychiatry have given me insight into how my non-conscious mind made me the way I was. I still struggle with the old demons that fueled my obsession with success. But now I am more able to enjoy small miracles, even if for only a few minutes each day. After spending so much of my life feeling bad about myself, daydreaming about fame, power and perfect relationships and fretting about the past, these small miracles help to keep me on the path toward a happier and more humane life.

How We Define Success

Europeans often delight in pointing out that the obsession with success is "an American thing." It isn't. First of all, I am from South Africa, a country at the other end of the globe from the United States. Secondly, across space and time, people have always found criteria for classifying others as *successful* or the reverse. All that differs from culture to culture are the ways in which success is defined.

It doesn't take long to understand different ideals of success, even if they are far removed from our own. Whom does the hairdresser in a small town gossip about? In a foreign country, whom do the children idolize? Whom do mothers want their children to marry? Whom do young men and women compare themselves to? Whom do people elect as their leaders? Whose are the faces on the covers of popular magazines?

I have had the fortune to work, live and travel in numerous countries. Growing up in apartheid South Africa, my version of success was political and religious power. But when I became a medical doctor in a rural area of the country, I saw that my definition of success was not shared by my patients. For them, royalty, fat wives and large herds of cattle were the pinnacle of success. When I moved to England, I discovered that ideals revolving around old money and an Oxbridge education still force many people to affect upper-class accents. On a tour of France, I discovered that much of Continental Europe still values old family names, "sophistication" and academic accomplishments.

Despite the tenacity of traditional measures of success, we see that American consumerist values have begun to make headway into every society on earth. Today South Africa—despite being a developing country at the geographical bottom of impoverished Africa—can lay dubious claim to anorexic 16-year-olds, middle-aged men in luxury cars and women who love nothing more than to compare the designer labels on each other's clothes. In France, modern mega stores on the historic Champs-Elysées cater to the material pleasures of Frenchmen who still prefer to think of themselves as enlightened intellectuals. My friends and colleagues assure me that the same holds true in Sydney, Hong Kong, Shanghai, Moscow, Tokyo, Caracas and Buenos Aires.

Today, thanks to movies, television, the Internet and other media, the rich and famous, bold and beautiful, smart and sassy, powerful and presidential, are symbols of success everywhere.

Success of Our Success

Prior to the credit crisis and ensuing recession, the United States was more successful than any other nation in the history of the world. Since the 1960s, the inflation-adjusted income per capita has tripled. Today, more Americans have college degrees than ever before. An obsession with beauty products, diets, fashion and cosmetic surgery have made Americans more focused on their appearance than any other generation in history. Thanks to video cameras, YouTube and social networking sites like Facebook, anybody can enjoy his or her 15 minutes of fame.

But what has been the success of our success?

To answer this question, we need to understand what people expect that success will bring to their lives. Personally, I slaved to attain success for three reasons: I was convinced that success leads to happiness. I also believed that the most successful people in our society were the best examples of humanity—those at the top of the food chain deserved all the resources in this life and a five-star reception with champagne and caviar in the next. Most importantly, I honestly believed that success would bring meaning to my life. When I die, I thought, my success will have justified why I have lived.

But despite all of their successes prior to the financial crisis, many Americans actually experienced a drop in happiness. Statistics show that the rates of depression, loneliness, obesity, anorexia and children struggling with social skills (e.g., Asperger's syndrome and ADHD) have increased significantly. Suicide among teenagers and young adults has increased threefold; suicide among baby boomers is also increasing. The percentage of people who claim to be happy has remained stuck at a dismal 30 percent. Success seems to have little affect on our happiness. In fact, recent studies indicate that incomes in excess of about $50,000 per year cease to have an affect on Americans' happiness levels.

After ten years of therapy, I know that the times when I think that I am a better human than other people are really the times when I feel the most terrible about myself. I also know that during those moments, I do not embody full human consciousness. I may *seem* human, but I am not acting humanely. Our successful leaders are certainly not the best examples of humanity. If they were, how would it have been possible for us to do so much harm to our planet and ignore our human legacy? Can people really believe that they are the best examples of humanity just because they are paid more or are prettier than their neighbors?

There are no statistics that measure the correlation between success and a life of meaning, but the wisdom of the ages prevails. From Icarus and Midas to *Citizen Kane* and Bernard Madoff, the moral is clear: Fly too high, and you'll end lonely, empty and in despair. In my own life, I have found that success has never brought me meaning or self-esteem. If anything, the more I accomplished, the more lost I felt. My story has been echoed by many overachievers whom I have met from all over the world. Success does not bring meaning. If anything, it distracts us from asking the tough questions about what makes us human and why we are here.

Universality of Happiness

During my travels, I have witnessed happiness in people talking rugby around a braai in South Africa, discussing philosophy around a pot-roast in England, analyzing ice hockey games over barbequed burgers in Canada, arguing about movies around foie gras in France and screaming for the New York Giants around a turkey on Thanksgiving Day. People from every culture enjoy group gatherings, often centered around a table of food. Everywhere, family and friends are important.

And in every country I've visited, I have discovered a few individuals who truly are passionate about what they do. Success cannot bring us happiness, but being successful does not necessarily spell unhappiness. In South Africa, I was taught by a brilliant professor of cardiology, who, unbeknownst to his friends, happily spent hours a week caring for the elderly and destitute. In America, I had a client—a successful executive—whose love for his family, his employees, cooking and life was always evident.

To me it is clear: Success is cultural, happiness is universal.

Our Culture

So why is the world so obsessed with success? Why do 81 percent of younger generations believe that getting rich is one of the main life goals for their generation, a significant increase compared to older generations? Why are there people in every city, village and town all over the world who are anxious about their comparative lack of success? Why do they sit up for hours with friends and family and say, "If only I was rich" or "If only I was pretty"? Why do people, whether they have it all or aspire to it, breathe success into their nostrils from their first yawn in the morning until they go to sleep at night.

A culture hinges on who we aspire to become and how we raise our children. In our modern culture, many of our role models are the richest, prettiest or most famous. As our leaders and celebrities, they are our inspiration. But many of them are successful because they must be successful. Without success and admiration, their true inner struggles and unhappiness will surface, beating them into pulp. Driven by their fear of failure and craving admiration, they often reach the top of the ladder or the center of the spotlight, from where they tell us what will make us happy. And we believe them.

As our culture has changed, we have changed the way we raise our children. On the one side, there are parents who view their children as status objects: dressing them in high-end clothing and fighting tooth and nail for spots in the best kindergartens. On the other side, there are parents who have replaced parenting with pleasure: indulging their youngsters with potato chips, soda, video games, unlimited television, the latest toys. Good parenting is now seen as placing the child's need above all else. The impact of excessive pleasure and admiration on a child's developing brain is enormous and the long-term impact on a child-turned-adult's happiness and humanity is devastating.

When Success Betrays Happiness: The Goals

By delving into the fields of neuroscience, child development studies, positive psychology and clinical psychiatry, this book investigates five key questions: What does make us happy? How do parents nurture happy children? Why does success fail to make us happy? Why are our culture and our leaders so obsessed with success if it continues to fail us so miserably? How do societies and individuals cure the addiction to success?

Section I

A Meaningful Life

Chapter 1

Searching Our Brains for Happiness

The mask of my success fell from my face for the first time late one Friday night, nine months after I started my new career as a management consultant in Manhattan. Earlier that evening, I had watched *Goodwill Hunting*, a feel-good Hollywood movie. Everyone left the theater with big smiles on their faces; I felt as if I had looked death in the face. I stumbled back home, my eyes never leaving the pavement. As much as I wanted to be alone, solitude terrified me.

In my Upper East Side apartment, I drank a few beers in an attempt to lift my spirits. But after the initial buzz wore off, my mood darkened even more. I prescribed myself sleep, but my revved-up brain had no interest in rest. Instead, question after question pounded through my mind in a loop: What do you want to do with your life? Why can't you find love? When I was unable to answer these questions, I became filled with self-loathing: You're useless. An idiot. You'll never find happiness.

Philosophers—from Plato and Aristotle to Mill, Locke and Freud—tell us that our need for happiness is natural. "All humans want to become happy and remain so," Freud said. Here in America, Thomas Jefferson went one step further. Taking his cue from Enlightenment philosophers, he chose to make "the pursuit of happiness" an inalienable right rather than "the pursuit of property"—his original choice. His selection of words gives the impression that happiness is a diamond hidden deep in the earth and all we need to do is dig hard enough until we find the diamond, retire and live happily ever after.

I believed that happiness was a diamond that could be mine for the taking. For most of my life, I fantasized about an event that would miraculously transform my life—a great accomplishment, a perfect love, worldwide fame. But my dark night of the soul revealed that all my achievements had done nothing to bring me happiness. All the little diamonds in my pocket that I had worked so hard for were incapable of giving my life meaning.

So, at the end of the day, what does bring happiness to our lives?

As a child during World War II, Mihaly Csikszentmihalyi, renowned positive psychologist and former head of psychology at the University of Chicago, witnessed the best and the worse of humanity. He saw that many people whom society had admired before the war became utterly helpless and despondent in the face of adversity, while others, whom society barely noticed, maintained purpose and good cheer.

To understand this contradiction, Csikszentmihalyi has devoted his life to understanding the human condition and what is worth striving for. Of the best of humanity, he writes,

> These are people who, regardless of their material conditions, have been able to improve the quality of their lives, who are satisfied and who have a way of making those around them also a bit more happy. Such individuals lead vigorous lives, are open to a variety of experiences, keep on learning until the day they die and have strong ties and commitments to other people and the environment in which they live. They enjoy whatever they do, even if tedious or difficult; they are hardly ever bored and they can take in stride anything that comes their way. Perhaps their greatest strength is that they are in control of their lives.

The best of humanity do not pursue happiness by chasing material success; they bring their happiness to the circumstances of their lives. They know there is no diamond to be found, no miracle solution, only the happiness within that can reflect light onto the confusion of the outer world.

Walking on a footpath next to the sea at Onrus, a small resort town in South Africa, I saw words written on a tile, "The best of humanity do not wait for the storm to pass; they dance in the rain."

Believing is Seeing

But how do the best of humanity manage to dance in the rain? How can you look at the chaos of a massive tragedy, such as World War II, and feel as if you have control over your destiny? How can you not only be happy, but also make those around you happier? How do you stare the worst of humanity in the face and still have hope?

If being happy in the face of war is one mystery, then being unhappy when the world is safe and prosperous is another. I have had a life of unusual privilege and luck. I have never had a day's hunger, a debilitating disease or severe trauma. I have traveled the world and studied at two respected universities. Over the past decade, I have lived in New York City, a gilded age in the metropolis's history. Manhattan has been safe, prosperous, fun, filled with opportunities and packed with beautiful people. So why did I live like a hermit, stuck in my apartment, struggling with loneliness, depression and thoughts of suicide? Why could all my hard work and success not make me happy? Why couldn't I snap out of my negative mood?

The solution to this paradox is thousands of years old: "It's not things that trouble us, but the views we take of them," said Epictetus in the first century.

A person with happy views about life can look at the devastation of World War II and manage to find points of beauty among the heap of rubble. A person with negative beliefs about life can look at all the opportunities that New York City has to offer and still feel that life is unbearable. To be happy, we must learn to change how we view what happens to us.

Our Filters of Life

Evolutionary biologists and neuroscientists tell us that we mammals, unlike reptiles, can learn from our past experiences—a major advantage. Where reptiles rely on their instincts to guide them, we as mammals have memories of past experiences to steer us. Our brains are constantly sorting our experiences through the lens of our memories in an attempt to reconcile them with past experiences. Our memories filter data from our five senses before passing them along to another part of the brain, which creates our conscious reality.

Muddy water poured through a clean filter gives pure water. But if pure water is poured through a contaminated filter, it tastes awful and makes us ill. Similarly, happy memories form a happy filter that creates a happy reality; negative memories form a negative filter that creates a negative reality.

Years ago my brother Francois and I joined in Manhattan's annual Halloween Parade—an over-the-top celebration of the bizarre and creative. We had barely started walking when a television crew came over to interview me. The bright lights felt like lasers and it seemed as if the whole world was watching me parade down Sixth Avenue in a foolish monk's outfit. "This is not what responsible citizens do," I admonished myself. "You are supposed to be a man of status. A doctor." Instead of being filled with life, joy and exuberance for being part of such a wonderful parade on a perfect autumn night, I was overcome with guilt, shame and fear. In return, I started to ridicule the parade as childish and a waste of taxpayers' money. At that moment, the best lawyer in the country could not have convinced me otherwise.

Research shows that humans only scan the world for enough evidence to support our existing point of view. If we find a few data points to reinforce our experience, we stop questioning—our assumptions have been affirmed. If evidence demonstrates that our reality is negative or harmful, we write it off. If people disagree with us about our views, we either believe that these people do not have all the facts at their disposal or that they are biased. Psychologists call this naïve realism. Once our brain forms our reality, it goes out of its way to keep reminding us that our view of the world is the truth and nothing but the truth.

The best of humanity can be resilient even in the face of tragedy because they possess happy filters that make them see the world as a fundamentally happy place. Once they are happy, they only need a few data points to keep their positive outlook in tact. My years of struggle, despite all the opportunities I had, proves that I had negative views about life and only need a small amount of confirmation to keep my life in darkness. If your filter is dirty, all your accomplishments, possessions and relationships will look like an outhouse.

Understanding that our happiness does not depend on how we look, what we achieve or what we possess in life, but rather how we view what we have, allows us to have hope. To be happy, we need to change the memories that comprise our filters.

Our Brain's Rewards

The human brain works mysteriously. Over millions of years, it has developed a regimen of activities that we must accomplish every day in order to ensure our survival. We do these tasks without conscious thought and only because our brain rewards us for completing them and punishes us if we do not. Like a carrot dangled before a donkey, our brain uses rewards to encourage us. For example, you work hard and forget to eat. But your body needs energy, so your brain makes your stomach growl or sends an image of pasta to your mind. Now you consciously start to feel hungry. You prepare some food to eat and after the meal, the brain says, "Thanks, mate!" and rewards you with a sense of pleasure. This reward is important because the brain wants to make sure you listen to it in the future. While we are usually unaware of it, the truth is that we only do things in life because our brain rewards us for doing them.

Pleasure, admiration and happiness are the three primary carrots that our brain uses to encourage us. In our modern world, we often confuse the three. I used to think that when I was sitting at a bar drinking my third beer or having sex with a pretty one-night-stand or eating a hamburger and chips, I was happy. But I was not. I was experiencing pleasure. Similarly, when I made it to the top of the class or earned a big bonus or was envied for taking a crowned beauty to a ball, I thought that I felt happy. Actually, I was experiencing the feeling of being admired.

Recently, I visited my family back in South Africa. I played golf with my brothers, whom I deeply care for, went horseback riding, threw a party for friends and family, dine-and-danced and visited with old friends. I gave a speech on the futility of chasing success; appeared on a radio talk show; even enjoyed a holiday romance with a wonderful woman. During these moments, I was fully engaged with life, people and activities that I enjoy. And this time, I truly felt happy.

I heard happiness expressed best by a young boy on the day of Barack Obama's inauguration. When asked how he felt to see an African-American president, the boy, also African American, said, "I feel full."

Pleasure and admiration are rewards for taking from the world; happiness comes when we deeply, intimately and vulnerably relate to the world, others and ourselves. When we allow the world in, we feel alive and full.

There are other differences too. Stripped from all its hype, happiness, unlike pleasure and admiration, is one of eight primary emotions. Emotions comprise a complex system of information organization, which is crucial for survival, communication and problem solving. They are a thousand times more powerful than intellect—and a million times more informative than pleasure or admiration.

But like all emotions, happiness is fleeting.

A Happy Mood

I used to be convinced that one day I would attain a level of existence in which I felt happy all of the time and be forever free from negative emotions, such as anger, sadness and fear. I felt really surprised to discover that even the best of humanity do not experience the emotion of happiness every second of the day—in fact, they too feel sad and angry on occasion. The best of humanity appreciate that life is not a blissful paradise and that no one is immune to the pains and unfairness of life. They also know that all emotions are essential for living a full life. So, they feel everything that life throws at them, but they never try to hold their emotions captive, not even happiness. They appreciate, manage and learn from every emotion.

What they do enjoy is the ability to recover from life's knocks and return to a baseline of happiness that is significantly higher than most people's. The idea that we all have a set happiness point or mood that we return to is well researched. Studies show that whether people win the lottery, become paraplegic, marry or have children, the short-term change in their happiness is short lived and they eventually return to the same level of happiness they had before fortune or fate struck.

While possessing a happy filter cannot guarantee a life free from pain and tears, it does allow us to have a happy mood that we can return to time and again.

The Human Animal

I've always loved studying the brain. When I began my search for meaning, I intuitively knew that the brain would hold the key to the many big questions I had about my life and about life in general. At medical school, I was taught that the brain comprises the brainstem, cerebellum and cerebrum, with the latter divided into the left and right hemispheres. When it comes to understanding how the brain determines our behavior and our consciousness, the work of renowned neurologist Dr. Paul D. MacLean made the most sense to me. Dr. MacLean has shown that, as animals evolved, the brain did not simply enlarge over time like an expanding balloon. Each new brain has added to—but not replaced—the previous brains. Today, our brain consists of four different brains: the reptilian brain, the mammalian brain, the primate brain and the human brain.

The automobile offers us a good analogy. The best cars today still have the basic design of the Ford Model T first developed in 1908. Mid-century, the car was changed to increase fuel efficiency and comfort without changing the idea that a car has four wheels, two axles and a steering wheel. Today, we have added computers to increase safety and comfort. Every stage of development was essential in the design of the modern car, but every stage added to the original design.

For the sake of simplicity, let's divide the brain in two parts: the animal brain (compromising the reptilian, mammalian and primate brains) and the human brain.

The first and foremost goal of our animal brain is to help our genes survive. Over millions of years, our animal brains have been finely tuned to seek food and shelter, to procreate and to help us to flee or fight attackers. To ensure that we persist with these survival activities, our animal brain rewards us with pleasure. Since pleasure signifies success at survival, our animal brain is always seeking more and more pleasure—and sooner rather than later. In the animal brain's view, the more activities we do to bring pleasure, the more our chances for survival increase. Our animal brain is greedy, easily bored, hedonistic and very selfish.

Our animal brain also tells us that life is a zero-sum game: When one person wins, another loses. When we succeed in moving up the ladder, our animal brain rewards us with a sense of admiration, one of nature's most powerful drugs. When we fail or lose our standing, our animal brain punishes us with shame.

Our Human Brain and Our Humanity

Years ago, I cut out all meat, sex, alcohol and swearing from my life. Giving up all these earthly pleasures made me believe I was more human—and *at least* a touch closer to God—than everybody else. Today I know that I was really trying to compensate for my inner chaos by controlling my external behavior.

My attempt to define what it means to be human and then mandating that it was the definition for all to follow is, in fact, very common. Over the centuries, our leaders—either in the name of gods, God, politics, science or industry—have commanded us to follow their vision of what it means to be human. Our willingness to trust them has caused millions of people to die in war or genocide, or to live like scared animals in psychological cages. We are no different today. All that has changed is the message: To be the best of humanity, be rich and famous, bold and beautiful, smart and sassy.

During my medical studies, I spent many hours studying the Diagnostic and Statistical Manual of Mental Disorders, commonly known as the DSM. This manual, created by the American Psychiatric Association, allows for the reliable diagnosis of mental disorders. With my interest in human behavior, I enjoyed memorizing all the criteria for different conditions. In my final year, examiners could have interrogated me on any mental illness and I would have had an answer.

But one question would have dumbfounded me: What is normal mental behavior?

Fortunately, over the last 20 years, science has stepped up to the challenge of defining what exactly it means to be human. Today three different fields of study— positive psychology, neuroscience and clinical psychiatry—provide us with answers based on fact, rather than movies, fear or superstition.

A few years ago, a group of prominent psychologists set out to revise the DSM and in the process created the field called positive psychology. For three years, they searched for all the virtues that humanity has celebrated across space and time. They read Aristotle, Plato, Aquinas, Augustine, the Bible, the Talmud, Confucius, Buddha, Lao-Tze, Bushido, the Koran. They concluded that temperance, wisdom and knowledge, justice, courage, love and humanity and transcendence are six virtues at the core of our humanity.

From the late 1930s, Harvard professor George Valliant ran two rigorous psychological studies to determine what virtues or "mature defenses" lead to joy in living, marital satisfaction and a subjective sense of physical health. His research suggests that the best of us non-consciously respond to pain, conflict and uncertainty with altruism, humor, the ability to postpone attention to an impulse or conflict, future-mindedness (planning ahead to avoid future pain) and sublimation (putting unwanted feelings into culturally useful activities, such as art, inventions and sport). The best of us can keep going when the going gets tough.

Using brain-imaging to understand how the human brain works, neuroscientists discovered that our human brain enables us to think about the future, commit to long-term goals, focus our attention, learn from mistakes, be compassionate and empathetic, have consciousness and exercise free will. When the human brain is wrongly wired, we struggle to show even a single human virtue.

Dr. Daniel Amen, a clinical neuroscientist and psychiatrist, specializes in brain-imaging. "When I meet a person whose brain works right, I am likely to see someone with a prosperous, fulfilled, loving and connected life," he writes. "When I treat someone whose brain does not work right, more often than not the history I take reveals a life that is associated with struggle, pain, isolation and failure."

Upon hearing this, a smart friend asked, "Don't we think with our brain, but feel with our heart? Aren't we both our hearts and our minds?"

The brain uses our bodies to make us aware of emotions. We may have heartache or butterflies in the stomach, but it is our brain telling us that we need to seek care from others or that we need to prepare ourselves for something exciting.

We are our brain and our brain is us.

Happiness and our Human Brain

Tuesdays with Morrie, one of the best-selling memoirs in history, tells the story of Morrie Schwartz, a popular sociology professor at Brandeis University, who, after being diagnosed with Lou Gehrig's disease, spent time reflected on his life and coming death. If we evaluate him by our six essential virtues, Morrie was a fine example of what it means to be human. Perhaps not surprisingly, he was also very happy. It was no fluke that one of the best examples of humanity also enjoyed a happy mood, even while experiencing many painful emotions as he died from a slow and painful disease. Research shows that happy people are kinder and more altruistic than others and that people who give more than they take are on average happier than others. Our happiness, humanity and human brain are tightly linked. We have gotten warmer in our search for discovering what tasks bring us happiness and a happier filter.

The research on how and where the human brain processes happiness is still in its infancy, but a few studies give us some clues. Brain scans show that people who have a healthy left human brain—the area in charge of language, logic and linear thinking—have a positive outlook and approach life with happiness and zest.

Since most of us are products of an educational system that stresses our left-brain abilities, we are relieved to hear the left-brain is so closely tied to our happiness. But we ought to be concerned for two reasons: First, we may know overachievers with intimidating IQs and backpacks filled with elite degrees who are the most miserable people on earth and who struggle to show a single human virtue, even while on exotic vacations. Second, we are not searching for the part of the brain that is in charge of our mood, our long-term view of life. We are searching for that part of the brain that is in charge of the short-term reward of emotional happiness.

Dr. Mark George from the National Institute of Mental Health did just that. He observed that when people experience the emotion of happiness, their right human brain and the temporal-parietal area of the cortex (which controls our memories and orientation in space) is involved. Our right human brain orchestrates the emotion that we call happiness. It also harbors the center of the self.

For the longest time, the idea of the self seemed just fluff to me. After all, the self has been around since Socrates stated, "Know thy self"; couldn't this archaic term be another thinker's version of "The world is flat"? In recent decades, self-help books and grandiose self-help gurus have given the self a negative rap. But I have come to realize that understanding the self is crucial to understanding humanity and my struggle for happiness. Finally, neuroscience convinced me to take the concept of the self seriously.

At the University of Zurich, researchers asked participants to take part in the "ultimatum game." Participant A must divide $20 with Participant B. Participant B must then decide if he wants to accept the offer. If Participant B rejects the offer, both lose. Participant A, wanting to pocket as much money as possible, typically leaves the least amount of money on the table that he believes Participant B will accept.

When mentally healthy people are in the role of Participant B, they typically refuse offers of $4 or less. They would rather receive nothing than have their sense of self insulted by such a ridiculously low sum. But when neuroscientists suppressed the activity of the right human brain, Participants B accepted all offers. In these situations, they argued that any money is better than no money; who cares about being insulted? Without the right human brain, all of life's decisions became objective cost/benefit assessments. Without the right human brain, we have no sense of self and self-worth.

So the self is no airy-fairy concept: Without one we would think like baboons. (Many people confuse the self with the ego, false self or being selfish. To minimize the confusion, I will use the term Real Self to describe a strong healthy self.)

The Real Self

Throughout my life, I was tormented by the big questions: Who am I? What is my calling? Who will I love and marry? What is my purpose in this life? How do I feel good enough about myself? How to have courage to persevere when life knocks me around?

Today I know why I struggled with these questions. When I asked the existential questions of life, I had no Real Self to whisper the answers.

My psychiatrist, Dr. James Masterson, a professor of psychiatry at Cornell University and a preeminent researcher on the self, writes that somebody with a healthy Real Self "recognizes that he is somebody who lives, works and loves in a certain way, and who takes for granted that the somebody is a worthwhile, competent human being, not immune to the sufferings of life, but capable of withstanding them and growing because of them."

Animals, lacking language, have at best a limited awareness of their existence. Even though some evolved animals can reason, and some like the higher apes and dolphins can recognize their own image in a mirror, we as humans spend significantly more time trying to make sense of our selves. Thanks to language we can create a sense that we exist and are an entity who works and loves in a unique way. We can reflect on our dreams and aspirations, why we behave the way we do and why we are alive. Thanks to the Real Self, we can have self-image, self-esteem, self-confidence, self-knowledge and self-worth.

The Real Self is that little voice inside our heads that advises us on what to do, when and how to do it. The Real Self soothes us when we fail and congratulates us when we succeed. The Real Self is our company when we are alone and is the part of ourselves that we share with loved ones in intimate moments. The Real Self inspires us to embrace challenges, change, failure, novelty and ambiguity. It is our source of wisdom when we struggle with the questions of what we can change in life or what we should accept—to paraphrase the well-known Serenity Prayer. The Real Self holds us accountable for our moral decisions. It allows us to have empathy and fight for justice and ethics. The Real Self is what we transfer to our children to give them a life of autonomy, self-confidence and self-esteem.

The Real Self and Our Security

"I think, therefore I will survive," I believed. I had many reasons for doing well at school and pursuing many degrees: The need for admiration was huge, but so was the need for security. My brain convinced me that a good education and advanced degrees would always ensure that I had steak and wine on the table and survive whatever life threw at me. Many people I know have other ideas about which accomplishments will make them feel secure about the future. Investment bankers talk about having $5 million in the bank at all times. Some men pump up their muscles to feel strong enough to take on any challenge. Many women spend a lot of time and energy on being skinny, pretty and youthful.

Neuroscientists who study the human brain in an attempt to understand why we became human are convinced that our brain developed out of our need to regulate our emotions so that we can interact socially. We are human because we can cooperate on long-term tasks, learn from and teach one another and build knowledge based upon what we have learned. We are human because we needed culture to increase our chances of survival. The evolutionary biologist David Sloan Wilson believes that over the last 80,000 to 100,000 years, culture has been equally as important as genes in shaping our behavior. According to Wilson, humans as social animals are genetically oriented to be part of culture. But many animals, especially mammals, work within groups because chances for survival, especially during infancy, increase when members work together. So certain animals help those that share their genes (called kin-altruism) or help those that help them (called reciprocal altruism). Even though the groups work together, selfishness still drives cooperation.

So what makes us different from other animals?

John Nash, the Nobel Prize winning mathematician and economist, has described our human ability and tendency to make decisions based on what is both good for the individual and for the group. In many situations, all benefit. The Nash-equilibrium is the foundation of game theory, a field of mathematics that can predict human behavior in politics, sociology, economics and evolutionary biology. Survival of the fittest is for the animals; united we stand is for humans.

I want to emphasize an important point: We are not human because of superior tool-making and cause-and-effect calculations. We are not human because we are smarter than other animals. We are human because we learned that cooperation with non-family members significantly increases our survival rates. The Real Self is essential for us to intimately interact and cooperate with other people.

When we need to be resilient and overcome difficult obstacles, the Real Self whispers, "Yes, you can!" When we fail, it says, "Good for you for trying! Maybe next time. Learn from your mistakes!" When we are alone, the Real Self tells us, "You are alone, but not lonely. Someone soon will be in your life." When the going gets tough, it is those with a healthy Real Self who get going.

When we suffer from loss or trauma, it is the Real Self that soothes our pain and helps us to manage our lives without loved ones or without limbs. The actress Cate Blanchett summarized the role of the Real Self best: "It's like when you experience intense grief—you often have the deepest insights because the dead wood's been cleared out. When you're absolutely exhausted, somehow the work you've been consciously trying to do gets done on a different, deeper level." It is the Real Self that does this work.

There are a few other tools the Real Self gives us to survive and find security in life: We can learn from the future by having a gut-feeling on how to deal with problems; we can excel at long-term planning; we can adapt better than any other organism; and we can create a reality that takes the edge off the harshness that life throws at us.

So when Csikszentmihalyi found that the best of humanity's "greatest strength is that they are in control of their lives," he was not referring to control of physical surroundings. The best of humanity are not tenacious control freaks who actually succeeded in organizing their physical surroundings. Nor are they extremely successful people with gold in bank vaults or elite degrees against office walls. In the chaos of World War II, no one had control over the world and many of the most successful succumbed to despair. Control over our lives is a state of mind. It results from the faith we have in our ability to cooperate with the right people and to rely on the other tools that our human brain has given us. The best of humanity believe that they control their lives because they trust their Real Self. Hope, faith and a belief that we can master life and the future comes from non-conscious memories found in a strong Real Self, not a strong résumé.

The Real Self and Humanity

When I was a young teenager, my parents gave me a framed copy of Rudyard Kipling's masterful poem, "If." The poem discusses all the virtues that we need in order to become mature adults and say goodbye to our childish ways. This poem and the strong Calvinistic culture in which I was raised propelled me to live an outwardly righteous life. In high school, I received a coveted prize for possessing outstanding character and leadership abilities. Today, I know that had I been born in Nazi Germany, I too could easily have been swept into the SS. There is a major difference between *displaying* human virtues and *embodying* them. The former is easy when the fields are ripe with harvest, the latter quite difficult during drought and famine. Our character and virtues should not come from pleasing parental or political authorities; they can only come from within.

In his well-known experiment, Yale psychologist Stanley Milgram convinced participants to help him teach students important new tasks. He explained to the participants that giving students electric shocks after they made a mistake would significantly help the learning process. He informed them that a shock of 450 volts would kill the students. Milgram then stationed actors in the next room to be the "students." At 180 volts, the actors were instructed to shout, "I can't stand the pain!" and at 270 volts to scream in agony. The experiment started. Despite the screams, all participants shocked the "students" up to at least 300 volts. When Milgram instructed the participants to give the potentially lethal dose of 450 volts, many protested. But Milgram persisted and was able to convince two-thirds of participants to go all the way. The study was replicated all over the world with nearly the same outcomes. Most people are actually prepared to kill a human in the name of a goal that was sold to them as important by a person in power.

But it is important to note that even though two-thirds of the participants in the Milgram experiment shocked their "student" to death, a third refused to listen and walked away from killing their "student." The latter, when the moment arrived for them to say, "This is what I believe and I will not go further," had the guts to stick to their conviction. This third lived up to their human values. In contrast, the majority, when asked to kill a student, obeyed out of fear of being embarrassed, different or wrong.

I have no doubt that if I had participated in the Milgram study, I would have shocked the student to death. After all, people in power know what they are talking about. You must obey a professor, a president, a billionaire, a celebrity or a priest. Or so I thought.

Researchers are convinced that all humans are born with moral intuitions. Instincts that drive us to need fairness, empathy and attachment are in our genetic make-up. But it is clear that many of us do not live up to our most basic human drives. The main difference: the strength of our inner moral compass, the Real Self.

The Real Self and Transcendence

Actors are encouraged to choose an audition monologue that portrays something about who they really are, called the "This is Me" monologue. I use a speech from *Long Day's Journey into Night*. In my monologue, Eugene O'Neil describes how, while sailing to Argentina, he had a transformative experience:

> I became drunk with the beauty and the singing rhythm of it, and for a moment I lost myself—actually lost my life. I was set free. I dissolved in the sea, became white sails and flying spray, became beauty and rhythm, became moonlight and the ship and the high dim-starred sky. I belonged, without past or future, within peace and unity and a wild joy, within something greater than my own life, or the life of Man, to Life itself! To God, if you want to put it that way.

I have a need to transcend the smallness of my life, to find a sense of purpose and meaning that explains why I must endure the arrows that life shoots at me. My need for meaning is universal. Our earliest ancestors often danced for hours with drums to connect with their forefathers or had many rituals to serve their gods to bring meaning; today we all have our unique ways of feeling that we belong to something bigger.

Today, religion and work are the two places where the most people seek meaning. In his book, *Healing the Hardware of the Soul*, Dr. Daniel Amen, who is both a Catholic and a brain researcher, writes, "Our spirituality is influenced by how the brain functions. It has been my experience that when the brain is healthy for people with religious beliefs, God is experienced as loving, compassionate, forgiving and present. When these people struggle with brain problems, God is often perceived as angry, vengeful, controlling, rigid, judgmental and distant. Brain physiology impacts our perception of the world, including our perception of God."

After reviewing the work of prominent researchers on the brain and transcendence, the political commentator David Brooks concluded that the mind indeed "can transcend itself and merge with a larger presence that feels more real."

The ability to relate our deepest, most vulnerable and authentic self to others, the world, the human spirit, evolution or a higher being depends on a healthy Real Self. The Real Self is the door to our soul. Realizing that this belief can cause significant controversy in religious institutions that believe the soul is separate from the body and brain, Dr. Amen says that he believes that God has given us the knowledge of the brain to help religious people enjoy the magnanimity of God, not his punishments or his absence.

For those who seek purpose through their work: Research done by Mihaly Csikszentmihalyi and Jeanne Nakamura shows that when people follow their calling in life, they reach a state they call "vital engagement." During this state, people have "a relationship to the world that is characterized both by experiences of flow (enjoyed absorption) and by meaning (subjective significance)." In the next chapter, we will discuss the essential role the Real Self plays in allowing us to find our calling and to pursue it until we reach a place of vital engagement.

Many people also find transcendence in the appreciation or production of beauty in nature, music, art, drama, film, sport, science or mathematics. Whether we observe or participate, we need a healthy Real Self to enjoy the moment, smell the roses, hear the rhythms in music or appreciate delicious food and wine. We can start to focus on the abundance of life only when the Real Self tells us that we are safe in the moment and that enjoyment of all life has to offer is possible.

Transcendence, like happiness, lies in our ability to lose our sense of self and relate to the outside world or activities. It is an experience of being caught between two powerful poles: our inner self and the mysterious, magical and powerful energy outside our skin. It is a dynamic relationship, not a static belief.

Real Self and Temperance

I have had many evenings when I came home from a long day at the office in which all hell had broken lose. Clients screamed at me, colleagues betrayed me and the subway was packed with sweaty, obnoxious people on a sweltering New York summer's day. At home, two voices would go off: "Put on your sneakers, go for a run, come back and eat a healthy salad or sushi and go to bed early. Tomorrow you will be rested and ready to tackle the day." The other voice insisted, "It was a long day. You need a cold beer. Just one cold beer and you will feel much better."

The second voice often won. But there is nothing like a cold beer for people controlled by our animal brain. So after one beer, I would have another. Then I would become hungry and open a bag of potato crisps. Then I will have another beer. Later I would order in a cheeseburger. Throughout this time, I would feel fantastic. I would know that I made the right decision. Until the next day when I would be hung over and tired from an alcohol-induced restless sleep and overindulging in comfort food.

We are in a daily fight for our humanity against our animal brain and its instincts and desires. The Real Self is not always in charge, even for the best of humanity. When the Real Self wins the daily battle, we feel confident, competent and cared for while we live out our human values. When the animal brain wins, we become selfish and make pleasure and admiration our main goals in life. The battle for control of our brains is crucial. That is why, as old-fashioned as it may sound, I see temperance as one of our most important human virtues. Without the ability to manage our animal desires, we cannot live up to any of our other virtues.

The battle is not a fair contest. Our animal brains are millions of years old; our human brain, a youngster of tens of thousands of years. We share 98 percent of our DNA with chimpanzees. Looking at the brain's anatomy, we see that 70 percent of our brain is animal brain and the neural pathways that convey our "animal" needs, desires and feelings look like the muscle fibers of a bodybuilder. The neural pathways from the human brain that control our animal urges or sooth our fears look like the muscles of a baby. Our Real Self is David; our animal brain Goliath.

A culture based on our human values is important to help our Real Self control the animal brain. Our current culture flaunts pleasure and admiration. Our role models are symbols of excess or starvation; we are bombarded with messages to buy products that will bring us pleasure or admiration; and parents use sweets to please their children and designer clothes to decorate them. Our Real Self is taking a beating more than ever. No wonder we are aching for meaning and happiness.

I don't want to leave the impression that puritanical societies are right and that all pleasure and admiration are evil and ought to be eradicated. The positive psychology movement defines temperance as the appropriate and moderate expression of appetites and wants. It is not to suppress motives, but to wait for opportunities to satisfy them so that we do not harm ourselves or others. Neuroscientists are also clear that a healthy brain is an integrated brain where all four brains (the reptilian, the mammalian, the primate and the human) work in harmony together. The Real Self ensures that all four brain areas work together and are rewarded appropriately and moderately.

Happiness is...

At the beginning of the chapter, I asked how we humans could be happier. What I found is that we need to change the filter through which we view reality by increasing memories of times when we have felt truly happy. I also found out how the emotion of happiness is linked to the Real Self, which is the most essential aspect of who we are. All very interesting. But we still don't know what we can do to increase our happy memories.

The next few chapters show how I discovered that self-expression, self-share and self-care create happy memories and strengthen the Real Self.

Finding this out made all the sense in the world to me: Happiness, humans' most sought after reward, is given to us to encourage us to strengthen a brain area crucial to our identity, survival, humanity and spirituality. Happiness is psychological growth. And that should also be our definition of success.

The next time you scream, "I want to be happy!" do not expect the skies to offer up a quick cure. Don't expect a major event, great success or a profound romance to miraculously make you happy. Like an athlete daily training his muscles, we need to daily strengthen our Real Self. In return, our brain rewards us with happiness and these experiences are encrypted into our long-term memory. More happy memories form a happier filter that allows us to be happy with what we have.

Chapter 2

Live for a Passion

After weeks of cloudy weather, Washington Square Park was packed with people soaking up the first sun of spring. I sat next to a pretty NYU student, who seemed oblivious to the miracle of nature's awakening. Then I saw why and groaned inwardly. On her lap, organic chemistry formulas stared up at her. I cringed as I remembered wasting many similar beautiful days studying organic chemistry and other subjects I secretly loathed.

"Pre-med?" I asked.

"Trying." She smiled shyly.

"Why medicine?" I prodded.

Kristen was hoping to become a doctor, like her father in Boston. She said that she wanted to help people, especially people in developing countries. As she talked about her future, I saw that she had almost no body movement; her eyes were opaque, lifeless; her voice monotone. Kristen looked as if she were wearing a mask.

"So, are you taking any fun classes?" I continued my interrogation.

Kristen started to tell me about her voice lessons. "It's amazing how my teacher can give me one small hint that has such a huge impact on the quality of my singing. I always leave the class so full of energy. I love that class."

While talking about her voice classes, Kristen moved her whole body with vitality and her eyes and voice were as colorful as the tulips of early spring. Talking about her passion, this pretty woman became beautiful. Later she mentioned that she would love to work with children.

"So why on earth do you want to become a doctor? Why don't you study voice, teach children, see where such a career takes you?" I asked.

"Because there's no money in teaching," she said flatly.

Kristen was luckier than I was. In her early twenties, she knew what she wanted to do. She just didn't give herself the permission to do it. Even in my thirties, I had no idea what I wanted to be when I grew up. Showered with opportunities, I was drowning in too many choices. At times, I wished that I came from a family that owned a farm or a restaurant, so that I might be forced to keep the family concern going. All this, while knowing many people with the family farm or restaurant who wished that they had *my* life.

My Left Brain's Lies

When I had to decide on my career path, I relied on my logical-and-linear left brain for guidance. I concluded that I had the intellectual abilities to become a doctor; that being a doctor would earn my parents' praise and society's respect; and that medicine would ensure a good income and a lifetime of job security. My aptitude tests reinforced my decision. No life coach, positive psychology signature strength test, career councilor or the Pope could have convinced my left brain otherwise. They probably would not have tried to, either. To many, being a doctor has the benefit of being one of the few "helping" professions where one can actually be financially well off. But what they may not realize is that being good at something and getting paid well do not guarantee happiness or meaning.

After two years of medical practice in rural South Africa and provincial Canada, I got out of bed as my first patient arrived at the clinic where I worked in Reston, Manitoba. Medicine had left me numb and unfulfilled. When a patient came into my office and complained about being tired, I had to pinch myself to keep from screaming, "You are tired?! Do you know what tired is? Let me tell you how tired I am!" Even delivering babies or treating victims of car accidents could not stir passion into my life. Saving people's lives could not save my dying soul.

Searching for a way out of my melancholy, I again consulted my left brain for help. This time I concluded that, since I had always enjoyed challenging leadership positions, I should obtain an MBA. My plan was to combine my higher education and areas of expertise to work somewhere like the World Health Organization. Rather than curing one patient at a time, perhaps I could cure entire nations at a time! When I arrived at Yale, all the smart people seemed to be interested in the lucrative investment banking or management consulting jobs. So my left brain changed gears again: "Your signature strengths are to help others and to think analytically. As a consultant you can help companies and enjoy problem solving. Consulting skills will also be an asset wherever you go." So when a consulting job came knocking, I embraced it. But within months of starting my job as a management consultant in New York, I knew my left brain had led me astray once again. The sad truth was that I cared even less for management consulting than I did for medicine.

It was then that I realized that my left brain could be a real whore. I also became convinced that I could not live a life devoid of passion. The harder I searched, the more people tried to convince me that passion is a luxury. But passion is one of only a handful of traits that separate us from animals. If it were a luxury, would it not have disappeared from our brains over the millennia? After all, through self selection, we lose that which we do not use.

The Need for Passion

Recently, I had a magnetic resonance imaging (MRI) scan to investigate the cause of my persistent backache. If you've ever had an MRI, you know that the chamber they have you lie in is a claustrophobic's version of hell. To distract myself, I kept a mental dialogue going in my head. One topic I reflected on was how an MRI works. In medical school, I learned that the human body consists of billions of atoms spinning randomly in every direction. By using magnetic fields, radio frequency and computers, the MRI manipulates the energy from hydrogen atoms to form images of the cells and tissues that make up our bodies. An MRI can only function because my body is made of atoms that are constantly giving off energy and recharging themselves with new energy.

This led me to wonder: "Can the smallest particles of our bodily existence give us a clue as to what the most complicated collection of atoms, also known as humans, needs to do in life?"

Later on, I read that the smallest particles in our bodies are so small that they do not appear to have any qualities of their own. They only "exist" as part of a relationship with other tiny particles. Quantum mechanics states that matter must increase and multiply in order to fulfill all possibilities. "To fulfill all possibilities" struck me as another driver in our lives. We, like our smallest particles, are driven to expand to our full potential.

This idea turned out not to be new at all. Abraham Maslow, the famous twentieth-century psychologist, researched mental health at a time when most of his colleagues were focused on mental diseases. He wanted to know why his two mentors embodied the best of humanity, while other people seemed to stumble toward...nowhere. Researching the lives of his mentors and of many other outstanding humans, he noticed similar traits and patterns. He concluded that the need for self-actualization—to become everything one is capable of— drives all humans. But he found that only one percent of people actually reach their full potential in life, almost always in middle-age or later.

Carl Rogers, another renowned psychologist, disagreed that becoming one of the one percent of self-actualizers is the ultimate goal of life. Instead, he argued that our goal should be to become *self-actualizing*. Since not everyone possesses the same level of mental health, not everyone will become self-actualizers. The good news is that our *attempts* to expand to our full potential are more important than actually reaching self-actualization.

Child development and intercultural psychiatric, psychological and evolutionary research all strongly support the idea that we are innately driven to be the most that we can become. I particularly enjoyed Harvard psychologist Robert White's description of our need to achieve—not to be confused with a need to overachieve. He believes that all of us have a need to "make things happen," just like we need water to survive.

There is one difference. When we drink water, we reach a point at which we have our fill. We are rewarded with pleasure and we stop drinking. We never reach this point in our need to achieve. The brain does reward us for reaching incremental goals, which psychologists call the progression principal, but we never feel that we have quenched our thirst for pushing the boundaries of our potential. We are driven to expand knowledge, craft and expertise. That is why Csikszentmihalyi found that the best of humanity "lead vigorous lives, are open to a variety of experiences, keep on learning until the day they die." To our brain, life is indeed a journey on which we need to keep expanding our limitless potential.

History is filled with examples of brave men and women who left the safety of their homes, the warmth of fireplaces, cupboards filled with food and land ripe with harvest to fight an enemy ready to take away their freedom, but not their livelihood. Nelson Mandela was not a poor man when he decided to take on South Africa's National Party and its apartheid laws. He had a law practice, a home, a wife and children. It was his belief in the freedom of all people that set him on a course of action that could have killed him. In the end, the cause took 27 years of his life. Here in the United States, the constitution safeguards liberty as a right that is equal to life. Why would people sacrifice their lives for freedom if survival of our DNA is supposed to be our primary motivation? Why do studies show that living in a free democracy adds significantly to a person's happiness?

Nikki Giovanni, one of America's most loved poets, sees herself as "a Black American, a daughter, a mother, a professor of English." When asked why she, in her youth, became such a staunch activist for black and women's rights, she said she wanted to be happy, safe and to contribute. Later she added, "I wanted to be me."

The best of humanity will do whatever it takes to push themselves to fulfill their unique potential.

Flow

I recently met a Wall Street banker admired for his work and successes. When he asked me what I do for a living, I explained that I was writing a book on happiness and success. He asked, "So what is one thing that you have learned that makes people happy?"

"You must live up to your full potential," I replied.

"I like to learn new things, to get better at what I do. I work hard. My clients often give me compliments and my company pays me a lot for my successes. Am I living up to my full potential?" he asked.

I too have spent many hours in my life working hard to achieve. Add to that the gallons of cortisol my adrenaline glands excreted in reaction to stress at work or the painful isolation that I experienced in the middle of New York City and on the Canadian prairies. I did believe that I was living up to my full potential. "No pain, no gain," was how I justified my stress-filled life. Today, I know that despite my strong résumé, I had actually been stifling my potential.

Planet earth is 3.5 billion years old. Given this timeline, humans are minutes old. The criteria our modern culture use to measure success: seconds. We have no idea where we come from and no idea where we go when we die. To measure our potential in terms of manmade rewards is either foolish or grandiose. Or both.

Modern man's first reaction to the question "Am I living up to my full potential?" is to search for hard data. First, we look at our success or the lack of it: Do we have wealth, beauty, elite degrees, articles in coveted magazines, civil prizes, admiration, fame or successful children? Then we look at how hard we work: the 100 hour weeks; the one day of vacation we took to see the doctor; the few nights we saw our kids before they went to sleep; the youthful age of our first heart attack; the number of stress cigarettes we smoke; the amount of alcohol we need to wind down. We add this all up and drink another glass of champagne to congratulate ourselves on our productivity or drink five beers to drown our sorrows.

I set out on a journey to discover my passion. For five years, I took painting, photography, creative writing, poetry and playwriting courses. In 2002, I decided to take an acting class to improve my playwriting. On the first day, terrified of certain embarrassment, I made sure to tell everyone that I was not an actor, but a writer. I survived the ten-week course and even managed to have a bit of fun. On the last day of class, we had a performance that was open to the public. My scene partner, Patrick, and I had worked hard on a scene from *Long*

Day's Journey into Night, Eugene O'Neil's masterpiece. As we walked on stage, I prayed that a freak earthquake would suddenly swallow the theater.

But when the scene started, my deer-in-headlights feeling vanished. I was acutely aware of Patrick, the text, the audience and my own self. I felt confident and in complete control. Our ten-minute scene ended after ten seconds, or so it felt. I had lost myself during the scene. I felt as if I were swimming in a river in which space and time dissolved. When the scene ended, I walked off stage without searching for admiring eyes to tell me I was good enough. It didn't matter.

Mihaly Csikszentmihalyi's life-long quest to know "what is?" and "what could be?" for humanity led him to discover the fascinating phenomenon of *flow* or optimal experience. He describes *flow* as a non-thinking experience where one feels deeply engaged with an activity, does the tasks effortlessly, experiences an unknown sense of control, loses the sense of self and loses track of time. *Flow* is an experience Maslow found to be common in all self-actualized people. So when we ask, "Am I living up to my optimum potential?" we need to count how often we experience the state of flow in our daily lives.

"Pleasure marks the achievement of biological growth, whereas flow marks the achievement of psychological growth," writes Csikszentmihalyi. When we follow our passions, we experience flow, grow psychologically and strengthen our Real Self. In return, we experience happiness.

Passion lies in those authentic activities that we choose and that lead to many moments of flow and happiness, leaving us with a stronger Real Self. A stronger Real Self allows us to push our potential even further, allowing for more happiness and an even stronger Real Self.

Passion and Self-Esteem

An old business school friend sent me an email with a connection to a YouTube video. At first I ignored it as just another piece of mass email. But my gut encouraged me to open it up and look at the clip.

On the surface, Paul Potts seemed an unlikely participant in the *Britain's Got Talent* show. During interviews before the performance, Paul said, "By day I sell mobile phones, my dream is to spend my life doing what I feel I was born to do"; "My voice has always been my best friend. If I was having problems with bullies at school, I always had my voice to fall back on"; "I was always a bit different—I think that's the reason I struggle with self-confidence. When I'm singing, I don't have that problem. I'm in the place I should be."

On stage, Paul looked like a man about to be executed. When a judge asked, "What are you here for today, Paul?" he answered, almost in tears, "To sing opera."

The judges pulled faces like a bunch of kindergarten kids told they had to eat their broccoli. Then Paul began to sing. Jaws dropped, smiles replaced the masks of cynicism, tears rolled, young adults jumped up and down. The Brits starts to scream as if they were at a football game. Paul's performance traveled the world on the Internet.

"All my life, I felt insignificant, but after that first audition, I've realized I am somebody. I am Paul Potts," Paul said in an interview before winning the final round of the contest. Discovering his passion and sharing it with the world brought Paul flow, which strengthened his Real Self, which increased his self-esteem.

I watched the video clip a dozen times within 24 hours; more often than not, tears were flowing down my cheeks. Inside, my own Real Self was screaming to get out and play. Months later I signed up for a singing class.

Research shows the close connection between a healthy Real Self, flow and passion. Researchers gave a group of 500 teenagers beepers, called them at random times throughout the day and asked them what were they doing at the moment, their thoughts, their emotions and their level of engagement. They found that the 250 participants who experienced flow frequently had hobbies and interests, engaged in sports and worked hard at school. These children measured high on all levels of psychological well-being and were the people who make it to college, develop deep relationships with others and live healthy confident lives. Their success was not based on pleasing parents, but on being engaged in what they do. In contrast, the 250 teenagers who seldom experienced flow, who hang out at malls and watch television a lot, measured lower on almost all levels of psychological well-being than the "high flow" kids.

Passion is to the Real Self what enriched uranium is to a nuclear bomb.

Passion and Humanity

As a medical doctor and then as a management consultant, I had the drive to always be the best. I was often envious of others' achievements and when they failed, I would support them, but I always had a voice celebrating their fall from grace. Within theater, I have discovered how much I enjoy it when people break through acting barriers and progress. As a director, I love helping people to find their truth as an actor.

People who follow their passions and develop a stronger Real Self always care as much about their chosen field and its people as they do their own progress. They live up to the most fundamental human legacy: to trust and cooperate with non-family members so the group can survive and increase its collective potential.

"None of the movies that I've made throughout my whole life would have been possible...without somebody first believing in me, and I really believe that being a mentor to talented newcomers is a very time-honored tradition," said Steven Spielberg, after accepting the Cecil B. DeMille Award at the Golden Globes for lifetime achievement in film. He recalled how Sidney Sheinberg, former head of Universal Studios, had told him, "I will be there for you in success, but I will also always be there for you during the tough times."

One winter, Subrahhmanyan Chandrasekhar was asked to teach an advanced class in astrophysics. Only two students signed up. At the time, Chandrasekhar lived 80 miles away from the University of Chicago, where he taught. Everyone assumed the class would be cancelled. An 80-mile haul in the middle of winter through back-country roads for two students would be too much effort, or so most people thought. But not Dr. Chandrasekhar. He loved astrophysics and he loved teaching. So, he taught the two students twice a week for a whole semester. Both students later won the Nobel Prize for physics, an achievement their teacher also eventually received, but only after his students received theirs.

The obligation to mentor can even be seen in the cutthroat world of corporate America. After decades of researching leadership and human motivation, David McClelland, the renowned Harvard researcher, identified four motivations that all humans innately possess, but don't necessarily follow: the need for achievement (meeting or exceeding a standard of excellence or improving personal performance), the need for affiliation (maintaining close friendly relationships), the need for personalized power (to be strong and influence others, making them feel weak) and the need for socialized power (helping people feel stronger and more capable). For most of his life, McClelland believed that our need for achievement is the most crucial for personal, societal and national success. Later he revised his opinion and concluded, "The most effective leaders were primarily motivated by socialized power."

I do not want to leave the impression that great leaders are those who are overly focused on charming others or being liked. This type of CEO is more focused on people's reactions to what they do ("They admire me!" or "They like me!") than getting the job done. The best CEOs typically have both a strong task focus (hard workers, analytical thinkers, persistent, efficient, detail orientated, resolute, conscientious, focused on incremental successes) and people focus (humble, self-effacing, effective coaches and mentors, assertive team leaders).

Great leaders like to encourage others to reach their full potential. They know it makes sense both from a business and humanity perspective.

Passion and Spirituality

During class, two of my acting teachers read a letter that the famous dance teacher and choreographer Martha Graham wrote to Agnes DeMille: "There is a vitality, a life force, a quickening that is translated through you into action, and because there is only one of you in all time, this expression is unique. And if you block it, it will never exist through any other medium….Keep the channel open…" With this letter, teachers encourage us to be open to the magic that comes from a life force greater than us.

To tap into something magical and spiritual is not the only gift for following our passions. Researchers have found that people who follow their passions find meaning in their lives. They feel their work is a calling, they are doing God's work or they are a channel for a higher being.

Passion and Success

"Don't aim at success—the more you aim at it and make it a target, the more you are going to miss it. For success, like happiness, cannot be pursued; it must ensue...as the unintended side-effect of one's personal dedication to a course greater than oneself," Victor Frankl, the Austrian psychologist and Auschwitz survivor, wrote in *Man's Search for Meaning*.

We all have a strong drive for achievement lurking within us. The best of humanity, however, want to succeed not to receive rewards, but because they care about what they do and want to contribute to something larger than their own lives.

The good news is that those who follow their passions are more likely to succeed than those who do not. Anders Ericsson, a researcher at Florida State University, studied expert performers in sport, art, business and games and concluded that the key difference between them and the rest of us is that expert performers desire to be good at what they do and practice extremely hard to improve their skills. What makes them to desire to be good? They love what they do.

Others studies also show that achievement depends more on grit—the determination to accomplish an ambitious, long-term goal despite the inevitable obstacles—than on innate talent. In fact, IQ accounts for only 25 percent of differences in job performance or grade point average. Quoting the "ten-year rule," researchers explain that those who are highly successful in all areas of life often have dedicated themselves to their goals through ten years of hard practice and work. And what makes one person grittier than another? Passion that inspires is the leading contender. It sure is easier to be gritty when you like what you do.

Copernicus, Galileo, Isaac Newton, Antoine Lavoisier, Gregor Mendel, Albert Michelson, Albert Einstein and, more recently, Andrew Miles, renowned Princeton mathematician, all made their contributions to science while working in unrelated fields. To them, it was "fun," hobbies or something they just had to do to express their unique Real Selves.

Compare this to Ozymandias, the antihero of Shelly's famous poem. The narrator talks of discovering a broken sculpture of this once powerful and successful ruler and on the pedestal, the following words appeared:

'My name is Ozymandias, King of Kings;
Look on my works. Ye Mighty, and despair!'

But the power of time and nature have left this statue of arrogance in ruins:

Nothing beside remains. Round the decay
Of that colossal wreck, boundless and bare
The lone and level sands stretch far away.

Parents take note: Your children may be more successful if you allow them to do what they want to do. In return, following their passions will increase their self-esteem, love life, humanity and spiritual life.

Finding a Passion

"I guess I need some direction in how to find my passion. I'd like to have a career where I am giving back to the world and using my potential to do so. Ideally, I'd like something that is a real calling, not just a job. Basically, I feel like I need some sort of decision-making and information-seeking algorithm," an overachiever wrote to me in an email.

We are often confused when to call work a job, a career or a calling. Research shows that when work is a job, you do as little as possible to get through the week; have little interest in advancement; collect your check; and go home to spend your money as you see fit. Work is about money and money is security.

When work is a career, you constantly compete against your own high standards, other colleagues' performances and rival companies' profits. The goal is to win, often at all costs. So you work hard and late. You do not mind cutting corners or even turning a blind eye to inappropriate or unethical behaviors. Promotion, prestige and large paychecks are the carrots that keep you going.

Work is about money and the pecking order. Often the rewards justify the hard work, but you always feel there is more to life.

When work is a calling, we are engaged in what we do for the sake of doing it. The reward does not lie in the money or status, but in the doing.

When we see work as a job or a career, we can easily figure out what jobs to take. Where can I make money? Where can my need for overachievement—as opposed to achievement—be rewarded with money or status? An algorithm to find a job and career is easy; to find a passion, impossible.

In my twenties, I seldom went to the theater, though I occasionally watched movies and television. To me, there were more practical things to do: Acting was a job for those not prepared to work too hard. Actors were divas or sluts, hippies or attention seekers, and were best avoided. As a student, I once declared, with breathtaking arrogance, that all Bachelor of Arts degrees ought to be banned from universities. If it's not practical, then it's a waste of money, I thought.

If you told me then that I would one day find my passion in the theater and that I would write, act, produce and direct a play that would be reviewed by *The New York Times*, I would have cracked a rib laughing. Such a prognostication would have been on par with telling Donald Trump that he would one day become a nurse or Tiger Woods that he should really think about boxing. No aptitude test, thinking, talking or books could have brought me close to considering the theater as a livelihood. No "decision-making and information-seeking algorithm" would have helped me. For if we use logic to make decisions about our career paths, we tend to rely on the same old criteria: Will it please my parents? Will it bring status and money? Do others think that I am good at it? Will this amazing job opportunity present itself again? Trusting the left brain is risky. It will always give us misconstrued messages, botched from our egos, parents and culture.

Sadly, only 29 percent of workers in the United States feel engaged with their work, 15 percent in Germany and 10 percent in Singapore. From surveys and informal conversations, I estimate that more than 60 percent of medical doctors and lawyers would do something different today. This number is the same for actors; it may even be higher. Many people are in their work situations for all the wrong reasons. In the process, they miss out on the positive rewards from following their passions.

So how do we figure out what our passions are? If flow and passion are a function of our Real Self, then the Real Self must have the answers.

Passion and the Real Self

The movie *Goodwill Hunting* triggered my dark night of the soul. For years I wondered, "Why that movie? Why that night?"

Just like me, the protagonist struggled to find passion and intimate love. Unlike me, he found both. So, out of yearning, my brain collapsed in despair. But there was another reason.

Upon seeing the movie, my fragile Real Self started running naked through my non-conscious brain, screaming, "Eureka, eureka! You're an actor/writer, you're an actor/writer." From the newspapers, I knew that the movie's lead actors had also written the screenplay. I thought nothing of it at the time, but my Real Self was tickled pink. It knew all along that I am a writer/actor. I, on the other hand, had no idea. My Real Self's outcry of joy woke every demon sleeping in my numbed brain. They came out with a vengeance, hoping they would suppress—like they usually did—the uprising in a few seconds. Only this time, my left brain ran out of lies. My suppressed passions began to fight my demons. The first of thousands of dark nights of the soul followed.

We cannot communicate with the Real Self via logic and language. To take guidance from the Real Self, we must understand what it is made from and how it communicates.

When you listen to a self-help guru giving advice on how to live your life, your brain becomes filled with memories of positive advice. Someone can ask you afterwards, "How can I be happy?" and you might answer, "Read *The Secret*" or "Think positive thoughts." When someone asks for your date of birth, you can say, "June 12." This type of memory, called factual or explicit memory, can be recalled explicitly, using language.

But when you ask Tiger Woods to explain his swing, his answer will likely be very unsatisfactory to you. Most of his knowledge lies in his muscles, rather than conscious thoughts that can be expressed through words. Or when you remember a lover tenderly caressing your body, you can't find the words to explain just what made it so wonderful. But the memory of the touch is recorded in detail. This type of memory, called in-your-bone, muscle, kinetic or implicit memory, is made from emotions, sensations and pictures.

The Real Self is made from muscle memory. Neither logic nor vocabulary can touch this part of the brain.

There is a time-tested childcare method that billions of parents have employed to care for their babies. Just like the Real Self, a baby cannot explain his wants. He doesn't have the awareness or the vocabulary to tell his mother that he is hungry. All he can do is cry. So the parent starts running through a list of possible needs: Is little John sleepy, wet, cold or hungry? Through trial and error, she will rule out every possible cause. She will only stop when the baby stops crying and starts to coo.

This is how we communicate with our Real Self. To "listen" to its cries for passion, we need to open ourselves to many experiences and be aware of a gut feeling that might tell us we have found what we are looking for. William James described this gut feeling perfectly to his wife: "I have often thought that the best way to define a man's character would be to seek out the particular mental or moral attitude in which, when it came upon him, he felt himself most deeply and intensely active and alive. At such moments there is a voice inside which speaks and says: 'This is the real me!'" When we suppress this voice, we experience sadness, depression or a dark night of the soul.

In my own life, I had to be a doctor, consultant, student political leader, amateur painter, photographer, opera fanatic and poet before I stumbled upon the theater and heard my Real Self whisper: "This is the real me."

The positive psychology movement offers other criteria that people who have found their passions exhibit: a feeling of excitement while displaying it, particularly at first; a rapid learning curve as the strength is first practiced; a need to continuously learn new ways to follow one's passion; a sense of yearning to find ways to use it; a feeling of "try and stop me" from doing this; invigoration rather than exhaustion while using the strength; the creation and pursuit of personal projects that revolve around it; joy, zest, enthusiasm, even ecstasy while using it. I experienced all of this, with one exception: My learning curve in acting and writing were not rapid.

I would like to add a few more. As an actor and writer, I have been more willing to learn from my mistakes than as a medical doctor or consultant. In the past, mistakes brought shame, not resilience. I now also find pleasure in incremental successes as I learn more and more about the crafts of writing and acting.

Both Pablo Picasso and Steven Spielberg saw their work as an adventure. To them, every moment of creation is an opportunity to discover something new or try something that was never done before. People with a passion constantly ask, "What is?" and "What can be?" As an Academy Award-winning actress recently said after embarking on a complex dancing routine, "I don't know what I can do until I do it!"

The final, and arguably the most important, criteria are that people who pursue their passions enjoy a stronger Real Self. If people follow their passions, we should see an increase in their self-esteem, not in their ego; in the intimacy of their relationships, not in their arrogance; in their appreciation of being part of a greater force, not being the king of their little hills.

Passion in All Fields

The first time I ever understood passion was when I looked into the eyes of a shoe shiner who was polishing my shoes on a street in Istanbul. His dedication to his craft, focus on detail and the joyous smile on his face have haunted me for years. How can such a man have more joy than most of the highly educated professionals I know?

I know people who have found their passions as a caretaker for the elderly, a teacher of children with special needs, a basketball player, a teacher's aide to a blind student, surgeons, CEOs, psychiatrists. Political prisoners such as Victor Frankl and Bruno Bettleheim found passionate goals to follow every day, even while imprisoned.

We often make the mistake of believing that we must become artists to have passion. This is far from the truth.

I know medical doctors who see their profession as a job ("I make as much money as I can so I can retire early"), career ("I need to be the most published author in the country") or as a calling ("I want to find a cure for cancer" or "I want to relieve suffering").

Many people assume that actors and painters must definitely be following their passions. Who would choose to be an actor unless it was truly a passionate calling, knowing that most of them support themselves by waiting tables? Surprisingly, most actors I know are pursuing acting for the wrong reasons. Many of them approach acting as a job, wherein they receive admiration instead of money. Others are obsessed with acting as a career. They will never be satisfied unless they hug an Academy Award and thank their mothers in front of a global audience. Only a handful of actors see acting as a calling: something they must do to make sense of their humanity and of life, and by doing so, change audiences' lives.

Whether rich or poor, free or imprisoned, young or old, passion can be found anywhere.

Following Your Passion

Finding my passion in the theater was a long haul; following it has turned out to be even harder. I keep sabotaging my efforts and continuously find excuses to not audition: my South African accent, my lack of experience, my lack of income.

The best of humanity do not have this problem. They follow their passions with gusto. When Steven Spielberg's father told him to stop crashing his toy trains, the six- year-old took the family video camera and recorded the train crash so that he could watch it over and over again. He found a creative solution to a hurdle. When he was a young boy, he sneaked away from an official tour of a big Hollywood studio to explore the site on his own terms. His sense of adventure was rewarded: He met an editor who took the time to tell him about how films are made, a bonus the rest of the tour group did not enjoy. When he was twice rejected from film school, he kept making movies.

So what does Steven Spielberg have that I do not?

Researchers at the State University of Arizona wanted to see what the brain does when people are in flow. They asked ten amateur golfers to participate. First they were asked to hole 20 five-foot putts while their brains were measured with an EEG and their heart rates were monitored. They were also asked to rate their anxiety levels. Once completed, they were asked to do the same task again, but this time they were told that they were being videotaped by NBC. Afterwards, they were asked to repeat the 20 putts. If they matched or bettered the score of stage one, they would win $300; if not, they would *lose* $100. From their heart rates and self-reporting of anxiety it was clear that all ten had equal amounts of stress. But only five won the $300. The ones who succeeded were able to maintain equal brain activity in the left and right brain, while those who choked got caught up in their left brains. They started to analyze their swing, remember tips from coaches and mentally attempt to control all 24 elements found in a golf swing. The winners, in contrast, focused on visualization, sense activation and focusing on smooth movements—all right brain activities.

Compared to me, Steven Spielberg has a healthy right brain. If we were to monitor the sensations, emotions and pictures in his right brain, we would probably see that his right brain whispers the following to him:

"You are unique. You must live up to your full potential. Follow your passions. Feel all your emotions and learn from them. You can deal with failure and rejection. You can learn from mistakes. You must enjoy what you do, not only the rewards of doing it. Celebrate your small success. You can enjoy mastery over your life and passions. Loved ones, mentors and even strangers will support you to become the best you can be. Give back." Where do the whispers come from?

From the non-conscious muscle memories found in his Real Self.

Obsession versus Passion

During my final years at medical school, I studied from early in the morning until I could not face a book; then I kept going. But it was not passion that drove me. I was obsessed. On the surface, it is very difficult to differentiate between those who are passionate and those who are obsessed. But a closer look reveals many differences. Passionate people work hard because they enjoy what they do; obsessive people are pulled by the rewards, pushed by their ambitions and afraid of their inner demons. Passionate people enjoy close human contact and mentor others; obsessive people avoid intimacy and care more about perfection than people. Passionate people take care of themselves; obsessive people are always stressed and crave instant gratification or admiration for the hard work they put in.

Csikszentmihalyi observed that there are two types of people who seldom experience flow: Those who are constantly preoccupied about how others perceive them, who are worried about giving the wrong impression or doing something inappropriate have a very difficult time enjoying their lives. The same goes for narcissists or people who are perpetually self-centered. "A self-centered individual is usually not self-conscious, but instead evaluates every bit of information only in terms of how it relates to his desires," he writes. "Both lack the attentional fluidity needed to relate to activities for their own sake. Under these conditions it is difficult to become interested in intrinsic goals, to lose oneself in an activity that offers no rewards outside the interaction itself."

Since I was both self-centered and self-conscious, I seldom experienced flow and was unable to find passion. I overachieved because I was obsessed with admiration. Today, when I hear of a successful businessperson who treats his employees like objects or of an Oscar-winning actress behaving like a diva, I know they are obsessed. They are drawn by the rewards, not by what they do. Overachievers may have won the lottery of obtaining material success, but we are often incapable of finding our true passions, without the help of intensive therapy.

To distinguish whether a person is obsessive or passionate is difficult, but essential. Mistakes lead us to marry the wrong people, work for caustic leaders or, even worse, pay the wrong people to help us with our struggles. Many psychiatrists, yogis, motivational speakers, psychologists, executive coaches and self-help gurus seem passionate. But often it is their obsession with their own pain that motivated them to help others in the first place. The consequence: Millions of people pay thousands of dollars and waste valuable time stroking the egos of obsessed therapists or coaches.

The line between passion and obsession can blur. In his book, *The Search for the Real Self*, Dr. Masterson analyzed the lives of the philosopher Jean Paul Sartre, painter Edvard Munch and writer Thomas Wolfe. These artists expressed their inner pain and demons through their passions. They did not—like most overachievers—use obsessions to run away from their pasts, but to face them. Their creative outlets gave them temporary relief and meaning. But using art to deal with our demons can never be a permanent cure. Soon the hurt comes knocking again, often with vengeance. We are forced to be obsessive about our passions to keep ourselves psychologically afloat. Thomas Wolfe wrote boxes and boxes of notes; Edvard Munch produced 50,000 drawings and paintings in his lifetime; and I am sure Sartre never stopped thinking and writing about loneliness and nothingness. Despite their incredible productivity, all three artists had lives filled with interpersonal chaos. The arts can keep us afloat, but they cannot cure us.

Our Culture and Passion

Our materialistic and meritocratic culture is a large stumbling block in our search for passion. People always ask, "How are you going to support yourself?" Their question assumes that everyone wants to have a big house with luxury cars. Or they may say, "By the *sweat of your brow*, you will produce food to eat until you return to the ground..." With this, they imply that loving or hating your work is irrelevant, as long as it brings money. To them, passion is a luxury, not an essential.

The most scathing criticism we face typically comes from our own culture. A friend from South Africa called me up one day and said, "You know people here think you are a bit crazy." I told him it was the best compliment anyone had ever given me. On a recent vacation to South Africa, a retired man told me that normal people are just doing their day-to-day work and live simple lives, hinting that I am still an irresponsible child. I am all for simplicity, but boring lives are another thing. After I started to explain the thesis of my book to her, a South African interrupted me and sarcastically asked, "What do you know about success?" Add to that the "knowing" and contemptuous smile from others when I told them I am an actor and writer, I can understand why so many of us never follow our passions. Without my therapist and an ocean between me and my country of birth, I feel confident that I would still be treating sore throats.

People criticize others when they are dissatisfied with their lives, when they wish that they were doing something other than being propped in front of reality television, beer in hand. They wish they could live full lives.

Passion and Money

Money kills passion. When overachievers think about following their passions, they often say, "I know I would love being a photographer or documentary filmmaker, but there is no money in it!" or "I love teaching children, but it pays almost nothing." They are right. Very few people are rewarded with vast fortunes—as Steven Spielberg has been—for following their passions.

I went from a good salary to no salary and borrowing money from my brother. I went from eating at great restaurants and buying all the high-end clothing I wanted to avoiding high-end restaurants and shopping for a pair of jeans every two years, gratefully accepting hand-me-downs from my brothers. I had to cut down on opera and Broadway tickets. I love the apartment I live in, but I must soon leave it to find something cheaper. I am not thrilled with moving or changing my lifestyle. Some days I behave like a two-year-old, throwing tantrums because life is not rewarding me for all the hard work and sacrifices I have made to follow my passion. When my unpaid credit card bill and my enormous rent keep me awake, I sooth myself by remembering that when I had no money concerns, I struggled with who I was and what I would do with my life. Both situations are hard. But I know which one I prefer.

In better moods, I am filled with gratitude. My passions have made me more confident, happier and more connected to others and to life. This, while money, management consulting and medicine had made me miserable.

I also often remind myself of an unknown actor—most of us are!—who told an interviewer of her times of excess and of scarcity in the theater world. But she never went hungry. The right jobs—both acting and odd jobs—appeared at the right moments to help her through tough times. Her life was hard, but she had no regrets.

I compare her story to a successful businessman whom I know well. When he retired with his millions, he reflected, "I feel worthless. Nothing I have done has had any real value. And I am still worried that I do not have enough money."

The dilemma of following one's passion and living a comfortable life is real. But based on what I have learned, I am convinced that following your passion and doing what it takes to guarantee an income that covers basic food, house, health and security is a better life than living in luxury and only doing your job for the sake of money.

The Cost of No Passion

With so much riding on us to follow our passions, our brains have a powerful way of punishing us for ignoring them: regret. Studies show that regret is one of the most common complaints in old age. "I wish I studied further"; "I wish I took that business opportunity"; "I wish I followed my love for teaching"; "I wish that I learned how to paint," people say, whether surrounded by wealth or poverty. But the regret is not only for a work life without meaning. Since passion ignites our self-esteem, love relationships, humanity, health and our experience of life and Life, ignoring it brings regret. A life of passion leaves us filled with gratitude; a life of ambition leaves us empty.

The Cycle

If we want to live full, meaningful, happy lives, we have no choice but to follow our passions. It is our human legacy. When we follow our passions, we push ourselves harder to achieve goals that are important to us and experience many moments of flow. During flow, our Real Self grows psychologically. A stronger Real Self allows us to enjoy self-esteem, happiness and meaning. We start to believe we are in control of our lives. We are more able to live up to our human values. We also start to experience our place on earth, both as unique individuals and also as part of something greater. Passion is not a luxury, but an essential part of our human legacy.

But herein lies the dilemma: To find and then pursue our passions, we need a strong Real Self; to strengthen our Real Self, we need a passion.

Chapter 3

Enjoy Intimacy

Paul Durose was in the prime of his life when he began experiencing daily nausea. Originally from Canada, he had come to New York to work in the financial sector. Paul knew more about most things than any other person I have known: Art, wine, countries, politics, business—you name it, he could talk about it. Before it became all the rage, Paul had started his own hedge fund; the fund and Paul did very well. He worked hard, occasionally made time to play tennis and hang out with friends. On a club crawl one evening, he introduced me to vodka gimlets. The gimlets added fuel to an intense and most enjoyable conversation. One glorious autumn day, Paul threw a wonderful cocktail party on his terrace. He cleaned the place for days, had new pots of plants and fresh flowers brought in and ensured that caterers kept our stomachs full with delectable appetizers.

But Paul's nausea turned out not to be from a bug he picked up on his last trip to India. He had liver cancer. Soon after his diagnosis, Paul and I talked about life. He told me how, through the lens of his disease, all the time that he had spent at the office and his many successes seemed blurry. All he could remember clearly was playing tennis and enjoying good conversation with the people he cared about most.

"My best memory? The cocktail party I had. To see all the people I know in the city on my terrace. What a highlight!" he reflected.

Paul died last summer at the age of 40. I keep his funeral pamphlet on my fridge as a reminder of how short life is and what really matters. And whenever I drink a vodka gimlet, I remember Paul and I sitting at the bar at the Mercer Kitchen solving the problems of the world.

On a recent trip to South Africa, I came across the In Memoriam section of a local newspaper. A picture of a happy 24-year-old woman caught my attention. I never met Michele Brear, nor do I know anything about her family. But the letter her family wrote to her on the two-year anniversary of her death struck a chord:

> You showered us with love and then suddenly you were gone. We often speak your name. All we have are memories and your picture in a frame. We love you and miss you always.

Mom, Dad, Charlene, Michael, Donovan, Noreen, Jason, Zoe and Kelly

I can only imagine that the memories they carry in their hearts are the laughs of the family around dinner tables, the adolescent tears of unrequited romantic love and the shouts of delight in childhood. Two years after we are gone, all that is left of our lives are the memories of intimate interactions, a photo and a name. I noticed how the family ended the letter by listing all the family members' names. Through shared intimate memories, Michele is still touching everyone in her family.

In the shadow of death, we finally realize that our relationships, especially our intimate relationships, are what matter. After death, they are all that we leave behind.

Intimacy: A Survival Need

Jean, my nephew, is almost a year and a half. He walks everywhere his chubby little legs can carry him. He has developed a personality and can connect visually and with baby language. But boy, when Sylma, my sister-in-law and Jean's mother, shows up, delight erupts over his face. Without her, he sometimes fusses as if his life depended upon it. Jean requires intimacy with his mother.

A relative in her eighties, widowed for more than 20 years, and increasingly losing her memory, was placed in a high-care old age home. I visited her the day she moved in and listened with sadness as she talked about the years of loneliness that she has experienced since her husband died. "You know, I don't understand why I haven't met someone else during these years. It's been very lonely. I really hope I meet someone here. I met a man whose wife is dying. Maybe he and I can get together." My aunt, facing the final act of her life, still seeks intimacy.

John Bowlby, the twentieth-century British psychiatrist and father of attachment theories, explained our need for intimacy. He said that we first need intimacy from our parents and then later from other relationships. Our need to make intimate emotional bonds is "a basic component of human nature, already present in germinal form in the neonate and continuing through adult life into old age." He believed that intimacy is on par with food or sex, and that "the relationship exists in its own right and has survival function of its own."

Our need for intimacy is not a "nice to have" in life. Whether aged one or 91, we need intimacy because we need protection, comfort and support from others. Intimacy to our hearts is like oxygen to our lungs. We need someone to share our lives, to hold us together when we want to fall apart, to celebrate our joys when we reach a goal, to enjoy the beauty of life when we witness two butterflies make love on a flower or to sit in a bar and get tipsy with Belgian beer and laughter. It is as important as food and water.

Logically this makes sense. If we became humans to cooperate, to care for one another and to support one another, then the foundation of our existence depends on this need to be fulfilled. We are born to take care of one another. This begs the question: If we do not give or receive care, are we still truly human?

Intimacy: A Definition

Despite his busy medical practice and a full family life, Etienne, my eldest brother, took the 24-hour door-to-door trip from Cape Town to New York for a three-day visit to attend the first play that I produced. The morning he arrived, I took him to The Grey Dog, my favorite coffee shop, on Carmine Street. We were just talking about "koeitjies en kalfies"—pleasant and superficial topics— when we suddenly entered into a level of conversation unfamiliar to us. People around us disappeared. The noise, rather loud, became a faint hum. I focused on Etienne's eyes and voice. I heard his words surfing on waves of honesty and vulnerability as he told me of the joy he feels at being a father to his three sons, and the camaraderie of working with his new colleagues and the struggles common to most people in midlife.

I, in turn, shared my own pain of the last decade: the loneliness, the times I thought of suicide, my failure to find a social network and love in New York. Etienne did not jump in with advice or attack me for being foolish. I felt no judgment. He just listened to me, and because of that I felt understood. Then we both had a moment where, despite being in a very public place, we sat with tears in our eyes for no other reason than being acknowledged for who we are: vulnerable human beings in a beautiful but tough world. We enjoyed a moment of painful joy and joyful pain. We both knew that we had supported the other for being who he is, not for what he could mean or do for the other. When I left the coffee shop, I felt energized to tackle my demons, to enjoy the day, to perform my best on stage that night.

Intimacy is allowing someone into the most secret chambers of your heart and soul, telling them, "Come into my being and see who I am at my most vulnerable level. Come and see my pain, my dreams, my fears." No wonder Susan Batson, acting coach to the stars, call intimacy "in-to-me-see." But intimacy is more than just seeing into another. It is the moment where the well-being of the other becomes as important as our own. It is where we love our neighbor as much as ourselves. It is the moment where we have as much empathy for the other as we have concern for our own failures and success.

Intimacy is to be real, vulnerable, authentic, ourselves in the moment. This state allows others to acknowledge, shape, understand, read or see us for who we are. When someone witnesses us like this, we feel connected, inspired, energized, alive, known, strong, real and accepted for who we are. Intimacy provides a feeling of safety to grow, to push our boundaries, to expand our potential and to become more actualized. The more actualized we are, the more intimately we experience other people and life.

My moment of intimacy with Etienne that day revealed three important points: Emotional intimacy between two humans is independent from sexual intimacy. Intimacy is at the center of all happy relationships, may it be with siblings, parents, romantic partners, friends, colleagues, community, nature or a higher being.

Secondly, Etienne and I are two Afrikaner men who played competitive rugby in a culture where we were told that boys don't cry and the only real men are macho men. All of us need intimacy…even men.

Thirdly, most of my interactions with Etienne had little to do with the words we spoke. Our bodies and minds communicated with one another on a level more mysterious and magical than we could put in words. We were in flow with one another, where strong currents were communicating and our words waved on the surface.

Intimacy, Existence and Self-Esteem

I have often woken up overcome by a feeling of isolation. A cup of coffee, the newspaper, music and stretching exercises barely impact my mood. But the second I walk out of the elevator and ask the doorman, "How are you?" and he says back to me "Good. How are you?" I feel a little better.

Scientists and philosophers for centuries have told us that nothing is constant except change itself. The Greek philosopher Heraclitus said, "You never step through the same river twice."

Einstein's theory of relativity, Bohr's quantum physics and Heisenberg's Uncertainty Principle support this belief at the most minute level. All three theories help to explain that we cannot predict both a particle's place and speed at the same time. What is even more interesting, as soon as we look at a particle, the energy of our attention impacts the movement of our smallest brothers and sisters. Nothing is fixed. Life is a whirlpool, not a dam.

If atoms, the building blocks of all life, are made of particles that are not fixed in space and are constantly changing, how can we humans be expected to have a rigidly constant existence? Just as the tiniest particle only exists because of its relationship with other particles, we humans also need to be recreated every millisecond by our relationships with others and with the external world. Hegel called this relationship the dialectic.

Peter Berger and Thomas Luckmann, two well-known phenomenological sociologists, believe that conversation holds our sense of the universe, our reality, together. When we speak to one another—even just to say, "How are you?"—much more is at stake than a question that seems to be only about our well-being. First, by speaking to the doorman, I am affirming his existence as a human being. I show that I am friendly. I also reaffirm the cultural habit of asking people about their well-being, and our sense of culture is kept alive. When the person says, "How are you?" back to me, my world is in turn reaffirmed.

Knowing we exist is the minimum goal of our daily personal interactions. If we did not constantly keep this type of "conversation light" going between people, the two sociologists argue, we may start to have doubts as to whether the reality we have created really exists. This implies that we might start to wonder whether we exist too, at least on a philosophical level. "Maybe it only appears that we exist, but, in fact, we are not here. I don't know anything. Nobody knows anything," Anton Chekhov wrote in one of his plays. Every day, we struggle to believe that we truly exist, whether or not we are conscious of it.

Recent studies show that even though New York City has the highest percentage of any major city of people living alone, people are not so alone as they can be in less populated areas. Even the suicide rate in Manhattan is lower than most counties in the United States. Just a walk to the coffee shop immediately puts us in the company of others who confirm our existence. But knowing we exist is not sufficient to living a full and healthy life.

Intimate Friendship

My journey through my non-conscious mind often felt like climbing Mount Everest without gear. Throughout the past ten years, I have had a few moments where I felt that I just could not go on. Then miraculously the phone would ring. Paralyzed by my thoughts, I seldom answered. But when I checked the message, I would year, "Hi Pierre. Stephan here. Just thinking of you. Hope you are well." Those calls meant the world to me.

Researchers took 34 students, strapped heavy backpacks on them, and told them to hike a hill. Before they did, they asked them to guess how steep the hill was. Those who were alone guessed the hill to be much steeper than those who had a friend standing next to them. Those participants who were standing next to a long-term friend guessed the hill to be less steep than any other participants. Good friendships are crucial for us to live up to our full potential. But it is also essential for our survival.

Women with ten or more friends are more likely to survive breast cancer than those without close friends. What was important was not whether the friends lived close by or how much time they saw one another, but just having friends. Another study showed that married men without friendships had a much higher chance of a heart attack or a fatal coronary disease. Lack of social support was the second most predictive risk factor after smoking!

Older people in old age homes love to play bridge. Some researchers believe that keeping mentally engaged like this can help to delay the onset of Alzheimer's. But it does not stop it. So when a person starts losing her memory, other players start to stop playing with them. "People stop playing, and very often when they stop playing, they don't live much longer," another player said.

Without friends, life can quickly become meaningless.

Intimate Love

James, a close friend, has struggled with his self-esteem for ages. Today, after five years of marriage, he told me how he has come to feel "okay" about himself. "I know my wife loves me, whether I have wires for legs, a mirror for hair or a stiff upper lip on some days," he said. "Since she is okay with who I am, I am okay with who I am too."

Researchers asked 10,000 men from Ohio, "Does your wife show you her love?" For ten years, the researchers carefully followed the participants' health. Those who answered yes had fewer ulcers and chest pains. They also lived longer. Other studies show that people who feel supported and connected are less likely to have depression, suicidal thoughts, heart disease, hypertension, cancer and anxiety.

Observing great couples, researchers found that they exchange 100 or more caring behaviors throughout the day that make the other person feel loved, valued and affirmed. Whether spouse, partner, parent, sibling, child, colleague, we need people to make us feel that we are loved, or, as a therapist said, we are cared for, that we count and that we are competent.

Intimacy and Emotions

I used to avoid emotions at all cost. I was convinced that the best of humanity wake up in the morning, check their emotions at the door and stay cool, calm and collected throughout the day. So I would feel embarrassed if I shed a tear, raised my voice or felt fear. "Logic and linear thinking are what real men care about. Emotions are for the weak," I thought.

But it turns out that emotions are the best tool we have for surviving the whirlpool of life. Our left brain is a cheap calculator compared to the old and wise supercomputer that lives in our right brain. Our left brain provides us with conscious knowledge that we acquire in our lifetime; the right brain connects us with the non-conscious knowledge that we have gained in our life and with the wisdom gained through millennia. Our left brain is a mid-level accountant, our right brain with its gut feeling, Socrates.

Our right brain is not written in verbal language; the operating system is coded in emotions, sensations and pictures. For us not to drown in the whirlpool, we need to feel all of our emotions and sensations intensely. A tell-tale sign of someone with a healthy Real Self is that he or she experiences emotions spontaneously.

After coffee with Etienne that morning in The Grey Dog, I had a surge of feeling alive. I felt open to all the beauty of life and ready to go on stage that night to give my best performance. I felt present in the moment and ready for the future, a feeling very uncommon for me at the time. That moment of intimacy had changed something in my brain and its lenses.

The brain in love has become a fascinating topic of research for neuroscientists. Using brain scans, they search for the part of the brain that is activated during romance. One study caught my attention. Brain scans of people who have been in relationships for longer than two years—arguably those where intimacy is at play—differed from those in the grips of infatuation or romantic love. Specifically, the group enjoying intimacy activated two parts in the brain, called the anterior cingulate and the insular cortex. The anterior cingulate increases emotions, attention and working memory; is associated with happy states; increases awareness of one's own emotional state; allows us to assess other people's feelings during social interactions; and is associated with split-second emotional reactions to a win or loss, thereby judging the value of a reward. The insular cortex takes data from the body regarding external touch, temperature and internal pain; monitors activities of the stomach, gut and viscera; brings about "butterflies," and other gut reactions; and processes emotions.

Intimate relationships increase our awareness of emotions, ours and those of other people, which leads to a sense of connection with others and the world, a feeling of aliveness, the opportunity to use our "gut feeling" more effectively and greater self-esteem and confidence. No wonder women, in a study on beauty, said they feel beautiful (read: confident and alive) when they feel loved. This was independent of how physically attractive they judged themselves to be.

Intimacy makes us feel more alive and better able to experience more of life. But to simply have heightened emotions is not sufficient—many people with mental health disorders also experience greatly heightened emotions, to the detriment of their safety and relationships.

Intimacy and Our Story

I have seen many Broadway shows over the years. I often went alone or with people I knew only casually. Last year, Simon, a fellow businessman-turned-actor, went with me to see the production of Anton Chekhov's *The Seagull* on Broadway. The play, directing and acting were all superb. I laughed, cried and nearly exploded at a fellow patron who sighed loudly every time I laughed at the Chekhovian jokes. I felt alive with emotions, both positive and negative. Afterward, Simon and I could not stop talking about the play. I witnessed his enjoyment of the play and he was witness to my joy. Our moments of intimate sharing confirmed our passion for the theater and inspired us to keep going despite the odds against either of us "making it."

During the tough moments of my life, I often feel like I just can't go on. It feels like the world is conspiring against me to block everything I am trying to do, leaving me feeling humiliated. The best way I have found to overcome this feeling is to talk to people who have my best interests at heart, whether my therapist, a brother or a close friend.

To me, a tell-tale sign of a great relationship is when I can cry when I need to. From a man who detested tears, I now view tears as essential for living the good life, which can still really hurt sometimes. The more we deny the hurt and the less we cry, the more we live outside reality and away from our humanity. Crying washes the eyes for another person to see deep into us: to see and share in our pain and joy. Crying with somebody whom you know cares for you is a thousand times more powerful of a healer than crying alone or not at all.

Intimate relationships are essential for us to weather the thousand shocks our bodies and souls receive in this life, providing emotional buffers to attacks on our existence, whether physical or psychological. During moments of loss, loneliness, failure or death, our intimate relationships carry us through and make us stronger.

The Beatles, in their song "Hey Jude," gave a wonderful version of intimacy.

Hey Jude, don't let me down.
You have found her, now go and get her.
Remember to let her into your heart,
Then you can start to make it better.

A quote on a sugar packet in South Africa perfectly summarizes the role of intimacy in our lives: "Friends and family double our happiness and share our sorrow." This of course is only true if we have intimate relationships with our families. In contrast, dysfunctional families often double our sorrow and halve our happiness.

Intimacy and Self-Actualization

After Paul Potts won *Britain's Got Talent* in 2007 after years of struggling as a singer, his wife Julz, in an interview, said, "I am quite happy for him. I've been quite supportive always. That's what he wants to do and obviously I'm going to back him 100 percent."

"It must be very tough. He's had some knock backs along the way. It cost you a lot of money," the interviewer said.

"But at the end of the day, it makes him happy, and if it is going to make him happy, then one needs to make sacrifices for that."

When asked whether they ever thought of giving up after all Paul's struggles, she said, "Never at all. If he wants to do it up until he was 90, we still would be in the same position, still would be doing it. He needs to be doing what he loves."

Then she told the interviewer how Paul sang at their wedding: "There wasn't a dry eye in the house."

Intimacy is not only important for artists putting their emotions and vulnerability on display. Not long ago, I met Doug, a man with pools of humanity for eyes, in a deli on Broadway. Not long into our conversation, he said, "I want you to come over to meet my wife. She was just made manager at McDonald's and tonight is her first night on the job."

I watched his eyes as he introduced me to her. The pools of humanity became an ocean that was reflected back in her eyes. I have no doubt that the couple's mutual adoration played a big role in her moving up the ranks.

Sandra Murray, a researcher of romantic illusions, asked couples to rate themselves, their actual partner and an ideal partner using a questionnaire of strengths and weaknesses. Friends of each partner also filled in the same questionnaire. Murray then searched for the discrepancies between what people thought about their partners compared to what their friends thought.

In unhappy marriages, people tended to be much more critical of their spouses than their friends. Unhappy love is a highly critical magnifying glass. In happy and stable relationships, spouses rated their partners much higher in their strengths than their friends did. Happy love seems to make us blind and create a bit of fantasy, but one with a good outcome: Murray found that positive illusions become self-fulfilling. People strive to be the ideal that their partners believe them to be!

How can love make us blind? Brain scans of people in love show that there are a number of areas in the brain that love switches off. These areas are the parts of the brain that deal with negative emotions and social, moral and "theory of the mind" tasks. The researchers hypothesized that love—I would call it intimate love—decreases our critical social assessment of others and sooths away our negative emotions.

"Our chief want is someone who will inspire us to be what we know we could be," Ralph Waldo Emerson said. Nothing is more inspiring than people who believe in us or who are prepared to make personal sacrifices for us to reach our full potential.

Intimacy and Our Life's Story

I caught Max, the doorman at my apartment building, admiring photos of lovely women in a popular fashion magazine.

"I love women," he sighed. "I love their bodies. All the different shapes! I even love their minds. So complex. But, boy, I love digging into it. You may as well know what you are getting into. I know men are not supposed to do this, but I do. And women dig it. Boy, and do they broaden your horizons. They open you up in ways you never knew existed."

Max hit on many important aspects of great relationships: They don't depend on a specific body shape or measure of beauty. The interest lies in the other person's mind. Or, in the words of a Hollywood actor who was asked how it's possible that he still loves his wife so much after years of marriage, "Because

I fell in love with her eyes the first time I met her. I still am in love with them." People who are in great relationships fell in love with eyes and minds, not breasts and bank accounts. The beauty of falling in love with someone's eyes is that when old age, sickness or failure comes knocking, the eyes will still be shining.

Max hit on another important point: All great relationships broaden our horizons. Partners who intimately care about us want to understand us better. Because of their wish to understand us, we start to enjoy clarity to our thinking and improved self-reflection and understanding, key attributes to living a full life.

One of the first cultural activities performed by our early ancestors was telling stories at night around the fire about what happened throughout the day, who acted bravely, things people learned and affirming that all will ultimately be well, even in their highly uncertain world. They also spent a lot of time talking about where the clan fit into the broader scheme: Who was who in the family tree. The Old Testament is filled with pages upon pages of family genealogies, which ensured that people enjoyed a sense of connection and continuity, of being an essential component of the story of their family.

Over the millennia, modern humans began to tell ourselves these stories in order to develop what psychologists call a coherent narrative. We are driven to tell a story that makes sense given our past and present experiences. Intimate relationships help us to tell a more realistic story of our lives. We need people who want to dig into our stories to find the pearls that we have forgotten and to help us to cut out the rotten pieces that distort our views of life. Intimate partners help us to be better, more positive and more realistic story-tellers of our lives. Without intimate relationships, we come to believe in Hollywood stories; we see our lives as imperfect compared to the lives and relationships portrayed in movies and on TV. Intimate relationships help us to keep our feet on the ground as we reach for the stars.

Intimacy and Marriage

It makes me sad that I have never come close to being married. But what sometimes feels like a curse seems to be more common than not these days. The percentages of people who never marry are growing in double digits. The time spent married among all Americans has decreased and most people say that they can live alone happily. 79 percent of people say a woman can lead a complete, happy single life and 67 percent of people say that men can.

Those who do get married seem to want to get out of it very quickly.

Couples who get divorced enjoy, if they are lucky, three years of romantic love. Romantic love brings magic, excitement and a vision of a perfect life. But romantic love was never designed to last. When the chemistry is extinguished by life's realities, couples start getting frustrated with their marriages and stop having sex. On average, another three years pass before they seek divorce. The seven year itch is for those who married for chemistry, not for intimacy.

For some reason, many people believe that the best way to fix a "chemistry-free" marriage is to have children. But here the news is even worse: At least 25 studies show that, on average, there is a significant drop in marital happiness after the birth of the first child. With a drop in romance, happiness and sex life, 50 percent of couples ultimately file for divorce.

So why get married at all?

As dismal as these statistics are, there is another side to the coin. Research is very clear: People who are happy tend to be married, live in a wealthy democracy and have a rich social network. Happily married couples are healthier, live longer, drink less and are less violent. There is more.

James, a down-to-earth friend with a healthy Real Self and intimately in love with his wife, said to me, "My wife and I are now married for 13 years. Our love is stronger than ever. Even in bed. They can come and make a porn movie." Comfortable with their sexuality, my friends still make love as if lust were discovered yesterday. This continued enjoyment of sex is found in roughly 15 percent of couples, who contribute to nearly 50 percent of all sex in a given year. Happily married couples have more sex than any other demographic.

But it is not only sex that intimate couples enjoy. They too enjoy romance until death do them part. Romantic love comes from sharing novel experiences. That is why researchers found that successful marriages have partners who create novelty by investing attention in each other and really learning about the thoughts and feelings and dreams their partners have. We are all endlessly complex, so the search to understand the other will remain an endless journey. In the process, our marriages will never get stale. Great couples also work hard at finding joint adventure, like traveling together, visiting museums, learning a new skill or going on hikes. But the biggest source of novelty: Each partner must constantly work to discover new potentialities in themselves. Each partner must push his or her personal boundaries. Great couples have passion for what they do at work and play. They believe in their partner's passions as much as their own. Passion brings growth, growth brings change, change is novelty and romance loves novelty. This is why I want to marry a woman with passion for her calling. Being a good mother and wife will then follow.

Intimate couples also do not experience a drop in happiness when they have children. They plan for or welcome conception. They also never stop caring for one another, nor do they sacrifice time for their passions and with friends for the sake of their children. They know they need to be energized by their own lives if they want to energize their children's lives. So they work hard to save their marriage for their children's sake. As their children grow older, intimate parents keep adjusting their relationships with their children. Studies show that when parents maintain intimacy and interest in what their teenagers do, feel and experience, rather than on their grades or jobs, teenagers feel happy, strong and satisfied with life.

On the other hand, caustic marriages can have more negative health effects than being alone. The difference: the level of intimacy between two couples. Intimacy is such a crucial part of happy marriages that almost all relationship courses or therapists have one goal in common: Teach partners to see and appreciate the other partner's dreams, fears, pains and joys.

We live in a culture obsessed with Hollywood love, chemistry, feeling good all the time and beauty marrying big bank accounts. But if we are searching for long-term love that will help us to maintain our identity, deal with life's blows, fulfill our potential and create the perfect environment for our children to grow in, we must assess our future partners on the following criteria: Do they make us feel competent, cared for and that we count? Do they make us feel more alive with emotions? Do they double our happiness and halve our pains? Can we cry in front of them? Are they crusaders for our passions? Do they help us to bring clarity to our lives?

If the answer is yes, research suggests that we have a stronger chance of enjoying a happy marriage, raising healthy children, maintaining romance and enjoying good sex. Without intimacy, we will be bored in three years. If we are lucky.

Many people have opted against marriage for cohabitation. "What is a piece of paper anyway?" they ask. If the act of getting married is seen as being what our mothers want, our résumés need, the state demands or making our friends envy us, then marriage licenses are bad toilet paper. When getting married is seen as making intimate commitment vows in front of a caring community of friends and family, the impact is much more significant. If our existence depends on our intimate relationships with family and friends, and we honestly vow to marry another person in front of them, it is the non-verbal commitments that count. Studies show that people who are happily married are healthier than people who happily cohabitate. Intimate relationships do allow us to take better care of ourselves. Our bodies rejoice when another person tells us in front of all the people she loves: I promise that I will make you feel competent, cared for and that you count. I promise I will care for your passions as I will for my own. I promise I will double your happiness and halve your pain. I promise I will make you understand yourself better.

I want to get married. I want someone to "in to me see." I want her to share my pain and celebrate my joy. I want her to see my confusion and bring me understanding. I want her to see my self-hate, and help me sooth my demons. I want her to see my anger, acknowledge it, and help me to make sense of it. I want her to see my fears: of unrequited love, of death, of the future. By seeing it and holding it witness, she will sooth it. I want her to see the potential I have as a mature man, as an artist, as a husband and father, and believe in it even during the many days that I will doubt myself. In return, I want to be there for her in exactly the same ways.

Intimacy and the Real Self

Neuroscience research on the developing brain also gives us a hint as to what happens in our brains when people are intimate. Researchers found that when a mother and a young baby gaze at one another, significant activity is observed in the right prefrontal cortex (the location of the Real Self). These interactions bring about changes in the baby's pupils, while the mother may experience her nipples becoming wet. During these moments, a baby experiences an increase in opiates in the area of the Real Self. Intimacy forms the Real Self. But remember: At this point a baby still only has baby-speak. He has no language to communicate with his mother. Our earliest intimate relationships are built on non-verbal communication. First, it is the caring touch and soothing voice that support the baby. Then later, it is a mother's gaze. Magically, the gaze carries messages to the child's brain not unlike our cell phones receiving message through thin air. This right-brain-to-right-brain interaction or Real Self-Real Self interaction is the cornerstone of intimacy and essential for normal development of the Real Self. Non-verbal, Real Self-Real Self communication remains the most important part of communication with intimate partners throughout our lives.

There is plentiful clinical proof that intimate relationships impact our Real Self, even in adulthood. Researchers scanned two groups of patients, one with obsessive-compulsive disorders and the other with social phobias, before and after they underwent ten weeks of therapy. Good therapy always has intimacy as its foundation, regardless of the technique utilized by the therapist. In both groups, scans showed an improvement in the right brain function of patients after therapy. Now if these patients, with average Real Selves, can improve their right brains with minimal therapy—after all, the therapy was only ten weeks—imagine the powerful effect that two healthy Real Selves can have on one another's right brains.

To me it is clear: A healthy brain allows us to enjoy healthy love and that healthy love in return leads to a healthy brain. Lucky for those who were given that cycle in life!

Intimacy and Happiness

If intimacy strengthens the Real Self and happiness is the reward for strengthening the Real Self, we must expect our brain to reward us with happiness for being in intimate relationships.

A University of Illinois study showed that strong ties to friends and family and a commitment to spending time with them are the most salient characteristics of the ten percent of students with the highest happiness rates.

When asked to list their major sources of happiness, respondents in a separate study answered (in descending order of importance): relationships with children, friends and friendship; contributing to the lives of others; relationship with spouse/partner or love life; degree of control over one's life and destiny; leisure activities; relationships with parents; religious or spiritual life and worship; and family gathering periods, such as Christmas and New Year's. Six out of the eight are directly connected with increased social interaction with others.

Asked to keep a daily log of what makes them happy, researchers found that sex and social interaction are the leading contenders.

Robert Biswas Diener, called the Indiana Jones of positive psychology for his worldwide travels in search of happiness, concluded that happiness from the most traditional cultures to the most modern depends heavily on close family and other human relationships

Based on her research, Sonja Lyubomirsky from the University of California advises people to do the following to boost their happiness: Invest time and energy in friends and family; practice kindness to others, whether friends or strangers randomly (allowing an hurried motorist pushing in front of you) or systematically (every Sunday bring supper to a person in need); thank a mentor or person who meant a lot to you at a crossroads in life; forgive those who harmed or wronged you in the past.

The list of research is longer. But to me it is clear that our brain wants us to connect with others. If we do, we live happier lives.

Intimacy and Our Humanity

One morning, when I was a management consultant, I walked into my Park Avenue office to find Elizabeth, my assistant, fighting back tears in the kitchen. Concerned, I asked her what had happened. Elizabeth told me that that day was the first year anniversary of the death of her beloved sister. With contorted eyes expressing unbearable pain, she told me of her agony a year ago when she received the call that her sister had unexpectedly died. As she fought her own tears, I felt my own eyes well up.

I imagined the pain of losing one of my brothers. The death of one of them would scar me forever. Afterwards, in my office, I reflected on the incident. First, I had an inkling of what Elizabeth felt and thought (in science speak, I was able to mentalize Elizabeth's inner state). But just as important as understanding what she felt and thought, I was able to feel what she felt. Her pain became my pain. This level of empathy was entirely new to me and only possible after many years of therapy.

Here in New York, a friend told me of how a very arrogant and self-centered woman once confessed her painful past and loneliness to her. Even after this moment of self-disclosure, this woman has continued to maintain her bitchy demeanor, whether at work or play. But my friend constantly defends her.

"The one time she opened up to me is now branded in my brain. I now see her hurt more than her theatrics."

When you see eyes, you don't see a person as boss or employee; when you see eyes, you do not only see bitchy behavior; when you see eyes, you don't see disabilities; when you see eyes, you don't see the turban around the head; when you see eyes, you do not steal money from employees and stockholders; when you see eyes, you see the potential of all people to be part of the human family.

But if you can't—if you do not have a healthy Real Self—you will see differences and use them to elevate yourself to hide your lack of self-esteem. If you cannot, you will use people as objects and pawns. Prejudice is the inability to see another's soul, mixed with a false sense of superiority. Prejudice is animal brain territory; shared feelings are human brain domain.

I showed in the chapter on Passion how the best of humanity help others live up to their full potential and support their passion. Good bosses or colleagues do not necessarily show tears, but they do try to understand, to support, to validate and to keep our own growth at heart. To love our neighbors as much as we love ourselves means that we should help others feel competent, cared for and that they count. We all need relationships at work to help us grow too.

But it is not only our intimate relationships with people at work and in love that count. Study after study shows that mentally healthy people have a wide network of family and friends with whom they keep in contact, while also contributing to the community. Sharing ourselves with the whole community, including the poor, hungry, old, sick, young or dying, is an aspect of intimacy that we understand as our obligation to other people. We have been doing it for thousands of years.

George Bernard Shaw wrote, "I am of the opinion that my life belongs to the whole community, and as long as I live, it is my privilege to do for it whatever I can…I want to be thoroughly used up when I die, for the harder I work—the more I live…"

Prerequisite for Intimacy

A fellow actor asked, "You say intimacy is essential for happiness and humanity. Why is it then that most of us struggle so much with it?"

Our ability to interact with others comes from our right brain, specifically our Real Self. Intimacy is initiated and managed by the Real Self for the purpose of strengthening the Real Self.

To understand what it takes to be in an intimate relationship, we need to discover the non-verbal knowledge that is stored in the right brain of someone who is great at intimacy. Like we imagined putting a translator in Steven Spielberg's brain, imagine you do the same to someone whose relationship you admire. Someone like Morrie Schwarz, whose memoir shows how he enjoyed many intimate relationships with a wide range of people throughout his life.

The whispers that the best of humanity hear about how to approach intimate relationships can be separated into two groups: beliefs about the self and beliefs about other people.

During intimacy, the best of humanity have a right brain that whispers to them: "You are unique, autonomous and separate from others. You are safe and capable. You can sooth yourself when you are alone and know people will come into your life. You know the importance of all your emotions, how to feel them, manage them, make sense of them and share them with others to increase understanding and cooperation. You do not need people to feel good about yourself. You need people to share your life."

When the best of humanity looks at another human being, they hear, "People are physically and emotionally separate from you. They have their own dreams and fears that are different from yours. They have both "good" and "bad" traits. No one is perfect. You are competent to understand their feelings and thoughts, to see how they differ. You can and must empathize with how they see the world, their actions and their feelings. You know when to trust and when to run from people. People believe in you. You know the right people will validate and support your fears, dreams, joys and pains. You will not be boxed in or rejected for who you are and for following your dreams by temporarily moving away from loved ones. You know how to find a good combination between autonomy and intimacy. You know all relationships are filled with conflict. But you know you can deal with conflict in such a way that you, the other person and the relationship are much stronger afterwards. You know some relationships may end through death, misunderstanding or distance. But you know how to mourn properly as to free you emotionally and prepare you for a new relationship.

The best of humanity know that our animal brains will always tempt us to cheat on our partners. The animal in us wants to sow oats or seek adventure. They know lust never goes away, but they know they can look at the menu and not order. They also know that if they cheat, intimacy will be nearly impossible. Guilt destroys vulnerability and intimacy. The best of humanity know how to manage their jealousy. They know that jealousy is an unrealistic fear that someone will abandon us. They know what requests they can make to feel more secure in their relationships.

Most people are seeking love. Some do even have realistic expectations of what love is. But all the desire and factual knowledge in the world will not help if we do not have the non-conscious memories in our Real Self whispering to us about who and how to love.

Culture of Crying Alone

Americans have only two people, on average, whom they trust to share important matters with; 25 years ago this was three. 25 percent of Americans feel they have no one to talk to. We are also less likely to join groups, such as churches, unions or bowling alleys. Some researchers are fighting to demonstrate the importance of Internet networks or the importance of loose ties with similar minded people.

Loose connections and Internet networks tell us we exist. But for a happy life, we need caring eyes and a tender touch more than words on a screen or over the phone. With increasingly fewer intimate connections, more of us are joining Sartre in saying, "Hell is People." Hell is people not connecting intimately with us.

I have spent most of the last decade struggling with loneliness. Many weekends, I speak to nobody except the doorman or a waiter. Friday evenings often leave me with a tearing pain in my chest. To survive our brain's worst punishments, I make sure I stay busy. I have tried working until I dropped from exhaustion, daydreaming, chasing women or drinking, drinking and drinking. I have had to fill the lonely New York minute.

In a particularly unpleasant sounding experiment, researchers asked kids to evaluate the quality of cookies. Half the participants were taken aside and told that nobody wanted to work with them, meaning that they would have to evaluate the cookies alone. The other half were told that everyone loved them, but they would need to work alone, because it was not practical to work together. Researchers then counted which group ate the most cookies. The group that thought nobody wanted to work with them ate nine cookies; those who felt loved ate four and a half.

The cookies we need to battle our loneliness determine a lot of our daily behavior.

My Xmas Tree of Life

I sometimes think of my life on earth amongst the vastness of space and time to be the equivalent of a Christmas tree on a dark night. The existence of my tree depends on the number of lights brightly burning. If there are no lights, I am not visible. I do not exist. Nor will any silver or gold decorations or candy sticks matter.

Weak lights are loose connections, a doorman saying "How are you?" or having bar, restaurant and club friends in New York. Weak lights bring a sense that I exist, but they do not tell me who I am and what I am worth. Weak lights make me feel as if I am a blur in life.

Bright lights tell me who I am. A bright light is an intimate relationship I have, a relationship that energizes and uplifts me. A relationship that keeps on informing who I really am and that I am good enough.

For most of my life, I had a lot of decorations and weak lights on my tree. This tree never made me feel I was good enough, especially during dark moments. Gold on a tree in day glitters, but in the darkness of existential despair, it does not matter how popular or powerful you are. Today, a few bright lights allow me to breathe easier about life. But I am still afraid of stormy winds.

In my future, I want my tree lit with lights from many people from all walks of life. I also want to be a bright light on many people's trees. I know that when my tree is chopped down, the memories of intimate moments will still energize the lights on other people's trees. What better legacy is there than helping someone to shine brighter, become the best they can be and help them when life hurts.

Chapter 4

Take Care of Yourself

Once during an acting class, my teacher exploded at me. "You're not being present enough, you're not willing to let go and you're not listening to me!" she raged. After the scene was over, I felt surprisingly fine. "I am here to learn," I told myself.

But all of five minutes after leaving the class, my demons appeared in the back of mind: "You stupid fool. You will never be able to act. She's right. You are a failure."

"I better go to the gym," I told myself, knowing that my negative voice would leave me cowering unless I worked it out.

But the gym didn't help. So I tried another self care strategy: going to dinner at my favorite wine bar. I downed my first glass of wine as if it were water. My attempt to take care of myself was being subverted by my need to escape. And despite the wine, my mind kept spinning with hostile thoughts. I felt desperately alone in the middle of the crowded wine bar, surrounded by a blur of noises and shapes. I felt unseen, unappreciated, not understood. I did not exist. So I gulped down more wine, ate a rich pizza and ordered sweet deserts to comfort myself.

On my way home, I stopped off at a few more bars. After many, many drinks, I finally stumbled into my bed. Sleep finally hushed the demons that overwhelmed my mind.

The next day I was useless. Tired, hung over and grumpy, I wasted 12 hours trying to feel better, hours I know that I would pay a lot of money to have back when I come to the end of my days.

Life is challenging—the understatement of the century. If we look at humanity's collective struggle over the millennia, life has never been a walk in the park. At the same time, we are driven to push ourselves to fulfill our full potential by taking calculated risks and connecting intimately with others. People who live full lives encounter failure, loss, conflict or heartbreak nearly every day. We do not always have people around to care for us in the midst of our struggles. We need to be able to take care of ourselves—but every day, not only when life punches us.

There is a rhythm of expansion and contraction in the universe: Birds migrate for thousands of miles, but come home to breed. Cells, even cancer cells, move far and wide in the body only to return to their original location to self-seed. The tiniest particles in an atom expand to their full potential but ultimately return back to the core where they recharge.

Whether we call it self-care, self-seeding or self-charging, all humans need a place, both physical and psychological, where we can return to energize our mind, body and soul, to count our blessings or to lick our wounds. How effective we are at self care determines the quality of our passions and intimate relationships. Self care is crucial for finding happiness.

We Are Our Brains

As a junior doctor in South Africa, I worked at a rural referral hospital in the province of KwaZulu-Natal. There I met John, a medical doctor, who was much older than me but who nevertheless had a marked inability to control his impulses. Every Thursday, I would assist a reserved-to-the-point-of-being-nunlike surgeon during her morning surgeries, while John provided anesthesia. Usually, John would end up swearing at the surgeon, throw her the middle finger and call her terrible names, best not repeated. After surgery, he would stand at the window of our hospital's tearoom and gaze out at the African bush. One day, a friend walked into the tearoom, saw John contemplating the outdoors and said, "Morning John!" When John did not answer, my friend said, "Nice day, isn't it?"

Without changing his expression, John replied, "Nice day for a suicide."

Earlier in his life, John had been a top student in anesthetics and happily married. Then a motorbike accident damaged the frontal lobes of his brain. John recovered and was able to continue practicing medicine effectively. But the injury completely changed John's character and personality. His brain injury robbed him of who he was. Years later, I learned that John had killed himself.

In my days of practicing medicine, I have treated a few Alzheimer's patients. As the disease suffocates a patient's memories, she stops recognizing her loved ones and ultimately herself. The patient's personality evaporates along with her memories. Remember the research subjects who allowed their right brains to be paralyzed by TMS technology? They lost their sense of self-respect and self-worth and life was reduced to a game of cost-benefit.

Our brains allow us to say "I am Pierre" or "I am Susan." They determine our every conscious and non-conscious goal and inform us how to behave toward other people, life and our planet. If how we act is who we are, then we are our brains.

On hearing this, a friend with an Ivy Leagued education asked, "But don't we think with our brains and feel with our hearts?" We don't. The brain uses our hearts and our guts to make us aware of our feelings. Even lust comes from our brain. No wonder some researchers call the brain our biggest sex organ.

Self care is therefore brain care, especially Real-Self care and its building blocks: emotions, sensations and images.

Emotion Care

For most of my life, I tried to be an Elliot. The famous patient of the behavioral neurologist António Damásio, Elliott was unable to feel any emotions after having a brain tumor. For many of us in the Western World, this condition would not necessarily have been undesirable. After all, we are taught that to make rational decisions void of emotional interference is the key to a successful life, right?

But Damásio found that Elliot was at a loss on how to navigate life. When he had to work, he would sit for hours trying to figure out what type of pen to use. In restaurants, he focused on the knife, forks and lights, but could not make a decision about what to eat. Without emotions, Elliot had no idea how to go about making decisions, whether trivial or important.

Dr. Masterson writes that the Real Self gives us the capacity "to experience a wide range of feelings deeply with liveliness, joy, vigor, excitement and spontaneity." But when I told a friend this, he said, "Wow. I can't take more emotional spontaneity from my wife. It is hard as it is." To feel all emotions fully is healthy; to express all emotions fully is not. The ability to delay action is one of the most important criteria that separate us from animals.

People who are emotionally intelligent know how to make sense of their emotions. Over time, their emotions allow them to get to know themselves better and become more decisive about who they are, what they want from life and what to do to get it. Emotion care is to become emotionally aware, in order to become self aware.

Emotion care is one of eight strategies that happiness researchers tell us to cultivate in order to sooth ourselves during times of crisis or unhappiness. They suggest a range of advice from religion to secular beliefs and wisdom such as "this too shall pass" and "that which does not kill me will make me stronger." The trick is actually believing them. And the only way that we can believe in these tools is having a healthy Real Self.

Listening to interviews with great sports players, you often hear how they compliment themselves for dealing with tough moments in competitions, and for winning. Emotion care also means taking the time to congratulate ourselves when we accomplish our goals. It is not vanity when our compliments to ourselves are based on accurate assessments of our accomplishments.

My friend Andre Haasbroek gave the perfect definition of emotion care when he told me, "You must be your own best friend." Indeed, a good friend usually does know when to compliment and when to sooth.

Sensation Care

One Saturday evening, I went to the opera with my roommate, Pablo. We sat in the high altitudes where the cheap seats are and where all the tourists go so that they can say they have been to an opera. The performance had just started when I heard a woman behind me begin to sniffle. I tensed up. "Please not a sniffer. Please, please!" My cries to the opera gods were in vain. The woman had allergies, and like so many people with allergies, she had no clue how frustrating her sniffling was. Not long into the opera, all I could focus on was the next sniff. I felt homicidal. "Goddamn tourists! Do they not have any opera etiquette?" During intermission, Pablo asked me if I was enjoying the opera.

"No way," I said. "I am only hearing the woman behind us sniffling."

Then I had an idea. I decided to take a bunch of napkins back to my seat and offer them to the four women sitting behind us.

As we got back to our seats, we heard that the women were speaking Spanish. Pablo, fluent in Spanish, offered to talk to the women on my behalf.

"Ladies," Pablo started in Spanish. "One of you has a cold and it makes it hard for us to listen."

"No, No. It's not us," all four blurted out almost simultaneously.

"Well, it must be one of you."

Three of the women began to point to the fourth one.

"It's her. She's got allergies."

Pablo kindly gave her the napkins, thanked her sincerely and sat down. When the opera began again, all was quiet in the Met. Finally, I could disappear into the magic of the human voice.

I went to the opera to enjoy an aural and visual display from some of the world's top artists. Taking my ears and eyes on a date is a good example of self care. Plato thought children should learn music before anything else. Music brings "soothing patterns of sound to restore order in their consciousness."

But just listening to music is not good enough. To really listen, Csikszentmihalyi says, we must pay attention to how the music creates a sensory experience, then appreciate what feelings and images we feel based on the music we hear. Finally, for the experts, listen to the structure underlying the work and how harmony and dissonance are achieved. When we focus our energy and attention on active listening, the Real Self is strengthened.

Director and screenwriter Terence Davies says of Bruckner's Symphonic Cycles 1-9: "I couldn't live without them. They give something so sublime that they restore my soul."

But to listen to music at such a sophisticated level demands a strong Real Self. My fragile Self was easily ambushed by the poor woman sniffling behind me. People with a strong Real Self are better equipped to focus on their joys without getting distracted.

Any activity that stimulates our sensory organs and transports us to a new sense of reality is important. The positive psychology field tells us that we can experience transcendence by appreciating the beauty and excellence of nature, music, art, drama, film, sport, science and mathematics. The list of self-care activities is much longer. The only criteria: being fully engaged and experiencing flow.

My friend Karen became completely blind late in life. This did not stop her from traveling across the country to attend a weeklong improv camp. Months after we met at the camp, I told her about a trip I took to France to watch the Rugby World Cup with my brothers. She wrote back, "I am glad your travels and rugby were all good. I can't wait to get back in the saddle for globetrotting. Although I can no longer see the sights, I can eat the food, visit with the people, hear the music and language and feel the environment in ways I have never before experienced. It is a good goal."

Sensation care is learning how to see and smell fully, to hear and feel completely. Life is rich, but unless we train our senses, we are only conscious of a small slice of life. Sensation care is learning how *not* to settle for scratching the surface of what life has to offer; to make time for all our senses; and to learn how to concentrate so that a sniffling tourist does not upset enjoyment.

Happiness researchers advise us to make an effort to really enjoy the sweetness of a peach, the caress of a spring breeze, the sight of two lovers, to take "mental photographs" to view when we are down and out. But it is also clear that sensation care is not listening to an iPod constantly or playing videogames every chance you have. Sensation care is deep involvement with what you are observing, rather than an escape from life.

Benjamin Franklin summarized sensation care this way: "Happiness consists more in small conveniences or pleasures that occur every day, than in great pieces of good fortune that happen but seldom to a man in the course of his life."

Visual Care

"The eyes are the windows to the soul," is a well-known saying. Neuroscience has caught up with the belief. Research shows that the hub of our Real Self lies in the right orbito-frontal cortex. This part of the brain links who we are and what we feel with the part of our brain that is in charge of analyzing what we are seeing. So a healthful visual diet is extremely important in taking care of the Real Self. It should come as no surprise that our brains enjoy walks in nature, whether we are a small child with ADD or an elderly businessperson.

For millions of years, our daily visual diet comprised our natural environment and the eyes of family and friends. It was a world filled with three-dimensional data. Today, we spend much of our time staring at two-dimensional screens. We barely connect intimately with one another and communicate primarily via email, Twitter or text message. We fill, or our minds are force-fed, visual junk: commercials, videogames, porn, gossip magazines and photos of stars and celebrities, to mention a few. Research shows that many of these activities bring pleasure to our minds. But would you eat ice cream non-stop for five hours and believe that your binge will leave you feeling great? So why do we do that with our visual diet? Since we see what we believe and believe what we see, we must mind what we watch every day of our lives.

Language Care

Two years before Nelson Mandela was released from prison, I was elected President of the Student Council at the University of Stellenbosch, a prestigious South African university that had delivered many former prime ministers. 1989 was an exciting year in South Africa. We were still stuck with apartheid, but times were changing. To say that Nelson Mandela should be released from prison had become accepted on the campus.

During the year, 18 of us, against the university and government's wishes, traveled to Zambia where we met many of the African National Party leaders, who were still in exile. On our return to campus, all hell broke lose. We were called traitors. I even received an anonymous telegram saying, "The ANC is like a snake. Hopes it bites and kills you." We also had to face many challenging meetings among liberal students, conservative students and university leaders.

At one tense meeting, I was forced to make some impromptu remarks. In those years I could make good speeches, but I was horrible on the fly. My remarks sounded as if I was a two-year-old still learning how to speak. Two members of the Student Government came to me afterwards and said, "You will go down in history as the Student Government President with the worst grasp of language!"

At its core, language is how we symbolize and interpret emotions and sensations. Language helps us to label our feelings, create space between ourselves and our feelings and allow us to reflect on our behavior. Being conscious of our feelings and learning from them is essential for having a human consciousness. Higher-order human consciousness exists when we are aware of other people's unspoken emotions and can use this knowledge to increase communication, trust and intimacy.

Working on feeling your emotions and then expressing them with the right language is an important part of self care. But language is not only important for our emotional life.

When I walk through snow, my senses inform me there is white, cold, soft, grated ice laying on the grass. My mind translates this experience into the word "snow." Snow is now conscious and has meaning. I use this information to decide whether to build a snowman or to fetch a shovel to clean the pavement. Someone from rural Africa who has never seen or heard of snow may not have any idea what it is. To him, it would simply be "white stuff" of uncertain origin to be treated with suspicion. Without the vocabulary or informed senses, the snow would have no meaning to him. In contrast, an Inuit from Alaska would look at the same snow and give it one of many names that his culture has for snow. Since their survival depends on being acutely aware of different types of snow, they have both the senses and vocabulary to experience snow on a very sophisticated level. Language creates the world we live in and the possibilities that we see. If we want to experience more of the iceberg of our non-conscious life, we need to learn how to feel more, train our senses and learn the vocabulary to make our experiences conscious.

In the famous Nun Study, researchers asked 678 nuns upon taking their vows when they were in their early twenties to write autobiographical essays. They then followed them for more than 50 years, searching for signs of Alzheimer's disease. Since nuns living in convents experienced the same routines, food, weather, etc, as each other, researchers tried to see what variables may cause Alzheimer's. They found that they were able to predict who would get Alzheimer's based on the nuns' essays. Nuns who wrote with positive emotion, many details and with many thoughts merged into few words, lived longer, lived happier and had significantly lower incidence of Alzheimer's.

Our effective use of language in describing our experiences, especially our emotional and sensorial experiences, correlates with a healthy and happy life. This also explains why happiness researchers advise us to count our blessings by writing a weekly gratitude journal in which we write down things we are thankful for: whether it is flowers in bloom, our child's first steps, a day in nature. Using language to describe our emotional and sensorial experiences helps us to make sense of our lives, to tell a coherent narrative of what has and is happening to us. The better we can tell the story, the more it becomes a self-fulfilling prophecy: We become more unique. That is why some philosophers believe language give birth to us, we do not give birth to language.

In my local coffee shop, I met a world-famous writer whose intellect and writings are much admired. I have enjoyed his work, but I never felt I had a sense who he was. Often his writings left me with a "so what?" feeling. I closely observed this famous man of letters. He had almost no natural movement in his body. When I heard him ordering his coffee, his voice was monotone and lifeless. This man can write, but he is having a tough time living fully and spontaneously. He can impress people with his intellectual use of language, but he is unable to make his emotional and sensorial experiences more conscious. This also holds true for many politicians known for their gift of language. Many of the worst dictators in history were wonderful orators. They could use language to describe images that influenced the hearts and minds of their followers. But they used language as a tool to impress and persuade, rather than to make sense of their own experiences. Their inability to symbolize their emotions and sensations enabled their grandiose fantasies of themselves.

Animal Brain Care

When I sat at the bar drinking wine as if it were water and eating pizza and chocolate mousse to comfort my sorrows, my human brain was not in charge of my actions. The animal brain was let loose to order and consume whatever I could get my lips around.

Humanity has designed many products that stimulate our animal brain's need for pleasure and admiration. In our human history, sweets, alcohol, cigarettes, drugs, videogames, porn and luxury products are relatively new. But to our animal brain, anything that brings pleasure and admiration is perceived as important for our survival. Our animal brains want everything that brings admiration and pleasure and they want them now. But giving in to a life of pleasure and admiration harms our Real Selves.

"Healthy people appropriately enjoy pleasures," Dr. Masterson writes. Neuroscientists tells us that a healthy brain is one in which all four brains (the reptilian, the mammalian, the primate and the human) are integrated and work in harmony together. We need to give our animal brains their dose of pleasure and admiration, but when the animal brain drives our decisions, we weaken our self.

Self care means feeding our animal brains, but not spoiling them.

Habit Care

If, ten years ago, I had to face a teacher screaming at me in front of other students, I would have gone numb, plastered a Pagliacci smile on my face and become a puppy eager to make my teacher feel that she is God's gift to the universe. If I failed to get any compliments from her, I would have gone home and stared at the wall while I drank alone. I would have found all the excuses in the world to never go back to class.

I was not aware of my numbing and avoidance behaviors. I just believed this was the correct way to behave. If others cried while a teacher screamed at them, I thought they were histrionic. If they defended themselves against the teacher, I thought they were disrespectful.

Two observations have helped me to understand my own behavior: "Humans are a collection of habits" and "Humans do not do what is good for them, but what is familiar to them."

My reaction to failure or embarrassment was habitual and comfortable, because it was all I knew.

It took me years of therapy to start having a strong enough self to become aware of the emotion called *shame*, label it, identify its sources and then make an effort to combat the attacking voices by going to the gym. Sure, I failed miserably that day in the bar. I often still do. But I did put up a fight, a fight I now win more often than not. I hope that soon, I will be able to face moments of failure, identify shame, work out in the gym, call a friend and go to a movie. I want my new non-conscious habit to be reaching out to friends, not the bottle or comfort food.

Self care is finding ways to make our non-conscious habits conscious and then identify new ways of living and practice them until they become non-conscious habits. Growing from our experiences is the key to a happy life. Dr. Masterson defines creativity as "the ability to replace old, familiar patterns of living and problem-solving with new and equally or more successful ones." Later he continues, "We may need to learn how to view things differently to eliminate false impressions and replace them with accurate, realistic ones."

Self care is being able to get rid of habits that bog us down and replace them with new ways of living.

For the longest time I believed that all I had to do to change habits was to replace my negative thoughts with positive thinking, say positive affirmation a million times a day or tell myself to be more confident or my demons to go to hell. Today I know these attempts were a joke.

Our habits are formed out of many thousands of physical experiences that form our muscle memory. We cannot change muscle memory through factual memory or factual thinking. Factual knowledge brings awareness, but a change of habits takes years of practice.

Mind Care

After a vocal chord paralysis left me with a voice like Donald Duck's, I decided to start taking singing classes. Since then, I have learned two of my favorite Italian arias by heart. I do not expect to appear as a tenor at the Metropolitan Opera, but singing gives me great joy. And whenever I have a bad day, I sing my arias. When my brain recalls the tune and lyrics, my unquiet mind is frequently soothed. Singing my two Italian arias is self care to me, even though it may be torture to my neighbors.

Researchers tell us that when we learn stable mental content (the lyrics and rhythm of a song) to recall during moments of chaos, we can sooth our frantic minds. Exercising our memory is self care. This should be no surprise. Luis Buñuel said, "Life without memory is not life at all....our memory is our coherence, our reason, our feelings, even our action. Without it, we are nothing."

My other favorite tool to combat my chaotic mind is to solve problems. Many days when the demons attack, I tell myself: "Just finish the book. Or write a story." As soon as I sit down to focus on the task at hand, my mood lifts. Csikszentmihalyi stresses the importance of being an amateur scientist, poet, mathematician, musician, historian, biblical expert or philosopher. His research shows that people who take care of their minds by practicing their memory and problem solving skills are those who during extreme challenges "stood out as islands of sanity surrounded by the waves of chaos."

Mind care is finding hobbies, interests and games that make us feel like little children playing. Mind care is finding ways to do routine chores with a sense of adventure, for example, brushing your teeth with your non-dominant hand. A healthy mind is a challenged and playful mind.

Research shows that exercise is better than any product that we can buy. A good walk a few times a day can help executive functions as much as expensive tools. This close connection between the mind and the body takes us back to a philosophical debate as old as Aristotle: Are the soul and body separate?

Mind/Body Connection

Over the last few years, I have developed a severe backache that sometimes leaves my left leg numb. MRI scans show that I have a minimally herniated disc. A specialist recommended physical therapy and exercises to strengthen my core muscles. After almost a year, I have had some minimal improvement. But why does my backache and numbness come and go like an uncommitted lover? Why can I play golf with my brothers and feel fine and then weeks later when I am back in New York, simple exercises cause severe pain? Logic dictates that the more severe the exercise the more severe the pain.

Dr. John Sarno from New York University School of Medicine has shown that people like me suffer from TMS (tension myositis syndrome). He believes my mind is creating the inflammation in my back. My mind initiates back pain to avoid my non-conscious rage, sadness and emotional pain from pouring into my consciousness. My back pain is an emotional plug. His research shows that 94 percent of the 104 patients he treated in a TMS study had an abnormally high drive to be perfect and good. In my vocabulary, 94 percent of his TMS patients were success addicts like me. In his work, he found that patients found more relief from their TMS pain by addressing the emotions in their non-conscious minds than from conventional medical treatment.

As a Western-trained medical doctor, I dismissed the claims that the mind can cause physical illness. If the car is broken, it is not the driver; it is the car. Today I have come to believe a wide range of diseases and even some cancers can be traced by to the mind and negative emotions. In my own life, therapy has helped me to get rid of Raynaud's phenomenon, Gilbert's syndrome, morning headaches, severe heartburn and hypoglycemia.

I used to perceive my body as 180 pounds of muscle given to me to carry my head around or to lift weights or to play rugby or to look good on the beach. To steal from James Joyce, I lived a few yards away from my body. Photos taken throughout my life show this truth. In every one, I have one big fat smile while I stand rigid and at attention. I look like a soldier ready to go to battle.

Today I know that my rigid body portrayed the rigid inner beliefs I harbored about life and myself. It also served as a warning to the world: "Do not come too close. I am not emotionally available. I fear intimacy."

I have no doubt that how we live in our bodies informs the way we see ourselves and the world and how we see the world and ourselves informs our bodies.

This close connection between our bodies and our minds starts from the day we are born. How and when a mother touches her baby creates muscle memory of sensations and emotions that forms the Real Self. That is why child development researchers have coined the phrase: What is physical is psychological to the child. This is true for adults too.

Body Care

I cannot think of a time in my life when I did not exercise at least three times a week. When I arrived in New York, I started to run nearly every day. I had to. Running kept stress from devouring my soul. Every day, I would join hundreds of other runners in Central Park, each in his or her own little world, complete with iPods. I never ran to enjoy the park. I was more like a machine made to transform oxygen into carbon dioxide.

It gets even worse. When you walk around Manhattan, you see a gym on almost every corner. From early morning till late at night, people run on treadmills and listen to iPods, watch television and read popular gossip magazines—all at the same time.

This form of exercise makes us look good in the clubs or at the Hamptons in the summer. I was so fit that I even ran the New York marathon with my brother Andre, one of the highlights of my life.

But for me, this type of exercising was never about self care.

Today, when I go for a run, I take time to stop and appreciate beautiful vistas. I often buy coffee, marveling at the Statue of Liberty and Ellis Island for the thousandth time. Often I walk back home and enjoy seeing a child cycling with his father or two lovers holding hands. Jogging has become more of a date with the world than an escape from the world. I also enjoy classes such as yoga and NIA dancing that help my body play.

Doing exercise for the body may help you *look* good, but doing exercise that encourages the brain to play makes you *feel* good about yourself—long after the endorphins wear off. Exercises that allow the mind and body to play with one another is taking care of the Real Self.

Stretching every morning has done wonders for my psyche. For half an hour every morning, I stretch my muscles, warm-up my vocal chords and sing or recite a monologue. After a night in the company of my demons, getting back into my body through warm-up exercises has become an invaluable tool in my fight for mental equilibrium.

Intimate touch is important for all people of all ages. We need to feel that others truly care for us. A brother who hugs me, a friend who pats me on the back or a woman who kisses me with care brings joy to my brain.

We often admire those who claim to only need four hours of sleep a night, but studies show that these people have a higher mortality rate than adults who sleep at least seven hours a night. Sleep also boosts our immune system and is essential for our nervous system to work well. Lack of sleep make us drowsy and grumpy, inhibits concentration, impedes our ability to do complex mental tasks, impairs memory and deters optimal physical performance.

Happiness researchers are clear: We must take care of our bodies by getting plenty of sleep, exercising, stretching, smiling, laughing, touching and being touched.

Food Care

My mother is a great cook, but for most of my live, I used to eat with my mouth and not my palate.

"It is astonishing—as well as discouraging—when guests swallow lovingly prepared food without any sign of having noticed its virtues. What a waste of rare experiences is reflected in that insensitivity," Csikszentmihalyi writes.

One day, a friend invited me to dinner. For the occasion, he bought a very expensive bottle of wine. I raved about the taste and used all the wine-lingo I could remember. My host was pleased. When he brought out a second bottle, I tasted it and said that I may even like that one more than the first. My friend told me that the second bottle was as cheap as a bottle of water at the local grocery store.

Research shows that those of us who love to give the impression that we are food and wine connoisseurs often do not experience the food or wine as well as we like to pretend. Doing any activity with the aim of impressing others prevents our ability to find flow and truly taste the wine or food. We are thinking with our left brain vocabulary, not enjoying with our right brain sense of play, emotions and senses. This is why researchers find it is easier to fool people who think they know a lot about food and wine.

When I feel depressed, my brain sees every fast food store in Manhattan. But today I know that having hamburgers, fries and ice-cream when I have the blahs provides short-term pleasure before it leaves me low on energy and feeling stuffed.

People with a strong Real Self know how to eat and drink in moderation.

They know how to resist the enormous portions restaurants serve people here in the United States. Obesity is as much a Real Self problem as it is being part of a culture celebrating excess and fast food.

When we eat and drink in moderation with appreciation and awareness, food and wine feed the soul. Add good company, and many people will swear that this is the reason why we are alive. They may be right: Some researchers suggest it was the discovery of fire that allowed humans to enjoy high protein diets. Cooking meals around the kitchen fire lead to a sense of community and mutual caretaking.

Sexual Care

I was brought up in a culture where it was a bigger sin to have sex before marriage than to discriminate against black people. No doubt my Calvinistic upbringing was at least partially responsible for making me uncomfortable about sex. I believed I had to be a virgin until I met the right one, who would surely also be a virgin. I never entertained the thought of marrying a woman who had had sex with another man. After all, women are different than men, right? Our brain is between our legs; women are angels and future mothers.

Since those days, I have encountered many other views on sex. I have heard a woman tell me that women do not care as much about sex as men, while the next night another told me that she is just as horny as any man she has ever slept with, if not more. I have heard women say that all men are rapists or objectify women while others complain about their husbands' low libido. I have heard men say that women that sleep around a lot are whores, but men can feel free to sow their oats, since that is how we have evolved.

Let's face it. Sex is confusing.

When researchers tracked the eye movements of men and women watching sex scenes, they found that both men and women looked at the porn stars' genitals equally. Interestingly, women looked less at the porn stars' faces during these scenes, looked longer and with more enjoyment at a man giving a woman oral sex and were more likely to pick up fashion details of the porn stars than the male subjects. Research also shows that women with high sex drives tend to be attracted to both men and women. Women can be turned on by seeing scenes where a man and a woman have sex, two women have sex and two men have sex.

In places like North America, Germany, Britain and Israel where women enjoy sexual freedom, men and women enjoy almost equal *physical* pleasure from sex; in Britain, Israel and France, men and women report enjoying nearly equal amounts of *emotional* pleasure from sex.

When it comes to casual sexual encounters, men are more likely to seek out sexy women, while women are more focused on accepting or rejecting those who seek sex with them. And reject they do. Women are very picky about whom they sleep with. While men seeking casual sex often let go of all their criteria of what they are looking for in a night of pleasure, women tend to have casual sex with men who fit the criteria they are looking for in a long-term mate. To women, casual sex is an informal interview, researchers say.

The research on men and sex is more predictable: Straight guys love straight girls, gay guys like gay guys. But not all men are as sexually excitable as their neighbors. Men with a high sex drive and low self-control are more likely to have sex without condoms. They also are more likely to treat women as objects.

In a study, researchers assessed 40 men and rated them on how aroused they were and how much control they had over their sexual urges. Then they placed the participants in a room where they watched pornographic material that ranged from "normal" to brutal and violent sex, while a device measured the penile responsiveness. All of the aroused men responded equally fast and robustly to both the violent and the "normal" pornographic material in contrast to those with a lower arousal score. But horny men differed in how long they watched sexual brutality: Those with a high level of control over their horniness quickly were turned off by what they saw, while the rest maintained an enthusiastic response.

Happiness researchers asked participants to carry a pager and to write down what they were doing and how they felt when they were beeped. Researchers then randomly paged them throughout the day and night. Having sex was one of the top three activities that made people very happy. Other research shows that people in good marriages have more sex than those of us who are trying to imitate *Sex and the City* and are happier and healthier. Research shows that mentally healthy young adults in countries where sex is accepted, do have a few sex partners while they experiment with their sexuality. They quickly discover what they like and have fewer sex partners than those of us with struggling Real Selves. Finally, Csikszentmihalyi's research shows that sex brings moments of flow when we intimately care for our partners. Sex, tender touches and emotional intimacy strengthen the Real Self.

The research has made me conclude that the best of humanity are comfortable with sex; enjoy a few sex partners early in their lives, but quickly figure out who they want to be with in long-term relationships; experience happiness when having sex; have sex more often than those of us who are single or in boring marriages; and experience flow while having sex with those they care for. Sex done right strengthens the Real Self.

The Real Self is also essential for being responsible about our sex lives; to treat our partners with respect and care; to ultimately find the sexual and intimate partners who we want to commit to; and to keep our marriages fun and romantic. It is also essential to avoid a life of feeling guilty about sex or becoming serial one-night standers to fill our loneliness.

Today I know I want to marry a woman who can kiss well and loves sex; has had sexual partners; enjoys a sense of adventure and play; can ask for what she wants in bed; and is equal in the giving and taking of sexual favors.

A Healthy Body

We live in a time where the human body is manipulated to fit popular magazines' versions of the ideal body. But what is a normal body?

Healthy people live fully in their bodies. They practice being present to their senses and emotions. They love to touch and be touched, good food and good sex. They love activities such as dancing and outdoor activities that encourage the freedom of movement, as opposed to routine movement. To them, their bodies are not objects to use and abuse, to lose weight, to beat a time, to run marathons or to pump for admiration. Their bodies bring them joy. In most cases, they have a body mass index of 18.5 to 24.9—the medically accepted range for most people. (The exceptions are muscular athletes or older people with muscle loss.)

Healthy people have a positive body image. For every positive bodily experience they enjoy, their brains (specifically their right parietal lobes) record and transform their bodily experiences into a healthy body image. Many enjoy being naked in front of their intimate partners. They do not rush to put off the lights or hide under bed sheets to avoid appreciative eyes from caressing their bodies. They enjoy the admiring eye of others without feeling "objectified." They enjoy physical and sexual intimacy with those they love. They do not harm to their bodies with mutilation, sexually risky behavior, obesity, self-starvation, relentless exercise or chemical addiction.

Thanks to a healthy Real Self, they treat their bodies like their best friends.

Clothes Care

For most of my life, I was told what to wear. More often than not, it was a suit and tie. So clothes never had any meaning to me. Once in corporate

America, a partner, after looking at my clothes, asked, "Are you sure you weren't a vet in rural Canada?"

In an interview, Roger Federer said, "Maybe seven years ago, when I started to date Mirka, it was, oh, God, you know, I had jogging shoes and a pair of jeans. Then I started to really enjoy dressing up. What is my style? Is it a suit? Is it casual? What is it? I'm young now. So I can make mistakes with my choices. It's a way to discover what I like, who I am."

When we dress to discover ourselves or to show the world our style, it is self care. When we dress in high-end labels to seek admiration from others, fashion and grooming are a form of self-flaunting.

Research shows that when women care about their personal style—which can be from clothes found in thrift-stores—their marriages are often happier. Psychiatrists will also tell you that seeing a patient walking through the door with attention to his or her clothes is typically a good sign of a depressed mind finding joy in taking care of the self.

Home Care

I go through phases where I write from morning till night, completely oblivious to my apartment. Then one morning I will wake up and feel uncomfortable in my own space. Only then will I notice the week's dishes in the sink and avalanches of paper on my desk, coffee table and floor. My home often reflects my inner mood. When I set out to clean my apartment, my mood lifts too. A clean home brings a new perspective on life.

Like all animals, we are territorial. We like to have a place to call our own. But our place communicates much more to the trained eye than anything we can do or say. Is it clean or messy, a museum or a pigsty, homey and personable or extravagant?

Having pets also has a positive self care effect. State University of New York researcher Karen Allen took a bunch of hypertensive, success-addicted stock brokers and put all of them on anti-hypertensive drugs and told half of them to get a pet. Six months later, during some stressful tasks, such as doing math or holding one's hand in ice water for a long period of time, those with pets showed less than of the blood pressure surge and made fewer math errors than their peers without pets. Allen believes it is because people feel less nervous around animals; animals do not judge and provide an object for their owners to shower with unconditional love. These types of studies show that pets, just by their presence, can help to lower blood pressure, decrease cholesterol, reduce loneliness and depression and increase the chances of survival after a heart attack.

A clean livable home with a pet is good self care.

People Care

Sam, a CEO from San Francisco, had an acerbic relationship with his employees. His perfectionism was destroying his company and I was called in to coach him. As part of my initial assessment, I interviewed his employees. They told me that when they made mistakes, Sam would change into a parental figure, scolding them for not performing as expected.

"Many of us are up day and night preparing for meetings with Sam. 99 percent of our reports are perfect, but he never says anything about that. He focuses on the one percent that was wrong. Then he would become like my mother. It was not what he says, but it is how he says it. I always leave the meetings sick to my stomach. For days I can't concentrate."

While speaking, the employee barely took a breath. Talking about his boss was filling him with fear. When I confronted the CEO about this rather strange behavior, he answered, "I would never give anyone a report full of mistakes, so how could I accept this from them? No, they are unethical and unprofessional. Give me their names, I can't work with people like that."

In 2005, researchers set out to examine the connection between the mind and the lungs of people with asthma. After inducing asthma attacks in their subjects, the researchers performed brain scans and lung tests on their subjects, who read words with different levels of negative emotional charges. At end of the test, they concluded that the subjects' emotions actually triggered the inflammation in the lungs. Angry or sarcastic words carry power and can force our body into a fight-or-flight situation. But people can influence our brains without a word being spoken.

Our minds, especially our right brains, communicate with one another as magically as a text message traveling to a satellite and back to earth. We do not even have to use words to transfer the message. Our brains pick up people's foul moods, negativity, gossip, pain, confusion and hatred.

Research have shown that chronic exposure to negative people increases the level of cortisol, a stress hormone that is linked to many psychosomatic and physical conditions, such as ulcers, immune disorders and certain cancers. In high levels over long periods, cortisol harms the brain. We need to know who is undermining our happiness and causing us ill health and shut them out of our lives.

But identifying these negative people in our lives may not be that easy. Our conscious mind may tell us to love certain people for they love us, but they may not be the people our non-conscious mind wants to hang out with. Traumatic experiences with certain types of people force our conscious minds only to see their best, idealized side. So how do we tell if someone is spreading negativity to our non-conscious mind?

Watch a bird or a deer under threat. It barely breathes as it tries to blend into the background and its eyes move quickly in all directions to scan for any danger. Our animal brain gives us a third option to deal with threat, called the behavioral inhibition system (BIS). In the layperson's language, we fight, flee or freeze. Simply put, our brain allows us to shut down our feelings and needs, to become puppets. In nature, this system is designed to be a temporary cure. In our human society, we have created environments where people are forced to continuously activate their BIS. Examples include abusive spouses and parents, or tyrannical work environments.

So when we look at which people are causing our non-conscious mind harm, we need to ask ourselves the question: Who makes us stop breathing at home or at work?

Self care is avoiding those who make you stop breathing and spending time with people who allow us to breathe freely. In order to do so, we need to become aware of how people impact our breath and how and when to say "yes" and "no" without feeling guilty, being selfish or hurting others. We need to know we have the right to stand up for our needs. A healthy Real Self acts as our observer and lawyer.

Community Care

Last summer I spent six weeks at the Atlantic Acting School. The school is well-run, employs many competent teachers and attracts students from around the world. It also has a strong sense of community. Combining my passion with a sense of community made that summer one of the best of my life.

We all need to feel that we belong to a community. We became human to cooperate, share, learn and make sense of life together. Without a community, we never can be whole.

For many, a religious community brings meaning and care. Studies show that when people participate regularly in faith-sponsored activities, they stress much less about finances, health or other issues than non-religious people. Other research shows that this may not be due to the depth of their religious convictions, but the quality and quantity of their participation within a community. Working, praying and believing in similar values with likeminded people may be a stronger cause of happiness than the religion itself.

Some scientists and philosophers even believe that humans are not only driven by self-selection (we are driven to have our DNA survive), but we may also be driven by group-selection (that all of us compete, live and die as a human family).

Bernie Madoff will always be associated with the greed and unethical behavior of our financial leaders. In a wonderful *New York Times* article, titled *If Bernie Met Dante...* Ralph Blumenthal argues, with the help of Robert Pinsky, American Poet Laureate and Dante scholar, that Maddoff belongs to the ninth and deepest pit of Dante's Circle of Hell. The pit is "where sins of betrayal are punished in a sea of ice fanned frigid by the six batlike wings of the immense, three-faced, fanged and weeping Lucifer," Blumenthal writes. Bernie betrayed his community, which gave him his energy and moral force. As Mr. Pinky puts it, "Dante was interested in what the soul could do to itself. To betray everything you're connected to is the bottom."

In Manhattan, especially during the summer, you cannot walk a block without an earnest young undergraduate stopping you to solicit support a horde of good social causes. Some days I am friendly to them, some days they annoy me more than an attention deficit disordered fly on my grandmother's farm in South Africa. The ones that solicit money for charities that help children always get me to think of my duty as a citizen of the world. So far, I have not pledged any money. A part of me says that I am an artist borrowing money to pay my way at the moment. One day when I have made it, I will sponsor 100 children. But I know this is a copout. Because later that night, I will probably think nothing of downing five $6 beers—the amount of money it costs to sponsor a child for five months.

Peter Singer, professor of bioethics at Princeton University, feels differently. In his book *The Life You Can Save* he argues the following: Human suffering is terrible. After all, imagine your child trapped in Sudan without water or food. So if we can do something to prevent suffering that will not cause us to lose a night's rest, it is ethically wrong of us to do nothing. Giving to aid agencies will help relieve suffering that we never want to experience. So if we do not give, we are not good citizens. We are acting immorally. We are doing something wrong. Dr. Singer himself gives 25 percent of his annual income to aid organizations.

We can lash out at the Madoffs of the world, but are we living up to our responsibilities as humans? Are we not betraying people who are part of the human race but are suffering terribly in this life? Do we not belong with Bernie in the deepest pit of Dante's hell for not giving a single night's worth of beer money?

TAKE CARE OF YOURSELF

Animal Care

I was raised on meat and potatoes. Braaing (barbequing) meat in South Africa is more important to our Afrikaner culture than any other activity, even church or rugby. Even though I do not eat as much red meat today as I used to, I still enjoy a steak. Where I can, I support organic meats. But most often, I eat what I get.

At the same time, I am acutely aware of the atrocities that take place in factory farms all over the world. Calves, pregnant hogs or egg-laying hens are forced into pens and cages that make any movement impossible. At slaughtering houses, animals are often killed with much suffering. Our addiction to meat causes extreme cruelty to other species on the planet. But for the sake of profit and our full bellies, we turn a blind eye.

Each one of our four different types of brains possesses its own level of consciousness. The reptilian brain has limited awareness of the world and uses instinct to survive. Thanks to emotions, mammals are slightly more aware of life. Primates are thought to have a budding sense of self and a high level of consciousness. No wonder countries like Spain are moving to give apes basic legal rights. Humans, due to our sense of self and ability to make our emotions conscious, are the most conscious beings on the planet. The best of humanity even possess a higher form of consciousness: They can be aware of the minds and hearts of others around them.

Now if I had lived most of my life in total ignorance of my emotions and a complete lack of self, was my level of consciousness not on par with a reptile? If true, would other mammals that have full access to their emotions, like the calves, pigs or wild deer we eat, not be on a higher conscious level that I operated on most my life? I may be human because I have the spark of a sense of self in me, but if that spark is locked up in a cellar of my non-conscious mind, was I truly more conscious than the pig I am eating?

There are other concerns too. Jeremy Bentham, a famous Enlightenment philosopher, asked the following about animals, "The question is not, Can they reason? Nor, Can they talk? But, Can they suffer?" Animals have all the emotions in place to suffer. Farm factories know it and to ensure higher quality meat have designed many guidelines to ensure that animals are not stressed before they are killed. They know afraid, traumatized cattle lead to tough steak and low sales.

We need to make sure we treat all animals, even those we eat, with the same respect we would treat our dog or cat. Or, if my philosophical argument is right, with the same respect we give our cold, caustic self-centered boss sitting next to us at the office. Fortunately, there is a strong movement all over the world to ensure that animal rights are protected. Fast food companies, based on consumer demand, are listening. But much more needs to be done.

Time Care

At rush hour in Washington, DC, hundreds of thousands of people run at breakneck speeds to catch the subway trains. One day, only a few heard the music played by a young man in a baseball cap. A child and an older man listened for a few seconds before the river of people forced them to keep floating along. It turned out that the young man was Joshua Bell, one of the world's foremost violinists. As part of a *Washington Post* project, he agreed to play for free for all to hear. Nobody took the time to enjoy the moment. Here in the Western World, every minute of our lives seems to be spent on being efficient, filling the full minute by working toward goals. Since the world is 3.5 billion years old, we need to wonder why we feel so compelled to be part of the rat race.

Working in rural South Africa, I doctored many people who had a different sense of time. Many patients would arrive at the government hospital early in the morning and patiently wait their turn, often until early evening. Few ever complained. Other times someone would say, "See you at 1 p.m.," only to arrive at 3 p.m. with a big smile, but no apology. When my patients asked one another "How are you?" they prepared themselves to talk for a long time. Here in the US, "How are you?" means "Hello. I'm in a hurry. Sorry."

An anecdote, possibly an urban legend, shows the difference between "African time" and "US time": An American businessman arrived at a border crossing between two African countries. After waiting for hours, he finally saw the customs official.

"Please, Sir, I'm in a hurry. I'm late for an appointment," he pleaded.

The official responded, "Sir, you may have the watch, but I have the time."

Self care is having both African and American time. On some days, we need to sit a bit longer to enjoy the spring sun over lunch, listen to subway performers or really ask others how they are. Or, as my brother Andre suggests, we need to play with our children so we can re-experience how endless a summer afternoon feels for a child. And some days we need to get the job done. The Real Self helps us to choose which experience of time is important for our goals and the people we care for.

Uncertainty Care

During a Caesarean section in rural South Africa, I pricked myself with a needle. Anxiously I looked at the patient's charts. My worst fear came true: The patient was HIV positive. I freaked out. "I will almost definitely get AIDS. Goodbye a life of love, of having a wife and kids. Goodbye travelling and seeing the world," I told myself.

Against protocol, I decided not to report the incident to the administration. I rationalized that the chances of getting AIDS from a needle prick are not that high nor had the prophylactic use of anti-viral therapies been well-researched at that time. I thought that if I just ignored the incident, I would forget about it.

Our minds do not forget these incidents. Over the next six months, at the most awkward of moments, the uncertainty of my HIV status appeared. Often, it was while meeting a romantic interest. How could I have sex if I did not know my HIV status? But I did not want to know my status for I was convinced I was HIV positive. But uncertainty trumped my fear of the worst of news.

I visited a private pathologist in town for an HIV test. I wanted to know before the whole hospital knew. The day my of my results, I shook like a leaf in a hurricane as I opened the envelope. "HIV 1 and 2: Negative." I began to cry. I immediately drove to the golf club and ordered great food and a glass of wine. I was given another lease on life.

For six months, uncertainty destroyed my peace of mind. Like Hamlet, I found out that the worst stress is the time between thought and action, the time of uncertainty and endless pondering.

Researchers told participants that they would be given 20 electric shocks. They told some participants that all the shocks would be intense and others that they would receive 17 mild shocks and three intense shocks at random. The results showed that those who did not know when the intense shocks would come sweated more profusely and had faster heartbeats than those who knew every shock would be intense. Uncertainty breeds fear.

A life with Huntington's disease, a neurodegenerative disease, is tough. So for many people at risk, the question is: To know or not to know. Researchers found that people who opted to undergo genetic testing to learn their fate and were told that they had a high likelihood to develop the disease were much happier a year later than those who did not want to learn their risk.

Harvard psychologist Daniel Gilbert tells us our mind has a psychological immune system, a system that allows us to deal with the great setbacks that we as humans have experienced over millions of years of evolution. But here is the trick: The psychological immune system only kicks during significant events in our lives involving huge failures, diseases or pain. The chronic stress of uncertainty is not one of them. Our brain may help us to deal with an HIV diagnosis much better than it helps us to deal with the stress of uncertainty. This is why research shows our worst fears of the future, when they are realized, are never as bad as we expected.

People with a healthy Real Self will face whatever life throws at them. The Real Self allows us to mourn the news, to change the way we see the world, to adapt our behaviour, to lower our standards, to become more real and to find a new level of peace and happiness amongst the worst of news.

Uncertainty care is therefore searching for and facing your worst fears and then hope your Real Self is strong enough to help you adjust to a new way of living.

But there are some things we cannot know. Daniel Gilbert writes that one of the main reasons many Americans have been less happy and more depressed since the start of the recession is not the decreasing figures in their monthly bank statements. People are less happy because of the uncertainty of the future that looms in front of them. With the exception of the best of us, uncertainty kills happiness. So what can most of us with weak to average Real Selves do to combat the caustic effect that uncertainty has on our consciousness?

Palestine today is arguably one of the most uncertain places in the world. Palestinians do not have a legal home, face 60 percent unemployment, endure food, fuel and water shortages and suffer from intense overcrowding. That is still the easy part. Surveys show that 70 percent of all children have witnessed a killing and that 30 percent suffer from posttraumatic stress disorder. Dr. James Gordon and his Center of Mind-Body Medicine decided to help these stressed minds that are struggling with debilitating uncertainty. He and his clinicians teach parents and children the following techniques: "slow deep breathing to quiet anxiety; guided imagery to seek intuitive solutions to intractable problems; words, drawings and movement to express and share their feelings." All of these techniques directly access the right brain and allow people to move away from the frantic chatter in their left brain. A quieter mind allows people to focus on the here and now, on what they can do in the moment to survive physically and mentally. It stops the traumatic past from infecting the present moment and the uncertain future.

These techniques have helped stressed mothers to breastfeed their babies and teenage children to stop throwing rocks at Israeli tanks at the risk of being killed. Finally, the Mind-Body team teach people to be there for one another. Dr. Gordon reflected on how a Gazan clinician told him, "In our Scripture, it is written that when you do not have hope, you look for it in the face of your friend."

What is good for Gaza must surely be good for all of us who are worried about our economic future, our ability to pay for our children's education or when we will be able to go back to buying $300 Prada shoes or bottle of vodka at Gold Bar. Maybe these techniques need to be taught in the White House, the gilded offices on Wall Street, the mining towns of Wales and at Welgemoed primary school, the primary school I attended in South Africa.

When we face uncertainty, a healthy Real Self allows us to act with courage. It allows us to focus on the moment and on what we can do to master the situation, not what we hope others will do to rescue us or wishing it all would just go away. Finally, if the worst happens, the Real Self helps us to adapt, to grow and make the best of what happened to us. Resilience, a universally admired characteristic, is a product of a healthy Real Self.

Tensions of Life Care

"Longing for the ideal, while criticizing the real is evidence of immaturity. On the other hand, settling for the real without striving for the ideal is complacency. Maturity is living with the tension," Rick Warren wrote in this book, *The Purpose Driven Life.*

Johns Hopkins sociologist Andrew Cherlin writes that one of the main reasons why Americans face such high levels of divorce is that couples are not able to deal with the tensions created by a culture that celebrates both the intimacy of marriage and our drive for individual freedom and self-fulfilment. Couples struggle to deal with the innate tensions within all humans for wanting both intimacy and autonomy.

A life well lived is a life that confronts the tensions of many opposing needs and instincts we face daily. We need to actualize our full potential, but not forget to enjoy the moment. We must accept life's realities, but work toward a better life. We must live for self-expression, but know when to spend time with those we love intimately. We need to be parents to our children in a fast-paced world, but find time to keep our own relationship healthy and romantic. We need to take time for self care, but also find time to care for loved ones. We must take care of our families, but also find time to take care of the community. We need to seek moderate amounts of pleasure and admiration for our animal brains, but know when they begin to overpower our human brains and our happiness. We need to focus on reality, but know how much fantasy to add to avoid becoming depressed.

Research tells us that when we face a situation where we have too many options, we must not rely on our cold, rational left brain. This brain is good for us when we have a few options. But when we are overwhelmed, we must listen to our emotions, to our gut feeling. We must listen to our Real Self.

A Take Care of Myself Day

Wise people facing death often see life clearly. To me, one of the most beautiful descriptions of self care comes from Morrie Schwartz. When he was asked at the end of his life, what he would do if he had one day of health again, he answered, "Let's see....I'd get up in the morning, do my exercises, have a lovely breakfast of sweet rolls and tea, go for a swim, then have my friends come over for a nice lunch. I'd have them come one or two at a time so we could talk about their families, their issues, talk about how much we mean to each other.

"Then I'd like to go for a walk, in a garden with some trees, watch their colors, watch the birds, take in the nature that I haven't seen in so long now."

In the evening, we'd all go together to a restaurant with some great pasta, maybe some duck—I love duck—and then we'd dance the rest of the night. I'd dance with all the wonderful dance partners out there, until I was exhausted. And then I'd go home and have a deep, wonderful sleep."

That is the best example of self care I have ever come across.

The Cycle

The best of humanity know how to take care of themselves to ensure they live full lives. These moments of self care bring more happiness to their lives and a stronger Real Self. But people who struggle with finding happiness also struggle at self care activities. We often attack ourselves with negative thoughts, comfort food, alcohol, drugs, abusive company, disastrous relationships or sleeping only a few hours per night. We often move from one addiction to another, never finding moments of being at peace with who we are of what the moment has to offer.

The difference: The best of humanity have thousands of non-conscious muscle memories in their Real Self whispering to them about how to take care of their mind, body and soul.

Chapter 5

Creating a Positive and Humane Reality

It was the last Friday in January 2004 and my last day in corporate America. I was walking away from more than my Park Avenue office, regular paychecks, office politics, suits and ties. I was leaving behind a life of toeing the line to please superiors and colleagues. I was leaving behind a life of fulfilling expectations—other people's expectations, not my own. I was challenging my beliefs about who I am or ought to be and what life is all about.

As I walked into my apartment building, I saw the superintendent talking to the doorman. I gave them a friendly greeting, but the superintendent ignored me. Suddenly I was overwhelmed with fear. "He knows I resigned from my job. He knows that I will not have a regular paycheck. He's going to notify the real estate company. They will evict me. What will I do then? It is impossible for foreigners to find apartments in this city without a steady paycheck. I am doomed. Doomed!" I went into my apartment and rather than celebrating my freedom, I sat around worrying about what I would do when I got evicted. The future seemed dark and frightening.

The reality was that the super didn't know me—and he still doesn't. And even if he did, he would have had no way of knowing that I had resigned from my job.

So why did I, a man with a medical degree and a Ivy League MBA, panic for absolutely no reason? How was I able to create a reality that had very little to do with the truth?

Reality and Self-Perception

As a medical student, I was asked to examine a few severely anorexic patients. I can vividly recall the first time a patient told me with all the conviction in the world, "I am fat." Even when she was being force fed, she still saw herself as ugly and fat.

Now I understand why. It is nearly impossible for us to see ourselves objectively. Rather, our self-images are dependent on the inner realities that are shaped by our brain. We see what we feel about ourselves, not how others see us.

In order to demonstrate to his students the impact of a right parietal lobe brain injury on the reality of a patient, a neurologist pointed to the patient's right arm and asked her to whom the arm belonged. The woman, completely sane, correctly identified the right arm as hers. When he pointed to her left arm, she said she didn't know. When the neurologist asked her to identify the wedding ring on her left hand, she said, "It's mine." This woman could not recognize her left arm as her own, even in the face of concrete evidence. No amount of interaction or willpower will make her understand that her left arm belongs to her.

Every moment of the day, we create a subjective reality about our worth, our looks and our body image. Even our bodies are a fabrication of our brain!

Reality and People

Years ago I went out to a bar with two friends. I spotted a woman from across the room whom I was immediately attracted to.

"Wow. Look at that one at the bar. Now she's my type," I told them.

"So what's your type?" one friend asked.

"Sweet. Innocent. Caring."

Both men looked at me, stunned.

"You must be kidding me," one friend blurted out. "That woman will take you to the cleaners. There's only one-way traffic with her and that is pleasing her 24 hours a day."

For the life of me I had no idea what they were talking about. I ignored their advice and approached the woman. Weeks later I had to confess that they were right.

In our sessions, Dr. Masterson has told me a number of times that I could walk into a room with 20 potential partners, 19 of whom are good, caring, mentally healthy and eligible, but I will invariably sprint for the one that is not good for me. All this, while my brain tells me I have met the woman of my dreams. My brain doesn't allow me to see people for who they really are.

During a couples therapy session, a therapist videotaped a conflict between a husband and wife. Afterward, the wife said that she thought she had behaved with stoicism and control. But to everyone else in the room, she was approaching Mars on the scale of bitchiness—an observation she appreciated only after watching the videotape.

We do not see people. We *experience* people and our brain sees what it wants to see to justify our feelings.

Reality and Conscious Will

Over the years, some people have laughed at my foolish reactions to the world and to my dating life.

"Come on," they say. "Just grow up."

With these words, they indicate the common belief that we all are equally conscious of what is happening to us and have a perfect conscious will to make good decisions. When we behave outside the norm, we want to damage ourselves, to hurt others or behave childishly. So we need to be punished, ridiculed or avoided.

More often than not, I don't feel as if I'm truly in charge of my life. If I did, I would be in a great intimate relationship, have children, enjoy a big social network and run to every audition I see. I would live my life with resilience and optimism. I know what to do, but for some reason, I cannot do it. Every time I attempt to reach for one of these goals and enjoy a breakthrough, I experience an enormous breakdown that leaves me feeling hopeless and isolated. I frequently do not have the conscious will to fight these feelings.

Dr. August Kinsel did some interesting experiments during his years working at the U.S. Medical Center for Federal Prisoners. He noted that, in his work on animals, some creatures react with extreme violence when they perceive that their territories are invaded. So he designed some experiments to determine whether personal comfort zones are the same for all people. His results showed that violent criminals felt threatened at a distance that most other people feel safe and comfortable. A typical person will allow you to enter his space to about an arm's length from him before he begins to fight or flee. A prisoner is ready to fight at two arm lengths away.

Our brain creates a reality, then we exercise our options based upon that reality.

Reality and Morality

I was born and bred in apartheid South Africa. For the longest time, I believed that apartheid was moral and just. We had a right to keep blacks separated from whites. After all, we all have a right to choose those whom we want to have as our neighbors. Fast forward a few decades, and I am arguably on the more liberal end of most debates.

The latest research has some good news: We are all born with moral intuitions that are shaped in our early years. Even children know when something is right or wrong. Why do all humans have moral intuitions? We became human to survive as a group by helping with the raising of children, division labor, fighting common enemies and being there for one another emotionally when the going gets tough. It is in our genes to value tradition, respect, equality, loyalty, altruism, empathy and cooperation. We want to be on the side of what is right and good.

Research shows that in the United States, liberals see fairness and prevention of harm as the most important variables in any moral argument; conservatives use respect for authority, loyalty and avoidance of disgust as the foundation for their moral arguments. (Disgust, an emotion unique to humans, helps us to avoid any form of outside threat, may it be a physical threat, such as from bacteria-ridden feces, or perceived social threats, such as unfamiliar cultures with different value systems.) Both sides believe they are acting morally, but both often have completely different viewpoints. Their intent is the same (to be moral), but because of differences in their created reality, they will oppose, if not hate, one another.

To my mind, belief in the apartheid system was not immoral. At that time, my mind created a reality whereby I believed moral behaviour was based on authority, loyalty and a desire to avoid feelings of disgust. I cannot be embarrassed by what reality my mind created for me then. But today, my stronger Real Self allows me to base my sense of morality on fairness and prevention of harm. It makes me feel part of the human family, all 6.7 billion of us. But I still have many moments where my mind says, "Listen to authority. Be disgusted with those who do not look like you." Consciously, I hate those beliefs; but they love my reality.

Reality: A Murderer

Sadly, and even embarrassedly, I admit that I am no stranger to having thousands of suicidal thoughts over the years. After fantasies of fame, suicidal ideation has been my most frequent lover.

There are moments that I am 100 percent convinced that I will never find love or a passion that will pay my bills. I know, as sure as the earth revolves around the sun, that my life will remain dissolved in an eternal emptiness. Then my mind will ask, "If this is it, why keep going." In these moments, my conscious mind believes life is useless, but my non-conscious mind keeps fighting.

After keeping this horrible secret to myself for so long, I have started to tell others about my suicidal thoughts. Their response: "But you have so much to live for!" often leave me feeling nauseous. If only they knew how useless any conscious thought or advice is during those moments.

English poet and critic Al Alvarez failed at killing himself. He later wrote that suicide is "a closed world with its own irresistible logic....Once a man decides to take his own life he enters a shut-off, impregnable but wholly convincing world where every detail fits and each incidence reinforces his decision."

Then there were times when I consciously wanted to live, but a force above, beyond and within me had a different idea. While my mind screams for help, my body feels convinced that jumping to my death is the only way out. These are moments when I wrap my arms around chairs, put my feet under carpets, lean away from the abyss calling me—all in an effort to not kill myself. In these situations, my non-conscious mind wants to end it all, while my conscious mind fights it. A quarter of all suicides have this impulsive nature.

Our drive to live is the strongest of all our drives. Yet, our brain is capable of creating a story that can override it. It succeeds 30,000 times a year in the United States alone.

But it is not only in killing ourselves that our non-conscious mind shows its strengths. Research shows that the majority of murderers feel that they acted rationally in taking someone else's life. To their minds, murder in their predicament was on par with having ice cream on a hot Sunday afternoon in Central Park.

Creating reality is by far the most important task our brain accomplishes every day. For many of us, it is a case of life and death.

Created Reality

Donald Winnicott, the twentieth-century pediatrician, once noted that "Life is difficult for everyone from the beginning. From what do difficulties arise? First, from the mental clash of two kinds of reality, that of the external world, which can be shared by everyone, and that of each child's personal inner world of feeling, ideas, imagination....Throughout life there must always be distress in connection with this essential dilemma."

There exists in our brains three realities at any given point in time: the inner reality (our conscious and non-conscious feelings, thoughts, beliefs), the external reality (the physical world with people we experience in the moment) and the created reality, which is a mix of the other two realities.

When I left corporate America, my inner reality was filled with fear: "I am not supposed to be free from pleasing others. I am not supposed to do what I want to do in life." My inner life was freaking out. But here is the trick. I had no conscious awareness that my inner reality was going berserk. All I felt was slight anxiety. So my brain searched for an explanation for my massive levels of non-conscious fear and when my super was unfriendly, my brain said, "Aha, this is the cause of your anxiety."

The conflict between the husband and wife let loose her demons of past rejections into her created reality. The demons, bypassing her conscious mind, filled her created space with pent-up anger. Her brain looked for a cause in the real world. It saw her husband.

"It's he who has caused you all this pain," her created reality informed her.

So with aggressive body gestures, shrieking voice and sarcastic comments, she attacked; all the while she consciously thought she was behaving rationally.

To me it is clear: Our created reality drives our behaviors. Most of our created reality is non-conscious, so we often behave first and then rationalize our behavior after the fact. If the created reality is warped, as it is for me, you can beg, threaten or compliment someone to think more of themselves, treat others better or live a fuller life and nothing will happen unless our brains can learn to create a better created reality.

I have so often in my life, during times of struggle, thought of leaving a city or country, believing it will give me a fresh start to life. "A change is as good as a holiday," I believed. Or I believed a new place would bring new love. But despite a number of moves in my life, across three different continents, I never felt an improvement. We take our created reality with us wherever we go. We can run from the present, but we cannot hide from the chaos our brains create.

Reality: The Paradox

My confused created reality has caused me millions of moments of pain and unhappiness. But I am not alone. Harvard psychologist Daniel Gilbert set out to discover how our brains help us find happiness. His conclusion: Our brains actually confuse most of us, leaving us only to occasionally stumble upon happy moments.

But does this make sense? If happiness is such an important reward for humanity, can the brain really be such a liability? The real answer lies not in how the brain confuses most of us, but in how it helps the best of us.

Csikszentmihalyi found that the best of humanity can be happy in the face of disaster. They can fill their creative reality with data that make them feel optimistic while they are witnessing hell on earth. And that is exactly why we are given the ability to create our own reality. If we feel hopeless about life's struggles, our created reality can make us see the best of life and remain positive. We can be optimistic and increase our chances of surviving, instead being overwhelmed by stress.

This is why some philosophers have called our ability to choose our attitude in all circumstances our ultimate freedom. No one can take away our positive creative reality. We can always remain resilient and happy, even in the face of disasters.

Thousands of people receive implantable defibrillators every year. This devices monitors life-threatening arrhythmias and gives the heart a shock when they are detected. These devices save lives. But imagine that a defibrillator is misprogrammed: It shocks you every time your heart is beating normally, but does nothing when you heart goes into a serious arrhythmia. In this hypothetical scenario, your defibrillator will cause your death sooner rather than later. A device, designed to save lives, can indeed cost lives too.

Our created reality is like a defibrillator. When programmed well, it can save our lives and allow us to live a life of happiness and meaning. If misprogrammed, it can shock us when we do what is good for us, or it can do nothing, or worse, it can give us the wrong shock when we are battling life. A misprogrammed created reality makes us see our superintendent as a serious threat, our spouses as rejecting us when they are only disagreeing with us or a kind researcher an arm's length away from us as a potential killer. People who kill have misprogrammed created realities, but for them, their behavior makes completely sense.

Humanity's biggest gift can also be our worst curse.

Creating a Reality

We know that we create a reality by mixing data collected from our inner world with data from our external world. To understand how the best of humanity create a positive and humane reality, we need to figure out what data they use. But, first of all, we need to figure out where they mix the data.

Researchers have found that his area lies in the prefrontal cortex of the right human brain and have called the space many different names, such as Potential Space, Background of Living, Mental Space, Play Space, Analytic Space, Space for Cultural Experience or the Creative Space. I like to call it the Creative Space since we are constantly creating and recreating ourselves, others and reality.

I am no chef. But I am sure if a chef had to choose one bowl to use in his kitchen for the rest of his life, he would choose a large stainless steel bowl. There are plenty of reasons: A large bowl can be used for large or small ingredients in tiny or huge quantities; the large bowl makes it easy to put the ingredients in and mix or pound them; the stainless steel provides fast conductivity for ingredients that need to be heated or cooled over water; a stainless steel bowl can never break.

The best of humanity have a creative space comparable to a large stainless steel bowl. A large creative space allows for a lot of data to flow in from both the inner and outer world. The more data we put into our creative space, the fuller we live and the more in touch with reality we are. There is place for a little bit of everything. A big bowl also allows for the ingredients to spread out a bit and for air to travel into the bowl. A chef can always see how much of each ingredient were used in his recipe. Similarly, a large creative space allows us to view which data came from the inner world and which came from the external world. Healthy people do not confuse the superintendent with Hitler; they know what belongs to the past and what comes from the physical present.

When one cooks for a lot of people with small dishes, one is always in a hurry. Mixing ingredients will need to be repeated a number of times. But a chef with a big bowl can take his time. He is in no hurry to make quick decisions out of necessity. And so it is for the best of us: They can delay action when need to.

A great creative space is an excellent conduit for all types of data, cold or warm. The best of us know we need to be open to all types of data, allowing them to keep in touch with the physical present.

A great creative space is also resilient. It remains constant among the changes we face: the changes in our inner or external worlds we face every microsecond; the ups and downs of our material fortunes; father time reshaping our bodies; the many hats we wear during the day as child, parent, colleague, friend and spouse. The creative space allows us to experience ourselves as the same inner person with the same inner core regardless of what happens to us. The strength of this space determines the resilience and moral fortitude that the best of humanity have in life. It also gives us a sense of freedom in the world. We are who we are regardless of what happens to us.

It is not surprising then that researchers claim that our relationship with the creative space is the single most important characteristic of our higher human consciousness. This is where we create the realities that inform our behaviors.

The recipe for a positive humane reality reads as follows: From the inner world, take data from the animal brain, the human brain, memories and fantasy.

From the external world, take data from the physical world, people and culture. Mix well and often.

The Needs and Instincts of the Human Brain

In the midst of my people pleasing days and fear of authority, I was elected President of the Student Council at Stellenbosch University. During the election, I aligned myself with the National Party, the ruling party of apartheid South Africa. The election was exciting because for the first time, a student from a far-left student group ran for office. He was labeled a communist for his leftist views. But then, in those days, everyone who was not for the government was thought to be either communist or crazy.

Against all odds, Mark made it onto the council.

The weekend after I officially became President, Mark called me up and said, "I want to talk to you about heading the political discussion portfolio on the council."

My first reaction was to burst out laughing. Who would give one's enemy the most sensitive position on the council?

But I told him that I would speak to him about it the next day over coffee. The next morning I woke up and had a clear conviction: Mark would be the best person to bring the widest range of speakers to the university. This would allow me to achieve one of my goals for the year: to allow as many of us to hear the truth of all South Africans on campus, not only government propaganda.

I had to fight people in authority to have Mark appointed. But, counter to my character at the time, I never gave in. I knew I was doing the right thing. I prevailed. Decades later, I asked Dr. Masterson how it was possible for me to have the resilience to stand up for what I believed, when I was such a pushover in general.

"Because your Real Self was not dead then. You ignored it. But that one time, you did not."

Alice Miller writes in her book, *The Drama of the Gifted Child*, that it is a miracle each time she sees how much authenticity and integrity her patients still have after years of denial and self-alienation.

Our human brain is constantly filling our creative space with advice from the Real Self: "Marry for love, someone who truly loves you. Do what makes you happy. Take care of yourself. Don't drink or eat so much or watch so much television. Take care of the earth and your community. Live up to our humanity. Trust your gut."

Research suggests that we are all born with genes encouraging us to behave morally and to live up to our full potential, follow our passions, love intimately and take care of ourselves. These needs and instincts float around in our created space. The best of humanity have a strong enough Real Self to listen and act.

The Needs and Instincts of the Animal Brain

Every day I am tempted to watch porn, daydream about love, eat a cheeseburger, drink ten beers, fall in love with emotionally unavailable skinny young women or criticize others based on their looks, their religion, their skin color.

My animal brain never stops sending its needs into my created space. It is especially in how we see other humans that our animal brain creates chaos. When we meet people for the first time, our brain immediately sizes up people based on how they look. Then we put them into impersonal categories, not dissimilar from seeing an animal and calling it a cow. This immediate classification of others had a life and death importance early in evolution. We had to know whether someone was with us or against us. Not surprisingly, the two major categories of stereotypes our brain assesses for are intent ("Is this person's behaviour benign or malign?") and appearance ("Is this person dangerous or trustworthy"). So our animal brains instinctively avoid angry and dominant people and move toward attractive friendly people.

If we feel we are safe, we keep looking for other criteria to judge: value ("Can this person help me get what I want and need?") and status. Research shows that the part of our brain that is active when we think of humans is not firing when we think of people who are homeless. We see them as objects.

When people's behaviors do not fit into our framework, we ignore the conflicting evidence. Hearing a bitchy comment from an attractive woman is ignored. We believe it is the exception, not the rule. When we are presented with many exceptions to the rule, we will keep the stereotype, but create a subtype. As a researcher explains, "Obama is not a black man, he is a black professional."

How do we fight our stereotypes? Bombarding people with information about the good, value and safety of another group has no impact. If anything, it may confirm prejudices.

Researchers observing the brains of people who view homeless people as objects asked the participants to focus on which soup a homeless person would like to eat. The area that make us see people as people, rather than objects, became active. No wonder Professor Haidt, author of *The Happiness Hypothesis*, explained that the only way to change minds is by opening hearts.

Great advice, but often very hard for those who lack a healthy Real Self and are dealing with a strong animal brain that prefers its prejudices to new ways of thinking.

Stereotyping is only one way our brain impacts our created reality. Every day, we are driven to act like animals. We never completely outgrow our terrible twos and the need for instant gratification and admiration. We all need a diet of both to enjoy life and to fuel self-expression and intimacy. But the best of humanity know our minds are in a constant battle to ensure the pleasures of the flesh do not destroy our lives and prevent us from living out our full legacy. It is also the animal brain that tells us that lust, gluttony, greed, laziness, wrath, envy and pride—the seven deadly sins—are cool.

Memories

Daniel Gilbert, the Harvard psychologist, says that, "We don't just treasure our memories, we are our memories." He shows why our memories confuse us to such an extent that most of us can only stumble upon happiness. Research show our memories are not very accurate. We tend to remember tidbits of information rather than actual events; we remember the best of times and the worst of times, but not the most likely of times; we remember closing moments of experience, not the full experience; we remember unusual instances, not ordinary moments. Often when we recall a memory, our brain rewrites it as a new fact. After a few rewrites we quickly forget where we heard the fact. The false rumor from a suspicious source becomes a verified fact on CNN.

When these memories are emotional, they are even more warped. And when we have experienced life threatening experiences or child abuse, our post-traumatic disorder causes terrifying memories to enter our created space at the worst of times. Our memories and their associated emotions confuse many of us and prevent us from living full lives.

Some might say, "Come on. It is only memories. It is not the present!"

Researchers monitored the brains of participants who were watching three movie clips. Afterwards, they asked them to recall a certain video clip. The brain, asked to recall what it had witnessed, fired in the same way it did when watching the video clip for the first time. Typically, this firing happened a few second before the participant was able to say consciously what video clip he was accessing. To our minds, memories are very real.

I attribute most of my struggles to non-conscious memories of how little respect my budding Real Self was given in childhood. These memories, I call them my demons, contaminated my filter of how I viewed myself, life, love and work. And for all the tea in China, I could not categorize them as belonging to the past. When my demons enter my reality, it feels as if the past is happening right now.

But this is not the case for the best of humanity.

An interviewer asked a physicist who had received a Nobel Prize what made him so successful. He answered that one of his earliest memories was of walking on his mother's favorite carpet with a glass of milk. For some reason he tripped and dropped the glass. Terrified, he looked at his mother. She smiled, consoled him and told him to fetch a glass of water and to walk over the carpet until he felt confident to do it without tripping. Once he told her that he was confident, she told him to go back to the kitchen and fill the glass with milk and walk over the carpet again. To this man, failure was never a screaming match. Failure was an opportunity to learn how to do things better.

This man recalled a single memory, but a mother who deals with a child's failure like this surely gave him thousands of memories as a baby and toddler that made him feel confident in who he is. Now, when he fails, these positive memories of failure pour into his creative space and allow him to remain positive and to learn from his mistakes.

The best of humanity also have millions of muscle memories of self-expression, intimacy, self-care and transcendence. A created space filled with these types of memories comprises the filter that allows the best of humanity to exhibit all the capacities of the Real Self and to create even happier memories.

Fantasy

In my thirties, I believed that the world would give me everything I wanted if I was only prepared to work hard for it. I believed that overcoming obstacles was only a matter of "how" and "when," never "if." I believed I was immune to death and its predecessor, old man time. When people close to me died, I quickly found ways to distract my attention. When Father Time started to scratch wrinkles into the skin of those close to me, I focused my attention on the areas that were still smooth. Like a child I believed, and sometimes still do, that my parents and brothers are immortal and that they always will be around. Like a child, I believed that what I did not see did not exist and could not harm me. Like a child, I believed that I would live happily forever. Like a child, I believed life and reality to be that of a typical Hollywood movie where organized plots and a fixed reality always lead to eternal happy endings. I still sometimes do.

Donald Winnicott writes, "Why is it that the ordinary healthy person has at the one and the same time a feeling of the realness of the world, and of the realness of what is imaginative?"

In an experiment, undergraduates were told to control a green light. But there was a catch. Some were given control over the green light, while others had no control over whether it went on or off. After the test, all were asked to assess how much control they had over the light. Depressed students had a realistic view of how much control they had in both scenarios. Happy students had a realistic view of when they were in control, but they still claimed to have control a third of the time they didn't.

Fantasy gives mentally healthy people the illusion that they have control over their destiny, or, as psychologists would say, they have a sense of agency. Hope and faith are the product of good memories mixed with a touch of fantasy in our created space.

Two of my favorite American plays are *A Streetcar Named Desire* by Tennessee Williams and *Death of a Salesman* by Arthur Miller. In both plays, the protagonists live fully in a fantasy to escape the reality of their past and present lives. But in both plays, real life starts to intrude on the fantasies of the characters. In both cases, reality wins. In *Streetcar*, Blanche, unable to face reality, withdraws into a world where she fantasizes about her past, her status, her sophistication and her love life, all to escape her unimaginable pain. The cruel Stanley makes sure to burst each of her fantasies and at the end of the play, Blanche is sent to an asylum. In *Death of a Salesman*, the father commits suicide rather than face life without the help of his fantasies of being the best salesman, husband and father. Blanche DuBois and Willy Loman preferred madness and death to facing reality.

Those of us with many painful memories in our created space need a lot of fantasy to get through the day. In the process, we make decisions based on fantasy, not fact, wishful thinking, not truth.

Thoughts

I am a skeptic when it comes to believing that changing our thoughts can change our minds, our lives and bring us eternal happiness. Like everything in life, it has a place, but for me, positive thinking has had little effect on how I deal with conflict or find love.

But it is still a powerful force in how we perceive reality.

32 people volunteered to taste strawberry yoghurt. Researchers then put off all the lights in the room so the participants would focus only on taste. But instead of strawberry yoghurt, they gave them chocolate. 19 of the 32 claimed

to love the strawberry yoghurt.

When students were told to think of a professor before they wrote a test, they outperformed those who were asked to think of a criminal. How we are primed can make a big difference in how we perceive reality.

People and the Physical World

Our sensory organs pick up millions of bits of data from the ever-changing and endless external world. Life is filled with abundance and we are barely skimming the surface. We also know now that other people significantly add to our creative space via right-brain-to-right-brain communication, which fills our creative space with positive or negative data that influences the way we see ourselves and the world. David Brooks of *The New York Times* summarized it best when he wrote that our brains naturally and automatically mimic the neural firings of people around us.

When therapists help couples with relationship issues, they usually acknowledge three clients in the room: each partner and their relationship. Good therapists realize the history of a relationship informs each individual as much as their behavior in the here and now. The history, downloaded from memories or the other person's right brain, significantly affects the way we see ourselves and the other.

Parents and people in power are a particularly significant source of data. We listen when they convey information to us verbally or non-verbally. We may decide to rebel, but their impact is powerful. Parents in particular know which buttons to push to have our created reality washed with feelings and memories that force us to listen to them. Our fight to free ourselves from our parents' control and expectations are as old as humanity. It is also our most important fight in our search for happiness. Good parents are great for our lives; hurtful parents, who were hurt themselves as children, can destroy our lives.

The Imperfect World

One summer morning, I went to Washington Square Park and sat down in the first spot of sunshine I saw. Soon, I smelled something off. I turned around and noticed I was sitting next to four homeless men enjoying the sunny day. One said, "You should hear what my family did. My mother called the cops on Christmas. They took me to prison. Just me and chicken noodle soup. It took my mother until New Year's Day to realize that I needed my meds. So she called them up and said, 'Oh, by the way, he's bipolar.'"

Later he talked about his life as a vagabond and his alcoholic blackouts all over the United States. "I lost it here. I lost it there. I lost it everywhere."

One of the many bands that congregate in the square on weekends began to play. The man started to dance: free, uninhibited, laughing. His friends watched, smiling fondly. In that moment, the imperfect man with a history of mental illness and drug abuse was loving his life. He had friends, compassion, support for his past and a body eager to dance. I felt inspired by him.

Years ago, upon realizing I was sitting next to a homeless person, I would have left immediately. But now, my occasional willingness to embrace the imperfect world has given me many moments of joy. After all, what joy it is to see this man, struggling to survive in a city of excess and success, experience a moment of peace and freedom that so many highly successful and admired people rarely do.

Each day, we are reminded that life is not fair. Someone begs for a penny as we exit a subway, we watch Hurricane Katrina devastate New Orleans, we watch another American soldier's family receiving the worst of news, we see pollution in the rivers.

Dr. Masterson writes that those with a healthy Real Self realize that the world is neither completely fearful nor filled with endless pleasures. It's a place where poverty, death, sickness and pain literally lie around every corner. Life is filled with both safety and danger, good days and bad days, success and failure, comfort and pain, power and powerlessness, birth and death, intimate relationships and loneliness.

Life is ambiguous. Those who try to deny its imperfections cut themselves off from obtaining all the information they need to make positive and realistic choices for themselves and their communities. You can run, but you cannot hide from life's truth.

With the gift of imagination that we share with other primates came another important tool to survive tough moments in our lives. We are able to deny reality. We can block from our created reality that which we do not want to see or experience. In short spurts, denial is good and a normal part of the grieving cycle. We need to come slowly to grips with the trauma or deaths that have befallen us. But if our lives are built on denial and fantasy, we are doomed for emptiness and unhappiness. If we wipe out our wrinkles to deny we are becoming old, we avoid the opportunity to make better use of the limited time we have left. When we deny that there is a beggar at the subway, we deny our obligation to help others. When we deny that our relationship with a spouse or boss is causing us a sense of loneliness and stress, we can live for decades in a state of numbness and rob ourselves of better love and life.

My life has been built on denial and fantasy. It had to be: Uncomfortable with who I was and what life was offering me, I had to deny all reality, imperfection and death. The best of us do not live in worlds that are either perfect or disastrous, spend time on black–or–white thinking, or see people as either saints or sinners. The best of us are adept at seeing beautiful colors in the grey of life.

The Mortal World

Mark, a successful professional in Manhattan, was recently diagnosed with cancer. After successful surgery, he went back to work. But the surgery and disease had left him very thin and pale. Mark told me how bizarrely people reacted to his return. Many avoid him; some spoke to him, but avoided any discussion of his cancer; and some wanted to know all the details of his cancer, but never asked him how he was doing. They filled their brains with facts rather than feelings.

If you had asked Mark's co-workers if they had thought recently of death and eternity, they would have said, "no." But their reactions show that their creative reality was filled with existential fears.

A close cousin to the mortal world is the imperfect world.

Our brain wants us to entertain death on a more regular basis. Our brain is the little bird that Buddhists believe sits on our shoulders, whispering: "Is today the day? Am I ready? Am I doing all I need to do? Am I being the person I want to be?"

Accepting that I will die, that my body will age, that I will lose people close to me is a challenging task. I have moments where I embrace the truth, only to distract myself with petty concerns. Our society's obsession with youth is a hysterical attempt to avoid the inevitable: We will grow old—unless illness, violence or accident gets to us first—and die.

Death scares me.

Hodgon Louw, the father of a close friend, died a few years ago. Hodgon was one of the most fulfilled people I have known in my life. His relationships with other people and with nature were honest, caring and joyful. When I said goodbye to him a few weeks before he died, his shining eyes struck me. On his death bed, he was burning with life. He told me how he enjoyed how his family took care of him: Hodgon was connecting with people in death as he did throughout his life. I believe he knew that he existed across space and time. Hodgon had what psychologists call the "continuity of being." He knew that inside of him there is an inner core that never changed as he transformed from a baby to child to teenager to lawyer to husband to father and to grandfather. He knew that that inner core would not change even after he stepped out of his body.

From discussions I read of the last days of both Pope John Paul II and Morrie Schwartz, I am convinced that they too had these shining eternal eyes. If an Afrikaner Protestant, a Polish Catholic and an American Jew can embrace death in similar fashions, then we know those who face death bravely have been blessed with a belief in their continuity of being, a gift from the Real Self. In my analogy, they had a large stainless steel bowl as a creative space.

The Real Self reminds us of death to motivate us to use every moment of life to fulfill our unique potential and connect intimately with others. But it also allows us to feel that our lives are part of life across space and time.

Culture

When I was growing up, I believed that to have premarital sex was a worse sin than racial discrimination; that the ANC and UDF—political organizations that opposed apartheid—were part of the communist threat; that we, the Afrikaners, were God's chosen people for Africa; that "meisies" (girls) must remain virgins until married and, as the weaker sex, must be protected; that music, choir, art and theater were for "moffies" (homosexuals); that "staan jou man"—a man must be tough and never show tears or fear. Today, I laugh with embarrassment at these beliefs. This, while some smart educated Afrikaner men and women continue to live their lives believing them to be God's truth.

After I left South Africa, I worked and lived in Canada, England and the United States. On the surface, all three cultures seemed fairly similar to my own. In all three cultures, English is an official language; leaders were mostly white men; Western values and Christianity played a significant role; alcohol was a culturally accepted anti-depressant. So one would think that white South Africans, Canadians, Brits and Americans have a lot in common. But I learned that we differ so substantially that I often wished that we had a different color skin for each culture (purple, green, yellow or red). At least then I would not make the mistake of believing that because we look and sound so alike, we are so alike.

Our culture dramatically influences our created reality.

Culture and Our Emotions

My Afrikaner culture has seriously affected the way I experience emotions. Crying was out for all men; anger was out for "gentlemen"; fear was not a word at all.

Researchers asked Asian Americans and European Americans how happy they felt during a period of weeks. The results: The Asian Americans were slightly happier than the European Americans. But when all the participants were asked a week later to recall how they felt the previous week, the Asian Americans reported that they felt less happy than what they had initially reported. This is particularly interesting since Asian social beliefs place less value on personal happiness than European American beliefs.

Culture influences how intelligent we are with our emotions, the foundation of our lives.

Culture and Our Sensations

Researchers at the Stanford University School of Medicine conducted an experiment in which 63 children between the ages of three and five sampled all the same foods. Everything was from McDonald's, but only half of the products were branded with the familiar "Golden Arches" packaging. The other half was wrapped in unmarked paper. The kids were asked to taste both the branded and unbranded food. The kids strongly favored the food wrapped with McDonald's paper. The lead author of the study, Thomas Robinson commented, "Kids don't just ask for food from McDonald's, they actually believe that the chicken nugget they think is from McDonald's tastes better than an identical, unbranded nugget." Two factors played a significant role in how strongly children preferred McDonald's wrapped food over the unbranded food: the number of television sets they had in their homes and how often they ate at McDonald's. Dr. Robinson continued, "It's really an unfair marketplace out there for young children. It's very clear they cannot understand the persuasive nature of advertising."

But adults are also manipulated by advertising. Researchers enrolled 67 volunteers, determined their preferences for Coke or Pepsi and scanned their brains while they first drank unlabeled drinks and then labeled cola of their preferred choice. They found that the main reason why people prefer one cola above the other was not the taste. After all, Pepsi and Coke are nearly identical chemically and physically. The difference came from an area in the brain that is actively involved in our perception of culture.

There are many other examples: A brownie on china tastes better than the same brownie on a paper plate; wine with a phony pedigree or with a fancy name taste better than the same wine without the cultural trappings.

Culture influences how we experience the physical world.

Culture and Our Thoughts

I had the fortune of seeing the Royal Shakespeare Company's production of Arthur Miller's *The Crucible*. Astonishing acting and set design emphasized the strong theme of the play, in which a young girl claims that there are witches in the community, in order to deflect punishment from herself. Powerful judges, preachers and intellectuals all fell for the young woman's fantasy, precipitating the Salem Witch Trials. Soon the whole town was caught in a culture of mistrust and witch hunting. Before the fantasy ended, many people were punished and sentenced to death. When people are swept up in fear, they lose all perspective on reality.

Arthur Miller wrote the play in 1953 as a protest against the paranoid fantasies perpetuated by Senator Joseph McCarthy's persecution of communists, both real and imagined. There have been many other Abigails and McCarthys in the world: Nero, Napoleon, Hitler, Stalin, Mussolini and Mao Zedong, driven by their own inner fears stemming from childhood, created cultures of paranoia and violence that influenced the behavior of hundreds of millions of people.

Marketing professionals use polling in order to figure out what issues are popular or how to sell unpopular policies to the mainstream public with the right catchphrases. Politicians hire people who know how to shape our realities and influence our decisions about issues in a way that benefits them and their party base. Two political scientists aptly called their book on how US Presidents use and abuse polling: *Politicians Don't Pander: Political Manipulation and the Loss of Democratic Responsiveness*.

For those of us with fragile Real Selves or who find our sense of morality in trusting authority, our culture and its leaders can easily brainwash our thoughts and influence our behavior.

Culture and our Animal Brains

In apartheid South Africa, we were fed a good dose of fear. We were told that blacks were communists and the antichrist and that they would come to our homes and kill us. If we *let* them rule, we would become like the rest of Africa.

After September 11, 2001, the United States was on alert for more attacks. Many of us were perplexed that the government always increased terror alerts as they tried to get bills passed regarding military spending or during re-election campaigns.

In both countries, fear worked to subvert rational reasoning and force people to become sheep, following our leaders for protection. Fear strengthens our animal brains, which overpower our human brains. We become a herd.

Herd mentality is the term scientists use to describe the driving force among bees, birds, fish and wildebeests. It allows them to move gracefully in the same direction even though only a few members know where they are going. No complex decision-making process determines group behavior; two simple non-conscious drives are at play. First, most animals seek to stay in the group for survival reasons. Secondly, a small number are driven to move in a preferred direction. When a group balances these two drives, herd mentality appears. Interestingly, the individuals that move the group do not look different from their naïve followers. Most animals do not even know who the leaders are. They just follow the direction of their nearest neighbors. Animals move in herds in order to keep up with the Joneses. As a researcher from Princeton noticed, "[This study] demonstrates the power of the little guy. You don't need avowed leaders, you don't need complex signaling."

Nor do you need a majority to move the group. Through computer simulations, researchers found that at a crucial point, adding new leaders to the group had no impact on where the group went. But the minimum percentage of leaders needed to predict behavior was not fixed; it depended on the size of the group. In a group of ten virtual buffaloes, 50 percent of the herd had to be leaders, while in a group of 200, only five percent needed to lead. The tipping point changed as the group increased in size. In the United States, a country of 300 million, the percentage of people dictating our behavior is small. And in a world of 6.7 billion, power lies in the hands of the few.

In *Superclass*, David Rothkopf writes, "They number six thousand on a planet of six billion. They run our government, our largest corporations, the powerhouses of international finance, the media, world religions and, from the shadows, the world's most dangerous criminal and terrorist organizations. They are the global superclass, and they are shaping the history of our time."

By strengthening our animal brain through fear or the lure of products for pleasure and status, our leaders influence our culture and our created reality.

Csikszentmihalyi writes, "One must particularly achieve control over instinctual drives to achieve a healthy independence of society, for as long as we respond predictably to what feels good and what feels bad, it is easy for others to exploit our preference for their own ends." He continues, "As long as we obey the socially conditioned stimulus-response patterns that exploit our biological inclinations, we are controlled from the outside. To the extent that a glamorous ad makes us salivate for the product sold or that a frown from the boss spoils the day, we are not free to determine the content of experience."

Culture and Ethics

Here in the United States, research shows that cheating in schools and colleges has drastically increased. Copying from other students went from 26 percent in 1963 to 52 percent in 1993. During the same period, crib notes use during exams went from six percent to 27 percent. A survey of 25,000 students from 2001 to 2008 showed 90 percent of students, regardless of sex or demography, cheated. A culture of success tells students that high grades are more important than the process of learning. To many, cheating was justified.

Another study showed that when schools counter the culture of success with a culture of integrity by instituting honor codes or emphasizing honesty, cheating dropped significantly. Students in these schools behaved more ethically in the workplace after graduation.

A culture shapes the created reality of our ethical behavior.

Culture and Our Role Models

I am fortunate to call Nelson Mandela, one of the twentieth century's most remarkable people, a fellow South African. Nelson Mandela stands for everything humanity should aspire to. A man who had courage to stand up for his convictions, who forgave his captors and oppressors and who, upon release from jail, contributed to society. He could have made millions of dollars by making speeches all over the world. Instead, he focused on helping others and living a simple life.

His influence on white South Africans was remarkable. Within years of him becoming President, people who had formerly expressed racist tendencies spoke his praise around campfires, braai or rugby events.

One man changed the minds of many people.

Recall the Milgram experiment? Milgram also conducted an additional experiment in which participants witnessed other people refusing to shock the "students." Witnessing people who refused to torture another human empowered 90 percent of participants to say "no" too. Compare this to 66 percent who decided to give a fatal shock in the absence of positive role models. Those of us with a fragile Real Self are pawns in the hands of role models.

Albert Bandura studied two groups of children to show how modeling others influences our views of the world. Group A observed how an adult violently handled an inflatable doll; Group B saw the same adult handling the same doll non-violently. Each child was then left alone in the room and filmed. Children from group A were significantly more violent to the doll than children from group B. We learn by observing other people's behaviors and the consequences of these behaviors.

People want to imitate the behavior of a role model admired by society. Role models carry more weight than your average Joe. A very sensitive diagnostic of a culture's mental health: Who are its role models?

Culture and Our Self-Esteem

For most of humanity's struggle, skinny was not a beautiful characteristic. In contrast, full voluptuous female bodies have been celebrated for ages. Greek and Roman sculptures, Renaissance paintings of the Madonna and child, Rembrandt's voluptuous models and Marilyn Monroe photographs show we have always loved full women's bodies.

Within 50 years, humanity has moved from idealizing full fertile women to skinny young women—girls, really—as the standard of beauty, wiping out tens of thousands of years of how humans viewed beauty.

We have a few clues to the sudden rise in skinniness. First, 50 years on top of millions of years of existence shows that evolution as the cause is highly unlikely. I believe that the only way we will understand why this has happened is to look at skinniness as a commodity, like smartphones or hybrid vehicles. Skinniness as the standard of beauty is a human made concoction. It is a cultural phenomenon.

The impact: Women all over the world are sacrificing enjoyment of food to fit the pictures they see on popular magazines, believing it will bring them happiness and self-esteem. But their attempts are futile.

When *The Real Truth About Beauty* study surveyed 3200 women from across the globe and rigorously evaluated women's assessments of their own beauty and that of society's perception of beauty, the results were shocking. Only the minority of women see themselves as above average in appearance, and only two percent claim to be beautiful. The study concluded that women today are less satisfied with their beauty than with almost every other dimension of life except their financial success.

Ideal Culture

Ask graphic designers how they create their best work, and they will say: "Give me some rough outlines of what to do, but then let me have the freedom to do what I want to do within the guidelines."

Ask them their worse fear: "Someone saying: Surprise me!" or "This is exactly what I want you to do." Too much freedom or too much structure kills creativity. Freedom within structure brings joy.

An ideal culture follows the same principal: Give individuals the freedom to self express, find intimacy on their own terms and encourage citizens to take care of themselves. In short, allow citizens to be free to pursue happiness in their own way.

But too much freedom is not good for us either. Left idle too long, our brains tend to revert to animal consciousness. Scans show that when women are asked to think about nothing, they revert to goals and activities innate to our mammalian brain (bonding, relationship and children). Men, on the other hand, think of activities innate to our reptilian brain (sex, sports and games).

We need structure to direct our energies to something worthy not only for our own psychological development, but also to the betterment of all people. Structure helps us to live lives with meaning, spirituality and actualizing values, rather than instant gratification of our animal needs.

Research shows that the healthiest communities in America are those where parents will address the inappropriate behavior of children who are not their own. We need a community to keep us all focused on our humanity. Without it, we will revert back to an animal consciousness!

Cultures differ in another way. Researchers showed American and Chinese people a fish tank with fishes of various sizes. Then they asked the participants about what they saw. Americans tend to describe what the biggest fish in the tank is doing, while the Chinese focused on the tank itself, the context in which the fish are swimming. Americans see individuals and categories; Chinese see context and relationships. From this and many other research, it is clear that in some countries all that matters is the welfare of the individual; in others, all that matters is the welfare of the group.

The ideal culture of today focuses on individual freedom and the right to self-express, self-share and self-care. But it never forgets to remind its citizens that we are humans first and foremost and to take care of the group. Both the individual and the group are equally important. The ideal culture provides structure to its citizens by upholding the human values that have been celebrated across space and time: temperance, wisdom and knowledge, justice, love and humanity, courage and transcendence.

Such a culture will not evolve soon. Many of us will suffer from our culture's insistence on maximizing our individual pleasure and admiration. Some people, like Morrie Schwartz, advise us that if the culture does not work for us, we should not take part.

There are a few problems with this advice. Our current culture is metastasized to all parts of our lives. See what effort it takes not to see or hear one commercial on a single day. Those of us obsessed with the admiration of our current culture are the ones with a weak Real Self. We need the culture to boost our confidence. To walk away from our materialistic culture is for us the equivalent of a diabetic walking away from its insulin.

Our culture needs to adapt in order to help people.

A Positive Humane Reality

We have laid out the table for the feast of living in a positive humane reality. We have identified the importance of the large stainless steel bowl and all the ingredients for the meal. But how do we mix the data? And who will do it?

The recipe for a positive humane reality is as follows: A handful of data telling us to find our passion, find intimate relationships and take care of ourselves. Three hands filled with positive memories about ourselves, people and life. A pinch of fantasy to create the idea that we are in control of our lives. A pinch of pleasure and admiration to keep our animal brains happy and fed.

From the outside world, take little bit of death and imperfection. Add two fists filled with positive people. Mix it all with five cups of a positive human culture.

After mixing it all thoroughly, sit back and enjoy a delicious meal called life.

There is only one major problem: We are not in charge of how our reality is created. I cannot today decide to follow the recipe above and become happy. My reality is first formed and my ability to make decisions comes second. Even if I want to say "yes" to my human needs and positive memories and say "no" to my animal needs, traumatic childhood memories, excessive fantasy or caustic people in my life, my brain more often than not does the reverse.

And here lies the real problem for most of us struggling with life: We are not in charge of our own unhappiness.

Who is in Charge?

For the longest time, we believed that all humans had conscious will and that we determined all of our decisions. Philosophers equated our lives to that of a rider on a horse. We direct where we go. We can control our non-conscious mind with all its instincts, memories, needs and wishes.

But some philosophers and neuroscientists are now believing that the horse is in control. Our non-conscious minds tell us what to do and all we can do is justify our behaviour after the action. We are lawyers to our inner non-conscious selves and its unpredictable moods.

I believe both arguments address the extreme. We differ in how much control we have over our created reality.

When I succeed in a goal and receive compliments, my created reality is filled with admiration that makes me feel as if I am God.

When I try to be intimate with another person or follow my passions, my created space is filled with demons, non-conscious childhood memories telling me I am wrong for following my human legacy.

When I faced the atrocities of apartheid, my created space was filled with moral intuitions telling me that I must obey authority and be loyal to my culture.

When I deal with pain, conflict or uncertainty, my non-conscious memories tell me I am helpless to deal whatever life throws at me made me feel empty and hopeless with suicide the only way out.

When I spend time with caustic cold gossipy people, my created space is filled with negative images of myself and life.

When I feel lonely, my created space is filled with an unbearable desire to eat comfort food, drink beer, chase women or watch porn.

Context provides the stimuli that determine which memory, fantasy, instinct or need becomes dominant in my created space. This reality causes my behavior that I justify later.

There are people worse off than I. Some people facing pain, conflict or uncertainty trigger psychotic defenses. They experience paranoia, hallucinations or megalomania. From the outside they look crazy to us, but to the person screaming to himself in Washington Square Park, losing all connection to reality is better than dealing with a perceived reality that scares him to pieces. Crazy people are hurt people trying to cope the best their brain allows them to.

Then there are people much better off than I am. Throughout their day, and during particular during moments of stress (conflict, uncertainty and pain), their created reality is filled with millions of positive non-conscious memories that tell them they are good-enough regardless of what happens; they can deal with failure; they must seek passion and intimacy; and they must take care of themselves, their families and the community. Thanks to a healthy Real Self, their brain non-consciously forms a positive, humane reality regardless of the context they find themselves in.

Chapter 6

Parenting a Happy Brain

I have delivered more than 75 babies. Upon making their debut, not one of these newborns has ever said: "Hi mom. Hi Doc. Sorry I'm a bit late. The traffic in the tunnel was slow. I'm hungry as hell. Is there a free breast available?" Language is not the only human capacity babies lack at birth—they lack all of them. They have no identity, sense of self or capacity to empathize. They have no idea about how to relate to others, whom to trust, whom to reject or how to be altruistic. Nor do they possess logic or experience a day full of disappointments or memories of good times. A newborn baby is more like an amoeba than a person: He moves away from that which brings pain and toward that which brings pleasure.

Brain scans explain why. When a baby is born, he has a fully functioning animal brain, but an underdeveloped human brain. At birth, the humanity of babies is still just a spark.

In essence, humans have two births. After nine months of pregnancy, a mother gives birth to a child's physical self. But over a period of three years and through three distinct phases, primary caregivers give birth to a child's psychological self—the Real Self. With the birth of the Real Self, the child becomes human.

Building Blocks

In *Anton*, the biographical play I wrote about the life of Anton Chekhov, I imagined Dr. Altshuller, Chekhov's friend and personal doctor, telling the great playwright: "The Romans believed we mature like trees. So let's look at the inside of a tree. If you take a tree—an oak tree, for example—and you cut it horizontally, like this, you will see all the growth rings have the same shape. So if the Romans were right, our inner rings too stay exactly the same regardless of how cultured or educated we become." Later he continues, "The only way it all makes sense is if some memories are more important than others, Anton. Maybe our first inner ring, our first memories of our first experiences drive who we are. And unless an oak tree falls on our head, we will stay who we are forever and ever."

Memories are the most important building block that a baby has in developing his humanity. Since our memories build on one another, our first memories are indeed the most important memories we possess. But babies do not have factual verbal memory at birth because they don't have access to language. All they have is muscle memory, which documents their experiences of what causes pleasure or pain. If we are our memories, we are our earliest muscle memories.

If a baby did not cry after delivery, I would tap the soles of his feet. A baby has contact with the external world through his five senses, which, when stimulated, would make him breathe and cry. When hungry, cold or afraid, a baby feels sadness and fear, which he expresses through crying. He has several other emotions at birth that enable him to experience and communicate with the world. But a baby has no control over his instincts, needs or emotions. A baby doesn't cry to manipulate others, but to express needs. When new parents ignore their baby's cries, they are ignoring the only tool she has at her disposal to communicate with them. Babies are also born with the capacities of imagination and denial. Life is not fair, so humans have perfected the use of fantasy as an essential tool to escape negative events and cling to positive hopes and outcomes. Finally, we are also born with the innate drive to make sense of our experiences and what they say about us, other people and the world. We have a drive to discover a sense of self.

When I began my search to discover the inner workings of the human mind, I was focused mostly on the lives, choices and behaviors of adults. But I learned that the Real Self begins to be formed before we even have the words to name our surroundings, desires and emotions. The kernel of the Real Self is formed from the non-verbal muscle memory of emotions, sensation and experiences we had with our primary caretakers. How they physically and emotionally nurtured us forms the happiness filter through which we view our own lives, other people and life itself.

Research is very clear that primary caretakers play a dominant role in our mental health. Specifically, the fascinating field of attachment studies has shown conclusively that the mental health of a primary caretaker is the most important determinant of the strength of a child's Real Self. Happy and humane primary caregivers nurture happy humane children who mature into happy and humane adults. (For a discussion on the history and science of attachment theories, please see Appendix A.)

Ideal Primary Caretaker

Throughout the millennia, primary caretakers have almost always been the mother. Society has changed and today we have fathers or nannies who act as primary caretakers. The debate over to what extent men can act as primary caretakers is sensitive and controversial. The key issues are: Can a man take over the strong emotional bond that is shaped between mother and child *in utero*? Can men be taught the natural skills women have at reading a child's facial expressions, touching a child with gentleness or soothing the child with soft and high voices? Are some men more capable of nurturing than others?

Some sociologists claim that the drastic increase of non-maternal care in the first 18 months of life is the single biggest threat to Western civilization. Others claim that men definitely can be taught the skills needed to be a good-enough primary caretaker.

The answers to these questions are not clear. With a child's future at stake, more research needs to be done and guidelines or support given to those men who by choice or fate are the primary caretaker for a child in the first 18 months of her life. To acknowledge the sensitivity of the issue, I will mostly use the term primary caretaker, unless studies focused specifically on mothers.

A compilation of research suggests that the following criteria define the ideal primary caretaker: The person is in a happy, long-term intimate relationship; makes intimate partners feel they count and are cared for; enjoys a wide social network; enjoys a passion outside the house that he or she pursues with purpose and perseverance; takes care of physical health and appearance; is emotionally intelligent; is educated; is older than 25; lacks psychological distress; possesses sufficient income; and enjoys reading and learning.

But the most important criterion is the caretaker's ability to provide positive caregiving to a child. (For a list of activities that the National Institute of Child Health and Human Development has identified as positive caregiving, please see Appendix B.)

The Art of Parenting

I have never been a parent, though I obviously was once a child. I am also an adult who has struggled for a decade to figure out what happened in my childhood that has caused my brain to let me behave in such weird, dysfunctional ways. I have studied the latest research on early childhood development over and over again in order to explain the science that shows which types of nurturing lead to a healthy Real Self and a life of happiness.

I am not oblivious that secondary research of other people's studies has many difficulties, especially since I haven't had the benefit of raising children of my own. I have limited ability to truly understand the complex tasks and challenges involved with raising children today. I have been told by friends that I sometimes give the impression that nurturing a healthy Real Self is like baking cookies. Just follow the recipe and you should be fine. But this is obviously not true.

For the longest time, people believed that all newborn babies came into the world with a *tabula rasa*—a clean slate—on which new experiences are piled to form their unique personalities. But today we know that children enter the world with innate attitudes towards life. There are two major reasons: genetics and in-utero experiences.

A recipe of how to nurture a Real Self can easily ignore how genes or in-utero situations contribute to each child's uniqueness and make parenting an art, not a science. Some children will need more nurturing, some may need less.

Such a recipe can also leave the impression that raising children is a daily to-do list without any fun, an obligatory task, similar to paying taxes or cleaning out the refrigerator. But happy parents will tell you that parenting is a gratifying and enriching, though rarely easy, experience.

The true art of parenting lies not in following guidelines for each phase of development like a roadmap, but in knowing your child, her personality and her unique needs.

Phase I: A Bubble of Safety

One of my favorite things to do in the summer is to swim under water for as long as I have breath, enjoying the blue quiet. As I climb out of the pool, the noise of New York City hits me. I move from a sense of calm to chaos.

At birth, babies experience a similar shock to the system. The external world is a surprising place and, like most people, they would probably prefer to go back to the safety of their previous existence if given the choice. Their instincts tell them to find someone who will provide security, food and comfort. With his first mouthful of breast milk, a baby tastes security for the first time. He will most likely continue to think of the world as fundamentally scary for as long as he depends on others for his basic survival, which goes far beyond a chug of milk here and a change of diaper there.

In a famous experiment, Harry Harlow, a therapist, placed baby monkeys in a cage with two fake moms: one was an object made from wire that gave milk and the other was covered with soft terrycloth, but did not provide nourishment. Even though the wire "mom" was the only one that could actually provide sustenance, the monkeys became much more attached to the soft terrycloth mom. They would cuddle with it and run to it when frightened. Attachment theorists Clive Bromhall and John Bowlby have said, "Primate babies need food, but primarily they crave warmth and comfort or attachment" and "an attachment is as much a prerequisite for emotional survival and health as food and shelter is for the physical world."

Good primary caretakers understand that emotional safety and care are essential, so they step between their child and the external world to provide physical and emotional protection. They create a safe bubble for their child to live, eat, experiment and learn. This bubble is created by spending a lot of time bonding through touching, caressing and talking in soft voices. When the baby cries, he is soothed. Consistent presence, care and routine create the—let's face it, false—impression that the world is safe, predictable and kind.

Budding Self

Babies at birth are not yet aware of their existence—at least not on a philosophical level. They have no self awareness and no sense of boundaries. The tender touch, constant attention and presence of caregivers teach a baby that there is a "me" inside her skin, and a "non-me" outside her skin. Caring touch creates the foundation of the capacity called "continuity of being," an emotional and psychological backbone that helps a person to feel worthy and loved while riding the roller coaster of life. Our most basic conception of our sense of self lies in how we were touched as babies.

Once a baby achieves a certain level of self-awareness, he moves on to the next philosophical plane: "I exist and I have needs that I want met." When I lived in London, I assisted a few cardiac surgeons with open heart surgeries. What an experience to see them tinkering with hearts as if they were deflated balloons. The invention of the bypass machine made open heart surgery possible. Before the surgeon operates, he connects the patient's main blood vessels to a machine that takes over the duty of the patient's heart and lungs.

Since a newborn baby has yet to develop a human brain, caregivers serve as the baby's bypass brain. Sensitive caregivers know what a baby needs before she even cries most of the time. Crucially, they pretend to the baby that he himself has identified his need and asked to have it satisfied. This is why we often see primary caretakers engaging in a specific type of one-sided dialogue: "*You* are hungry. That's why *you* are fussy. Do *you* want your food now?"

Primary caretakers also serves as their child's emotional regulator. Upon seeing a child crying, the primary caretaker feel her own sadness welling up. Her reactions mirror the baby's own feelings. So she first calms her own sadness and then soothes her baby's sadness and then names it, "I can tell that you are feeling very sad right now!" When primary caretakers empathize with their child's emotions, the baby learns that all of his emotions—positive or negative— are acceptable and can be regulated, in addition to learning what they are called. Since emotions are the fulcrum of life, this gift from caring primary caretakers cannot be underestimated. After all, no self-awareness can take place without emotional awareness. However, this is not to give the impression that caregivers ought to be brooding hens. Everyone needs alone time, including babies.

Just as a parent's hand on a child's bicycles does all the work, but creates the impression for the child that he is in control, so do primary caretakers give babies the feeling of what it feels like to have a human brain. They start to develop a sense of agency, an inner voice that tells them that wanting and needing is a natural part of life and that they can manage their emotions.

Our Memories: A Video Store

Utterly helpless—humans are the most helpless species at birth—a baby has no option but to trust that someone will be there for him. To a baby, failure of care means rejection and certain death. As adults, we know that moments of temporary rejection do not have a life-and-death impact on the child. But to the baby, any slight hint of rejection triggers a survival instinct developed over millions of years of mammalian evolution.

Shockingly, no primary caretaker is perfect. But good primary caretakers know that the intent to be 100 percent compliant with a child's unexpressed needs combined with immediate repair of misunderstandings and conflict are more important than achieving perfection. So when they fail to meet a child's needs or sooth his fears, they set out to repair the misunderstanding: "Oh, I'm sorry, I didn't hear you cry!" Their goal is to keep alive the fantasy that the child is in charge of his life.

The baby deals with these mistakes by keeping what amounts to two sets of records, two separate DVDs, in his memory. The Heaven DVD is a record of his primary caregivers as being perfectly attuned to his needs and of him as being special and perfect. In this movie, he appreciates that conflict happens, but all will be resolved immediately. In the Hell DVD, his primary caregiver rejects him all around and he feels abandoned and unworthy. So obviously he clings to the heaven DVD as representing the truth and suppresses the Hell DVD deep into his psyche. Through fantasy and denial, he believes only the Heaven DVD exists. He must suppress the other DVD, for the thought that his caregivers reject him is unbearable.

Nine-Month Exam

During the first nine months, a baby is filled with the fear of rejection, has a limited sense of self, lacks proper boundaries, has a deflated self esteem and obsesses over the pleasure of food and touch. She sees her primary caretaker as a source of food, safety and an object that makes her feel whole. Without the primary caretaker, the child believes her life is at stake and that she is worthless. But a good primary caretaker delivers. After thousands of moments of touch and care, the baby starts to have new non-verbal beliefs about herself, life and people.

Remember the little device we put into Steven Spielberg's right brain to translate the sensations, emotions and images into language? If we do the same for a well-nutured nine-month old baby, we will hear her say, "Based on my experiences with my mother, I know I am safe and people care for me. My mother is emotionally available, acknowledges that I am a little person and loves that I am starting to explore the world on my own. I like it when she talks to me, instead of about me— 'Do *you* want *your* food now?' That's cool! She makes me feel I am somebody with needs, and that when I express these needs, someone will take care of them! How cool is it to want things from others. If everyone is like my mother, I know they can be trusted. And the world is a fantastic place. Whatever I want, I get. When my mother and I have problems, when she is not there for me immediately, I don't get so upset anymore. Boy, I used to think that it was a major catastrophe if she wasn't there for me as soon as I started to cry. Thanks to my newfound level of sophistication, I can be okay without her for a small period of time because I know that she will be back."

Since babies do not have the ability to speak these beliefs, scientists designed a test, called the Strange Situation Test, to evaluate the level of attachment between primary caretaker and baby and how safe the child feels in the world. (Please see Appendix A.)

Phase II: Grandiose Bubble

Once a baby feels safe and emotionally, physically and neurologically one with his primary caretaker, his next major goal appears: He wants to explore his own mind. Two events activate this need. Most primary caretakers are fascinated with the minds of their child. They love to "wait, watch, wonder and hold witness" to the birth of their child's unique personality and passions. Good primary caretakers want their baby to become who he wants to become; the misguided primary caretakers want him to become what they want; and the worst primary caretakers really couldn't care less. But let's focus on the good primary caretakers. The baby thinks, "If my parents think that I am so great, I must be pretty awesome. Maybe I should figure out why!" Curious and caring primary caretakers' interest in a child's mind is the psychological forceps for a child's human brain, Real Self and unique personality.

Because primary caretakers often fail to completely soothing a baby and her needs, misunderstandings do occur, which help a baby to realize that his mind is not the same as his primary caretakers' minds. This helps him to establish his own uniqueness. These two events force the baby to search for his mind in his primary caretaker's eyes (psychologists call this facial mirroring). It's important for primary caretakers and babies to stare deeply into one another's eyes. They know that when the baby feels as if he is understood by someone else, he will begin to understand himself. As famed child researcher Donald Winnicott puts it, "The baby looks at the mother and sees himself."

Eye contact serves another major function. The baby is tapping into his primary caretakers' Real Self and downloading information from her mind. Not unlike a wireless message sent to our phones or computers, messages are sent from the primary caretaker's right brain and Real Self, without a single word being spoken, to her child's right brain and Real Self. This relationship is the child's first experience of an intimate relationship. The primary caretaker's Real Self and beliefs about life pour into her baby's brain. One of these beliefs: The baby is special, great and perfect. All good primary caretakers think their children are the best.

The adoration for his mind and the near perfect attunement to his needs releases high levels of natural opiates into the baby's brain, especially the right brain. The baby is now as high as a kite on admiration.

13-Month Exam

During the Grandiose Bubble period, the child still is still plagued by fears of rejection, albeit to a lesser extent. He has a budding sense of self, but does not feel whole. He lacks proper psychological boundaries. Despite these limitations, the child has an inflated self-esteem. He sees his primary caretaker as an object, a source, a servant who brings him admiration and pleasure, makes him feel special and perfect and makes him feel whole. Without her, he is worthless.

If we dropped the translator into his right brain, we will hear the following whispers in the 13-month-old toddler: "I am perfect, special and fantastic, thank you very much. My mother is perfect too. I like looking into her eyes, which make me feel understood. We are on the same page all the time. We are one. Everything I want, she gives. She loves me unconditionally. Boy, life is pretty good. I am the master of the universe."

He sees all other people as he sees his primary caretaker: perfect, responsive to his every need, an extension of himself, an added arm. He does not even have to communicate his needs to others; people just know! He is unable to intimately connect with others because he has no self to share. He also has no concept of compassion and empathy. As a result, he has no idea of good and bad, ethics or morality.

At this point, the baby is a full-blown narcissist.

Phase III: Becoming Human

Researchers designed a study in which they left children in a room with candy and told them not to eat any until an adult came back. Some children could not control their need for instant gratification and ate the candy without permission. Follow-up studies showed that these children struggled to reach important psychological milestones later in their lives. Many primary caretakers understand that, after their child's first birthday, it is time for her to stop acting the part of a greedy little baboon and learn to control her endless appetite for pleasure and admiration every second of the day.

During the Separation or Socialization Phase—let's call it the Becoming Human Phase—primary caretakers become socializing agents. They gradually and carefully begin to provide real-world experiences so that the child can experience both challenges and boundaries. They persuade him to inhibit tantrums, to develop bladder and bowel control. Parents restrict their own nudity before the children and prohibit unnecessary nudity from the child. Primary caretakers also begin to make it clear that their needs are important too—the child is not the only person in the world who counts.

The baby's days of endless freedom and being the center of attention are forever over. Instant gratification and acting without thinking are for the grandiose bubble, not real life. Used to an endless supply of pleasure and admiration, toddlers must adjust to this new way of living and act out—hence the terrible twos.

Terrified Twos

A good primary caretaker, however, views the terrible twos as the terrifying twos. Primary caretakers know that being a toddler is a constantly challenging state. First, despite his secure attachment to his primary caretakers, toddlers are still very anxious of being abandoned. We never completely outgrow that one. His primary caretaker's new prohibitions rekindle his original fears. Secondly, he fears losing his romance. Who can't understand that! Who in his right mind does not want to stay in a state of euphoria? This is serious landmine time for young humans. Almost everything he does or wants to do fills him with anxiety. On the surface the child may appear as confident as Donald Trump, but underneath fear rules. Studies show that a "terrified two" has a significant increase in the stress hormone cortisol. But, as we shall soon see, this stress is the labor pain of the Real Self.

Primary caretakers do not become taskmasters overnight. They empathetically, kindly and gradually begin to frustrate the toddler's need for instant gratification by setting boundaries and creating challenges. When a toddler explodes into a tantrum, primary caretakers do not see him as a little devil who needs to be screamed at or beaten. They realize that he is not being purposefully difficult, he is only afraid and confused. They know that punishing a child for doing something wrong will force the child to avoid what he is doing, rather than informing him about what he ought to be doing instead. They believe in positive reinforcement of good behavior, not negative reinforcement of "bad" behavior. They also know what it takes to instill virtues into their children. They are patient, but firm.

Guardian of the Real Self

In the chapter on passion, we saw that people will sacrifice their lives in order to actualize their full potential. This drive to expand and grow motivates toddlers to venture off away from their primary caretakers. They become explorers of their environment and increasingly push themselves to take more risks. For them, every electric outlet is a fascinating uncharted territory. Their drive for exploration adds two more fears to their list of worries: "Will dad be there for me when I do what I want to do?" or "Will mom cling to me and prevent me from living up to my full potential?" This need to explore and then come back to a home base filled with caring people who are interested in our adventures remains the same whether we are one year or 101 years old. Good primary caretakers encourage their babies to seek and follow their own interests and spend some unstructured time alone. They know that their support will determine how the child will manage the natural tensions that exist between self-expression and intimacy in all relationships.

We are Our Rewards

In an experiment, researchers asked nursery school children to make drawings with special markers. After they played for a while, the researchers gave some children "good player" awards; the rest received no award. Some time later, the researchers brought the markers back into the classroom. The researchers then monitored which children drew with the markers and how the drawings looked. They concluded that those children who were given awards was less willing to draw or drew poorly compared to those who were not given the awards.

Barry Schwartz, a professor of psychology and author of *The Paradox of Choice: Why More Is Less* explains why: "Children draw because drawing is fun and because it leads to a result: a picture. The rewards of drawing are intrinsic to the activity itself. The 'good player' award gives children another reason to draw: to earn a reward. And it matters—children want recognition. But the recognition undermines the fun, so that later, in the absence of a chance to earn an award, the children aren't interested in drawing."

The biggest *aha!* I have experienced in my search to understand human behavior was learning about the role that non-conscious muscle memory plays in who we are, how we behave and how happy we will be in life. Even conscious will, faith and hope in the future are based on early childhood muscle memory. We are controlled by our own memories and habits. I also came to appreciate how little we will do if our brain does not reward us. Look at the lethargy of a depressed person, who sees life as stripped of all rewards. For healthy people, there is a reward for every task we accomplish. If we do the same task over and over again to achieve a certain reward, we create muscle memory that informs our behavior. We can conclude: If we are our muscle memories, we are first and foremost the rewards we chase.

A good primary caretaker realizes that she must be careful in how she rewards her small son or daughter. Even though all primary caretakers want to say, "Great job. You are so smart!" good primary caretakers know that often these compliments may hurt the child in the long run. They know that a child can quickly become addicted to compliments and will continue doing what brings him the most admiration for his success. Compliments of success and talent may destroy the joy of doing. These primary caretakers are also acutely aware of the folly of rewarding children with sweets, toys or money for completing tasks. It is fine if you want a Pavlovian dog as a child, but if you want to have a self-directed human, bribes are a recipe for disaster. But this can be harder than it seems. As a mother said, "I like to tell my daughter how wonderful she is because then I feel wonderful too!"

Good primary caretakers should consider complimenting a child's joy in doing a task or his effort more than his success or talents. This approach sets in place the implicit belief that happiness is the journey, not the destination; the doing, not the having or the achieving counts.

Recall the Nobel Prize-winng physicist whose mother encouraged him to walk over the carpet with a glass of water after he spilled the milk? A good primary caretaker does this hundreds of times a day. When the child fails, his primary caretakers soothes his anger, fear or sadness and encourages him to keep going, teaching him that failure is part of life and learning and trying again is the only way out. Their support makes the child feel that failure is a learning experience and that resilience is a valuable characteristic. Recovery from failure is rewarded too.

Goodbye Mommy

After many, many tantrums, confusion, frustration, encouragements and victories, children begin to believe that they are competent and unique. "I do not need mom around me all the time to feel whole or to feel safe. I can live without her holding my hand all the time." He gradually separates emotionally and psychologically from his primary caretaker. Supporting the separation, the primary caretakers are non-consciously telling the child: "I have complete trust that you will be able to live life without me being with you all the time. I give you my blessing to become who you want to become without me interfering. I believe you can take care of yourself, especially when you fail or when you are alone. You also know when to rest when you are tired."

Up until this point, primary caretakers have acted as their child's brain. Metaphorically, a large part of the baby's mental space was occupied by the primary caretakers' mind. After separation, there is now an empty space. This space becomes the created space in the child's brain wherein the child will create reality and the story of his life on earth. Feeling secure about who he is and his ability to deal with life, a baby can now begin to edit his memories, his Heaven and Hell DVDs, in his creative space to create a positive, humane reality. He does not need to believe in a perfect world anymore. He can move away from black-and-white thinking and beliefs about himself, others and the world. He can stop having grandiose beliefs and its opposite: worthlessness. He can now see his primary caretakers for who they really are: people separate from him, both good and fallible, both caring and reprimanding, both a supporter but also someone who needs support.

The New Me

Seeing his primary caretaker in this way allows a baby to see himself in a similar fashion. He starts to feel that he is unique, autonomous and separate from people, but like all people, his is part of life, not the center of life. He must follow his passion and live up to his full potential. He has learned that he has both talents and shortcomings. He will experience success and failure, so he must treasure small successes. A separation brings humility and the ability to deal with frustration, disappointment and loss. The socialization phase also teaches children that they can enjoy mastery over their life and passions; but to do so, he needs to know when to enjoy moderate amounts of pleasure and admiration and when to follow his passions. He has also learned that loved ones, mentors and even strangers can support him to become the best he can be. "After all, Mom did it thousands of times!" his right brain argues.

His positive experiences of sharing his emotions with his primary caretakers encourage him to feel all his emotions, share them appropriately and honestly with others and learn from them. Memories of misunderstanding with his primary caretakers and how they dealt with conflict encourages him to become more and more aware of who he is. He also knows he can deal with conflict, failure and rejection.

The process of separation shatters a child's need to be one with his primary caretakers, to fuse with them mentally to feel whole. He feels whole from inside; he does not need the outside world to tell him he is perfect and special. After thousands of moments of exploring, failing, standing up, trying again, being encouraged, his self-esteem is now inside his own brain, not in the external world. He now has muscle memory to back up his claim that he can master life, ambiguity and the future.

The New Other

Separation and a new way of seeing his primary caretakers allow a child to change his view of all people. Now, the toddler can say, "People are physically and emotionally separate from me. They are not part of my bubble. They have their own dreams and fears that are different from mine. They have both 'good' and 'bad' traits. No one is perfect. I am competent to understand their feelings and thoughts, to see how they differ from me. I can and must empathize with how they see the world, their actions and their feelings. I know when to trust and when to run from people. People believe in me. I know the right people will validate and support my fears, dreams, joys and pains. I will not be boxed in or rejected for who I am or for following my dreams by temporarily moving away from loved ones. I know how to find a good combination between autonomy and intimacy. I know all relationships are filled with conflict. But I know that I can deal with conflict in such a way that the other person, the relationship and myself are much stronger afterwards.

"I have also learned that people are not there to give me all I need all the time; they too have needs. I need to suppress my need for instant pleasure and admiration in order to interact with others as equals. Pleasure is cool, but self-expression and human connection are cooler. I have learned I need to give to others too."

The New World

With new beliefs about himself, his primary caretakers and others, babies begin to see the world in a more realistic way. They start to see the world as neither completely fearful nor filled with endless pleasure, a place filled with both safety and danger, good days and bad days, success and failure, comfort and pain, power and powerlessness, birth and death, intimate relationships and loneliness. He starts to see life as ambiguous and uncertain, but a place where mastery over our lives is possible if we can focus on both short-term enjoyment and long-term planning. He realizes life is not a Hollywood fantasy.

To Reality

With a Real Self in place, toddlers are now ready for the final phase: It is time to learn more about reality, the external world and people. At this point, toddlers know that people have different needs, but they are still convinced that all people see the world as they do. For example, in an experiment, children watched as their friend Maxi hid a chocolate and then left the room. After Maxi left, the examiner hid the chocolate in a different place. Maxi returned. Researchers then asked the children in the class where they thought Maxi would look for the chocolate. Three-year-olds know that Maxi wants the chocolate as quickly as possible, so they answered that Maxi would look where the examiner hid the chocolate, not where Maxi hid it. The reason: Three-year-olds still cannot understand another person's beliefs and reality; they still cannot mentalize or take an intentional stance; they cannot figure out that Maxi will act according to Maxi's belief of reality (i.e., chocolate is where he hid it before he left) and not their belief of reality (i.e., that the chocolate is where they saw the examiner place it).

Toddlers learn to negotiate reality as formed by their inner and external worlds. A psychologist provides the following example: A father tells his son dressed in Batman gear to clean his room. His son answers: "Batman does not clean his room, but I will later." The reason is that a child of three is still in psychic equivalence mode or in pretend mode. In psychic equivalence mode, he feels all his ideas and fantasies are reality, and therefore always true. He cannot understand it is a "movie" he is watching concocted by his inner world. To him, the "movie" is reality. In pretend mode, he may know that his ideas are representational, i.e. a "movie," but he does not test the reality of the ideas. He likes to stay in his fantasy.

Parents start to connect the two worlds by sometimes pretending to be part of the Batman fantasy, but also to be the parent of the real world. As Dunn said, "Only gradually, through the close participation of another mind which can simultaneously hold together the child's pretend and serious perspectives does the integration of these two modes give rise to psychic reality in which feelings and ideas are known to be internal, yet in close relationship with what is outside."

By age four, a child starts to learn that people do not act based upon his view of reality, but according to their own unique belief of reality. Now, with the same chocolate experiment, children realize that Maxi will look for the chocolate where Maxi hid the chocolate, not where they know it is. The child starts to know that his actions are caused by beliefs and desires that belong to him and him alone. He starts to attribute different goals, desires and beliefs to the actions of different people. He also embraces the idea that there is not one reality in the world; reality is everyone's reality thrown in a bucket.

At this point, the child has moved from the pleasure principle to the reality principle, from animal brain dominance to human brain control. He can trust non-family members because he has learned first to trust the primary caretakers and then other relatives. Due to separation from the primary caretakers, he can delay gratification and admiration and learn appropriate language skills to improve social interaction. During the reality phase, he learned to connect the inner and outer world and to mentalize or understand and empathize with another person's thoughts, feelings, wants and beliefs.

By now, toddlers have all the muscle memory that is central to a strong Real Self and becomes a member of the human family.

Capacities of the Real Self

I mentioned in an earlier chapter how I was awarded a top prize at school for my character and ethical behavior. I then admitted that had I been born in Nazi Germany, I easily could have joined the SS. I was *displaying* human virtues, not *embodying* them. We embody human values when beliefs about ourselves, others and the world, as found in the muscle memory in our right human brain, support our universal human values.

By the age of three, mentally healthy children possess the muscle memory that tells them to follow their passions, enjoy intimate relationships and take care of themselves. They see that these goals are more gratifying than chasing pleasure or admiration. They also possess the ten capacities of the Real Self that help them to follow these goals and to live up to their human values.

The following is a list of these capacities taken from the book, *In Search for the Real Self*, written by my therapist, Dr. James Masterson, one of the world's foremost opinion leaders on the Real Self. In brackets, I state the human virtues that correlate to each capacity of the Real Self.

The first capacity of the Real Self is the capacity to experience a wide range of feelings deeply with liveliness, joy, vigor, excitement and spontaneity. The Real Self does not block feelings or deaden the impact of emotions but provides a sense of what is appropriate. [Wisdom and Knowledge; Temperance]

The second capacity: The Real Self acknowledges and maintains a person's self-esteem. It helps the mentally healthy to identify and acknowledge that they have effectively coped with a problem or crisis in a positive and creative way. When the world does not support a mentally health person's self-worth, the Real Self will help him or her to understand that they are still worthwhile individuals, entitled to setting and reaching their goals. [Wisdom and Knowledge; Courage; Justice]

The third capacity: The Real Self helps people to be creative. Creativity is defined as the ability to replace old, familiar patterns of living and problem-solving with new and equally or more successful ones. The mentally healthy adapt to the constantly changing environment or to the loss of loved ones. They rearrange intrapsychic patterns that threaten to block self-expression and constantly identify false beliefs they have about themselves, others and the world in order to become more creative and express more of their potential. [Wisdom and Knowledge]

The fourth capacity: the Real Self soothes painful feelings and to know when and how to avoid painful feelings. [Wisdom and Knowledge; Courage]

The fifth capacity: The Real Self allows the mentally healthy to be alone without feeling abandoned. They know aloneness is not the same as loneliness and that they can find meaning in life, since meaning comes from within. [Wisdom and Knowledge]

The sixth capacity: The Real Self allows for self-activation and assertion. Healthy people identify their own unique individuality, wishes, dreams and goals and then are assertive in expressing them autonomously. [Wisdom and Knowledge; Courage]

The seventh capacity: The Real Self makes and sticks to commitments to relationships and career goals when it is clear that it is a good goal or relationship. [Courage]

The eighth capacity: The Real Self provides the capacity to express the Real Self fully and honestly in a close intimate relationship with another person with minimal anxiety about abandonment or engulfment. [Humanity and Love]

The ninth capacity: The Real Self provides the capacity to expect appropriate entitlements. Healthy people expect to enjoy mastery and pleasure and to have the environment provide them with both. They know they can master their lives and achieve what is good for them. [Transcendence]

The tenth capacity: The Real Self provides a sense of continuity of the self. Healthy people recognize and acknowledge that they have a core that persists through space and time, whether up or down, in a good mood or a bad one, accepting failure or living with success. These people have an inner core that remains the same as they grow and develop. [Courage; Transcendence]

Early Bliss

In an earlier chapter, I argued that happiness is a reward for self-expression, intimate moments and self-care. These activities create happy memories that allow people to create a happiness filter that helps them see life, others and themselves in a positive light. Our earliest experiences shape both our abilities to follow those activities that make us happy and give us a filter that allows us to see life and our passion as positive experiences. Our early years form our happiness thermostat, our happiness baseline. No wonder attachment studies show that happy primary caregivers nurture happy children who become happy adults.

From Baby Speak to Language

I am in an elevator and a mother and her baby enter. I make eye contact with the child. "Blah, blah, blah," he says, obviously trying to communicate with me.

"What are you saying," I asked in my best baby voice.

"Blah, blah, blah," the baby says.

"He says *door*," the mother helps me out.

"Oh, door!" I said to the baby. He was satisfied.

How did the mother know "blah, blah" is "door" in baby speak?

We know that language is a key element that separates us from animals. We also know that our ability to label our sensations and emotions is essential for self-awareness, a healthy Real Self and a happy life.

From the NICHD study, we see that caregivers who exhibit positive caregiving attitudes help to teach language to a child through the following activities[1]: repeating the child's words; commenting on what the child says or tries to say; answering the child's questions; encouraging the child to talk by asking questions that the child can answer easily, such as "yes" or "no" questions or asking about a family member or toy; encouraging the child to learn or have the child repeat learning phrases or items, such as saying the alphabet out loud, counting to ten and naming shapes or objects; explaining what words or names mean; and telling stories, describing objects or events or singing songs. Through these activities we all learn language. But it is not only what we are taught that determines the quality of our language and our ability to make sense of our minds; other people's minds contribute as well.

No one understands a baby's mind better than his primary caretaker, especially if she has a strong Real Self, attempts to be perfectly attuned to her child and spends a significant amount of time with him. Her ability to understand his mind and her own, to put language to his needs, is the first step in helping the child to grasp the abstract symbols used to indicate inner emotions and sensations.

Within the safety and grandiose bubbles of early childhood, a child does not have a lot of impetus to learn how to communicate. He gets what he wants without asking for it.

But when a child emotionally separates from his primary caretaker, he cannot rely on her to automatically know what he wants. This forces the child to step up his language acquisition. The development of language has significant advantages for the separated self: It continues the ongoing individuation from the primary caretaker, connects the baby with other people and allows him to

1 What follows is quoted almost directly from the NICHD study.

start narrating a conscious story of his life experience that can be recalled in the future.

Recall the famous Nun Study that showed that those nuns who wrote with positive emotion, many details and with many thoughts merged into few words, lived longer and happier with significantly lower incidence of Alzheimer's than those who gave factual accounts of their lives. I believe it was the healthy nuns who enjoyed a separated Real Self that could observe and enjoy life better while at the same time having the right vocabulary to put their senses and emotions into words and into their conscious minds.

Full human consciousness, self-awareness, enjoyment of life's abundance and coherent use of language are difficult without a healthy separated Real Self.

Parenting After the Early Years

Researchers are clear that even though the first three years of a child's life are crucial to a child's Real Self, the years leading up to adulthood can still undermine it. A person spends his childhood learning how to put his Real Self to work in the real world: how to behave, how to interact with others, how to turn his passions into activities that satisfy him.

In adolescence, most teenagers start to fight their parents in the important battle of their lives: control over their destiny. Teenagers must discover their own unique identity away from their parents.

Dr. Masterson writes, "Outwardly they may appear to be auditioning their friends and acquaintances for their personality traits, values, sexual preferences and compatibility, but inwardly they are seeking to learn more about themselves."

This is another tough time for a child. Brain scans show the brain is undergoing another serious pruning session. No wonder teenagers can sleep for days. Life is mentally and physically exhausting.

Most parents, even the mentally healthy ones, believe they know what is best for their children. They know who they should be friends with, who they must date, when they should have sex, what they must study and what career paths they should follow.

Good parents know this is a time for a child to learn through trial and error. We only can learn about ourselves through deciding about a course of action, doing it fully and then learning from it. Parents who command their children to follow their advice seriously undermine this learning, making their children dependent on other people to direct their lives.

Research shows five characteristics of families that nurture teenagers who are significantly more happy, satisfied and strong in most life situations than their peers. The first one is structure: Children know without any ambiguity what parents expect from them. The goals and feedback are clear. The second is intimacy: Children know their parents are more interested in what they are doing, feeling and learning about themselves and life than in whether they are getting the grades or accomplishments to get into top schools or jobs. The third is freedom: Children know they are free to experiment, even going against their parents' rules. But they also know there are serious consequences for their choices. The fourth characteristic is supporting passions: Children know they are safe, both physically and psychologically, to unselfconsciously follow their passions and interest. Their parents support their passions as much as possible. Finally there is encouragement of psychological growth: Children feel encouraged to take risks and fail, to take on increasingly complex tasks to push their potential, knowing that if they fail, a kind and caring hand will pick them up and congratulate them for trying.

Good families provide children freedom within a structure that celebrates passion, intimacy and our human values.

Life after Teenage Years

Scans show that the brain goes through another slight pruning session around 28. At this point, the Real Self is fairly fixed. The way we see ourselves, others and the world remains fairly constant. The good news is that the brain never loses its ability to rewire throughout life. Under the right circumstances, the brain and the best of us can change. In fact, Erik Erikson showed that all mentally healthy people continue to undergo a number of changes until old age.

Throughout life, two questions non-consciously force people to consider changing either their relationships or career: "Am I strengthening my Real Self to its full capacity?" and "Do my work, relationships and culture allow me to express my Real Self fully in the physical world?"

If the answer to any of these questions is "no," your innate drive for self-actualizing will leave you restless. If you can say "yes" to both questions, thank your primary caretaker whose hand made you feel good-enough and cared for at birth and whose hand gently guided you away from her into the real world to become the unique person you were born to be.

The Other Parent

Even though the role of the primary caretaker is essential for a child, it does not let the other partner off the hook. For the longest time, men felt their role as father meant bringing home the bacon, doling out discipline, occasionally coaching a team and sleeping in the spare room if the child cries too much. But the role of the father is huge. First, the father must ensure that he strongly contributes to a home environment that enables strong bonding between the primary caretaker and child. He must also be the emotional reservoir for the mother. Giving birth to the Real Self is hard work for the mother even with a committed partner and a monumental task done alone or with an emotionally distant partner. Research shows that when men are sensitive and supportive of their wives' needs while they care for their newborns, the collective happiness of couples does not drop after the birth of the child. And a happy mother raises a happy child. Good fathers are also actively involved in day-to-day childcare activities, including changing nappies, bathing, going for strolls and especially bedtime. Primary caretakers need breaks.

But, just as important as it is to support and bond with the mother, a father needs to bond with his child. A father needs to give his child warmth, affection and make her feel that she counts. Harvard pediatrician Berry Brazelton wrote, "All of the studies that measure increase involvement of fathers in their babies' caretaking point to the gains in the babies' development." But it is not only babies who benefit from these intimate interactions.

Tiger Woods is known for his alpha male qualities on the golf course. To many, he is one of the most superb sportsmen of all times. But that is only part of his life. In a recent interview, Woods told reporters about his parenting duties, "I couldn't be happier than where I am right now. Having the two kids is just unbelievable, how much fun we are all having."

He spoke about what a blessing it was that his knee surgery took him out of golf for a while. His time away allowed him to bond with his daughter in a way that he never had before. Research shows that fathers who are more involved with their children tend to be happier with themselves as fathers and husbands.

Later, when the child starts exploring the world, the father becomes the safe version of the world away from mom. He helps his child to discover more of himself and the world. A good-enough father realizes he needs to help his child break the emotional umbilical cord. He *gradually* takes the child for longer moments away from the mother and blocks the mother's overprotective instincts. He is also instrumental helping the child understand what beliefs come from his inner world and what comes from the external world, and how to bridge both to form a realistic, humane reality.

Around the age of four, children begin to learn how the real world works. Traditionally, this task was one of the father's most important. Today, both parents seek out "teachable moments" in every day life to demonstrate social norms, how power works, a sense of justice, how to deal with all the bumps in the road and how to fight a fair and just battle for her passions, relationships and what is right. At this point, both parents are a guide to the complexity of culture. They emphasize that a good life is one lived between the tension found in wanting to self-express fully while also taking into account the direction of the community. Both the self and community are equally important.

Even though a lot of responsibility is on the primary caretaker's shoulders, it is clear that both parents are essential for a healthy childhood. In traditional families, a mother teaches a child about "being" (how to be ourselves, how to be with others, how to be in life) and a father teaches us about "doing" (how to chase our goals and stand up for what is important to us in our cultures). Each parent supports the other in his or her task.

Finally, and most importantly, parents are the dress rehearsal for real life. Children learn from how their parents interact with one another and with life and how they deal with the agony and ecstasy of following one's passions. Children learn a great deal by imitating their parents. They learn from actions, not words. If they see parents living without passion or without love, they believe such a life is the only life to live. We cannot become that which we have not experienced or witnessed over and over again.

Other Caretakers

Over the last 15 years, the majority of children have begun to receive some non-maternal care by six months. A study conducted by the National Institute of Child Health and Human Development found that in the first few years of life, the average child spends 27 hours a week in non-maternal care. In the first two years, most of the care takes place in family homes or child care homes and in the next two years, most care was center based. The researchers' main conclusion was that children who were cared for exclusively by their mothers did not develop differently than those who were also cared for by others.

Primatologist Sarah Hrdy writes in her book *Mothers and Others: The Evolutionary Origins of Mutual Understanding* that a major driver of evolution— she claims it is *the* driver—was humans' need to be cooperative breeders: We evolved out of the need to share the nurturing of children. Chimpanzees and gorillas will kill you before allowing you to hold their infants; humans pass babies around like so many bags of popcorn. In less developed tribes, like the Kung foragers in the Kalahari and the Efe foragers in the Democratic Republic of Congo, babies spend 25 percent of all time and 60 percent of daytime hours with people other than their parents. Without the influence of Western cultural biases, some parents spend 40 to 50 hours per week away from their kids.

Both modern-day research and history point out that primary caretakers do not need to stay at home all the time. But there are a few caveats.

The NICHD study showed that the most important variable for reaching milestones was parent and family characteristics. For example, children from families where parents were more educated, had higher incomes, are emotionally supportive and cognitively stimulated and where mothers are mentally healthy had better outcomes on all levels of comparison.

When researchers looked at what qualities determine good care, they found that centers that met accreditation guidelines and where positive caring was evident had much better outcomes than those centers with caretakers who did not meet these criteria. (See appendix B for the NICHD definition of positive caring.) Finally, children who spent more time in non-maternal care had more behavioral problems than those who had experienced fewer hours.

To me it is clear: A primary caretaker who has a healthy Real Self will want to pursue her passions outside the home after having a child. He or she will non-consciously choose caretakers who have a healthy Real Self to be their substitute or they will chose child care centers that fit the federal recommendations for good childcare and that emphasize positive caring. He or she will also know that working long exhausting days and coming home unable to provide positive caring to the child is not good for either parent or child. Good parents provide positive caring for their children whether in a center or after a day at work. The cost of negative or stressed caring on a child's developing brain is disastrous.

The Real Self Lottery

The data on what percentage of people possess a strong Real Self is limited. When I look at the percentage of Americans who find meaning in their work (20 percent), who will stand up under any circumstances for what they believe (ten percent) and who enjoy a lot of sex in their old age (15 percent), I have concluded that only around 15 percent of us are enjoying the gift of a strong Real Self.

Due to nature, nurture, culture and fate, most of us have a fragile or average Real Self. (Dr. Masterson defines fate as those events in the first three years of life that separate a baby from his primary caretakers for a whole host of reasons and that prevent a baby from moving successfully through all the phases of development.) Later in life, severely traumatic experiences can cause post traumatic stress disorder and may also significantly scar our memories and our lives.

We are not competing on the same psychological playing field. As a result, we are not all equally tickled pink with being alive or with our lives, nor do we all have equally strong conscious wills to deal with life. We can read all the books, listen to self-help gurus or get a PhD in psychology, but it remains very difficult to change our filters about life. The reason: Our filters are formed through hundreds of thousands of experiences early in our childhood. Reading a book will not change this, nor will the sincere and heartfelt apologies of parents who out of need, trauma or ignorance did not deliver in the first three years of life.

An End of Play Pamphlet

The theme of my play on the life of Anton Chekhov illustrated how the wrong childhood memories can destroy a child-turned-adult's life. In my play, Anton struggles with intimate relationships because of his memories of a clinging mother and an abusive father.

After each performance of the play, I asked friend to give the audience the following pamphlet to read at home:

Tandem fit arbor surculus. In time, sprout turns to tree.

Modern research has proven that the experiences of a child in his or her early years do indeed form an "inner growth ring" on which all subsequent development builds. Specifically, a report from the National Research Council and Institute of Medicine of the National Academies, called *From Neurons to Neighborhoods: The Science of Early Development,* presents evidence about "brain wiring" and how kids learn to speak, think and regulate their behavior. And in time, kids turn to adults. The following are direct quotes from the report:

> The long-standing debate about the importance of nature versus nurture, considered independent influences, is overly simplistic and scientifically obsolete. Scientists have shifted their focus to take account of the fact that genetic and environmental influences work together in dynamic ways over the course of development.
>
> From birth to 5 children develop foundational capabilities on which

subsequent development builds.

In addition to their remarkable linguistic and cognitive gains, children exhibit dramatic progress in their emotional, social, regulatory and moral capacities.

Early experiences clearly affect the development of the brain.

Children's early development depends on the health and well being of their parents.

Children grow and thrive in the context of close and dependable relationships that provide love and nurturance, security, responsive interaction and encouragement for exploration. Without at least one such relationship, development is disrupted and the consequences can be severe and long lasting.

Young children are capable of deep and lasting sadness, grief and disorganization in response to trauma, loss and early personal rejection.

Society is changing and the needs of young children are not being addressed. Interactions among early childhood science, policy and practice are problematic and demand dramatic rethinking.

But, as Jack P. Shonkoff, chair of the committee that wrote the aforementioned report said: "We're simply not taking advantage of how much we have learned about early development over the past 40 years. Work and family life are changing dramatically yet children's needs are not being addressed. This is not about blaming parents, the workplace, communities or government. This is about sharing responsibility, separating fact from fiction and using scientific knowledge to promote the well-being of babies and young children."

On what first inner growth ring is your life built? What inner growth ring are you passing on to your children? What are we as a society doing to support those parents with undetected defective inner growth rings to prevent them from passing on their loneliness, their melancholy, their self-destructive behavior and their fear of intimacy from generation to generation?

Tandem fit arbor surculus. In time, sprout turns to tree. Two trees form a community. All communities are our future.

Section II
Failure of Success

Chapter 7

Money is Impotent

When my brothers and I were growing up, my parents taught us that money makes the world go round. The rich enjoy every pleasure on earth, receive white glove treatment at airports and run for mayor, governor or president. They live in palaces on hills overlooking the world below and jet to exotic vacation spots. Their children gain admission to Ivy League schools and then, with minimal effort, find prized jobs on Wall Street, in Hollywood, on Madison Avenue or Capitol Hill. It all seemed so obvious: Money buys happiness.

So I was confused when it never worked out that way for me.

After the initial elation of earning a good salary wore off, I started to pick up my monthly paycheck in the same way I pick up my toothbrush. When I worked in corporate America, I enjoyed the excitement of bonus time for a while. But soon even bonuses lost their fun. A bonus became a carrot placed in front of me in December to entice me not to quit my job in April. I saw my income increase, but I experienced no increase in happiness or meaning.

When researchers look at the correlation between money and happiness, they find that in the United States, an annual salary of up to around $50,000 a year actually does contribute to our happiness. Beyond $50,000, an increase in salary loses its correlation with happiness. In Europe, with its strong social welfare system, €10,000 was seen as the critical point.

Another study showed that the extremely wealthy tend to be only a tiny bit happier than the rest of us. The difference is so small as to be insignificant. So it seems that money correlates to happiness only to the extent that we are happier when we know that we have enough to buy food, afford our rent or mortgage, pay the rest of our bills and have a bit left over for extras.

In many ways this should come as no surprise: Happiness has been around since we humans learned how to speak. The presence of money, a manmade invention, has been around for a comparative blink of an eye. But even if it does not make us happy, money does make the world go round and drives many of our behaviors.

Pleasure of Making Money

I have seen the excitement that investment bankers and traders experience as they talk about their day at the office. It's suspiciously similar to the expressions on the faces of gamblers at casinos. I have realized that this excitement is what I experienced the first time I received a bonus.

Brain scans reveal that the ventral striatum, one of the oldest structures in our reptilian brain, rewards us with pleasure for *making* money, as opposed to *having* money. The reptilian brain is obsessed with survival: finding food and drink to energize our bodies, shelter to protect us from intruders and disease and sexual partners to procreate.

Our reptilian brain sees money as a resource that ensures our survival. In America, our reptilian brain requires around $50,000 a year to be assured that its survival needs are met.

But now a conflict arises. The reptilian brain, never big on moderation, wants to continue its quest for more money. "More money means more pleasure and an increased chance of survival!" it screams.

A healthy Real Self, in control of the reptilian brain and its need for instant gratification, evaluates these screams: "What are we sacrificing in order to receive more pleasure?" it asks. "Are we sacrificing our happiness and our humanity for money?"

Without a strong Real Self, we blindly succumb to our reptilian brain's tantrums for more money. This is why studies show that people who value money above other goals are never satisfied with the money they make, regardless of the amount; their animal brain always wants more.

A few times, I have visited clubs in New York and London where the rich and famous go to drink, dance and be photographed by paparazzi. I have felt that sense of entitlement as selective bouncers waved me in. I felt that I had arrived in heaven when a gorgeous woman in skimpy clothes told us: "My name is Vera and I am here to serve you tonight." My eyebrows rose when I heard that we would be paying $450 per bottle of vodka, which would have cost $35 at the store, though for many, the price adds to the vodka's taste and the sense of privilege. "We had a table at the Marquee last night," is a phrase that carries a lot of weight in the city. I have also watched how men and women retreat to powder their noses: some with expensive cosmetics from their stylists, others with powder from their dealers. For many of these people, money, cocaine and champagne mix well together.

My brother Andre has told me that, during the recession, he has observed that investment bankers seem to miss the chase of the deal almost as much as the money itself. Bankers are addicted to doing deals.

Brain scans show us why: The area in the brain in charge of our need to make money is also the same area that dictates a drug addict's behavior as he takes care of business or inhales cocaine. No wonder studies show that people obsessed with materialistic goals are more likely to have dependency problems than those whose primary goals deal with self-actualization.

Making money can be a drug as addictive as any other.

Pleasure of Shopping

I lived in Reston, a small town in Manitoba where I had a medical practice, when I bought my first brand-new car. I was on top of the world. Even the bitterly cold Canadian prairie winter, with three feet of snow and minus 30 degrees Fahrenheit, was wonderful. I was in love with my car, with money and with life.

I enjoyed my new car for about a week before it became as important as an old pair of shoes.

Later, after I'd moved to New York, the purchase of an Armani suit, silk ties and an expensive watch gave me a similar sense of elation, which was followed almost immediately by disappointment. Today, if a fire were to wipe out all my possessions, I would miss my photos, my computer with my plays and the notes for this book, paintings that I made or bought and one old black cashmere sweater. Possessions, I've learned, don't do much for one's state of mind.

To me, all products and services can be grouped into four main groups. *Survival products and services* meet basic food, housing, education and healthcare needs. *Status products* are products and services that elicit a "wow" from others: a luxury car, a palatial home, high-end clothes, nights at exclusive clubs and massive engagement rings. *Pleasure products* include sugar, coffee, alcohol, videogames, television, drugs—manmade products that are not available unless processed. *Self-enrichment products* include those items and activities that help us to express ourselves (a camera if you are a photographer, a piano if you want to learn to play music); to find intimacy with others (an airplane ticket to visit friends and family, green fees to play a game of golf, acts of charity); to take care of our physical selves (a gym membership, a meal at your favorite restaurant); or to experience transcendence (a ticket to see Patrick Stewart in Macbeth, a hike in the wilderness, a trip to a church or museum).

Brain scans show that our reptilian brain is in charge of our desire to buy nearly anything, with the exception of self-enrichment products. The reptilian brain has never caught up with the last few thousand years of human development. It is clueless to the fact that humans have designed products that give us pleasure but have no survival purpose. Ignorant to the changing world and driven by an insatiable appetite for pleasure, admiration and novelty, it screams, "Shop, shop, shop! It's important for your survival!"

People with a strong Real Self evaluate every shopping urge to make sure they control their reptilian brains and spend money only on products that they need to survive, to bring pleasure and admiration in moderation, to further enrich their Real Selves or to take care of other people.

In an acting class, one of my fellow students faced a serious challenge. She had to act as if she was high on cocaine, but she never had the experience. She also did not want to try it for the sake of acting—a good idea. The teacher then had her recall the last time she had shopped for shoes. Through a focus on her sense memory, the young woman soon exhibited all the signs of someone high on cocaine. Another woman in the class jumped up and said, "I use it and that is exactly how it looks."

I know a very rich woman who owns her own plane, complete with pilot. I heard through the grapevine that she had significant trouble with cocaine and nearly lost all her close friends because of it. But she pulled through and today is drug free. But what amazed me was to see her shop in the luxury fashion stores of Manhattan. Every store display reduced her to a two-year old. "I want, I want, I want!" her behaviors shouted. She looked like a junkie in need of a fix.

Six percent of Americans experience uncontrollable urges to purchase, but do not care what they have bought, cannot remember what they bought and cannot stop shopping once they have started. Regardless of their financial situations, they are compelled to shop until they drop. Some researchers believe addictive shopping should be recognized as a mental illness and treated by psychotherapy or drugs. Shopping has the same destructive potential as other products designed to bring pleasure: alcohol, drugs, gambling and cigarettes.

People with a weak Real Self are in trouble in our consumer society.

Money and Admiration

John, after he graduated from college and entered the workforce, struggled with his self-esteem. Away from a milieu where his straight A's gave him a sense of self-worth, he became depressed and anxious. His annual bonus and raise in salary saved him. The more money his boss gave him, the more he valued his own life. To John, money is a golden star on his forehead that tells him that he is special and good.

In a study, researchers scanned the brains of 38 pairs of men while they estimated the number of dots appearing on a screen. If correct, they were promised a financial reward. After the test, researchers told participants whether they were correct, how successful their partners were and how much money each partner received.

The scans showed that when a person answered correctly and received his financial reward, the reptilian brain lit up. When the man lost and received no money, it had no activity. But when a participant was correct, received a reward and was told he received more money than his partner, the reptilian brain became a floodlight.

Researchers concluded that we are driven not only by the absolute amount of money we need to pay for necessary resources—the premise of classic economics—but also by our need to be comparatively better than others. Status anxiety—the term psychologists use—also impacts how we view money and what we will sacrifice to possess it.

At first blush, money may help us with our low self-esteem.

I read in the newspaper about a young man, called Pete—not his real name—who started his own company, sold it and banked his first $100 million. Immediately after he sold the company, Pete considered becoming a venture capitalist or an angel investor. But when a top venture capitalist firm invited him to join pitch meetings, Pete was not the nice guy in the room.

"I took this perverse pleasure in seeing if I could make someone cry," he told *The New York Times*.

He constantly challenged a friend to competitive games. Who was the most frugal? Who could do the most push-ups?

"No matter how many I'd do," his friend said, "he'd have to do that many plus two."

All Pete could do was start a new company with the aim of selling it for more than he had sold his previous company. "Otherwise, what have I learned?" he said.

Later in the interview, he said, "I don't know what I would do if I couldn't start companies. I'd probably think about slitting my wrists."

Today, Pete again works an average of 15 to 18 hours a day. Occasionally he goes out with his girlfriend, or, by the sound of it, he goes out with his Blackberry. All he seems to do is to answer e-mails and check his Web site.

In the article, one of Pete's friends bemoans the fate of the young rich: "All of a sudden, you have the luxury—or the curse—of being able to ponder the meaning of life. You ask yourself, 'Why am I not happier given how lucky I've been?'"

Pete made $100 million and was treated as a rock star. But all the admiration brought him no lasting happiness or confidence. He still needs to see the external world validating his fragile self each and every day.

Shopping for Admiration

I have met some very rich people in my life. What amazes me now is how, at the time, I admired everything they had to say. They might have been wealthy pharmaceutical executives, but because they arrived in personal limousines, their views on life were indisputable. They might have been well-dressed Wall Street tycoons, but because they arrived in a helicopter, they knew all there was to know about raising children. And like children, many of us are in awe of today's royalty: the rich. So we try to emulate their appearances and achievements. Marketers know this better than anyone.

Over the last few decades, society has moved from shopping for basic goods and self-enriching products to products with perceived status. The first two pages of today's newspaper had two advertisements for diamonds, three for high-end watches, four for high-end clothes and shoes and one for an exotic family vacation to a luxury island. Just because we have Louis Vuitton handbags, Prada shoes or drive a BMW, we feel a bit more special than others. This need for admiration and superiority screams against our most basic human values.

Money and Passion

Fashionable professions change with the times. When religion ruled the world a few centuries ago, parents wanted their sons to be priests, ministers or rabbis. After the Enlightenment, physicians, lawyers and schoolmasters became the flavor of the century. When I had to decide on a career, the choice was easy. Medicine. When people asked me why, I told them, "Because I care about people and want to help them." But that was only part of the truth. The real truth was that I valued the financial stability and prestige that accompany a career in medicine.

Shortly before the credit crisis, many parents wanted their sons and daughters to be in the financial services industry, even though they may have had no clue as to what investment banks, hedge funds or private equity firms actually do. The reasons are obvious: These jobs hand out compensation that is a whopping 20 times that of the private sector. Even with their funds bleeding money, the top 25 managers of hedge funds were paid a total of $11.6 billion. Not bad during one of the worst economic years in living memory.

Because of our reptilian drive for money and prestige, many people deny their passions. Many believe that they will work for a few years, make a lot of money and then retire to follow their passions. Most people get stuck in their careers or their brain gets used to the pleasure of making a lot of money.

And they don't stick around because their work is inspiring. People obsessed with money struggle to experience flow at work. Recall how Csikszentmihalyi found that to experience flow and psychological growth, we must do a task not for the reward, but for the joy of the task itself. To spend 80 hours a week for that big bonus is to live with the Real Self stored in a box in the garage.

A friend confided, "My mother does not care that I'm a published writer. She only cares about how much money I make. Money, money, money. That is all she talks about. She doesn't care that her comments are destroying me as a writer and a person. She wants me to make a lot of money so that she can brag to her friends about my income."

Many parents, some out of genuine but misplaced concern for their children's futures, will fight tooth and nail to prevent them from doing what they love if it doesn't bring a lot of money. Following our passions is hard enough; but it can be nearly impossible when our culture, family and friends are all obsessed with money.

Researchers tracked two groups of young people in Holland: those who studied business to make money and those who studied teaching. Decades later, the researchers found those who became teachers were much happier with their lives than those in business.

Money and Relationships

When I was an executive coach, I once met a Master of the Universe, a man with billions of private equity money under his control. His office floor looked like it belonged in the Metropolitan Museum of Art; his office, a war room at the Pentagon. Five huge computer screens constantly spat out data from all over the world. I was impressed.

His humanity impressed me less. As I entered, the Master did not get up to greet me. He was too busy looking at his computers. After I was introduced, he gave me one look, asked a question and kept looking at the screens as I talked. His look told me that I had failed some arbitrary first impression test. But at least he didn't scream at me.

I have met many people who work for people who are obsessed with money. Their accounts of how their bosses scream, shout, harass and throw tantrums made me believe they were describing a kindergarten classroom, not sought-after addresses on Wall Street, Park Avenue or Hollywood. The powerful and highly paid Masters and Mistresses of the Universe often have reputations for lacking interpersonal skills. They notoriously care more about profit than people. This, while Harvard's McClelland found that great leaders care equally about both, let alone what researchers have found to be our core human values.

During good times, employees in these firms know that if they make a costly mistake, they will be fired, given five minutes to clear their desks while a security guard frowns upon their every move, and then, in front of faces they have worked with for many years, they will be led out of the building as if they have committed a serious felony. The mistake may not even be because of negligence. Today's financial markets are so unpredictable that even a novice who throws darts at a list of stocks may receive a return on investment equal to those "in the know." Fate and fortune are stronger than talent and hard work. No wonder investment bankers say, "A hero today, a zero tomorrow." I have heard others equating their experience in corporate America to being modern day slaves or prostitutes. The only difference: Slaves and prostitutes do not believe the sugar-coated lies many leaders of money factories tell their employees.

During economic recessions or depressions it gets even worse. Management slashes without any remorse or humanity. During the recent layoffs, an investment banker said, "These are people's lives. It's not head count. We're not cattle." But in a culture focused on money, preventing the loss of profit is more important than the loss of its employees' peace of mind.

But it is not only the bosses to be blamed. An investment banker told me shortly after the crisis began: "I have lost all my faith in humanity. People are turning on one another. It is dog eats dog out there!" Even one's colleagues seem to be fair-weather friends.

I focus on the financial industry, but I have experienced the caustic effect of money in other industries, even in medicine. Here in Manhattan a favorite topic of dinner conversation is the number of hours people work per week.

"To clamber up the pecking order," *The Economist* reports, "some people slave away nights and weekends at the office. They gain in rank at the expense of their free time. But in making that sacrifice they also hurt anyone else who shares their aspirations: They too must give up their weekends to keep up. Mr. Frank (author of *Luxury Fever*) reckons many people would like to work less, if only others slackened off also. But such bargains cannot be struck unilaterally. On the contrary, people compete in costly 'arms races,' knowing that if they do not work harder, they will lose their standing to someone else."

Americans pride themselves on being the hardest workers in the world. But we end up living to work, not working to live. To live the American dream, many people spend more time at the office and end up with a nightmare at home. The pursuit of money and property is destroying families and its crucial role in strengthening the Real Self of family members.

Earlier in his life, Sam, a friend, was the epitome of respect, manners and kindness. Today, after ten years working a high-stress corporate job, I am frequently embarrassed by how he treats waiters in restaurants. If he wants a drink, he wants it now. He seldom says, "Thank you." He barely tips the minimum. Being treated as a pawn at work has caused him to treat others with the same level of respect.

I met Jim, a broker on Wall Street, in a bar in the East Village. On this Sunday evening, to escape his wife, his in-laws and his newborn twins, he went for a few lonely pints. After his third beer, he said, "I am still recovering from last year. I was laid off and for months had no income. My wife wanted to leave me. Her parents told her to get out while she could. Then I got another high paying job. Suddenly they all love me again. But how can you forget that?"

A culture obsessed with money makes many bosses, employees and even spouses treat others like disposable objects.

Money and Love

Years ago I was a coach at a dating service that helped men and women understand what first impressions they create on a first date. Alice, one of my clients, was a Type A investment banker. After an hour of our fake date, I closely observed her behavior. I then gave her feedback on what her main problems are with dating: She does not listen to the other, she tries to impress the other by constantly talking about her accomplishments and she never once spoke about her or my passions.

A few weeks later, I received a call from her. She wanted to meet for dinner and ask a few question. We decided on Pastis at 7 p.m. the next Wednesday evening.

On that evening, I waited for a fifteen minutes before her call came. She was stuck in traffic.

"Well, get out and take the subway," I advised.

"No, I am in my own car," she answered. "I have not used it for a while and thought it may need a bit of a drive."

I was perplexed. I know no one in Manhattan who rushes home from work to fetch her car to drive to a dinner date. It goes against all logic.

When she arrived, I understood: Alice was driving a brand new Mercedes Benz.

Researchers showed participants photographs of the opposite sex or told them stories about dating. Afterwards, they observed how men began to spend more money luxury items or vacations, while many women opted to volunteer for charitable work. From my experience with Alice, women also use luxury items to signal to strangers. But signal what? The researchers believe humans constantly want to signal our fitness as parents, friends or colleagues. We want to show others we possess openness, conscientious, agreeableness, stability and extraversion.

People who flaunt their money are trying to flaunt their personalities. They hope their possessions will impact the way they are treated. They believe that everyone is watching every detail of their appearances, careers or possessions. Our possessions will not only demonstrate that we are so well off that we have extra resources to burn, but also that we have personality and intelligence, Dr. Geoffrey Miller argues. But we have a consumerist delusion: Our possessions or elite degrees may get us the date or the interview, but conversations are a much more sensitive indicator of our intelligence and personality.

Having money to buy a desired personality seems to be another reason why so many people obsess about money. They feel that they are not good enough without the diamonds, watches or palaces at the Hamptons. No one will mate with them if they are not rich.

Money and Self-Care

Here in Manhattan, I often walk on busy streets crowded with tourists. For most New Yorkers, slowing down for anyone or anything causes a drastic increase in blood pressure, and when they are forced to slow down for a group of overweight people in sneakers and tracksuits, they are at risk of having a stroke. "Tourists," they mutter condescendingly before hollering, "Excuse ME!" When the sea of people refuses to part, they elbow their way through these "clueless out-of-towners." After all, a New York minute is much more important than a Midwest minute. We have work to do, milestones to achieve, money to make. We need to stay number one. There is no time to smell the roses or relax for one second.

Nancy, an artist who supports herself as a server at a trendy restaurant that attracts investment bankers and traders for post-work revelry, told me how "those people" change the ambience of the restaurant minutes after they arrive. The bankers and traders are demanding. Their comments often border on sexual harassment. They spend money on expensive food and wine. They drink like fish. They smoke cigarettes like cowboys. They snort cocaine like...well, like investment bankers. Beautiful hangers-on are part of their "cocaine and champagne" club.

After a day of fear, the reptilian brain will seek more pleasure and admiration after hours, or seek activities that shut down those cravings: a few drinks on the train home or mindless television to "calm the nerves." These goals become more important than taking care of one's mind and body or connecting with families eager for some human contact at the end of a long day.

A banker invited a friend, along with ten other bankers and their spouses, to a dinner party where the host graciously opened his wine cellar and asked people to choose any bottle of their liking. He made sure to mention that every bottle was at least $300. The circus started. People sniffed, gurgled, swallowed and spat. They described their findings with the vocabulary of a sommelier. Afterward, my friend, who grew up on a vineyard in Europe and knows his wines as well as Americans know baseball, said that only one person had any clue about wine—the rest had faked their knowledge.

Most people, especially those who can afford to pay the exorbitant prices at top restaurants, do not have the taste buds to enjoy fine cuisine. Trevor White, who has worked as a restaurant critic in Dublin, London and New York before he wrote his book *Kitchen Con*, agreed with me that many wealthy people do not appreciate good food, despite being self-described foodies. In his book, Trevor writes that "overrated, egomaniacal chefs, pretentious waiters and self-important critics" are conning most people in the food capitals of the world. If those who make and write about fine cuisine are clueless, imagine how clueless are those who buy into the deception—dropping thousands of dollars for a meal at a luxury restaurant.

To experience transcendence while consuming excellent food and drink, we need to have a strong Real Self and a relaxed state of mind. If our brains are overly excited by stress, pleasure or admiration, we can devour the best food in the city, but we cannot enjoy. Most people chasing money would be better off at Burger King than Balthazar.

Harvard lecturer, psychoanalyst and executive coach, Michael Maccoby writes that many of the CEOs he analyzed suffer from loneliness and isolation. Many wealthy people believe the best way to fight their isolation is to work harder, make more money and build higher picket fences. They withdraw from the human experience and see the poor, the sick, the illiterate as a nuisance. "Come on," they say, "I made it to the top, so can they. We all have an equal shot at life." To them, the widening gap between the rich and the poor may be a good sign. Their separation from the human struggle brings an enormous sense of isolation and robs them from the opportunity to care for the community, one of the most sacred of our human legacies.

The Lost Battle

One of the themes of this book is the daily struggle between our animal brain and human brain for control of our behavior, our humanity and our happiness. So far we know that to have a strong Real Self, we must daily strengthen it through moments of self-expression, intimacy and self-care. We also know that we need to minimize, but not deny our animal brain's need for pleasure and admiration to ensure that each part of our brain works in harmony.

We see that making and spending money strengthens the animal brain, soaking it with pleasure and admiration. At the same time, the money-obsessed ignore or neglect those activities important for a healthy Real Self.

A culture or person obsessed with money takes away David's sling and stone and leaves him to fight Goliath with his bare fist. David will lose. Our obsession with money caused a massive shift in our consciousness, happiness and humanity toward a lower level of living.

Human Consciousness

I have wondered: If I had been on Wall Street over the last ten years, would I have been a whistleblower and brought public attention to my firm misleading the naïve and channeling more money from the poor to enrich the rich? Would I have said "no" to bosses who treated me like a cow? Would I have used my huge bonuses to help the poor or spend them on exotic vacations, huge homes and lavish parties?

I would have gone along with the flow.

Rene Descartes, John Locke, David Hume, Immanuel Kant, George Berkley and many other famous philosophers over the ages have debated the nature of consciousness, where it is formed and how it impacts our behavior. Their answers are diverse and, like all good philosophers, they seem to not be able to agree on a definition of consciousness. All they can agree upon is that consciousness is the most important phenomena in the universe.

Consciousness is often understood as being the way we perceive ourselves, others and the world; an awareness that we are aware; a point of view; and a mental state.

For my own clarification, I see consciousness as a mental state that provides us with a point of view that influences how we create our reality and perceptions of the world; our created reality determines our behavior. I believe that there are six different states of mind with different points of view, perceptions and likely behaviors.

A favorite past time at Stellenbosch, my South African alma mater, is tubing down rivers pregnant with recent rainwater. You take an inner tube, drive to a place up stream, jump in the water and cling to the tube as the water takes you down stream.

Imagine doing this in a river where you spend most of the time in rapids, moments where all you care about is staying afloat. Your body is pushed around by angry water, most of which you seem to be swallowing. There is no time to think "Who am I?" and "What do I want to do with my life?"

When the river widens, you have moments where you can recover for a moment. But you still do not have the luxury of thinking existential thoughts. You are still part of the fast and furious river, but at least you now have time to think about and learn from your experiences. You think: What did I learn in the last rapid that I can use for the next one to make sure that I don't swallow so much water?

After ten minutes of being dominated by the river, you arrive at your destination. As you move toward the bank, you have a magical moment where you feel your feet touch the ground. You are still struggling to reach the bank, but at least you have moments where you can fight the water and stand up. This is still not a time to reflect on life, but at least you can enjoy the excitement of the moment.

You climb out of the water. On steady ground, you now experience the river differently. You have a distance between yourself and the river to observe it more objectively. You feel separate from the river. You notice that you are shivering. Without water crashing over you, you now have a choice of walking to the car, getting yourself a blanket and drinking coffee. You start to exercise conscious will over your actions.

A friend climbs out of the water. You see that she is shivering. You realize she must be cold too. You realized you never once thought of other people while you where in the river. All you cared about was your own survival and the flow of the river. You know how cold it feels to step out of the water. So, you take your friend's towel, jumper and coffee to her. She says "thank you."

After the sun has warmed you both up, you start sharing your experiences: the adrenaline rush during the rapids, the swallowing of water, the in-your-bone coldness. You both know, without a word, this experience made the two of you more connected with one another and with nature. Even though you are aware you have a body separate from your friend and from nature, you feel strangely at one with both.

Six Mental States

In the river of life, I often do not have time to be aware. I struggle psychologically and feel I will drown, so instinct takes charge. I have little control over what I do. My instincts play cat and mouse. I just hope for survival and to leave behind my DNA for the next generation. Our perception of life lacks conscious awareness and action is instinctual. To use a previous analogy, I do not have a bowl in which to create my reality. There is no separation between my inner and outer worlds. Instant action and gratification ensure survival. Reptiles live with this mental state.

Where the river widens, I have time to quickly figure out the best strategy to survive. My brain will think of all the rapids I have gone through, and based on my experiences of pain and pleasure, will give me the best solution to tackle the next rapid. My point of view is still focused on survival. The only difference: I now have instinct, emotions and memories of my experiences to guide me through the next rapid. I still do not have a bowl to create reality. I am still reacting to every stimuli in the environment, but I have learned that some are not life threatening, while others I need to fight, flee or freeze immediately if I want to survive. Mammals live with this mental state.

The moment I walk towards the bank and my feet touch the ground tentatively, I start to balance my worries about survival with thoughts of existence. My brain is not at peace. Survival is still key. But I am starting to get a sense that I am aware that I am aware and that I exist with unique thoughts and actions. I also can think about the future and another river with faster rapids that I want to do. In this mental state, I start to have a bowl in to which my brain is adding ingredients to create my reality. The bowl may be very small and made out of porcelain, but I am occasionally aware that I exist. I also can transport this sense of existence into the future. Primates live with this mental state.

When I step onto solid ground on the river, I become aware that I exist separately from the river and that I have options. With my feet firmly on the ground, I am fully aware that I am aware of my feelings, thoughts and actions. The river does not dominate anymore and I start to have options. This awareness of being aware is the most basic form of consciousness we as humans have. I have a stainless steel bowl to which I add all the ingredients appropriately. During the rapids, I only add animal instinct and needs to survive. During the widening of the river, I add memory and fantasy. I experience the data coming from the river: the cola brown water, the ice coldness, the blue winter sky.

When my friend walked out of the river, I was aware of her coldness and desire for a towel, coffee and a jumper. When I noticed this without any words being spoken, I entered a higher level of human consciousness. The moment we experienced intimacy based an awareness of what the other is feeling, we reach a higher level of consciousness. In this moment, feeling both physically and psychologically safe, I can fill my stainless steel bowl with the non-verbal feelings of my friend. I can mentalize her state of mind and make her world part of mine.

We reached transcendence in the moment we became one with each other and all of life, the moment our awareness of our own sense disappeared, not because the water flooded us, but because we reached another level of being. I can now allow for the deepest part of me flowing unhindered and unobserved through the bowl to the external world and back. It is as if the dam wall had opened all its doors and the river of life flows through unhindered. To enjoy the power of the now while forgetting our own sense of self is arguably the highest level of consciousness.

We all experience all different types of consciousness in our lives. Some of us are stuck in more primitive mental states. The best of us spend more time with their human consciousness. And even when they are in the rapids, they may be dominated by animal instincts, they have positive memories flowing in that tell them they can survive on their own and that soon they will be back on the bank. Their strong Real Self allows them to be aware that they are aware in most situations. And because they are aware they are aware, they have conscious will to act with intent, rather than reacting. That is why in the rapids of life, the best of humanity can still enjoy life and maintain their dignity.

The Reptilian Mind Set

According to the renowned neuroscientist MacLean, the reptilian part of our brain is in charge of our instincts, habits, order, power and familiarity. It is also responsible for social hierarchy, ritualistic displays, greeting, courtship and formalizing how we fight, display success or surrender. Since this brain is controlled by instinct and compulsive order, it is quick to react, but slow to learn.

We all possess reptilian brain instincts. A friend of mine told me his wife started behaving weirdly after she found out that she was pregnant. As luck would have it, I was reading an article on our reptilian brain instincts and I passed it on to him.

"'Establishing territory, preparation of home site, showing place preference,'" he read from the page. "Absolutely, man. Come to 17G if you need a case study. My wife is all reptilian brain at the moment."

The best of us know when to fill their created reality with reptilian instincts and behavior and when to override it. They know that each of our brains is important. The key is to make sure that one is not dominant, but that all work as an integrated whole. But some of us are stuck in different mental states.

When I read the list of behaviors that the reptilian brain is responsible for, I recalled seeing news clips of Hitler, Mussolini and Stalin showing their love for order, hierarchy and displays of might by having their armies march in front of them. These leaders seem to have spent their lives dominated by a reptilian consciousness.

The same image came to mind when I started to read of the greed, unethical behavior, vanity, showing-off, lack of interpersonal skills, grandiosity and need for power of the Wall Street masters of the universe.

Reptilian Ethics

Bernie Madoff is the poster child for everything that went wrong in the financial industry. While other bankers wittingly or unwittingly created a housing bubble, he created a Ponzi scheme and consciously lied to his shareholders. As he said in his trial, he knew it was only a question of time before he was caught, before reading an apology void of any emotion. Other facts about Madoff show that he had a knack for seducing others to trust him. He had a paternal image and created a sense of family, a social hierarchy, amongst his investors and employees. To become a Madoff client, you were made to believe that he was doing *you* a favor. He also had a few interesting quirks: He was obsessive-compulsive about neatness in his office. An employee once caught him vacuuming the carpets because he thought they were not clean enough. He also loved black and instructed everyone to have all photos framed in black.

There are many other Masters of the Financial Universe who love to display their perfection, wealth, power and brilliance at any and every opportunity. They also seem to live with two different sets of ethical rules: one for them and one for everyone else. People who live in primitive mental states, especially during times of stress, non-consciously believe that lies or hypocrisies are acceptable.

At his sentencing, Madoff said, "I made an error of judgment. I refused to accept the fact, could not accept the fact, that for once in my life I failed. I couldn't admit that failure and that was a tragic mistake."

Admitting failure is one of humanity's most noble actions. But when your non-conscious brain tell you that you must be perfect and the best, and you fail, your animal brain will scream: "Survival is all that counts; a lie does not matter."

To create the impression that only men behave this way would be wrong. Financial services employees of female bosses say that they play by the same rules as the men.

Reptilian Greed

The New York Times Magazine reports: "Until quite recently, very rich people had their money as of right, by virtue of their birth into a self-enclosed and self-regarding class. The wall between classes was almost impermeable: You could not get into the WASPs' clubs, nor live in their Park Avenue buildings. Now, by contrast, the superrich rise from among the ranks of the well-to-do. It's the dad in your kid's class who "does deals." But it's the new culture of display that ultimately gets the well-to-do goat. The old rich may have lived in 21-room apartments, but they drove dinged-up cars, dressed modestly, ate indifferently. When Deal-Maker Dad has the class parents over for a party, his private chef makes exquisite timbales. And his kid tells your kid that they have box seats for all the Yankees' playoff games."

Our greed has turned moments of celebrating the human condition into moments of showing off the depth of our pockets. Birthday parties, weddings or Oscar night are not about celebrating the gift of another year of life, the emotional union of two people or humans who have stretched their talent and potential. Greed has turned these events into an obsession about who is attending, who is catering, who is wearing what designer's clothes, how expensive was the wine, how beautiful the home. Even how we work or love is to show off, not to show our Real Selves.

In the dictionary, greed is defined as "excessive or rapacious desire, especially for wealth and possessions." Rapacious is defined as "inordinately greedy, predatory."

The close similarities between how financially powerful people behave and MacLean's discovery of our reptilian brain's functions, the close definition of greed with predatory and the neuroscience research that shows how making and spending money strengthens and pleases the reptilian brain allows me to conclude that a person exhibiting greed is a person stuck in a reptilian mental state. Unfortunately, they have no idea. Rationally, their actions are in perfect harmony with their created reality.

The Rapids

For most of my life, I lived like a Bernie or a Deal-Maker Dad. I lacked a sense of inner steadiness, a large stainless steel bowl, that would have allowed me to become increasingly more aware of who I am, what I want in life and why I should live up to my human values. I had to go along with the rapids of life, where it's all about survival. I had moments when I realized that I was caught in a rat-race, but being in the rat-race robs you of your sense of self and makes you believe it is all there is to life. You are not aware of being aware of how much you are hurting inside or what impact your actions have on others. You just instinctually let the reptilian brain tell you what to do. To cover your non-conscious pain, you tell yourself stories about how great you are, how much attention, admiration and pleasure you deserve in this life and that you are the only one who counts. To keep the story true, you work hard to possess accolades and possessions. Without them, you would realize that you are stuck in the rapids, filled with existential fear and about to drown. This is not a pleasant thought, trust me.

Some may wonder: How can you live like this but never feel your inner pain and confusion? How can people like Madoff not know that their greed and lies are being driven by fear?

Remember the woman who believed herself to be acting rationally even as she screamed at her husband? This is what happens to many of us. We suppress our true feelings. Without feelings, we have little awareness about who we are and what is happening in the real world. Without feelings, we can believe the lies that we tell ourselves and the world.

I love strawberry ice cream. Imagine I walk into an ice cream parlor with the assumption that there is no strawberry. So I order chocolate ice cream. Only after I take a bite do I see the sign for strawberry ice scream. I feel cheated. I made the wrong decision based on the wrong data. But this is still a nice problem. I knew strawberry ice scream existed, but I did not know it was sold in the parlor. But what if I never even knew that strawberry ice cream existed? I would not know how it tasted, when to ask for it or how much joy it would bring me.

Those of us living in a reptilian mental state have no clue what it means to have a human consciousness. Today I have a sense of human consciousness, but I cannot will it. Many circumstances throw me back into the rapids of life where I fight for survival with a reptilian consciousness. Besides, when people like Madoff, Deal Maker Dads and Moms and me try to live up to our humanity, we are devoured by our demons.

This is why earlier in my life I believe I could have lived the lives and lies of many investment bankers and CEOs. From within the rapids of our suppressed non-conscious inner confusion, all the greed, addictions, egos, hierarchy and grandiose fantasies make sense. It satisfies our reptilian brain's need for pleasure and admiration to overcome our survival fears.

The Fooled

I know and love many people who work in the financial industry. To claim they all live with a reptilian non-conscious state would be far from the truth and a gross generalization. What I do know that is that if you have an average Real Self, a medium- sized porcelain bowl, and you allow yourself to be in a culture that stokes fear and celebrates admiration and pleasure, you soon will find yourself in psychological rapids. Your created reality will be filled with fear-driven need for admiration and pleasure, often breaking the porcelain bowl and leaving you reacting like a reptile.

Dalton Conley, Chairman of New York University's Sociology Department, writes about how our mentality toward work has changed over the years. Before, we worked hard to make a lot of money so we could enjoy the good life. The people who worked the long hours were the low-income citizens trying to climb up the ladder. Today, it has shifted. The top 20 percent of earners are now working longer hours, an increase of nearly 80 percent. The more we earn today, the more we work. Dalton explains why: If we make a lot of money, the opportunity cost of not working is higher; those with a lot of money are not so worried anymore about being better off than those in the bottom half of society, they compare themselves to the top half of income earners. Since the very rich have become astronomically rich over the last few decades, those between the middle and the top feel left behind. A poll in New York found that those earning $200,000 had a higher probability of feeling poor than any other income group. Another poll showed that high-income women were more stressed than low-income women. From a humane, logical, rational perspective, this does not make sense; from a reptilian mental state focused on hierarchy at the cost of peace of mind, this make all the sense in the world.

This explains why, in the cities all over the world, those with a lot of money separate themselves from everyone else. It explains why people with money need to show off wealth and beauty, their sense of power and entitlement in restaurants and bars, the need to enrich one another with exorbitant bonuses that far exceed the annual salaries in many other industries that also require hard work and long hours. It also explains the disastrous track record many men and women obsessed with money have in love. When an obsession with money walks through the front door, love walks out the backdoor.

The Way Out

I met Cathrine within six months of arriving in New York. She was vivacious, without airs, spontaneous and funny. Among all the moaning in the city, her shining eyes were floodlights. Then she entered a career in finance. Within two years, I could barely recognize Catherine anymore. She became gaunt from the running around and stress, she dressed like the women in Sex and the City, she ignored calls, dated men who had deep pockets, but shallow personalities. Her life had come to revolve around making, marrying and spending money. One day in the elevator we spoke. I looked deep into her eyes. Catherine had mammon eyes. Her soul was dead.

A few weeks ago, I walked down the street and bumped into Catherine. She was her sparkly old self. This turned out to be because she was laid off six months ago. Despite the insistence of bosses and colleagues that she should immediately find another job, she had decided to take time off and discover what she wants to do with her life. Six months away and her eyes were her own again.

The good news is that for many, a reprieve from the rapid waters of pleasure, admiration and fear will bring back a sense of humanity and self-directed behavior. Many smart people got caught in the rapids and reptilian consciousness, but away from their work culture, they may find legs to walk toward the embankment.

Some will never let go of their obsession. That is why some bankers predict that some of their colleagues will not find a new lease on life during the recession, but will become angry and bitter. That is why banks inflated their earnings to justify their employees' enormous paychecks, while the rest of the country struggles. That is why many writers and politicians are crying out incredulously, "They do not get it. The gilded age is over, but they still want to live like it is the nineties. They meant nothing to society, not even to the economy, but they still believe they are worth millions."

For those at the top, "getting it" is impossible. First, the reptilian brain tells them to go for more at all cost. After all, it is now accustomed to millions as a reward. It is like telling a cocaine addict to be happy with half his current hit. Secondly, to admit that they do not deserve millions will awaken the six demons in their non-conscious mind that will devour their sanity and sense of self.

Donald Davidoff, a Harvard University neuropsychologist, explains why many financial executives run after they are caught for unethical behavior: Their self-esteem is linked to their wealth and power. When that disappears, they experience a "dissolution of their personality." Davidoff concluded, "They run not because of the threat of arrest but a loss of self."

The Dilemma

An obsession with money strengthens our reptilian brain and weakens our human brain. Individual incomes above around $50,000 cannot make you happier unless you are happy already. But what it can do is make you sacrifice our human values. All this, and our culture tell us that GDP, work, money and spending are our duties as citizens.

As scary as this is, there is worse news: If money makes the world go round and those in charge of money are not living up to their full human consciousness, can we expect the world to turn in the right direction?

Chapter 8

The Ugly Truth About Beauty

Once, when I was ten years old, my parents invited some wealthy friends of theirs for dinner. As is the custom, we children were summoned to greet the guests. I hated these moments: Pushed into a room to kiss adults reeking of wine, hug them and answer invariably dumb questions.

After I said my good-boy hellos, my mother's friend said, "Oh, my gosh. He is so handsome. The only thing off is his mouth. It's not very sensual."

I left the room, but her words stuck with me.

After the dinner party, I asked my mother: "What does *sensual* mean?"

"Why?" she asked.

"Well, Aunt Jen said my mouth is not sensual."

"Don't care what she says," my mother smiled.

But I did care. Not being perfect really bothered me and I wanted a sensual mouth, whatever that meant.

Fast forward fifteen years and my dentist informed me that I have a class-one bite and if I did not have a LeForte surgery to correct it, I would wear off my teeth within a decade.

"Like mine," he said, showing his set of teeth cracked and eaten halfway through. A visit to a mouth and jaw surgeon confirmed my fate. I hesitated. The surgery implied walking around for at least six weeks with my teeth wired together, sucking my meals through a straw.

The clinical case was strong, but what really confirmed my decision was the memory of what Aunt Jen had said fifteen years earlier.

"Maybe if I have the surgery I'll finally have a sensual mouth," I thought.

A week after I finished my final year of medical school, I had the surgery. I never felt more sick in my life, first vomiting buckets of blood and then having uncomfortable side-effects from an anti-nausea drug.

For all practical—but not clinical—purposes, I had cosmetic surgery. I fixed a part of my appearance I was not happy with. But the surgery didn't cure my need to be perfect, nor my crippling low self-esteem.

Perfect Girlfriends

Sonja, my first girlfriend at university, was slender, attractive and full of life. But, like most women, she was not a supermodel or an A-list actress. One day, while visiting a luxurious five-star hotel close to her parents' home, we went for a walk around a manmade lake. Away from the crowd, she took my hand. I tensed up; I hated this public display of affection. But she looked happy and I didn't want to disappoint her. For a while, we walked in silence. Chinese torture seemed more fun. We turned the corner and saw a large group of young people walking toward us. I dropped Sonja's hand.

Even now, I am mortified by the pain I caused a good person for no other reason than that she didn't belong on the pages of *Vogue*. I lacked the necessary self-esteem to truly see my girlfriend's inner beauty. Instead, I wanted a woman with external beauty who would bring admiration from everyone, even from strangers walking around an artificial lake. I believed that not only must I be attractive, but that everything and everyone associated with me had to be attractive as well.

Years later, I took a runner up in the Miss South Africa beauty pageant to a medical school ball. But even being seen with a crowned beauty has had little impact on my life: I am still waiting for lightning to strike.

My obsession with beauty is universal. If a Martian arrived here and saw our culture's propaganda in newspapers, magazines, advertisements, movies and televisions shows, he would believe that only beautiful people are great parents, spouses, friends, employees or citizens. Beautiful people are seen as being the best of humanity.

Americans spent $12.4 billion on cosmetic medical treatments and $49 billion on cosmetics and toiletries in 2005. This does not even include how much was spent on clothing. The current obsession with fashion among the rich and the poor alike tells me that having high-end clothes is part of what defines a beautiful woman in our society.

Skinniness Obsession

For most of my life, I mostly fell in love with skinny women. Curvy voluptuous women belonged in the centerfold of porn magazines or on calendars found on the doors of auto mechanics. My dating pool comprised skinny women with small hips, champagne–flute breasts and no sign of fat or cellulite within a thousand miles.

Our culture is obsessed with skinny. After the 2006 fall fashion show in

Bryant Park, *The New York Times* quoted one of the most sought-after casting directors for his views on today's models: "They're these faceless, sexless things," he said. "The editors say, 'I don't care about personality, I want blanks.'"

As a result, I have had many women telling me they are fed up with sacrificing their lives to be thin. All they think about is what they have eaten, what they must eat, what they will eat.

The obsession is also harming children: Studies show that 57 percent of girls and 33 percent of boys use cigarettes, fasting or skipping meals to lose weight. The use of diet pills has doubled over the last five years.

Youth Obsession

Until my eyes are burned when I am cremated, I will be turned into a lusty animal when I see a youthful beauty with bouncing breasts walking down the street. I am obsessed with youth.

Recently, on my way back from a trip to South Africa, I happened to be on the same flight as a couple with whom I had practiced medicine in Canada. With pride, they told me how they now are certified to remove wrinkles from patients. "This new technique is so much better than Botox. It removes wrinkles while ensuring the skin still shows expression. We heard actors are crazy about our technique."

If farmers in rural Canada pay hard-earned money to remove wrinkles and goodhearted doctors like my friends are only too keen to jump on the bandwagon, we can easily declare that youth is the fastest growing religion in the world today. Even my ENT surgeon has a sign in his office advertising his Botox and Resulin specialty! What next? The local deli? It seems everyone wants to stop the inevitability of Father Time's scratching.

In Los Angeles, a reporter described how she admired the thin beautiful body of a teenage blond wearing "It" jeans. But when this young teenager turned around, she saw with shock that the woman was many years above 60. In the city of youthful angels, the old are not allowed to grow old graciously. Newspapers report that some mothers dress like teenagers to be cool and "in" with their daughters and their friends. They want to be their daughters best friends, not older parent.

My obsession with youth seems to be "in."

Beauty and Happiness

A few years ago I dated Jenny, a model and one of the most beautiful women with whom I've ever shared a bottle of wine. One night, after a few drinks in the Meatpacking District, we went to her apartment in Tribeca. She warned me that her place was a mess. I joked and said "Can't be worse than mine." Well, it was. Ten times worse. A pigsty. But that's not why this experience is relevant. In her bedroom, she had four pieces of decoration on her walls. A Catholic cross, a photo of her mother as a young woman, a breathtaking photo of Jenny as a model on the cover of a fashion magazine and a self-portrait of Jenny. As an amateur painter, I eagerly walked closer to examine Jenny's budding artistic talent. Jenny had painted her hair, her neckline, her ears and her clothes with a skill far above the level of craftsmanship she claimed to have. I was impressed. But the face she painted for herself shocked me. Her face had no form, no line, no eyes. She had obscured her face with thick black oil paint. Jenny, an incredibly beautiful woman, loathed her own self.

Over the last three years, in almost every acting class I've taken, I have met women and men who, by today's standards, are pretty. Some of them make their livings as models. Yet, I have stopped being surprised by how little self-confidence many of them have or how unhappy they are with their lives. If they hate their looks, they also hate showing true sexuality on stage. Sure, they can play the flirty characters, but when the role demands a seductive character full of lust, the confidence evaporates.

Physical beauty cannot transform an inner beast into an inner beauty. If beauty had such power, why did Marilyn Monroe die of a drug overdose? Why did Kate Moss spend most of the nineties drunk and high, as she herself has confessed? Why did the reigning Miss America bravely reveal how she used drugs and alcohol to escape her inner demons? Why do so many pretty Hollywood actors check into rehabilitation centers? People with healthy self-esteems, love and happiness do not die of drug overdoses, nor do they stay drunk for the better part of a decade.

Research on beauty and happiness is scant. The only research I came across suggested that beautiful women have more opportunities in life, both in work and love. Attractive men are also more likely to be elected to positions of political power. But opportunities and power seldom translate into happiness if you are not happy already.

Skinniness and Happiness

Marilyn is an actor and a friend I deeply respect. I know the feeling is mutual. A few months ago she sent me the following email: "This is what I want you to do, for me. Every time you feel that loneliness, when you feel like the empty space is sucking you in—you get up, open your window and close your eyes. At that moment just breathe and think about what you have accomplished. You're breathing the air of New York, the capital of the world, the city of our dreams and a world of possibilities!"

With gratitude, I have often followed Marilyn's advice. Then I received an email: Marilyn tried to kill herself. I cried for my friend. I cried for myself.

Suicide and suicidal thoughts are common all over the world. It is even more prevalent in women like Marilyn, women obsessed with their weight.

I recalled how I too went through a period where I was obsessed with my weight. I ran all the time, drank only water, avoided red meat, ate very little food, lived almost in complete celibacy and withdrew from all major social life. Control over my body somehow gave me the illusion that I was in control of my external and inner life.

When my family expressed their concern over my skinny appearance, I felt a certain sense of accomplishment. Specifically, when one brother said, "Are you doing this because you think your body is the temple of God?" I just smiled. I knew what health was and obviously he did not. I finally felt different from them.

But in the process, I robbed myself of the full experiences and wonderful pleasures life has to offer. Even worse, I punished my own body and Real Self all the while my left-brain lied to me that I was taking charge of my life.

Life is indeed simpler if you only have to worry about what you eat and weigh; it leaves all existential and identity questions at the front door with the dirty shoes. An obsession with skinniness may keep the demons at bay, but it can never bring us happiness. Happiness is letting go of control and perfection, not clinging to some arbitrary weight to impress others.

Youth and Happiness

I have dated attractive women half my age. I have not found long-term happiness in the experience. The movie *American Beauty* perfectly illustrates that a fantasy of youth almost never brings any long-term happiness. The want is much more exciting than the reality, at least six months down the line.

Youth is the time in our lives where we transition from being children to adults. It is a period of seeking pleasure and admiration, of avoiding committed relationships so we can figure out our most preferred types of relationship and rebel against our culture to find our own voice in the community. Youth is a time for identity crisis and interpersonal conflict. Youth is the final contraction in the birth of a strong Real Self.

Youth is not a happy time.

Studies shows that happiness levels start to rise as people reach adulthood. For many, a happy life begins at 40. When we reach this point, we have shed many of our fantasies about life and begin to appreciate the finiteness of our lives. 40 bring a sense of reality that forces us to enjoy what we have, rather than wish we had more.

We become wiser and happier with age, not when we cling to our youth.

"If you've found meaning in your life, you don't want to go back. You want to go forward. You want to see more, do more," Morrie Schwartz said on his deathbed. "The truth is, part of me is every age. I'm a three-year-old, I'm a five-year-old, I'm a 37-year- old, I'm a 50-year-old. I've been through all of them."

Clinging to our youth or to a youthful beauty is like an Olympic sprinter clinging to his jumping blocks: He can have all the talent in the world, but he will not be able to show his talent. Nor will people like me experience the happiness of intimate relationships. After all, intimacy is about mature minds falling in love, not a youthful pretty face decorating the living room.

Cost of Beauty

"I spent most of my high school years fretting about my beauty and weight. There was this one girl we all admired. She was skinny and beautiful. Everyone wanted to be like her. At one point, my mother had to take me to a psychologist. She was worried about my weight and my obsession," a friend confided to me.

Adolescence is the time that the best of humanity figure out their interests and passions, not what size dress they ought to be wearing or how their looks compare to the "it" girls in class or popular magazines.

A few years ago, I watched a movie wherein a man said to a pretty woman: "Beautiful women are invisible." It took me a second to figure out what he was saying. When we see beauty, we see the physical attributes of a person. We see symmetry in face, luscious lips, large breasts, muscular biceps and strong jaws. We like pretty people for how they look, not for who they are or what their interests are. We see the shell, not the pearl inside. If you are not seen intimately, are you seen at all?

A beautiful friend told me, "Ask me anything about our culture and beauty. I'm a bit obsessed with it too. I know what's going on."

She did not have to tell me that she is into beauty and fashion. She spends hours putting on her make-up, even if it means being late for appointments. She compared her obsession with make-up to an artist painting a canvas.

Hours later, we were listening to music and she began to sing along, "I'm lonely and aching, and I don't know why?"

After a pause, she said, "All the music I listen to is about loneliness. I don't think this ache and loneliness will ever go away," she confessed.

"My wife used to be a model. She is very conscious of her looks. When we have sex, she needs to see herself in a mirror, or she has a panic attack," a man told me once.

Many people obsessed with their beauty struggle either getting into bed, being seen naked out of bed or having orgasms in bed. Sex, especially intimate sex, demands a person to remove the pretty mask, to reveal the body and its animal needs. Without mirroring from others, the beauty obsessed feel an emptiness or pain that feels like a black hole.

The joy of sexual care is not available for men or women obsessing with how the body looks rather than how the body feels in close physical contact with another human being.

Blanche DuBois is the protagonist in *A Streetcar Named Desire*. In the play, Blanche obsesses with her external beauty, her clothes, her sophistication, her accent and her wrinkles to fight off the ugly demons lurking under her skin. When she finally faces the truth, her mind leaves her body. She opts for madness over reality.

The ancient Greeks knew as much—the fable of Narcissus shows that when you love your own appearance more than anything else, you will wither away or drown in your own reflection.

Cost of Skinniness

From the day we are born, if not earlier, the body teaches the brain. In a world where we so often think of the brain as being in charge of life, the influence of the body on the brain is often overlooked. But, as we saw in an earlier chapter, the body forms our mind. Specifically, child development researchers have coined the phrase: What is physical is psychological to the child. With this, they mean that how and when you feed a baby and how you touch him create bodily experiences that are translated into sensations and then into emotions that inform the baby's developing mind. Good care of the baby's body forms the foundation of a positive body image and a strong Real Self. Later, when a baby starts to move around on his own, his experiences of exploring the world and the parental approval he receives for his efforts continue to strengthen both.

But the body's impact on self image does not stop in childhood. We all know how enjoyable exercise, healthful food and caring touch increases our creativity and self-esteem. In my own life, I stumbled upon many of my best creative ideas while I was showering, doing the laundry or exercising.

If what we do to our bodies impacts the real self, then what is the message that people send to their Real Self when they punish their bodies by withholding food or depriving their senses of foods they enjoy? What is the message if they run for long period of times on the treadmill or pound the pavement only to lose weight? What is the message if they smoke packets of cigarettes every day or use over–the-counter or illicit drugs to suppress their appetites? I would imagine the non-conscious message is, "I hate what life is doing to my body. Since I am what happens to my body, I hate myself. I must hate life."

It should be no surprise that anorexia patients have several severe co-morbid psychiatric conditions. They have among the largest suicide rate of all psychiatric illnesses. After all, if self-esteem shrinks, the self will weaken to a point where the normal pressures of life become unbearable.

But you do not have to reach anorexic levels before an obsession with skinniness can cause psychiatric complications. Research shows that when overweight, full-bodied or normal-sized women attempt to become a Paris Hilton, they often trigger a semi-starvation neurosis, a phenomena observed in people of normal weight who are starved. During this state, people fantasize about food and are riddled with anxiety, depression and suicidal thoughts. Researchers believe that we all have a non-conscious drive to have a certain bodyweight, arguably formed by genetics and the body image our brain forms within our parietal lobes. If a person tries to lose more weight than her body thinks is good for her, she may receive admiration, but anxiety, depression and suicidal thoughts will knock on her front door.

A Greenwich Village Pilates teacher told me that many of her skinny obsessed clients overcompensate for their withholding of food by shopping endlessly. In return, they amass significant debt that only compounds their problems. From a neuroscience perspective, her observations seem spot-on. If you take away the pleasure of food from the animal brain, you must reward it with shopping or multiple sex partners or drugs. Otherwise life is useless and void of pleasure. In the process, the self-esteem shrinks along with the body.

The skinny obsessed also struggle with infertility. Researchers studied the effect of stress, exercise and food starvation on monkeys. Dr. Berga from Emory University, leader of the study, reported her findings in *The New York Times* as follows: "We found that when we stressed monkeys alone, 10 percent stopped menstruating temporarily. When we added exercise and limited their food intake, again about 10 percent stopped menstruating temporarily. But when we combined stress, exercise and cut down on food, 75 percent became amenorrheic."

The skinny obsessed are often on regimens loaded with stress, self-starvation and excessive exercise. If a woman's fertility is at stake, we must know an obsession with skinniness is a cry against everything nature at its most basic is focused on: procreation.

Cost of Youth

For my fortieth birthday party, my brother Andre bought me an abstract painting of an area in South Africa called Lappiesland, a place of fond childhood memories. Before the gift, nothing in my apartment trumpeted my age. My apartment allowed me to escape reality and still made me feel like an 18-year-old boy. But now when I see the painting, I know I am living in a fantasy. I know old age and death are moving toward me like a linebacker toward a quarterback.

This often leaves me in a state of panic. I still have so much to do. I am scared of death and eternity. I am scared to grow old alone. I am afraid that I will never live out my dreams as an actor, find intimate love with a woman, feel my own child's little hand in my own or see his or her eyes filled with the joys of life. I want to object to life's unfairness. But time does not listen to any pleas, nor fall for any charm or give a hoot for any of our attempts to hide its effects on our bodies. Death is coming.

Years ago, a friend visited a women in her late seventies, who, in her youth, was a well-known and pretty Broadway star. In her apartment, everywhere my friend looked, she only saw busts and photos of the Broadway star in her twenties. In conversations with her, she seemed to believe that George Clooney was about to walk into her apartment and take her to bed. She even refused to eat cake so as not to add any weight to her figure. She never grew up.

An important part of maturity is acknowledging our own mortality so we can live more realistically.

Charlize Theron, Academy Award winning actress, model and fellow South African, once told Oprah that to remove wrinkles from one's face is the equivalent of burning one's photo albums. She explained: "We all go through a lot of turmoil and a lot of difficult things that maybe we'd want to forget. But you grow from those things and when you see those moments and those lines, it's not looking back at devastation. It's going, 'I've grown from this.' And so in a way…you've earned it."

Wrinkles show us we have lived. Wrinkles show us we are embracing the future and we are at peace with our past. Wrinkles should be badges of honor, not signs of shame. It is telling our Real Self that we are happy with the life we have lived.

Finally, what we do to our bodies impacts the Real Self. What is the message that people send to their brains when they allow doctors to inject chemicals in their bodies or cut them up to make them look youthful? You are not good enough for who you are. Reality is for old people, fantasy is for you. An obsession with beauty, skinniness and youth does not bring us happiness. If anything, it increases our pain. So why are we so obsessed with it?

Role of Physical Attractiveness

In his work on natural selection, Charles Darwin believed that beauty in animals and humans serves the sole purpose of sexual selection. Darwin believed that all beings do not possess a consciousness that can allow them to find a unique sense of beauty. At the most basic level, males follow beauty passively like a donkey follows a carrot. Females want to mate with alpha males to ensure a better gene pool, safety and a bit of status. Beauty is a carrot to non-consciously attract clueless alpha males.

In a study, a group of young men were asked to cross a long, narrow and moving suspension bridge high above a river. Walking over this bridge made the men anxious; they became physiologically aroused. While they crossed, an attractive young woman approached them and asked them to fill in a survey questionnaire. After they filled it in, she gave them her telephone number and asked every man to call her if they had more questions. But she did not approach all of the men at the same spot on the bridge. She approached half of the men while they were swinging 230 feet above the river and the other half when they were on steady ground after they crossed. The results showed that the men who were interviewed on the bridge were more likely to call the woman back than those interviewed on steady ground.

In his assessment of the study, Harvard psychologist Daniel Gilbert concluded, "Apparently, feelings that one interprets as fear in the presence of a sheer drop may be interpreted as lust in the presence of a sheer blouse—which is simply to say that people can be wrong about what they are feeling."

If our brain confuses beauty with fear and vice versa, we can deduce which part of the brain is activated when we see beauty: our animal brains.

I once dated a woman for a few months who could not stop focusing on putting on make-up. She was almost obsessive compulsive about how often she looked in the mirror and the number of hours a day she spent on her face.

A part of me felt that she was addicted to her beauty and her beautification. Reports also show there are people who are addicted to cosmetic surgery. A prime example was Michael Jackson. Any activity that points toward an addiction tells us that the rewards system in our animal brain is being activated.

A year ago I attended the fall fashion show at Bryant Park in Manhattan. The air of beauty was intoxicating. After I received my little gift bag, I watched the hustle that precedes the models walking down the catwalk. Television lights shone on the front-row celebrities and editors, the royalty of the show. Music started. One model after the other started to prance down the catwalk. Many of the models looked like young girls; some even looked like tall angelic boys. At the finale, the models as a group made a final walk before leaving the catwalk. As they left, an image of a herd of gazelles in the African veldt crossed my mind. There is something both majestic and primitive about watching a fashion show.

Beauty wakes up the animal in us.

Marriage of Beauty and Money

Power and beauty have had a long relationship. As children, we hear how Cinderella and Snow White ultimately marry their handsome rich princes. We were enthralled when Princess Diana and Prince Charles married. Since money, fame and political power are today's version of royalty, we buy every gossip magazine in order to read every detail about the wedding days of the rich and famous. Some rich and beautiful people are open about the relationship between money and beauty. Aristotle Onassis, the late Greek shipping magnate who had Jackie Kennedy and Maria Callas competing for his love, once said, "If women did not exist, all the money in the world would have no meaning."

Here in Manhattan, reporters asked a model, the third wife of Donald Trump, if she would have married her husband if he were not rich. She brilliantly answered: "Would he have married me if I was not beautiful?"

Some Internet dating sites exploit the money and beauty connection. One company only allows millionaires, CEOs, doctors, lawyers, benefactors, models, beauty queens, centerfold models, glamour models and fitness models to subscribe.

Darwin seems to be right. Beauty plays a role in attracting powerful alpha males. What constitutes an alpha male in the concrete jungle is different than the jungle of our ancestors. Research shows that many women are turned on by tall, smart, funny or rich men. Yesterday's alpha male is this morning's prince and this afternoon's Ivy League graduate working on Wall Street. Beauty is essential for mating if you live with an animal consciousness and you want to marry an object that will bring you status and security. In return, you become a sexual object and a trophy wife.

The good news is that Darwin was right only about those of us living with an animal consciousness. After all, we have already established that the best of humans have with a higher consciousness. They can walk out of the river of animal instincts and ancestral experiences and make decisions that are unique to humans. We can see another person's inner beauty and not react to physical beauty like low-level animals. We can indeed fall in love with someone else through sharing intimate moments, not just by looking great. The best of us, but not all of us, can indeed fall in love with someone's eyes, not their beauty, breasts or bank accounts.

Beauty does not only wake up the animal within us, it also helps those of us with animal consciousness to date and mate like animals.

Mirror, Mirror....

Here in New York, the search for beauty is conducted with a notorious religiosity in this most secular of cities. Female denizens of particular zip codes seem to fritter away most of their time by spending money on manicures, pedicures, bikini waxes, facials, massages, a 79th pair of black shoes, the new Wonder Bra, a Prada skirt, facials, massages, a class to firm the buttocks, diets, vitamins, lingerie and the latest anti-aging cream. Blond hair needs to be dyed black, straight hair needs to be curled and eyebrows need to be waxed. If the pursuit of their own beauty is not enough, they obsess about other people's beauty. They criticize colleagues' and friends' clothes or rave about the fashion at the Oscars. Beauty, fashion, beauty, fashion.

But it is not only to attract men.

Otherwise, why would some women "need" 50 pairs of black shoes that few people could tell apart? Most men would not know or care whether the label on a scarf said Hermes or Herpes. Why is it that when a man walks down Park Avenue in the company of a woman, other women check out the woman more than the man? Why are scientists so perplexed that some high-earning women are obsessed about their looks even if they make more money than most men? Why is it that a famous fashion designer said, "Women dress for women"? Well, because they do.

And why do men, once they reach a certain income bracket, suddenly start getting manicures themselves? Why do they spend hundreds of dollars to have plain white shirts tailored? They too buy into the culture of gold cuff links, carb-eschewing diets and expensive haircuts. And don't forget the ever-popular midlife crisis sports car. Men are not immune from the tyrannies of being attractive.

Beauty brings admiration; admiration tickles our animal brain.

As much as I, a beauty addict, hate to admit it, I could not find any connection between beauty and a higher level human consciousness, no matter how I searched. For the best of humanity, beauty is as useful as our coccyx: a symbol of an aspect of our physicality that played an important role thousands of years ago, but today has no use.

Role of Skinniness

I practiced medicine in KwaZulu Natal, a province in South Africa, where I frequently had to deal with babies dying from battery acid enemas given by witchdoctors who believe pain drives away demons that are causing disease; children dying from severe malnutrition; and members of the royal family receiving preferred care by the staff. It was also here that I saw the devastation caused by obstructed labor—a condition where either the baby's head is too big to pass through a woman's pelvis or a normal size head is stuck in a too-small pelvis. One day, we had to operate on a woman who had been in obstructed labor for days. By the time she reached us, her bladder and bowls were destroyed. Without the surgery, she would have died, an event that is still a sad reality for many pregnant women in developing countries.

As a skinny women addict, I could not believe how most African men would lust after women with full bodies, big boobs and childbearing hips. Not only that, many men frowned upon skinny women.

The reason for some men's fascination with full-bodied women is twofold. First, I was told, if you have a full body, you are either royalty or from a rich family. Your body advertises that you have more than enough to eat. Secondly, skinny narrow-hipped mothers often die in childbirth, leaving their children vulnerable to the stark realities of a life where people still struggle daily for food. Non-consciously, men know that hips that can bear children will serve them better in the long run.

KwaZulu Natal may seem a far way from Hollywood, Paris Hilton or Kate Moss. But this snapshot of the Zulu culture, through the lens of thousands of years of human struggle, is the snapshot of all of humanity. For most of humanity's struggle, skinny was not a beautiful characteristic.

Even in the Western World, full voluptuous female bodies have been celebrated for ages. Greek and Roman sculptures, Renaissance paintings of the

Madonna and child, Rembrandt's voluptuous models, and Marilyn Monroe photographs show we have always loved voluptuous female bodies.

In a recent experiment in England, researchers from all over the world gathered to see how modern science could help people date more effectively. They wanted to know why people meet and decide to enter long-term relationships. Personality compatibility questionnaires, computer images of faces calculating levels of masculinity and femininity and facial profiles were some of the data collected. All the major theories failed spectacularly. Scientists are still clueless as to why we want to bond with the opposite sex.

But one finding they made caught my attention. Researchers found that women with a high hip-waste ratio had more interest from more (but not all) men than any other criteria tested. Stripped from the influence of modern culture, most men prefer a full female figure.

This, and still within 50 years, we have moved from Marilyn Monroe to Kate Moss, from full fertile women to the skinny obsessed. In the process, we wiped out thousands of years of how humans viewed beauty.

The Control of Skinniness

A few years ago I had a date with Joan, a perfect case study of a woman who lived her whole adulthood in either the shadow of anorexia or in the light of praise for her skinny body. As a teenager in Los Angeles, she and two of her five best friends struggled with anorexia. After school, she dedicated her career to helping other women fight the disease. She studied with some of the best researchers in the field. After a number of years of helping anorexic patients, she left, exhausted by the effort.

When I asked her why, she answered: "In group therapy, when someone would say what laxative she recently used, or how she fooled her parents in their attempts to make her eat, I could see the girls take mental notes. They did not take notes to learn how to beat anorexia, but on what to do when they go home to lose more weight. They did not want to get better! They wanted to win the battle for the thinnest woman in the group. They use their bodies as a sport."

Medical research shows that anorexic patients are perfectionists, Type-A, often high achievers and have a need to be the best. Brain scans show that many anorexia patients have abnormal activity in the mammalian brain that disappears after therapy. I suspect that it is a sense of status and being the best that activates an anorexic's animal brain.

Some people may object to using anorexia patients as a proxy for fashionable skinniness. But after meeting many people obsessed with skinniness, including myself, I know that the only difference is a few pounds.

Months ago I met a very accomplished exercise obsessed medical doctor with experience in treating anorexic patients. When I explained to her my theories on why people obsess about skinniness, she quickly and adamantly said, "No, it is not only about seeking admiration. It is about control. The women think: If I can control my body, then no one can control me. The world can control everything, but they cannot control what I do with my body."

Some researchers support the idea that the skinny obsessed are filled with non-conscious anger and sadness and that they use controlling their body weight to control their non-conscious confusion. Others believe self-starvation is non-conscious anger from childhood that is used to attack the body and Real Self. Others believe such an obsession is a cry for help, a plea to their parents for an acceptance of their unique individuality and passions. The reality is probably that each of these reasons comes in to play in different ways for different people.

Skinniness has no evolutionary role. Today, it seems, an obsession with weight only serves as a psychological defense mechanism.

Role Of Youth

A while ago, I sat in a bar with a friend. I pointed to a younger woman I found attractive.

"Why do you find her attractive?" my friend asked.

"She looks innocent, kind and good," I answered.

"To me she looks like a blank canvas," she responded.

It suddenly clicked as to why I had such a fascination with youth throughout my life, even into my forties.

Our brains are constantly focused on identifying danger. We may think we are excited to go on a date, but like a parent, our brains fret about safety, even if we do not consciously know it. This is even more true for the people we meet.

Susan Fiske, professor of psychology and neuroscience at Princeton, studies how our brains stereotype people when we meet them for the first time. Our brains scan for signs of whether people look dangerous or have malignant intent. We want to avoid anybody that looks angry and dominant. She has also found that we tend to subdivide women into a few categories, one being the traditionally attractive. These are the women who "don't look dominant, have baby-faced features. They are not threatening."

The reality is that baby-faced young women and men are not necessarily trustworthy. Like all people, they too can take you to the cleaners. It's not exactly that our brains are lying to us; rather our non-conscious minds want to play it safe.

There are many reasons why I may fear older, more mature, non-baby faced women. Without a strong Real Self, my fear of intimacy causes me to be attracted to women who I see as a canvas, those on whom I can project my fantasies, those who will not rip me out of my bubble. A fragile Real Self also makes me fear growing up and marrying a mature woman regardless of her age or looks. Finally, a fragile Real Self prevents me from facing old age and death. Dating youth keeps up the lie that life is eternal.

Why the Beauty Obsession?

When I began to investigate my own obsession with my own and others' physical attractiveness, I was surprised to discover that my obsession was an attempt to recreate a childhood fantasy bubble in which perfection, beauty, innocence and eternity reigned.

Recall that during the union phase in early childhood, good primary caretakers create a bubble for their babies in which they nurture their human brains. One way they accomplish this, arguably the most important way, is how they look at their babies. If they look with intimate, caring and admiring eyes, their eyes become mirrors in which their babies experience themselves and everything in their bubble—their bodies, their parents, their toys and their home—as perfect and pretty. The baby feels perfect and beautiful for he sees himself and everything he touches as perfect and beautiful in his caretaker's eyes.

During the Separation phase, good primary caretakers slowly deflate this bubble to allow the child to develop a healthy Real Self, which allows children to have self-esteem based not on the mirroring in their parents' eyes, but on their joy and confidence of mastering their ability to self-express, self-share and self-care.

In some of the saddest research on the planet, a group of Canadian researchers conducted an experiment to see if parents care for their more attractive children differently than their less attractive children. Who would parents buckle up in the car? Who would parents allow to wander up and down the shopping mall aisle without supervision? Who would they not allow out of their sight? The results? The researchers found that parents were three times more likely to take better care of their more attractive children.

But when parents "take better care" of their pretty children by keeping a better eye on them in the shopping mall, they may be psychologically chaining their pretty children to them. Pretty children are more likely to be barred from exploring and mastering the world away from mom and dad. Their developing Real Self suffers. Their bubble never bursts.

If the bubble of perfection and prettiness never bursts, a baby-turned-adult will feel he or she is the most beautiful person in the world even if others' opinions would suggest otherwise. They will spend a lot of time on their looks. They need to be perfect and beautiful. With the help of what Dr. Masterson calls "a massive denial of reality," many succeed to maintain a fantasy bubble. I will add: It takes an enormous amount of energy to live in a bubble that needs to be created every minute.

If a bubble of perfection bursts too quickly without a Real Self developing, a baby may forever feel anxious about her self-esteem and looks; when the world admires her, she feels good and attractive, when she is without any adoring eyes or has salad in her teeth, she will feel like Jenny who thought her face was worthy of black paint. An obsession with one's beauty is an obsession with preserving a fantasy bubble.

The indoctrination of beauty as a sign of happiness and humanity continues even after the age of three. As a child, I listened to my parents reading me stories of how pretty Cinderella and Snow White escaped their abusive situations to finally find happiness in the arms of a rich handsome prince. The fantasy that beauty is the key that will unlock the prisons of our loneliness, confusion and painful childhoods continues long after we have graduated from bedtime stories to Hollywood movies.

I walk into an elevator and a pretty baby gives me a toothless smile. I bend down and say, "Ah, you are such a pretty little girl. Wow. Look at those eyes!" I look at the mother and say, "Wow! You have a beautiful daughter!" She smiles proudly and says, "Thank you!" as if she had sculpted the baby from scratch.

I had made mistake 101 in dealing with the baby. Remember, we become our compliments. I am sure this little baby hears ten times a day, "Oh, you are so cute." When this baby needs to separate from her mother to start her road to a healthy Self, she is probably complimented more for how she looks than what she is doing. "Be a princess" becomes the feedback, not "Be yourself" or "Be passionate."

Children brought up with beauty as their major attribute spend their later years dying of shame when they find a zit on their forehead, an unseen tear in their stocking or someone wearing the same outfit at a party. In addition, they also are obsessed with surrounding themselves with pretty people. Without other beautiful people complimenting their own beauty, they feel ordinary and empty. Anything that takes away from their being perfectly beautiful brings attacks of anxiety and worthlessness.

Alice Miller summarized it the best:

She no longer received constant affirmation of her attractiveness, which earlier had
served a directly supportive function as a substitute for the missing mirroring by her
mother. Superficially, her despair about getting old seemed to be due to the absence
of sexual contacts but, at a deeper level, early fears of being abandoned were now
aroused, and this woman had no new conquests with which to counteract them.
All her substitute mirrors were broken. She again stood helpless and confused, as
the small girl once did before her mother's face, in which she found not herself but
only her mother's confusion.

A developmental arrest leading to a fragile Real Self; excessive compliments
on how they look, not what they do; and cultural stories propagating the myth
that beauty is a virtue force many children to leave their childhood obsessed
with beauty. Many of us caught in our fantasy bubbles become the gods of
beauty and power in the real world.

Gods of Power

When French *Elle* decided to use models without make-up or Photoshop,
it became big news. Cindi Leive, the editor of *Glamour*, explained, "Fashion
magazines are always about some element of fantasy."

When *Vogue* showed an obese woman without clothes, Anna Wintour told
an interviewer that the point was to provoke readers. As Eric Wilson from *The
New York Times* wrote, "The implication here is that what can be considered
provocative image in a fashion magazine today is one that shows something
real."

Add to these statements the quote from a casting director that said editors
are looking for "faceless, sexless things" that are "blanks."

As an actor, I have often heard many actresses complain that they only
have a shot at getting great parts in movies when they are younger than 25 or
older than 50. Hollywood is not interested in mid-life women. Instead, we
often see pretty 22-year-old ingénues playing a 35-year-old mother, ignoring
the thousands of actress in their thirties bursting with passion, experience and
talent.

Whether in Hollywood, Madison Avenue, fashion houses or fashion
magazines, those who made it to positions of power have a warped, if not
primitive conception of beauty.

But they are not only to blame.

I know a lot of men and women who, like me, buy into the idea that young skinny and pretty are high in the hierarchy of humanity. We are often the ones with money and power who then marry skinny, young and pretty, perpetuating the myth that you need to fit the narrow definition of beauty today to find a mate.

Whether supplier or demander of this fantasy, we all have a few things in common: We are obsessed with fantasy, fear intimacy, need to be in control and perfect, live in a bubble and date with an animal consciousness. The Gods of Beauty are not the best of humanity.

The Market

Just as not all investment bankers and traders live with a reptilian consciousness, not all people obsessing about beauty, skinniness and youth are skinny monkeys dressed in the latest fashions. Many people with average Real Selves have been caught up in the fashion fantasy.

In our modern culture, most women receive 2000 images per week of what ideal beauty is. Probably totalitarian regimes do not indoctrinate their populace with such an intensity and frequency. We shake our heads in disbelief when we see think about communist or fascist countries that would post loudspeakers at every intersection, for to better indoctrinate the masses. But here in the land of the free, those loudspeakers of indoctrination are posted at every newsstand, grocery store checkout line and especially, the TV in our family rooms.

Society may say "beauty is skin deep" and "beauty is in the eye of the beholder," but society is also clear that the standard of female beauty is being young, skinny and pretty and dressing in fashionable clothes. Society has made women feel inferior if they do not fit a narrow and unrealistic standard of beauty. The result: research show that the majority of women are struggling with their looks, weight and wrinkles.

Our mere mortals are powerless to maintain a truly humane sense of beauty against the gods of beauty that have so much power in the media. They are literally brainwashing our created reality with unattainable images that leave women struggling with self-esteem. They just laugh it off: Fashion needs fantasy.

Real Definition of Fantasy

When researchers asked a group of women what personally makes them feel beautiful, they answered: "being loved"; "having a strong relationship or marriage"; "doing something they love"; and "taking good care of yourself." Men and women who follow the abilities of a healthy Real Self, i.e., self-expression, self-care and self-share, are in touch with their inner beauty. When they ask, "Mirror, mirror, on the wall, who is the most beautiful of them all?" their Real Self answers: "You are."

I am still caught in a fantasy bubble of beauty and youth. Over the years, I have made significant improvements on how I define beauty. But I am still struggling to see inner beauty more than external beauty. Even in a healthy culture, my struggle would have been Herculean. But our current culture keeps inflating my own fantasy bubble. Maybe I will never be able to put the fantasy of beauty behind me. But one thing I do know: I will never marry a woman, whether or not she meets today's standards of beauty, if she does not enjoy a passion, intimacy or self-care. I owe it to my children. I owe it to myself. I owe it to her.

Chapter 9

Love that Cures, Kills

I always imagined I would be 28 years of age when I would meet her. It would be love at first sight. I would just know. The dating process would be exciting and filled with a lot of kissing and cuddling. We would enjoy a fairytale wedding. Shortly thereafter we would have perfect children to share our pretty life together. We would live life free from old age, death or conflict; a life with perfect smiles and eternally youthful bodies.

When I turned 30, I started to get worried. What if I was wrong? But, I countered, "Good things happen to those who wait." Hollywood movies helped to support my beliefs that unconditional love exists and destiny would ultimately bring true love. So every class, vacation resort, airplane flight, subway ride or bar would see my transformation into a bee frantically flying from flower to flower. "Will she be here tonight? Is that her?"

Despite my enormous need and endless pursuit, my love history has been a horror movie. I most probably have kissed more individual women in my life than I have kissed the single woman I kissed the most while dating. Despite going on hundreds of dates, every date I had gone on seemed to be with the same type of woman over and over again.

Then it happened.

My Hollywood Romance

Tired after an overnight flight to London, I was just excusing myself from the table after a few beers with family and friends. The door to the pub opened. A tall, dark-haired woman with an enormous smile entered. Seconds became minutes, the bar's loud music faded into the background, drowned out by the African drum of my heartbeat. My legs remained stuck in a half-stand half-sit position. It was love at first sight. Ann walked straight toward our table. It turned out that she was the girlfriend of a friend's best friend. Chills raced up my spine as we shook hands.

The next day at a pub lunch, Ann was seated next to me instead of her boyfriend. It seemed to be another sign from the universe: She's the one.

Ann turned out not only to be gorgeous, kind and friendly, but also accomplished. She had an Ivy League Ph.D. and was heir to a massive fortune. But I knew none of this when I saw her walking through that door and fell in love with her. She could have been a local prostitute for all I knew.

For months, my friend, out of respect for his friend, refused to give me Ann's contact information. Then one day the news came. She had broken up with her boyfriend! I sent her an email. "Hi Ann, I hope this email finds you well. I enjoyed meeting you a few months ago. By the way, have you ever been to Istanbul? Please send me your telephone number and I will tell you why. Looking forward to hearing from you!"

The following day I received an email back. Ann said that she was very glad to hear from me and that she had been to Istanbul once before, but wondered why I was asking. She enclosed her telephone number.

I immediately called her. After a few uncertain moments, I asked:

"A friend of mine is getting married in Istanbul. I'm looking for a date. Would you be interested in coming with me?"

Ann paused for one second, and said, "Yes!"

I was ecstatic: I could add bold and adventurous to the list of things I loved about her. Finally, it was my turn. And high time too: I was 34 years old.

Our first morning in Istanbul, I woke up at 5 am, unable to sleep from excitement, nervousness and heightened energy. So I walked the streets of Istanbul while the old part of the city was still fast asleep. History was snoring, I was singing.

The weekend was everything I had hoped for and more. One night we had dinner in a hotel that had been an old prison, central to the movie *Midnight Express*. I had never felt so close to another woman. I felt whole, connected and at peace. More than ever, I was convinced that I had finally had found "the one." The symbolic significance of the place did not go unnoticed: In a prison that had seen the worst of humanity and animalistic torture, I had finally escaped my prison of loneliness. I had met my future wife.

We began to date long-distance, making frequent trips between London and New York.

A few months later, I spent the first moments of the new millennium hugging Ann as fireworks exploded around us. Not even Hollywood could have scripted a better moment.

When Ann dropped me off at the airport for my flight back to New York,

I had the strange feeling that she was relieved to see me with my suitcase in my hand walking toward the airport. I ignored my suspicions.

A month later, my love of the century ended. The fate that has befallen romantic lovers and dreamers for thousands of years had befallen me too. Ann broke up with me, citing, quite rightly, that among other reasons, she was tired of my constant psychoanalyses of life and people. She had a point. Our relationship made me anxious: Thinking and analyzing are my weapons against my fear of intimacy and rejection.

The breakup broke me. Extreme despair, emptiness and helplessness became my companions. Almost every single night for more than a year, I dreamed of being reunited with Ann. Many lonely nights the following summer filled me with desperation. I recall one night, standing alone on a beautiful Saturday evening in a public space next to FDR Drive, watching lovers kissing and eating ice-cream next to the East River. To block the pain, I looked away. Below me hundreds of cars were speeding toward the city.

"What if I jump?"

Romantic Love Defined

People kill themselves for it. People kill others for it. Those who don't have it want to find it at all costs. Those who have it want to keep it at all costs. Those who say they don't need it want it so desperately they can't even admit to it; admission would expose the unbearable pain of their loneliness. People sit in their rocking chairs in old-age homes filled with regret because of it. People create the most elaborate philosophies, religions and chemical substances to escape its painful absence. People waste their lives in search of money, fame, beauty and popularity, hoping that success will finally bring them a love that will cure.

The beauty of romantic love has been sung for nearly a thousand years. In the first poem I had to translate in high school from the Latin into the English, Catallus wrote to his beloved:

> Kiss me again and again.
> Let me kiss you a hundred times,
> a thousand more, again a thousand
> without rest, losing count, so no
> one can speak of us and say
> they know the number of our kisses.

Catallus was a man possessed by the euphoria found in romantic love. In addition to euphoria, scientists have documented that sleeplessness, loss of appetite, high energy, focused attention, drive and goal-orientated behaviors are common to all romantic loves. People in love also experience a great desire for sex and a need for sexual exclusivity. Emotional union, however, surpassed the urge for sexual copulation. In a research study, 75 percent of men and 83 percent of women said that knowing that their beloved is "in love" with them is more important than having sex with them. Scientists found that romantic love is a yearning for an emotional union that makes the lover feel whole. It also leads to a dependence on one another that encourages lovers to say "I love you" not because they really mean it, but because they really need to hear "I love you too."

Romantic Love and Happiness

I've learned that the love that nearly destroyed me is very common among many of earth's creatures. Birds fall in love, fish do a lovers dance and male frogs toe dance. Some animals enjoy love at first sight. They must, for many only have a small period in which they can procreate before winter comes or predators interfere with their courtship. When they fall in love, animals, like humans, experience nervousness and a loss of appetite.

Dr. Maclean and others have found that our mammalian brain constantly needs assurance of nurturing, a sense of belonging to a group, emotional security and feeling sexually desirable. This brain is activated by all the potent love tools popular magazines tell us will spice up our love life: touch, stroking, smells, chocolate, food, music and social contact.

Brain scans of humans who are madly in love show that romance lights up two main brain areas. The first is the caudate nucleus, a part of the reptilian brain that evolved 65 million years ago and is responsible for our reward system, for maintaining general arousal, sensations of pleasure and the motivation to achieve rewards.

The second area in the brain that is stimulated by romantic love is the ventral tegmental area (VTA), also a central part of the reward circuitry of the brain. It is filled with dopamine, which it delivers throughout brain and causes high levels of focus, fierce energy, concentrated motivation to attain rewards and feelings of elation, even mania. This part of the brain and dopamine are closely involved in all forms of drug addictions. People can indeed become addicted to the natural chemicals of romantic love.

Casanova was nothing more than a good-looking Italian obsessed with the romantic love chemicals found in his mammalian brain. But because our mammalian brain constantly needs novelty, we never remain satisfied. No wonder Plato said in the fourth century B.C. that the god of love lives in a state of need. A constant state of need very different from a state of happiness.

Romance: A Reward

I was truly convinced that my romance with Ann was my reward for decades of struggling with loneliness. It turns out that romantic love is a reward, but not the type that I felt I deserved.

The development of emotions was one of the most important milestones in the progression of life on earth. With emotions and memory, living beings were finally able to deal with the threatening external world through the recall of emotional experiences, rather than reptilian instincts alone. Living beings became freer. But there was a cost involved. We needed bigger brains to incorporate our mental abilities, to make sense of our emotional experiences and to store them properly in our memories. Bigger brains meant longer gestational periods, bigger heads at birth, earlier births to ensure that the head doesn't get stuck in the pelvis and a longer period of infant vulnerability after birth.

Nature had to figure out how to have a male stick around long enough to impregnate the female and protect her and the baby until the baby was more self-sufficient. Also, and very important, "romantic" love was also given to mothers so that they did not abandon their newborns. The emotional bond required between mating partners and then between mother and her baby is central to the survival of the more highly evolved species.

So nature did not play around. She gave us the biggest incentive to fulfill our obligations: the elixir of romantic love. A reward with a love-and-death quality on par with our need for food and water. But like all rewards, it was never meant to last a lifetime. It was designed for us to see, want and pursue mating partners; start the mating process; remain loyal up until we conceive a child; and then stay together until birth of the infant.

Romantic Love: Phase B

Nature knew that the euphoria and anxieties of romantic love would not help a newborn, whose survival demands that its parents work as a team. In order to facilitate the rearing of you, three percent of mammals, including humans, were given a new love, what I call *partner love*.

Remember how close, attached and fused you feel after having good sex with someone you care for? When we have orgasms, our animal brains give men a shot of vasopressin and women a shot of oxytocin. These two hormones are responsible for killing romance and replacing it with a love based on security, comfort and calm.

When a father holds his newborn baby for the first time, he also experiences a drop in testosterone levels. One can understand why couples complain that sex life is not what it was after the birth of their children. But for a short while at least, it is a good thing. Partner love forces couples to focus on their newborn instead of each other.

Who We Love

But why did I fall for Ann? Why did my brain go absolutely nuts when a woman whom I had never met walked through the door? To understand this, we need to revisit the psychological development of a baby.

A person is born with a drive to relate. Her instinct tells her that if she does not find attachment, she will die. Even though she knows she must connect, she does not know how. There is no self-help book on love in the womb.

We learn what love is through experience. The mammalian brain, with its gifts of emotions and memory, records all the feelings we had in our search for love as a baby. We saw in the chapter on nurturing that all mentally healthy children go through a romantic phase with their primary caretakers. (Since most of the research cited here was conducted on mothers and babies, I will use the term mother instead of primary caretaker.)

During the union phase, especially from 9-13 months, the relationship between mother and child is almost identical to unconditional romantic love. Child development research shows an increase in normal opiates in a child's brain as he stares into his mother's eyes; the mother, in turn, is alive with joyful emotions. Mother and child are smitten with one another. This is normal, very normal.

At the prestigious University College London, two researches, Drs. Bartels and Zeki, have done some very interesting research on romantic love. Setting out to chart the neural correlates of love, the researchers identified 17 people who were deeply in love. The subjects were asked to bring in a photo of their beloved and of three close friends. The researchers asked these people to relax, look at the different pictures and think of the person in the photo. This all happened while their brains were scanned using an fMRI. The researchers then compared and analyzed the brain activity of each person reacting to their beloved versus their friends.

Years later, the same researchers recruited 20 mothers with normal physical and psychological health for a similar experiment. This time, however, they showed the mothers pictures of their own children, of other familiar children, of their best friends and of other adults. Again they compared the mothers' brain reaction to each category of photo shown. Then they compared the data of the mothers' brain activity in reacting to their children with that of the in-love subjects from the first study.

"Both studies on maternal and romantic attachment revealed activity that was not only overlapping to an large extent with each other, but also with the reward circuitry of the human brain," they reported. They found that people in loving relationships activated specific areas in the brain and deactivated others. Love, both romantic and maternal, increased happy states, attention to one's own emotional state, ability to assess other people's states of mind (via anterior cingulate cortex), increase pleasure states (via nucleus accumbens), induce reward states in areas also active after enjoyment of food, drink, monetary reward, cocaine and sexual arousal (via striatum) and ability to interpret visual stimuli (via insula).

Maternal love and romantic love are close sisters.

Seeing Hollywood

Freud was the first to believe that most people project a fantasy upon people with whom they interact. Specifically, during intimate moments, we take a little bit of the real person in front of us, mix it with a lot of images and fantasies and create a person we want see. We transfer our non-conscious needs and emotions onto another. We therefore do not see a person for who they really are. We see them in the way we want to see them. And how we want to see them comes from our past love experiences.

Freud also believed that we mix memories of our parents with our beloved in order to finally resolve our childhood conflicts with our parents. Jung believed that we choose partners based on a non-conscious image that we have constructed of the opposite sex over the years. Modern thinkers on relationships, such as Harville Hendrix, believe that we form an inner non-conscious image of *all* childhood caretakers.

I believe people differ in what they are seeing. I believe the best of humanity see in their partners an image that is a mixture of their primary caretaker as well as all other caretakers, lovers and mentors they have had over the years. Those with an average Real Self choose partners based on an image of an average primary caretaker mixed with an overbearing or strict other parent. People with fragile Real Selves who obsess about romantic love choose partners based on their unresolved issues with their primary caretakers. But what are we trying to resolve or recapture?

The Romantic Bubble

The clue to this lies in what we feel in the present when we are madly in love. Research shows that those of us in love feel as if we are special, whole, manic and the center of attention. We see our partners as special too and as an automatic infusion of admiration. We feel the world is our oyster. We experience unconditional love.

Does this sound familiar? This is a perfect description of a one–year-old child enjoying the romantic bubble with his primary caretaker. Those of us obsessed with romantic love want nothing more than to reunite with our primary caretaker. We want to go back to the fantasy bubble of perfect and endless admiration. This why research shows that those in love are more interested in union with the lover than with having sex. This goes against all evolutionary theories that say that leaving behind our DNA is the most important drive!

So when those of us obsessed with romance fall in love, our minds say, "Hey, dude, that girl reminds me of the person who taught me about love. You better go for her." You focus on your target and she smiles back at you. Now you are no longer in control. Chemicals in your brain put you on an automatic pilot.

Romantic love comes from seeing someone whose right brain reminds us of the right brain of our primary caretaker. Shakespeare was spot on when he said: "Love looks not with the eyes, but the mind."

Dating Who?

We all have experienced that moment when we hear of a talented, kind young man dating a woman who treats him with contempt, even in public. Or we know a brilliant, sweet woman dating a man who treats her like his dirty socks. We cannot believe how these two could be in love. Yet, if you talk to them, they are smitten.

Recall that during the first year of life, a child keeps two sets of DVDs, the Hell DVD and the Heaven DVD. During the Heaven DVD, the child sees the mother as perfect and feels perfect for being one with such a mother. In the Hell DVD, he sees the primary caretaker as wicked and contemptuous and feels ugly and worthless. When we lack a Real Self to shape a more realistic picture of our primary caretaker, we go throughout life judging others, especially romantic partners, as either admiring or contemptuous, for us or against us. There are no grey areas. You are one or the other.

Things get even more confusing. A child tends to deal with traumatic childhood experiences in one of two ways: suppressing all bad experiences and living with an illusion of the past or reenacting the past traumas. People fall in love in similar ways.

Some of us will fall in love with a woman who resembles the idealized image of our primary caretakers found in our Heaven DVD. Our beloveds are as close to perfect as we can find. Even objective bystanders will say: "Wow, she is a catch." Some of us fall in love with a person who resembles the wicked primary caretaker: the cold, contemptuous person who never says a positive word and only expects to be served. Some of us occasionally fall for the one, sometimes for the other. The key here is not that the person we fall in love with needs to be perfect or safe for us to feel perfect or safe. The trick is that the hurt child within us wants to reunite with any one of the two maternal images. We either want to admire or be admired, or we want to work hard to finally find the unconditional love that a primary caretaker never gave to us.

Things can get even more complicated. There are people who fall in love not with a partner who brings admiration or contempt, but who brings safety and caretaking or rejection and humiliation. Since these personalities are not obsessed with success and admiration, they will not be discussed.

Regardless of what childhood need or primary caretaker image we are transferring onto our beloved, people addicted to romantic love are addicted to recreating the safety or grandiose fantasy bubble that they either never had or had but was burst before a healthy Real Self was formed. They are searching for the childish wish of unconditional maternal love.

Romantic Love and Passion

When I was in love with Ann, I was useless at work. I was floating on cloud nine, too intoxicated with chemicals to really focus on what I had to do. Even though I felt that I accomplished a lot during the day, I later realized that I was actually pretty unproductive. Not unlike being drunk and thinking we are smart, romantic love made me feel that I was the best employee, when in reality, I was just cruising by. When Ann broke up with me, I was even more useless. Romantic love did little for my productivity and even less to help me find my passions.

The reason should be obvious: If passion is the movement away from a primary caretaker to find our own life and discover our unique abilities, romantic love is exactly the opposite. Romantic love encourages us to move back to the past, whereas passion wants us to be grounded in the present.

Romantic Love and Intimacy

Marie told me of her recent relationship. "We emailed one another 40 times per day. I could not do anything else. I really needed this. It had been a long time since I felt this about someone. He wrote me a note saying how great it was, how wonderful I am. It was nice. It was great just to lose one's boundaries, to feel good. When I am like this, I can be so much fun."

Then I asked her where they had met. "In a club," she said. "There's something about being lonely and then going to a club and meeting someone who likes you. There is a story about it. Something to tell someone."

Later she said, "I am looking for someone who has youth inside and maturity outside. Like me. I'm so full of joy when I am in love. I want to feel that if he says tonight that we should travel for a few weeks, I will say yes and go. I will not settle for anything else."

Marie has a failed marriage and many other failed relationships to sustain her craving for "chemistry," for feeling admired and on top of the world. With nearly Pavlovian conditioning, Marie chose chemical love over intimate love.

Our whole society is saturated with Hollywood fantasies: Boy meets girl, boy buys girl flowers, they go on date, kiss on date three and eternal bliss follows. Love always has a happy ending. In the movies.

Divorce rates have increased over the last decades and are now close to 50 percent. As one divorce lawyer puts it, "Marriage is the first step along the road of divorce." I believe that one of the many reasons for this is our obsession with Hollywood romantic love. The median duration of marriages that end in divorce is seven years. Research shows that by the third year, couples heading for divorce begin to say, "We are happy and content, but we have no spark." At this point, most couples return to the baseline happiness they have had since childhood. The chemicals of the honeymoon period have been neutralized. The brain now starts pumping chemicals to form partner love.

But the calm and care of partner love is boring for those of us in the fast lane. It is like settling in a small town in the Midwest after having lived in Manhattan for decades. Our mammalian brain cannot accept this. After all, Hollywood tells us that chemistry, the spark, the excitement is the sign that true love exists.

After they reach the point of comfort, couples bear it out a bit longer, hoping a miracle will bring back the chemicals. When it does not, they divorce after another three or four years. Excited by the prospect of new love, they start dating again. The truth is, even if they meet another partner, they will again feel chemistry, marry and again feel bored after three years. When we lack a Real Self, our mammalian brain controls our romantic love experiences. A relationship solely based on romantic love will falter over time. Not surprising that the divorce rate of second marriages is 65 percent.

Our chase for chemical Hollywood love sets unrealistic expectations for our marriages. The result is that we do not do enough work to get to know the real person and never become intimate. Without intimacy, we remain kids in a candy store searching for the high, not adults in the real world searching for self-actualization.

Romantic Love and Self-Care

Self-care, in a nutshell, is avoiding anxiety-inducing experiences, eating well and healthfully, exercising, sleeping enough and spending a few minutes each day connecting with our Real Selves, via meditation, prayer, writing or whatever works. But when we look at the love sick, we see sleeplessness, loss of appetite, high levels of restless energy and anxiety about possible rejection. Romantic love forces us to kiss goodbye all that is important to our health! For some people, romantic love can be lethal.

The call came at 1 a.m. The nurse on duty asked me to rush to the emergency room. As I entered, the smell of burned skin and gasoline made me slightly nauseas. I moved to where the nurse struggled to insert an IV needle into a young man's arm. I examined the patient's body. Except for the souls of his feet, all skin was burned off his body. 90 percent burned plus third degree wounds: a death sentence. This handsome, athletic young man, after an argument with his girlfriend, poured gasoline all over his body and lit a match. I looked into his eyes. Frightened and in pain, they pleaded for a miraculous recovery. Maybe even for a chance to turn back time. Half an hour later his girlfriend stormed into the ER. All she wanted to know was "Why? Why? Why?" He died within 48 hours.

Love gone awry can cause people to do frightening, violent, horrible things. But what is more frightening is the knowledge that most people who stalk or murder lovers or ex-lovers feel that they are acting rationally.

Searching for Real Love

I have given up fantasizing that romantic love will save me from myself. But I have not stopped searching for love. I know I will never rest until I have found it. But having no more faith in Hollywood love, what is there to search for?

I have argued that to find happiness and enjoy a higher human consciousness, a healthy brain takes the best from each brain as circumstances dictate. Happiness is an integrated, harmonious brain where all brain-parts have good relationships with one another. What is true for happiness, is also true for real love. Real love requires that all brains work lovingly together.

Dove Love

I love going to sit in Washington Square Park to watch Fifth Avenue moms and nannies play with their children, bands making music, drug dealers dealing, doves mating and European tourists excitedly taking photos of squirrels begging for food. I also love the twenty-something NYU students parading to and from class. In spring, when layers of winter clothes come off, the flesh fest makes me almost crazy with lust. And believe me when I tell you that I do not lust for one specific woman, I lust after many.

I have no doubt that when I am 90, I will pay someone to push my wheelchair to Washington Square for this pleasure. But, I also have no doubt that the pleasure will be mixed with an incredible pain of longing and nostalgia. Watching Peter O'Toole's performance in *Venus*, the movie in which he brilliantly portrayed a dying old man who falls in love with an 18 year old girl, only to be used and abused in his love, left me struck with grief in anticipation of my day in the park.

Lust is common in all, whether we are the most conservative nun or the oldest man in the world. We may suppress our lust, but if we breathe, we lust. End of story.

Our strong but dumb reptilian brain is in charge of our lust. Through millions of years of evolution, it has learned that it is good for men to want to sow our oats as much as we can. I admit that I was surprised to learn what most women already know—that outside of cultural restrictions, they are equally as lustful as men. The only difference: Where men will lust mostly after beautiful women, they will have sex with any available woman. Women, in contrast, mostly lust after those who fit the criteria of an alpha male: Height, intellect, money or wit. Research today even suggests that women lust after and have more orgasms with rich men. Their reptilian brains want them to mate with alpha males. So the brain gives women an extra incentive to have sex with rich men!

At the reptilian level, our love is at its most primal. "Love" is all about bartering objects. Men give women status, security and sex, while women give men children, food and sex. Lust is the lubricant that brokers the deal. Fortunately, most people move beyond this level of love; but as we saw earlier, people obsessed with money and beauty often do not move on. They are stuck in a reptilian consciousness. Unfortunately, these also tend to be the marriages that receive the most attention in the media and movies.

Lust does not disappear when one is married, even happily so. Our reptilian brains are always on the hunt. For married men and women to be turned on by others is normal. What is abnormal is to deny this attraction. The biggest challenge is to cultivate lust in one's own relationship. Couples need to do what it takes to keep sex fresh, exciting and mutually satisfying.

Puppy Love

I have had the huge pleasure of dating a woman who lives for mammalian brain love. That woman told me, "I only have a few things in my life that make me happy: my cats, my music, sex, food and sleep." At her home, she gave me a kiss that made me weak in the knees. Her body felt as if it completely folded around me.

Even though I have argued so far that puppy love is for puppies, I do not want to leave the impression that all romantic love is useless. There is a lot of fun to be had in playing with a puppy. But to play with the puppy every day of your life will mean a waste of a life.

Our mammalian brain helps us to give our partners assurance of nurturing, a sense of belonging and emotional security. We also help one another feel sexually desirable. These are all extremely important fuels for life and love. So couples need to know how to turn on their own and their partner's mammalian brain through touch, stroking, smells, food, music and social contact.

Ape Love

Above the mammalian brain lies the primate brain (also know as the neocortex or new mammalian brain, which is crucial for our imagination, especially our ability to imagine the future. It is also in charge of the fourth type of love: Fantasy Love.

Recall how Sandra Murray, a researcher of romantic illusions, asked couples to rate themselves, their actual partner and an ideal partner using a questionnaire of strengths and weaknesses. Friends of each partner also filled in the same questionnaire. Dr. Murray then looked for discrepancies between what subjects thought about their partners compared to what their friends thought. In happy and stable relationships, subjects rated their partners higher in their strengths than their friends did. Partners had a fantasy of their lovers. The fantasy had a good outcome: Murray found that positive fantasies became self-fulfilling. People became the fantasy of their partner.

Research shows that many people, after watching Hollywood romances, have unrealistic expectations of relationships. When researchers questioned 100 students, after subjecting them to the movie *Serendipity*, more believed in fate and destiny than those who watched a David Lynch drama. The researchers claim the media's portrayal of perfect relationships is creating a fantasy of what real love and life are like. In real life, unlike in Hollywood, sex is not always earth-shattering, nor do our partners know exactly what we want when we want it. Indeed, fantasy love is severely abused as we try to escape from our own loneliness and the artificial expectations created by Hollywood.

Many people obsessed with success are also obsessed with perfect love. But perfect love does not exist. In a later chapter, we shall see how the brain of the success obsessed manipulates reality to fit their fantasies or uses fantasy to completely escape reality. Specifically, we will look at various sub-categories of fantasy love: Movie Love, Weekend Love, Blaming the Other Love, Loving the Weak and Prince and Princess Love.

Human Love

A few years ago, I attended a workshop conducted by John Gottman called "Marital Therapy: A Research-Based Approach." Gottman had approached his research on relationships with the following philosophy: Ignore everything that has been said or written or philosophized about love and focus only on what happens in the real world.

For over 30 years, he and his team have collected millions of data from thousands of couples during moments of conflict and ordinary conversations. Video camera recordings and physiological measurements ensured that they caught data normal observation would miss. With the data collected, they searched for what makes happy relationships work and others fail.

Gotmann defined a good enough relationship as one where a couple spends at least one hour a week drinking coffee, eating a bagel and just being friends. When I asked him what percentage of marriages fit that criteria, he answered: "There is no hard data. My gut says it is 30-40 percent of couples!" Here I believed in Hollywood love, but the reality is that most couples are not even friends. They live together like ships passing one another on stormy nights or they enjoy taking Strindberg's battle of the sexes to the next level.

For most of my life, I believed that the first sign of conflict with a lover meant that we were just not suited for one another. After all, good people should be able to be good to one another. Conflict is for barbarians.

Research shows that there is conflict in all relationships and that 80 percent of all conflict in a relationship comes from deep-seated beliefs and fears that will never be resolved.

We are wired to self-express, but also need intimacy and self-care, which sometimes means we need to go for a walk in nature alone. But we still need to put bread on the table and take care of the community. One can quickly see that when two people who live together need to do all the above on their own and together, misunderstandings quickly arise. "It is my turn to see my friends!" or " I did the dishes last night!" But what happens if you did do the dishes last night and it is your turn to see friends, but your partner needs your intimate care because she lost her job that day. Good relationships are a constant give and take, a negotiation for self-expression, self-care and intimacy.

Mature love is not unconditional love. Unconditional love, doing what we want when we want to do it and expecting our beloved to pick up our socks, is a childhood fantasy. Mature love is conditional love whose terms are daily negotiated, albeit non-consciously. Conflict abounds. The difference: The best of humanity know how to deal with it.

The way we deal with conflicts predicts how strong our relationships are. It is such a sensitive indicator that Gottman and his team can now predict with 90 percent sensitivity whether a couple's marriage will end in divorce by observing just a few minutes of how a couple deals with conflict. They even can predict whether the divorce will take place in three to five years or seven to ten years.

Great couples are not free from conflict, but they are great at conflict management. They can leave arguments with a "let's agree to disagree" and then storm to bed for passionate make-up sex. This, and I was hoping to ride into the sunset with Julia Roberts to experience eternal bliss free from even a raised eyebrow.

We need to create ourselves every day. We also need to find meaning in our lives. Great couples help one another with this task. Not only do they support one another emotionally during intimate moments, but they also work at making day-to-day day activities and events have meaning. Gottman talks about creating informal rituals (how to say goodbye in the mornings, eat together, go to bed together, initiate or decline lovemaking), formal rituals (how to deal with birthdays, getting sick, Thanksgiving, Christmas, Passover, Ramadan) or rituals of transition (how to deal with graduations and weddings). They key is that these rituals should be scripted, not left vague, and should reflect the couple's preferences, not necessarily what their culture dictates. Happy couples create their own culture.

Friendship, shared meaning and conflict management are crucial to having a good relationship. To experience a great relationship, two more ingredients are necessary. Relationship void of intimacy is a relationship that never will grow. Couples need to feel comfortable sharing their most vulnerable side, knowing that someone will be there for them through the ups and downs of life.

For a short while, I was a consultant for a company that assessed how people perform on a first date. I would meet with a client, chat with her over a coffee as if we were on a first date, take an hour to judge the woman's "performance" against criteria based on psychological research and then gave her feedback about what she did well and where she could improve. Even then I realized the irony that a man with the world's worst dating history was giving advice to others!

But I did learn that the key to all first dates, as well as to love, is to have people speak about their passions and then to fully support them. We want to be known for our passions. We want people in our lives who will help us to become the most we can become. Stripped from beauty and money, our passions tell us who we are. Research shows that when we are truly interested in another's passion, he or she will find us attractive regardless of our looks. The other person will say, "He is not that hot, but boy, he has got something." But all he or she has is a true interest in who we are and what we want to do with our lives.

I agree with Dr. Masterson that all great relationships have at their core the ability and want to take care of each partner's Real Self as if it was our own. Our partner's passions and goals must be as important to us as it is to them. A person void of passion will struggle to find great love.

Real Love

The Real Self is the mixer of Real Love. First, it encourages us to give free reign to our lust for our partners. It wants us to be porn stars in bed. We should never feel guilty for our needs or above our animal lust. The Real Self tells us that we have the right to enjoy the pleasures of good, playful and, if we want, dirty sex. But we should communicate our wants and dislikes clearly and honestly. We should give and take. We should make arrangements for how to decline a partner's sexual advances if we are not feeling up to it. It may be the most primitive part of our love relationships, but sex, combined with intimacy, can make us extremely vulnerable.

The Real Self allows romance in to the mix. It knows this brain loves novelty. So the Real Self encourages us to spend time together so we can get to know our partners better. Since we are small miracles and endlessly complex, no one will ever get to know us fully. There always will be pleasant surprises that a caring partner will find in us, even to our own surprise! This will ensure our partnerships never get stale.

If we are our memories, then the health of our relationship depends on the quality and quantity of shared memories. The Real Self encourages us to create new shared memories by taking fun and adventurous trips, eating at new restaurants, doing silly things or seeing new shows. Novelty feeds romance. I suspect it is the new, positive, happy experiences that couples share that keeps the filter through which they see one another clean, positive and happy, a big plus when life and love occasionally turn sour.

From our primate brain, the Real Self takes some fantasy. We must believe in our partners more than they do. We must make them feel like a million dollars, and in return, they will make us feel like two million dollars. This allows us to make them feel like three million dollars. The cycle is endless.

Our Real Self asks our human brain to add a lot of friendship, conflict management, shared meaning, intimacy and support for our passions to the mix. Throughout the course of a relationship, it is the human brain that keeps the relationship moving.

For those lucky to be in happy married relationships, the rewards are numerous. Studies shows that marriage makes people feel happier (super happy married people have the illusion that they are happier than they were before marriage, but their happiness scores do not actually change at all); be healthier (those who live together without marriage remain as sick as those that are single); have more sex than single people; and less likely to commit a violent act.

Finding Real Love

Even though I have a working definition of what realistic human love is, I am still perplexed at how to find it.

A few years ago, an Internet dating company approached John Gottman for help in predicting whether a first date will lead to a long-term relationship. After he mined his data, he was unable to make any clear conclusions. Lust, romance, friendship or a shared passion all could lead to healthy relationships. Or not. Other research shows that only 11 percent of couples experienced love at first sight. It seems to me that it doesn't matter where you start, it only matters whether you meet someone who helps you bring lust, romance, friendship and shared passion to the bed and table.

Logic and anecdotal evidence tell me that if good friendship, intimacy and shared passion are main ingredients of real love, then meeting a partner through good intimate friends or by following our hobbies, interests and passions are the best ways to find real love. From my experience, clubs and bars are difficult places to meet your future spouse. This is not from a lack of trying. I most probably have gone out 1000 times over the last 25 years hoping to meet Ms. Right in a bar. It can happen, but so can winning the lottery.

We can philosophize about love or read all the popular magazines with their "how to find real love" articles. There is a serious problem with any advice on finding love.

Earlier I mentioned how Dr. Masterson told me that I can walk into a room with 20 eligible women, of whom 19 are candidates for real love, but I will go for the emotionally unavailable one fighting to be the center of attention. The best of humanity do the exact opposite. When they walk into a room with 20 partners, 19 of whom are non-marriage material, they will instinctively know which person to focus their attention on.

Our right brains can communicate non-verbally with one another across a distance. When I saw Ann walking through the door, my right brain went nuts, but for all the wrong reasons. When a mentally healthy person's right brain goes nuts, it is for all the right reasons. They know in their gut what will work. They do not fall for the smooth talker, seductive prince or princess or fantasies of perfect love. They fall in love with another person's childhood memories. They fall in love with inner beauty.

Loving our Memories

When Shakespeare said we fall in love not with our eyes, but with our minds, he wisely intuited that our memories in our right human brain will make us behave in a certain way regardless of what we read, Oprah says or science tells us. Even in love, we go for what is habitual, comfortable, but not necessarily what is good for us.

If our right brain is filled with memories of a primary caretaker who provided us with many beautiful memories of self-expression, self-care and intimacy, we will find a partner who supports our Real Self and we his or hers.

If our right brain is filled with memories of a primary caretaker who hated our attempts at individuation and self-expression, we will find partners who will ignore our Real Self and use us for their unfulfilled childhood needs, or we will use them.

If our right brain is filled with traumatic memories, emotional, physical or sexual, we will fall for partners who will continue the abuse or we will transfer the power of the abuser onto ourselves and our traumatic feelings onto others, and hurt them to relieve ourselves of our trauma that relentlessly wants to be made conscious. But feeling those memories is like feeling the original trauma. So we would rather do it to others and find relief, at least temporarily.

Since we fall in love with and because of non-conscious memories, no morals or self-help guru will be able to break our patterns of love. We first need to mourn the lack of Real Self support or our most painful traumatic memories before we will stop loving others through a fantasy bubble or through reenactment.

To paraphrase Thornton Wilder: To have a love, we must love love. To love love, we must have love. Herein lies the dilemma for those of us still searching for someone to rescue us from ourselves. We must first love life and other people before we can have a love that will love us. To do this, we need, at a minimum, an average Real Self.

A Farewell to Romantic Love

In May 2006, I arranged to meet Ann for coffee while on a visit to my brothers in London. The last time I saw her I felt like Vanya in Anton Chekhov's play. I was a clumsy lover trying everything to receive a kiss from Ann, a kiss I needed to give me hope that one day we would get together, marry and live eternally happily together.

Six years later, I saw Ann walking through the door of a coffee shop. I still found her beautiful and charming. With her second child in her arms, we chatted for an hour over a cappuccino.

That day, I saw Ann for who she really is for the first time. Without the DVD of an idealized maternal figure projected onto her, I could truly enjoy all her beauty, charm and vulnerabilities common to all of humanity. By the end of our conversation, I too knew that the woman I thought would cure me, but whose rejection nearly killed me, was never the woman meant for me.

Today I know that when I experience love at first sight, enjoy a Hollywood movie on a first date, see the woman as my "dream girl" and want to marry someone even though we have never even lived and worked in the same city, I am deluded by my need for reunion or my need to escape reality. Feeling the chemistry of romance is wonderful, but if it is not supported by good friendship, fair conflict resolution and a desire to share our passions, I should run away, not toward. I cannot waste another six years of dreaming the impossible and improbable, while living the unbearable.

I say this, but then, the power of my mammalian brain—seeking romance— and my primate brain—seeking fantasy love—never ceases to amaze me.

Chapter 10

An F-minus for Elite Education

"I think, therefore I will be happy" was my motto throughout my life. I honestly believed that my intellect and a good education held the answers about life and happiness. So, for most of my life, from the moment I opened my eyes until fatigue tripped my brain, I thought about everything and anything I could.

I was intellectually so intense that, one night at Yale, a friend, after a few beers, said, "One day, when your wife gives birth, your baby will enter the world in *The Thinker's* position." He then mimicked the pose of Rodin's famous sculpture—a tortured man contemplating the meaning of life.

While traveling for a month in England, I spent two days in Oxford. I fell in love with the tradition, the prestige and the ambience of one of the world's oldest universities. But the visit also planted a seed: "If only I can obtain a degree from Oxford, Cambridge, Harvard or Yale. If only I can rub shoulders with the world's intellectual elite. If only I can know what they know, surely I will no longer have any self-doubt. I will take my place as a confident adult at the table of life, love and happiness."

At Yale

The Yale School of Management's focus on training leaders for management in the private, not-for-profit and public sectors closely fit my career goals. So when I received my acceptance letter, I was ecstatic. My dream of attending one of my "big four" had become a reality.

When I arrived at Yale, I committed myself to seeking an education, not just a certification that would allow me to find a high paying job. So, in addition to my business classes, I took classes in art appreciation, drama, philosophy and ethics. The latter was a ten-week lecture series by the then dean of Yale Law School on major contemporary ethical questions, such as capital punishment, abortion and euthanasia. His wisdom and insight still remain vivid in my memories, even though the details of his arguments have long since faded. Without a doubt, this lecture series epitomized the reason I came to Yale.

After my regular classes, I would rush off to every guest lecture who came through Yale. I listened to an astronaut describe the experience of leaving mother earth; Hillary Rodham Clinton; the philosopher Noam Chomsky; and Warren Buffet, one of the wealthiest businessmen in the world.

Outside the lecture halls, I engaged in vigorous discussion with students from many of Yale's graduate and undergraduate programs. The diverse backgrounds and nationalities of the student population were all I had hoped for. In my business classes alone, there were students from 52 different countries and almost every state in the United States. My closest friends were from Uruguay, France, Iran, Australia, Lebanon, California, Texas and Puerto Rico.

During this time, I met talented people who were amazingly well adjusted, as well as talented people who were certifiably crazy. I met people from meager means to people whose family fortune exceeded the annual GDP of South Africa. I met people who married those they fell in love with and people whose marriages had been arranged for them in childhood. I met people who wanted to protect the green forests and people who wanted to protect their green American dollars. I met people who needed to be the center of attention as they prepared for their careers on Wall Street and people who quietly, confidently and with great joy played the piano as we sang with falsetto voices and full whiskey glasses at our semi-annual fancy dress balls.

But my interest went beyond people and lectures. I listened with amazement to Izak Perlman and his daughter together on stage playing the violin and piano; struggled through the Bolshoi Ballet's terrible performance at the Schubert; fell in love with opera and hummed softly to myself as my friend Nicolas sang in an audience performance of Handel's *Messiah*. The jock in me ensured that I played indoor polo with my friend Pablo, rugby with a team that looked like the United Nations and rowed crew for my school's second team down the Charles River, before drinking a beer or ten, and appreciating a boob or two.

In May 1997, after two years of embracing as much as I could of what Yale had to offer, I walked up to be capped by Dean Garten. Earlier, thousands of students from all the schools had gathered in the Old Campus to celebrate the power and promise of education and the intellect. Actress Jodie Foster received an honorary degree, cameras snapped and blue skies symbolized wide-open futures and happiness to the fortunate graduates. Parents radiant with joy, were grateful that their sweat and labor—or family trust funds—had allowed their children to obtain an Ivy League degree, and with that, they believed, a ticket to a happy and fulfilled future.

Upon receiving my degree, my mother, who flew over from South Africa to celebrate my graduation with me, told me that I looked happier than ever. But underneath my black gown and white smile, I felt just as confused about my life. My time at Yale had showed me how little I really knew and how irrelevant my life appeared among all the wealth, brains, confidence, coveted degrees and beauty of those who find their way to Yale. I was lost, both in work and in love.

I give Yale an A-plus for treasured memories and top-notch teaching experiences. I give Yale an A-plus for opening doors that led to a good-paying job in Manhattan. I give Yale an A-plus for helping me to impress some pretty women in Manhattan, where the word "Yale" can be an aphrodisiac. But for the personal goals I had set for myself, I have no choice but to give Yale an F-minus. Instead of filling the black hole in my self-esteem and happiness, Yale made it darker, deeper and wider.

Self-Help Guru in Training

Having lost my faith in education, I formally set aside the snobbish attitude I had always had toward self-help books and started to study many of the popular books of the day: *The Seven Habits of Highly Successful People*, *The Celestine Prophecy*, *The Road Less Traveled* and a boxful of other books by self-help gurus. And when I say study, I mean *study*. I would read a book, underline the important parts, reread the book, summarize the book and try to practice the techniques that I had learned. But my self-help knowledge almost always failed to help me deal with conflict, love or passion.

When I lost faith in self-help books, I turned to psychology and postgraduate psychiatry books. But understanding the human psyche did not help me either. Even though I learned why the brain trips us when we try to achieve goals that are important to us, I was not able to use this knowledge to persist in the face of confusion and conflict. Despite all my efforts, I repeated the same mistakes over and over again.

After almost 30 years of believing to the point of a religion that the road to happiness is paved with education and the intellect, I was forced to concur with Oscar Wilde, who said, "Everything worth knowing cannot be taught."

Education and Happiness

Disillusioned, I began to debate the merit of education with hundreds of overachievers with degrees from the world's top schools: Cambridge, Oxford, INSEAD, Yale, Stanford, Columbia, Harvard, Princeton, Duke, Dartmouth and Penn, to mention a few. I found some graduates happy with their lives, but many had been just as happy before they had been capped by an Ivy League president. I found that, like me, many graduates were struggling despite all the golden stars on their resumes.

Cross-cultural psychiatric research shows that the percentage of mentally ill patients in all cultures, whether "primitive/traditional" or "cultured/modern," are the same. Despite all our education, 15-20 percent of all New Yorkers still struggle with their mental health, a prevalence on par with traditional villages in Africa, where people do not know or care about the Ivy League. More specifically, the United States has more educated people than it did 40 years ago, and still the level of happiness has not shifted. Despite all our education, the deep current of humanity flowing through all 6.7 billion of us is still struggling to express itself fully. The "primitive" seem to be as happy *and* as unhappy as the "cultured."

Happiness researchers have found that those who try to get as much education as possible do not increase their happiness at all. Martin Seligman, a professor from the University of Pennsylvania and one of the foremost researcher on happiness, has said, "As a professor, I don't like this, but the cerebral virtues—curiosity, love of learning—are less strongly tied to happiness than interpersonal virtues like kindness, gratitude and capacity to love."

Whether through the lens of experience, history or science, education seems unable to make us happier. Even elite education has no real impact its graduates' lives. A Harvard graduate wrote in her autobiography, "All I learned from Harvard was how to act that I was at Harvard."

Walter Kirn, Princeton graduate and author of *Lost in the Meritocracy: The Undereducation of an Overachiever,* wrote how his preparation for and admission to an elite school had limited impact on his life. The subtitle says it all.

But the best example of how elite education cannot sooth our unhappy non-conscious minds can be found in a fascinating study done at Harvard. For 72 years, researchers followed 286 men who studied at Harvard in the late 1930s. These men were picked as the most successful men of their years, put through hundreds of tests, and then regular follow-up tests over the years.

By age 50, a third of the participants had shown signs of mental illness, as defined by its main researcher, George Valiant, at least once, Arlie Block, one of the original researchers, complained to Valiant, "They were normal when I picked them. It must have been the psychiatrists who screwed them up!"

Harvard degrees did not help these "normal" and "successful" men to live a life of happiness and meaning.

Benefits of Education

I watched the opening of Oprah Winfrey's Leadership Academy in South Africa. Tears were flowing freely down my face as I shared the joy and passion of my fellow South Africans. Who can forget how the girls jumped up and down with joy and how they screamed with delight on hearing they were accepted into the academy? Who can forget the one girl's jaw dropping with shock when Oprah told her that she would pay for their university educations? Who can forget their belief in "girl power" to change the world? There was no pretense among the girls, only a raw drive and pulsating passion to escape their impoverished backgrounds through the power of education and then give back to their communities. I have seldom been so inspired by a program. Yet, here I am with a privileged educational background bemoaning the failures of education.

The first and foremost task of our brains is to ensure that our DNA survives. Human intellect and education have done a remarkable job in helping many people escape from hungry lions, bloody monarchs and dangerous infections. Today, humanity and nature are better dancing partners. Many communities are stable, safe and free from oppression. Many people are living longer and are enjoying a higher standard of living than ever before in history, even though we still are arguably enjoying the same level of happiness as we did thousands of years ago.

On the individual level, education helps people to escape poverty, suffocating cultures and demanding parents. Education opens the doors to a life of opportunities. But just as a mere $50,000 increases happiness, I believe that a solid basic education that allows people to enter the job market and better their lives is the only education that contributes to happiness. You do not need an elite education if you have a healthy Real Self. For with a solid basic education, a strong Real Self will create the opportunities to reach a higher quality and standard of life without a sacrifice in happiness and our humanity.

An elite education may open more doors and more opportunities and bring pockets full of money, published articles in *Nature* or *Science* or membership in the National Academy of Sciences. But if you are struggling with life, an elite education will not change the quality of your life or the lives of others. Elite education can inspire and enrich the mentally healthy, but it can never transform the mentally unhealthy. But elite education can indeed propel those of us struggling with our Real Selves and our humanity into powerful positions both in Washington and Wall Street. There is a high cost associated with putting people like us in leadership positions.

William F. Buckley, Jr. once said, "I'd rather trust the government of the United States to the first 400 people listed in the Boston telephone directory than to the faculty of Harvard University."

Education and Our Brain

Even before I read Descartes' famous quote "I think, therefore I am," I knew that thinking and having a high IQ are important attributes in our culture. In all my years of education, whether in primary or high school, medical school or business school, those gifted with cold reasoning skills were the ones who received praise in class or the trophies at award ceremonies. As a medical doctor and management consultant, I was rewarded with substantial paychecks for my ability to think. All the fuss encouraged me to conclude that it must be our ability to make tools and to think coldly and logically that separates us from other animals and drives the best of humanity to the top of the human pyramid.

Wolfgang Kohler, stranded on the Canary Islands during World War II, had some time on his hands. He used it to conduct experiments with chimpanzees. In one of his experiments, he cut a hollow bamboo stick into different lengths and thicknesses and left them within reach of the chimp Sultan's cage. Then, he left a banana out of reach. Sultan was no monkey. Soon, without any help or suggestion, he made a long stick from all the small parts by pushing the narrow part of a bamboo piece into the wider part of another piece. Before long, Sultan, using powers of logic and deduction, was eating a banana. Even a chimp can use his brain to make tools essential for survival.

The neuroscientist MacClean found that our primate brain is always curious, searching for novelty, new experience and new meaning. This brain wants, through cold reasoning, to make sense of what is happening to us, so it's strongly focused on the external world. In addition, this brain has in increased ability to process sight, sound and touch. It also allows us to imagine future events. Sultan knew that if he combined the two sticks together, he would, in the foreseeable future, be able to enjoy a banana.

The primate brain helps us to remember and make better sense of our past experiences, as well as to plan for our future survival. This is why the more advanced apes can be more flexible in their environments than other animal species.

So all the time I thought I was studying hard to become an elite human, I was really just practicing to become a smarter monkey.

Elite Education and Admiration

"When I was at Harvard"; "My son the doctor"; "My daughter at Yale"; "I am a professor at Princeton"; "I am Dr. So and So"—phrases that occur within five minutes of any conversation at any cocktail party whether in New York, London or South Africa. Donald Trump, in an interview with Larry King, mentioned a number of times that he went to the Wharton School at the University of Pennsylvania, which he claims to be the best finance school in the world and where he was one of its brightest stars. He then mentioned that his daughter had also attended this fantastic school. His elite education is as important to him as the gold letters on all his buildings all over the world. It also serves the same function: to stroke his status anxiety and his reptilian brain's need for hierarchy.

Parents of a certain income bracket push their children to overachieve at school to ensure they are accepted to an Ivy League university. They justify their actions by saying, "It's in their own best interest. They will have so much better careers if they do!" Many parents do mean well, but many are also obsessed with receiving the admiration of other parents for their "elite" parenting. Nothing beats gloating to other parents about how your child got into an elite school.

Companies also like to brag about the education of their employees. Both companies I worked for in corporate America mostly hired people from elite schools. They also paid well to attract the young bright things. Elite education has become a platinum credit card for the smart and a great workout for the reptilian brain.

Education and Passion

I know many academic overachievers who can solve complex problems, but one question still baffles most of them: "What do I want to do when I grow up?"

"I was definitely very stressed, and I worked very hard. Long nights studying, job shadows, college classes, internships, SATs, sports, all at the same time as balancing a social life. There is a sense of urgency and pressure," a high school senior in California told a reporter.

People who overachieve spend most of their school years working hard to make it to an elite school instead of using their youth to figure out who are they, what they like doing, what hobbies make them happy. Often they have parents who are more interested in how well they are performing than their day-to-day feelings, interests, passions or friends.

But the problem with finding passion starts before high school. Just as we tell little children how beautiful they are, similarly we tell them how smart they are. Our compliments have the effect of a weekend in Disneyland. Children love to be complimented more than anything else. So smart kids start to place their identity and self-esteem on their intellect. The cost: a false self that is founded on compliments for exploring the world and the self. Without a healthy Real Self, smart children will remain dumb to their real calling. The group that suffers most are those children who are both bright and beautiful. They are seldom appreciated for who they really are. I have stopped being surprised by how unhappy and confused those who appear to have it all are with their lives.

When overachievers need to decide upon a career, they often choose jobs at which a large paycheck and pleasing a boss or a client replaces pleasing a teacher or parents and an A on the report card. They are caught in the rat race up the ladder. After a lifetime of being rewarded for their academic results, they are too conditioned to break free of institutions that resemble our educational system. When some try to break away and ask, "What is my passion?" their neglected Real Self is unable to answer. Such an exercise is on par with trying to solve a calculus problem if one never learned how to add.

Education and Intimacy

A few years ago, I woke up one morning unable to speak. When I drank water, it ran directly into my lungs. Something was terribly wrong and I panicked: My future as an actor and public speaker was suddenly in ruins. I visited my general practitioner, a man I respect and trust.

That morning, we did not connect. I was convinced something other than a sore throat was at play. He disagreed. When he left the examination room without saying goodbye, I felt both enraged and rejected.

Then I replayed the events of my visit. I realized that I had played both doctor and patient during the consultation, forcing him to be an audience. I had tried to mask my emotional vulnerability with an "I know it all" attitude. Instead of trusting him and his opinion, I fell back onto my lifelong sense of self-sufficiency. After all, only I can help myself in this life. No one else is to be trusted, especially when I am not smiling, perfect and healthy. Even though I was right in my diagnosis, I was wrong in my attitude. So, instead of receiving the caring hand I so desperately needed that day, I received a cold shoulder.

As an executive coach, I frequently heard overachievers complain that they do not receive enough recognition for what they are doing or help when they need it. Taking lessons from my own life, I would answer: "If you look like you are always in control, why would someone offer to help you?"

Self-sufficiency is the password to many people cursed with brains. We think we do not need others to help us. We are smart enough to solve all our own problems. We have been rewarded from childhood for our brains and ability to figure things out. But in life, people who believe they are self-sufficient rob themselves of the most important human ability: The ability to share our pain with others and trust them to be there for us to help. The problem is that many of us call ourselves self-sufficient not because we can rely on ourselves, but because we *must* rely on ourselves. We are incapable of and fear intimacy, of grasping a caring hand stretched out to us. Without being able to trust others, all we have left to trust is our cold reasoning. We end up with cold inner lives.

"Intellectual men often have such difficulties with women," my teacher Liz Diamond said during my first theater class at Yale. I was taken aback by that statement. At that point in my life, I was still convinced that my intellect would one day solve all my relationship problems. To hear that other men, much smarter than me, still struggled with finding love shocked me. Liz turned out to be right. Not only did my intellect never help me find love, it became a huge stumbling block.

A few years ago, after a date with an ambitious hotshot vice president at a prominent investment bank, I received the following message from her: "I cannot get out of my bed. I feel like a train wreck. Our conversation gave me a terrible hangover and we only had one drink. They call *me* intense!"

The day I received the "Dear Pierre" call from Ann, she explained why she was breaking up: "I just can't take it anymore that you analyze me, my family and all of life all the time. It destroys all the fun!"

Indeed those of us who use our intellects as a crutch often see people through our analytical left brains. But if you dissect a frog into many pieces, is it still a frog?

An acquaintance once introduced me to a potential date with the following e-mail message: "His name is Pierre. He is an MD, MBA. From Yale! Have a drink with him!!!" Those eleven words summarized who I am.

As the leading playwright of the intellect-obsessed in Russia, Anton Chekhov received a lot of attention from women. In *Uncle Vanya*, he writes about the beautiful Yelena who married Serebryakov, a professor years older than her. But she is soon forced to admit to his daughter, "I'll swear to you that I married him for love! I was attracted to him as a learned, celebrated man. It wasn't real love, it was make-believe, but you see, it seemed real to me at the time."

But Yelena not only discovered that her love was a fantasy, but that her husband was extremely dumb in relationships. Their relationship was not to be admired.

I do not want to create the impression that men are the only ones obsessing about their intellects and elite educations. Today, both men and women have an equal driven to succeed academically. In many universities in the United States, women are now in the majority. In the time of Chekhov, this obviously was not the case.

People who obsess about school often fail in life. But that does not keep some of them from writing philosophies on life or "how to" books for the self-help generation. On an acting retreat, an actor confided: "My father has made a killing with books and speaking about relationships. He is on national television and radio shows. But he is a narcissist. He is never around. He cannot spell family, needless to say love. I hate him. But the world loves him for all his advice. To the world, he's an expert. To us, he is a liar."

Shakespeare's Ophelia was right when she warned her brother Laertes:

> But, good my brother,
> Do not, as some ungracious pastors do,
> Show me the steep and thorny way to heaven;
> Whiles like a puffed and reckless libertine
> Himself the primrose path of dalliance treads,
>
> And recks not his own rede.

Education and Self-Care

Whenever I woke up with demons attacking me, I would start studying, writing or thinking as if my life depended on it. Consciously, I would praise myself for being a hard worker and dedicated. But over the years, I have learned that my morning screams of "go, go, go" indicate an obsession and compulsion to avoid painful thoughts and feelings that still lingered from my demons' night visits. Worker and thinking bees are often hurt bees. For us, thinking is a band-aid to cover painful feelings.

The wife of a smart New York lawyer threatened her husband with divorce if he did not accompany her to her beloved grandmother's funeral. After years of resisting hanging out with his in-laws, he agreed. Not long after arriving at the wake, the man looked at all his in-laws and loudly proclaimed: "I am by far the person with the highest IQ in the room!" Apparently his wife filed for divorce days later. I suspect the presence of death made this man feel emotionally vulnerable. But instead of expressing his fears and reaching out to others for support, he buried his pain behind a mask of intellectual superiority. Many people obsessed with their intellect are unable to take care of their emotions. We need to control, if not block all our feelings. For if we allow ourselves to feel, we will feel our demons that will immediately throw us into an existential crisis. Feelings are no fun, but unfortunately for us, there is no real fun without feelings.

A woman I barely know told me how her boyfriend of five years, a man highly paid for his exceptional mathematical abilities, mumbles incoherent mathematical formulas to her whenever she approaches him for emotional and sexual intimacy. After five years, she finally was considering leaving him.

Sexual intimacy issues among the intellect-obsessed are as common as the A's on their report cards. People who live in their linear logical and orderly brains do not love the sweaty noisy fun of lovemaking.

We also do not live in our bodies. We can know everything there is about wine and food, but we often cannot enjoy the food as much as we enjoy throwing around the vocabulary of what we know. But to experience transcendence in life, we must live in both our brains and our bodies. As Goethe said, "All theory, dear friend, is gray; but the precious Tree of Life is green."

Add to this the high prevalence of underage drinking, self-mutilation, drug use or body-image issues among many Type A people and one can see that an obsession with overachievement is just as unhealthy to the body as it is to the mind and soul.

Education and Wisdom

So far we know why education cannot make us happy: It stimulates our primate brains and can distract us from pursuing activities that strengthen our Real Self in the right human brain, the activities that make us happy. But some may argue: Research shows that there is a connection between our human values and a happy life. Wisdom is one of our six human values. So why does elite education not contribute to the wisdom that will help us to live a happier life?

Scientists at the University of Iowa set out to assess the wisdom of the non-conscious mind. They asked gamblers to partake in a card game in which they had to choose cards from four decks, two blue and two red. Every card either won or cost them money. The gamblers' goal: to make as much money as possible. But what the scientists did not tell them was that the red cards were high-risk/high-reward. The only way to ensure a win was to pick low risk/medium-reward blue cards. In short, red cards were the new economy and dot.com stocks and the blue cards were Warren Buffet and Berkshire

Hathaway investments. The goal of the experiment was to see how quickly the non-conscious and then the conscious mind could figure out that only the blue cards would lead to positive returns. After the gamblers were connected to a diagnostic tool that measured their non-conscious stress responses, the experiment started. After picking up only ten cards, gamblers started to show a non-conscious stress response to the red cards. Their non-conscious knew something was wrong with red even though their conscious minds were still fast asleep. In turn, even though the gamblers were still clueless, they started to adjust their behavior by taking progressively fewer red cards. Only after picking up 50 cards did the gamblers consciously figure out that the red cards were weapons of mass financial destruction. The conscious brain woke up 40 cards later than the non-conscious brain.

David Brooks explains that when we face a complex problem with disparate facts, our brain tries to find a solution that explains all facts. To do so, we fortunately do not have a massive IBM computer in our brain. We have something much better. Our non-conscious mind, through trial and error, is in charge of finding the best and most comprehensive solution. First, our non-conscious mind creates a list of possible solutions. Since this list is hidden in our non-conscious mind, we have no clue as to what solutions are being put through the test. But the non-conscious mind lets us know through our emotions, which tell us whether we are getting hotter or colder in our search. As David Brooks put it, our emotions serve as our GPS. When our non-conscious mind final finds the ideal solution and shouts "Eureka!" it rewards us with dopamine. Consciously, we say, "I have got it!" get out of the shower and rush to our notebook. We then translate the answer into language to make it conscious. We then seek evidence in the conscious world to support our claims. Great decisions do not come from cool rational thinking taught at school or university, but from complex, non-conscious and emotional processes.

The presence of our non-conscious wisdom is evident. The source of the wisdom is less clear. I like to think that our non-conscious wisdom comes from all our experiences, from a non-verbal and non-conscious right-brain-to-right-brain interaction with those we trust; the collective unconscious that Carl Jung believed humanity shares; wisdom passed on from our ancestors through emotional DNA; or a higher power. I will never know this with scientific certainty. But what I do know is that emotions and sensations of the non-conscious mind are a thousand times more important that the logic or knowledge of our conscious mind. There is no wisdom without a "gut feeling." There is no wisdom in cold reasoning. There is no wisdom being taught in our school system with its emphasis on the logical, linear and non-feeling left brain.

Wisdom of Self

In the book *The Overachievers*, author Alexandra Robbins talks about a popular young girl stuck with a serious problem. She was admitted to both Duke and Penn. She had no idea how to make up her mind. So she signed acceptance letters to both schools and walked to the post office box, hoping the box would give her advice. It did not. So she threw in her application for one school. As soon as the envelope disappeared she was overcome with a sense of dread, convinced that she had made the wrong decision. She begged the post office to remove the envelope. They kindly agreed. With both envelopes in her hand, she again became confused. She had no way to decide. She inserted another envelope. Again she was convinced she had made the wrong decision. She again asked for the post office box to be opened.

Recall the patient Eliott, who after surgery, could not make sense of his emotions and could not make any decisions. But the young overachiever here did not undergo surgery that disconnected her from her emotions. Through nurturing and a school system focused on performing and thinking, rather than enjoying and feeling, her brain had done that surgery for her. I know the feeling.

For most of my life, I never allowed myself to experience emotions spontaneously, nor did I possess the vocabulary to make my emotional experiences conscious. My experiences of life filled one of four buckets: pleasure, pain, stress or numbness. None of these are true emotions. As a result, on a consciousness scale, I had more in common with a baboon than an evolved human being. But did I experience true emotions? Absolutely. All of the eight basic emotions common to all mammals, and the numerous secondary emotions only humans share, entered my non-conscious brain, from which— unbeknownst to me—they controlled my life. My obsession with education never helped me to become emotionally literate. If anything, with its focus on cold reasoning, I became even more distanced from my own feelings.

Daniel Goleman wrote an excellent book, *Emotional Intelligence: Why It Can Matter More Than IQ, which* discusses the importance of emotional intelligence: the ability to feel your emotions and use that knowledge to understand and guide you to make the right decisions. Emotional intelligence is seen as fundamental to what the Positive Psychology field calls personal intelligence. Without understanding our emotions, we cannot understand ourselves, our needs and wants in the moment.

Earlier in my life, making a decision about what to eat would propel me into a bundle of hopelessness. I would look at a menu but remained clueless about what I wanted. I would ask the waiter to please come back to me after everyone had ordered, hoping someone else's order would help me. It never did. By the time the waiter got to me, I was still unsure about what I wanted.

The post office overachiever and I are not alone. Michael Maccoby's research shows that the average person in the knowledge-service industry—typically smart people with coveted degrees from the best schools—possesses "no inner core that directs them," suffers from chronic anxiety and is constantly bombarded with questions: "Is this the appropriate answer? Am I doing OK? Is this working?"

In moments of rare intimacy or with the truth that lies in wine, a few overachievers agreed with my view that our educational snobbery and intellectual masturbation are band-aids for the emptiness and the insecurity raging inside us.

This lack of an inner core causes many overachievers to consider suicide. A well-documented research study showed that 55 percent of first year students at a respected college reported having at least one suicidal thought during their freshman year. Other studies show an even higher incidence of suicidal thoughts.

All my studies and an elite education never filled the empty core in my soul. Therapy has started to make me more emotionally literate. This has significantly helped my ability to order food at restaurants and make major career decisions. But I still have many moments when I experience a state of physiological arousal but have no idea what my heightened state of being is trying to tell me. Even worse, because I cannot label the feeling, I cannot understand whether the feeling is based on the reality in the moment or because of memories of past events. During these moments, despite significant conscious knowledge of how my mind works, I feel completely clueless.

Education and the Real Self

There is another reason why education cannot provide a Real Self, the inner core that directs us in life. Recall the first time you sat behind the steering wheel. Everything was a conscious effort that was verbalized in the brain: "Key in ignition. Gear in neutral. Push in clutch. Turn key. Release handbrake," etc. After many, many experiences, you now get into your car and the next minute you are in your office. Not once do you even think of how to drive a car, an activity that is now part of your "in-your-bone" memory (or what scientist call implicit memory). Muscle memory is automatic and reflexive and lacks consciousness. In fact, as you drive, you most probably are thinking of the jerk at the office or what you are going to have for lunch.

Now think of the last time you were driving along when a ball, or a cat, or a car suddenly moved in front of you. We hop that you reacted automatically and slammed the brakes. There were no conversations going off in your head, saying, "Oh, look, nice red ball with a two year old running after it dressed in a blue sweater. Now what must I do in situations like this? What did I read in the manual again?" If that were the case, the outcome would be tragic. But in almost all cases, the brain immediately, automatically and non-verbally helps us to apply the brakes. All this happens in milliseconds.

Once you avoid disaster, you stop to evaluate your experience. You tell the child's mother what happened and discuss what can be done to prevent this from happening again. You pick up your cell phone and call your best friend to explain to her what happened. If you have a good friend, she will listen empathetically to you. This will calm you down. Together the two of you decide it is not a good idea to drive faster than 30 miles an hour in a residential area. You both commit to never doing that again.

Suddenly, out of the blue, your friends says, "You know, this reminds me of Ted Kennedy, who drove his car off a bridge. What was the name of the bridge again?" To your surprise, you say immediately, "The Dike Bridge in Chappaquiddick." Your friend compliments your memory. (Scientists call this factual explicit memory.)

On your way home, your brain changes gears and lanes automatically while you think of what could have happened if you did not stop in time. At home, your husband asks you, "What happened to you today?" You tell him the story, recalling from memory what happened to you on the road. (Scientists call this autobiographical explicit memory.) This event and how you dealt with it are now part of the story you tell yourself about your life; a story you began telling the day you received your Real Self and the power of language.

Our brain possesses two types of knowledge: "how to" implicit knowledge and "what" explicit knowledge. The "what" knowledge can also be divided into factual or autobiographical knowledge.

When we look at the main questions our inner core and Real Self need to answer to live a full and happy life, we see that most of them are "how to" questions: How to value and care for ourselves (self esteem); how to empathize with people; how and when to trust them and how to relate with them (relationships); how to decide which goals to follow and how to follow them through the ups and downs of life (self-expression); how to learn from mistakes and how to adjust to life (creativity); how to stay aware of both our inner world and the external world (reality); how to adjust to feedback and life's lessons (creativity); how to nurture children (parenting); and how to stay calm when life rolls an unexpected ball in front of us (dealing with conflict, chaos, change or challenge).

Implicit knowledge or muscle memory found in the Real Self is written in sensations, images and emotions and was formed over thousands of experiences. This type of knowledge cannot be studied or taught. Doing, failing, learning over and over again is how we gain "how to" knowledge. "What" knowledge cannot become "how to" knowledge without a lot of practice.

The implicit "how to" knowledge given to us by primary caretakers and other mentors leads to a happy life. This is different from the verbal factual explicit knowledge we are taught in our education systems or gained from reading self-help books or listening to self-help gurus. We cannot study ourselves happier. Books cannot teach us more about ourselves. We learn about ourselves in the real world through trial and error.

Wisdom of Solomon

As a young boy, I loved the Bible story often referred to as the Judgment of Solomon. In the story, two women were brought to the wise king to resolve a dispute. Both had babies born the night before. One baby had died. In the morning, both mothers claimed the surviving baby was their child. Solomon then ordered the living baby to be divided in two, one half for each mother. When the one mother shouted that the baby belonged to the other woman, Solomon knew that she was the real mother. He knew that only a true mother (or at least a sane person) would have the compassion to give up her child rather than have him killed. So he gave her back her child. Although the story is more likely an ancient urban legend than a real life situation, it will serve well to explain how our brain helps us to live wisely.

During the time of Solomon's reign, there was no Oxbridge or Ivy League education. There were no computers, Wikipedia or Google. There were no massive libraries to go to for advice. One of history's wisest men had none of the skills and tools that we associate with being smart and wise.

Solomon had a few gifts. When he became king he did not ask God for a long life, wealth or revenge on his enemies. Instead, he asked for an understanding heart to judge people and to know right from wrong.

Our human brain gives us a few abilities to cultivate an understanding heart. Humans first and foremost have the ability to understand our own heart and mind. We can become aware that we exist and that we have unique emotional reactions to events. We have a sense of self.

Because we can understand our own mind, we also can understand another human being's mind. Solomon had what psychologists call the ability to mentalize. He was able to walk in a mother's shoes. But this ability to understand others' minds is not wisdom per se. Many politicians and marketers understand how our brains work, but use it against us. Solomon was not only able to walk in her shoes, he was also able to feel how it must be to walk in her shoes. He was able to empathize with the situation the real mother was in. But that was still not enough to bring him wisdom. He needed another tool.

Daniel Gilbert, author of *Stumbling onto Happiness*, believes that the key difference between humans and other animals is that we can imagine the future. We can, by imagining various outcomes, pre-feel our response to the outcomes, make informed decisions without going through the pain of doing and then learning. Gilbert writes, "The emotional experiences that results from a flow of information that originates in the world is called feeling; the emotional experiences that result from a flow of information that originates in memory (used when we imagine the future) is called prefeeling."

Solomon forced each woman to face three future scenarios: a life after receiving half a child, a life with the child and a life without the child. An animal would have had to experience all situations before it could make a decision based on what gave him the most pleasure or the least amount of pain. But this trial by error approach would have caused the baby to die. Solomon instinctively knew that each woman would pre-feel each of these scenarios and make a decision based on the resulting emotions. He knew that the real mother would rather endure the pain of giving up her child than to letting him die.

A monkey cannot empathize. A monkey cannot imagine the future. A monkey can definitely not empathize with another being that is prefeeling imagined future scenarios. We do not need education to be wise, we need feelings, mentalization, empathy and imagination.

Wisdom, Failure and Change

Life is change. The best of humanity takes change and ambiguity in stride. Whether they are caught in the midst of a war zone or in the tsunami of pleasure and admiration of Manhattan, they adapt to maintain a sense of self and an optimistic outlook. They know that they will adapt to the situations and failures that life brings to them. They will learn and grow and become stronger.

Even though I have lived in many countries and had many careers, I never approached change, ambiguity and failure with a sense of play and fun. In fact, these three musketeers stressed me out.

For the longest time, I had misread Darwin's belief that "survival of the fittest" drives all evolution. I assumed he meant survival of the *strongest*; but what he really meant was that those who are able to best adapt to their environments will have the easiest time surviving. The best of humanity are the best at adapting to what life throws at them. Rather than clinging to past knowledge, they are excited by the process of learning for its own sake. They want to learn from their mistakes. They want to learn from change. They want to push their own limits.

Their strong Real Self enables them to do this. Dr. Masterson writes that the Real Self has "the ability to replace old, familiar patterns of living and problem-solving with new and equally or more successful ones." The Real Self also helps us to constantly question the filters we have in life, to view events differently so we can remove false fantasies and replace them with accurate, realistic beliefs that fit the circumstances we are in.

Harvard professor Chris Argyris writes in an article neatly titled "Teaching Smart People How to Learn" that many "members of the organizations that many assume to be the best at learning are, in fact, not very good at it. I am talking about the well-educated, high-powered, high-commitment professionals who occupy key leadership positions in the modern corporation."

Argyris then discusses the reasons why: Overachievers, who seldom experienced failure in their lives, have no clue how to deal with it. Admitting to failure makes us feel like failures. So instead of embracing feedback, we become defensive, avoid criticism or blame other people or circumstances. If the world's best educated people cannot live up to life's most powerful drive—to adapt or die—then we can safely argue that education as we know it today does not serve humanity and life well.

But the need of overachievers to put life in neat little boxes has had far more serious consequences. David Brooks from *The New York Times* writes, "We got into it [the economic crisis] because arrogant traders around the world were playing a high-stakes game they didn't understand." He also explained how many finance whizzes believed that the Gaussian copula function, the formula that was supposed to accurately calculate risk, was foolproof. But it was not and the Tower of Babel came crashing down.

Life is so uncertain and unpredictable. Designing formulas to predict risk seems like building the Tower of Babel to avoid another deluge. One of the main victims in our search for smartness is wisdom. The arrogance and stupidity on Wall Street show us that our educational system is not preparing graduates for real life.

I have met a few of these mathematical geniuses on Wall Street. Their lack of interpersonal skills and emotional intelligence can be spotted from a satellite orbiting earth. If one is not in touch with one's own emotions, he or she cannot be in touch with real life. You will try to bring structure to a world that defies structure and formulas.

"There are no life experiences that would get you into Stanford. It's not what you've done; it's how you've experienced whatever has happened to you," an admissions officer told a reporter. Stanford has the right idea, one that both Wall Street and Washington ought to accept. Do not appoint people based on brains, but on their ability to adapt to what has happened to them. Test people for the strength of their Real Self, not intellectual abilities.

Elite Crooks

I was brought up in a Calvinistic culture where we were screamed at and beaten if we did not do what good Christian boys and girls should. Both at home and in the culture, we were told what was wrong and right, evil and good, and if we wanted to be saved (or at least save our burning buttocks), we had to adhere. After all, we are born with pure souls and if we misbehave we must be punished. The concept that beating and screaming at children to rid them of their demons is actually responsible for causing a child's demons is only now hitting the newsstands in South Africa.

After high school, I went to the University of Stellenbosch whose motto is "Pectora roborant cultus recti"—a good education strengthens the character. After six years of education, which included a few classes on ethics given by the dean of the Medical School, I took the Hippocratic Oath.

On my first day at Yale, we were all called in for a discussion on ethics. We were told that plagiarism and other unethical behaviors would not be tolerated. Throughout the two-year program, a few students, often out of ignorance, got into trouble. The school practiced what it preached.

After a lifetime of being told about good moral behavior for a Christian, gentleman and a man of character, I had to admit to myself that if I had been in Nazi Germany, I easily could have been indoctrinated to join the SS and commit unthinkable atrocities against other humans. I also have seen the unethical behavior of doctors, businessmen and lawyers. I have read of the many high-profile cases of grotesquely immoral conduct from top CEOs with stellar academic resumes. They are only the tip of the iceberg. But the immoral conduct of the intellectual elite is not new.

In his book *Intellectuals*, Paul Johnson points to the alarming fact that many German and Italian educated people, even medical doctors, were the first to follow Hitler and Mussolini, respectively.

The trust and respect that many uneducated people have for the educated, the priests, doctors, and accountants, is well documented throughout history. But from my experience, trust that is based only on degrees or titles is dangerous. Trust comes from observing behavior, not academic transcripts.

Scientists attempted to see the effects of the different brains on behavior by conducting brain surgery on monkeys. When they severed the connection between the body and the older two brains (reptilian and mammalian) but kept the primate brain intact, monkeys lost all their monkey behavior. But when scientist destroyed the primate brains, no major differences could be detected among the animals. If our primate brain, the focus of our educational system, has very little impact on behavior, we can conclude that education cannot make us men and women of character.

Origins of Morality

For a long time in my life, I had little patience for the homeless. I felt that everyone has an equal chance in life to make it. If you did not make it, then you are to be blamed, so do not come and beg from me.

We are daily confronted with moral decisions of how to behave to whom. Since Socrates, the question of what is moral behavior has been debated both with rigor and cold reasoning. When a solution was found, the smart informed the rest of us about what is fair and just. Reason and deliberation are kings. Many religions still hold this to be true. This is also why we believe the educated must be moral and ethical too. We constantly prove our views of the world right.

Researchers at Stanford asked 48 students, half of whom favored capital punishment and half of whom were against it, to participate in an experiment. They presented both groups with the exact same information: evidence for and evidence against capital punishment. After they reviewed the data, those who believe in capital punishment only found the data supporting their moral belief as credible. The reverse was true for the other group: They only found credible the data that showed that capital punishment does not work. Students believed the evidence that supported their original moral views. This did not change even after students were told to be objective. Only when they were told to consider that the belief opposing theirs may be true, did they look at all the evidence more open-mindedly.

"Moral judgment is not a single thing; it's intuitive emotional responses and then cognitive responses that are duking it out," a researcher from Harvard writes. Our emotional understanding and empathy fight our intellectual understanding and insight to lead us to moral judgments that can benefit all. Other thinkers believe that our emotional gut feeling of what is right or wrong comes from early childhood, clouds our views quickly and automatically and then we only use logic and reasoning to justify what our gut is telling us. Regardless of what camp is right, today we know that our emotions and conditioned moral intuitions play a much stronger role than conscious knowledge in how we make moral decisions.

Moral reasoning without empathy or emotions makes us susceptible to the moral theories of those in power. When Hitler says that non-Aryans are inferior, or the National Party (the South African political party that designed the apartheid laws) says that black people are communists or a danger to our lives, or New Yorkers say the homeless are an eyesore, people without empathy will not be able to fight unjust laws. They will adhere to the rules, not understand the pain caused by the rules.

We all have within us the seeds of prejudice. Here in America, I have met many people who do not make judgments based on the color of skin or a person's sex, but they do judge the size of the wallet or the skinniness of the body or the label on the clothes. Our need for prejudice comes from our animal brain's need for hierarchy, stereotyping and our need to belong to a group of people who are similar to us.

It is the human brain, especially the Real Self, that allows us not only to temper our need to be superior to others, but that also allows us through empathy to understand the value of all humans. Even more, those with a healthy Real Self also have empathy for all life's suffering. This includes the suffering of animals kept in unbearable cages so we can enjoy cheap pork or chicken, as well as the suffering of the planet from overuse and abuse.

Today, I have much more empathy for people with nowhere to live. I still am confused about whether I should give money or not, but I try at least to look everyone in the eye and acknowledge their existence. I often fail. But I know today that all people are not born with equal opportunities. Some of us have very fragile Real Selves. Others were smacked by fate from the moment they were born. I also know that all of us can, through a perfect emotional storm and life crises, end in places we never imagined.

But this does not mean I do not still have moments where I say, "Typical homeless guy," "typical woman," or "typical black person." But today I know that as soon as prejudice creeps into my consciousness, I need to figure out what is going on in my Real Self. Almost always, I find that my Real Self is under assault from my demons. During my moments of prejudice, the person I hate the most is myself.

Teaching Morality

With the unethical behavior in schools, Wall Street and Washington reaching frightening proportions, the call for teaching ethics to students has increased. In the United States, 18 states must provide programs that foster empathy, respect, responsibility and integrity. There are successes: Bullying on buses, fighting or detention for minor disruptive incidents such as chronic tardiness to class or running in the hallways is down in these schools. But the program does not work for everybody.

At one school that has an empathy program, a 12-year-old student told a reporter exactly what empathy is: putting yourself in someone else's shoes. So, he said, he tries not to call classmate names. But during the interview, he screamed at another student to shut up. A friend complained that the boy had kicked him in English class.

This is because not everyone has the roots of empathy in place. I did not. I had to learn it during therapy. In fact, when Dr. Masterson trains other therapists on how to treat success-obsessed people, he warns them not to expect to see any empathy from these talented and charming individuals. He emphasizes that it is not as if these people have empathy that they are too lazy to use or suppress for personal gain. They do not have the ability to empathize as a man without legs does not have the ability to walk. People with a fragile Real Self do not have empathy. Period. Without empathy, we cannot figure out what our prejudices are doing to others. Nor will it make us meet people who have opposing views and see them as humans first and proponents of a point of view second. Seeing our "enemies" as humans with their own needs, dreams and fears is one way researchers find people can change their moral intuitions.

The best of humanity has empathy and the conscious will to stand up for other people who are suffering. They have thousands of muscle memories of experiences where they enjoyed empathy from a caring primary caretaker who also encouraged them to make and then learn from their own decisions. Empathy and conscious will comes from having memories of empathy and conscious will. Without these memories, no school or teacher can ever help. The roots of moral behavior like the roots of the Real Self lie in the first three years of life.

The only way to teach someone empathy is to demonstrate empathy. When someone is interested in our minds and has empathy for our experiences, we start having empathy for ourselves. Empathy for ourselves allows us to love our neighbors like we love ourselves. Teaching people logic, language and linear thinking or Dante's *Inferno* or blasting them with data supporting the opposite view has almost no chance of changing a person's behavior or character. Teaching people to feel and understand themselves and others does. No wonder great teachers embody empathy for all.

A Call for Educational Reform

Dr. Kenneth Ginsburg, author of books on stress among teenagers for the American Academy of Pediatrics, advises parents to respect their children's compassion and generosity, not their grades or accomplishments. By doing this, parents can help children to be more resilient in life.

But the problem does not only lie with parents.

Einstein wrote, "A human being is a part of a whole, called by us 'universe,' a part limited in time and space. He experiences himself, his thoughts and feelings as something separated from the rest...a kind of optical delusion of his consciousness. This delusion is a kind of prison for us, restricting us to our personal desires and to affection for a few persons nearest to us. Our task must be to free ourselves from this prison by widening our circle of compassion to embrace all living creatures and the whole of nature in its beauty."

Our educational system is not freeing us from our prisons. It is adding to the thickness of the prison walls. We need schools where students learn more about themselves, their passions and interests and their unique emotional reactions to events. We need teachers who approach students with empathy for their misconduct and for what they do not know, while admiring what they do know. We need schools with strong cultures that celebrate all the human values, specifically self-knowledge and empathy. Then finally education may free us from our prisons and set us on a road of happiness and our humanity.

Stanford University's School of Education has a program that it is rolling out to other schools called Challenge Success. Dr. Denise Pope, founder of the program, told an interviewer, "College admission is how a lot of people are defining success these days. We want to challenge people to achieve the healthier form of success, which is about character, well-being, physical and mental health and true engagement with learning."

If academic institutions aim for these goals and teachers embody the human values, education may finally play a role in creating a happier and more just society.

Chapter 11

The Helpless Fantasies of Fame

When I was in my early twenties, I traveled through Zimbabwe as part of a student government trip to assess the changes that took place after the country's independence from Britain in 1980. One day we stopped at a kraal—a little village of homemade huts. Our guide told us that in one hut, a witchdoctor would tell your fortune for a small fee. Even though my religious Afrikaner culture deemed witchdoctors and fortunetellers to be the devil's work, I decided to take a chance. At the time, I was reeling from a painful romantic breakup and I needed hope and direction.

I remember the hut filled with human skulls, spears and animal fur. I remember darkness and smoke. An old man sat on the floor, looking up at me, eyes blinded by cataracts. That is what I remember. But our memories are fickle; they are photos of the past, often Photoshopped by our own narrative sensibilities and the passing of time.

The witchdoctor looked up at me and, in broken English, asked, "What do you want to know?"

"Will I become Prime Minister of South Africa?" I blurted.

As soon as I said it, I felt silly. How could I believe that a witchdoctor would know the future? Of all the questions in the world to ask—Whom will I marry? When will I die? What is my passion in life? Will I have children? —I wanted to know if I would become Prime Minister of South Africa.

The old man's eyes became more alive. His upper lip fought the urge to break into a derisive grin. He enjoyed my moment of childish hubris. He picked up a bag of bones, shook them, blew air into them and threw them on the floor. For an eternity, he studied the bones. Then, like Lawrence Olivier, he, after a dramatic pause, slowly and confidently said, "Of course you will."

Years later, on a visit to my brother Andre in London, I said: "One day, when I'm asked to make a speech at our high school, I will tell the students that tradition is good, but only if one knows when to break it."

After a pause, Andre asked, "So why do you think you will be asked to make a speech at the school?"

I smiled to hide my confusion. Why had I naturally assumed that I would become so successful and famous that my school would invite its "famous son" back to speak to the students?

The pursuit of fame, whether as a politician or a celebrity, has been the most intimate and consistent lover of my life.

My Fifteen Minutes

During my year as President of the Student Council of the University of Stellenbosch, a group of us, opposed to the general political sentiment of the campus, left for Lusaka, Zambia, where we were to meet secretly with senior members of the ANC, the banned political party of Nelson Mandela.

When news of our trip was leaked to university authorities, I publicly declared that I would *not* officially meet with the ANC. But on the tour, when I was given the opportunity to meet informally with a number of exiled ANC members, I gladly accepted. Laughing and drinking beer with men and women vilified as the antichrist opened my eyes to the indoctrination that I had been subjected to. But our meetings never remained secret. The story broke even before we returned to South Africa.

As we disembarked from our airplane in Cape Town, a wall of journalists and photographers greeted us. The next day newspapers had photos of us on their front pages. A few days later, we held a feedback session on campus to tell our fellow students why we went and what we had learned. That night, I appeared on national television news. Months later, a few student leaders and I were interviewed on a South African news program comparable to *Anderson Cooper 360*.

My brief moments of fame brought people into my life whom I never met in person. One person wrote a beautiful letter thanking me for being a voice for other Afrikaners embarrassed by the policies of apartheid. Other letters were less supportive. One read: "The ANC is like a snake. I hope it bites and kills you."

Fame had bared its teeth.

In 1993, I became the sole practitioner in a small town of 500 people in rural Manitoba, Canada. Like all small communities all over the world, the people in Reston loved their gossip. They used to joke and say, "We talk a lot, but we care a lot." I found this to be true on both accounts. To my surprise, I found that the biggest gossipers in town were the men gathering at six in the morning at a local restaurant for their morning cup of coffee.

One day, one of them came to see me for treatment. As I led him into the examining room, he said, "Congratulations!"

"For what?" I asked.

"On becoming engaged!"

"Really," I laughed, "please find me the woman's name and number!"

I was not surprised by his comment; he was the third person in four months who had congratulated me on being engaged.

These experiences gave me a small taste of what people who are truly famous must endure every day: the gossip about their love lives, the reaction to the gossip, the constant scrutiny and above all, the high burnout rate. In both situations, I could not wait to leave my positions of "fame." All I longed for was to live in a place where people did not know my name, a place where critical eyes would not follow me like spotlights. I understand why some celebrities burst out crying after discussing the negative influence the paparazzi have on their lives. The difference between my and their moments of fame: mine was a drop in the sea, but celebrities must live in the storm; I knew mine would be over in months, theirs will follow them for decades. Even as they face death, hundreds of insensitive camera lenses will document and broadcast their final breaths to the world.

The New York Times printed a picture of me in its review of the play I wrote and acted in on the life of Anton Chekhov. *The New York Times* was kind. The *New York Sun* ran a full article, accompanied by a huge photo, with the headline: "A Vanity Fair." The reviewer took me, both as a person and an artist, to the cleaners. For better and for worse, fame brought a magnifying glass to my life and my struggles.

The sweet and bitter tastes of fame had no positive impact on my self-esteem or happiness. Whether I was being discussed by the national news, early morning gossip or New York newspapers, I did not feel better about myself. In fact, I felt worse. Strangely, this made me want "to make it" even more.

Fame Addicts

From small towns in Canada to provincial towns in South Africa to major cities like London and New York, I have met fame addicts, young and old, striving to be the talk of the town. Whether as captain of a team, the star athlete, student government president, Rhodes Scholar, homecoming queen or the biggest gossiper, many of us want the local hairdressers to know our name.

New Yorkers see New York as the food capital of the world—if you can bake it here, you can bake it anywhere. Most of the world's famous chefs have opened a restaurant in the city. New York also has some of the most efficient, friendly, well-educated waiters, working eagerly for tips. Most of them are not career waiters; they are actors.

Of the thousands of actors who stream to New York and Los Angeles, only five percent will one day be paid to act and most will need to find other jobs to support their craft. The Bureau of Labor Statistics states that the middle half of all actors made hourly earnings between $7.75 and $30.76 in 2004. The lowest-paid 10 percent earned less than $6.63, and the highest-paid 10 percent earned more than $56.48. Actors with high incomes are the exception, not the rule. So what keeps thespians from running from acting as if from the plague? The dream of standing in front of the world and thanking their mothers for supporting their dreams on Oscar night. Fame is for the actor what gold dust is for the poor prospector seeking his fortune in a dry river bed.

I have a friend who is writing a screenplay. He told me over coffee in the East Village, "I still long to become a celebrity. I already dream of the interviews I will give, of people congratulating me and of my parents finally considering me a grown up." Jokingly he said, "Maybe then I will have cute women who want me to inseminate them with my genius!" At a time of job insecurity, a breakup with his girlfriend and static communications with his parents, the fantasy of fame keeps him afloat.

At business school and as a consultant in New York, I met a number of people who dream of becoming president or prime minister of their countries. One man was so adamant about becoming the top leader of India that he called himself "the JFK from Bombay."

Not one of these people, myself included, is qualified to hold office in a PTA, let alone in a country or corporation. They seek fame, not the opportunity to lead and make a difference.

I read of high school football players who refuse to tell their coaches that they have concussions out of fear of being dropped from the A-sides; of wrestlers who overdose on steroids to stay on top; of cyclists and baseball players caught using banned drugs during the Tour de France or before Spring Training. Some people sacrifice their long-term health for the lure of fame.

For millions of viewers, reality shows, such as *American Idol* or *America's Got Talent*, fuel the obsession of overnight fame and glory every year. Shows that allow for quick ascent to fame are popular.

In *New York* magazine, the journalist Emily Nussbaum, writes, "Kids today. They have no sense of shame. They have no sense of privacy. They are show-offs, fame whores, pornographic little loons who post their diaries, their phone numbers, their stupid poetry—for God's sake, their dirty photos!—online. They have virtual friends instead of real ones. They talk in illiterate instant messages. They are interested only in attention—and yet they have zero attention span, flitting like hummingbirds from one virtual stage to another."

She continued to show how so many young people obsessed with YouTube and Facebook have become public figures who have a lot in common with celebrities and politicians. She could have added to that some religious leaders, psychologists and television show hosts.

Many people today want to become famous for not doing anything except to publicizing their lives on the Internet as if they were the next hot thing.

Studies show that 51 percent of all Generation Nexters believe fame is a top priority for their generation; 40 percent of all people believe they will have at least one moment of fame in their lives; and 30 percent of people regularly daydream of being famous. 1-2 percent of people believe they cannot exist without fame. Many people seem to crave for their 15 minutes of fame.

Happiness and Fame

"Nice tie!" an onlooker yelled.

"Ah, yes, my bright tie," Bill Clinton said with a grin. "I like bright ties. You know, when you reach a certain age, all you've got left is bright ties and bullshit." Fame did not bring Bill Clinton peace of mind.

When George W. Bush spoke of his plans post presidency, he said, "Well, I will start the best institute to spread democracy around the world. When I am bored during the day, I will just go to the farm." Fame did not bring meaning to his life.

Famous businessman and Wall Street darling Jeffrey Skilling, Enron CEO, died of a heart attack after being found guilty for destroying a company and the pensions of his employees. Fame does not make us more humane.

Elvis Presley, at the height of his fame, overdosed because he felt he had no direction in his life after his mother died. Fame did not bring him happiness.

"Lurking behind every chance to be made whole by fame is the axe man of further dismemberment," the historian Leo Braudy wrote.

Even the ancients warned youth of the dangers of fame. As a student, I had to translate Icarus from the Latin into English. Even back then I understood, at least on an intellectual level, that if you fly too close to the sun, your wings will melt and you will fall from the sky.

Research also supports these anecdotal and historical examples of fame's futility.

When a psychologist analyzed the lives of Kurt Cobain, Cole Porter and John Cheever, he found that all three became more self-conscious in their work and interaction with others as they became more well known. But this increased self awareness was not an indication of enlightenment. Cobain killed himself at the age of 27. John Cheever was a notorious alcoholic. Fame brings a heightened scrutiny and focus on a confused and fragmented inner Real Self. Fame lets the demons out.

Surveys done in communities around the world show that a goal as subjective as fame, one that depends so much on other people's judgment, is psychologically treacherous.

Fame is incapable of curing unhappiness.

Fame and the Brain

At a bar in Greenwich Village, I heard a woman excitedly telling a few acquaintances about her most recent rock 'n' roll road trip to California. I watched her from a distance. She was vivacious, seemingly comfortable with her sexuality and confident. After our eyes connected a few time, I gathered my guts and walked over to her. I liked Jo instinctively. To be in the company of people passionate about what they do is always exhilarating.

"I've never felt more myself than when I started to sing for our band," Jo told me.

We talked about the arts, singing, acting and her journey to New York. She made fun of my vocal chord paralysis, which at the time still made me sound like castrated contra alto. Everything about Jo was wonderful.

"Do you want to see some video clips from our last tour to California?" Jo asked.

"Sure," I said.

Jo pulled out her video recorder and showed me only three clips, all of crowds screaming and cheering.

"Here they are asking for an encore," Jo said.

"Wow!" I was impressed. Jo not only has passion for what she does, but she also has "made it." But after a few minutes, I realized that there was not one image of Jo singing, the band joking backstage or the group having fun on the bus between cities. I started to wonder: "Isn't it odd that she would show a stranger screaming crowds of adoring fans?"

After returning her camera to her bag, Jo continued eating her bar food.

"You know what this needs?" she told the barman. "This definitely needs some more green peppers. Maybe even some onion. Yes. Some more onion."

Suddenly the rock star had become a food connoisseur. A very confident one too. I figured out what had happened. Jo was on an admiration high. The images of the crowds admiring her a few weeks ago were, to her brain, the equivalent of having a snort of cocaine. She was high on life, confident and a bit restless.

It is easy to see that Jo's animal brain was going crazy when she saw the images of her fans' adoring eyes. This brain wants us to feel superior to others and make us feel that we are omnipotent and omniscient.

What is even more interesting is to figure out how the brain caused this feeling of grandiosity and superiority.

Jo and her videos are a classic example of how the mind filters the present. When Jo watched the videos of her past experiences, her brain interpreted these crowds as screaming at her in the here and now. After all, time is a concept created by our human brain. For our reptilian brain, the stimulation of being famous brings the reward of admiration. Her videos of an actual event combined with the memory of it gave her a shot of admiration in the present. To our brain, what we watch or what we remember is often perceived as happening in the present.

One day, sitting in Dr. Masterson's office, I asked him, "I wonder if I ever will be cured of my wishes to be famous?"

"It's hard. Why would you want to if it is so much fun?" he responded.

Then I remembered my experience with Jo. Our animal brain gets excited about fame whether we experience it for real in the moment, through videos of past events or in the mind's eye of our imaginations. When we dream of being a movie star, the president or the world champion, our bodies react as if it is really happening. In return, the brain rewards us with natural opiates. We feel high from our fantasies of fame. After a fantasy of achieving fame, any of us would have the confidence to tell a barman what extra ingredients the food needs. Fantasies of fame bring almost as much pleasure as fame itself.

Seeing that fame, or even fantasizing about fame, is a product of our animal brain tells us that it will need increasingly bigger crowds or bigger fantasies to maintain the same amount of kick. We become addicted to fame.

Fantasy Bubble

Jo's experience of seeing adoring eyes as a pop star and my experience of seeing adoring eyes *in my imagination* as president of South Africa or as a Broadway actor share a common denominator: adoring eyes. During these moments, adoring eyes make us feel as if we are the center of attention and loved by all. It also makes us selfish and self-centered.

Fame or fantasies of fame bring back to us memories of a time in our lives when we were famous and constantly observed by adoring eyes; a time when our primary caretaker looked at us as if we are God's gift to the world. A time when we were 12 months old.

People obsessed with fame or daydreaming about fame are obsessed with reuniting with our primary caretaker. We want to be one-year-old child again, lost in fantasy, rather than an adult who deals with reality. We want to experience the pleasure of instant gratification and immediate action, not the human legacy of temperance and transcendence. We want to be the most important person in the history of the world, not just one of countless organisms that have comprised Life over the millennia.

So when an actor or politician tells you that he or she cannot wait "to make it," they are actually saying that they cannot wait to reach a state in which they feel constantly perfect and reunited.

Fame and Passion

I have been fortunate to have one of the most famous people of the twentieth century as my president. Nelson Mandela stands for everything humanity should aspire to. He is a man who had courage to stand up for his convictions, who forgave his captors and oppressors and who, upon release from jail, contributed to society. He could have made millions of dollars from making speeches all over the world. Instead, he focused on helping others and living a simple life. Mandela is still a role model to me and an inspiration for following your passion, not chasing rewards.

During an interview, a famous actor said that if he had not become famous in Hollywood, he would have traveled to every town in America to act. Acting is in his blood, not fame. Like him, those who follow their passions, do not care much about becoming famous. They care about what they love doing, regardless of where it takes them. If fame comes, it inspires them to work harder; they do not use it to escape life. Some people have used their fame to be role models for others on how to live life. They do not use it to be constantly in the news. When they lose their fame, they do not slit their wrists or drown their sorrows in drink. They keep doing what they love doing, even if the only adoring eyes watching them belong to the Real Self inside of them.

Beverly Sills, the most celebrated of American sopranos, said that the highlight of her life was singing Queen Elizabeth at the City Opera. That night, she told herself to not worry about the high notes or singing perfectly. Instead she aimed to only reach 85 percent of what she typically expects from herself and to find joy in discovering the body of Queen Elizabeth. In her attempt to *not* be the greatest, she delivered one of her best performances ever. When she ignored her need for adoring eyes, she tapped into her greatness, into her Real Self and into her true artist.

Dr. Masterson writes that the difference between mentally healthy people and the success obsessed is that when healthy people give a speech, they focus first on enjoying their topic of interest and sharing it with the audience, no matter how large or small. Fame addicts focus on adoring eyes, more than on doing. They focus on the result, not the process. Fame addicts cannot enjoy flow and psychological growth. As a result, they can work hard at a passion, but because they do it for the fame and not the enjoyment, their hard work never strengthens their Real Self.

Fame also forces the famous to start living up to the standards the masses set for them. They are forced to meet the audiences' demands, not their Real Self demands. Often, when they follow their authentic whispers from their Real Selves, their fans react with disdain. People want their celebrities to do what they have always done, rather than evolving their craft. A lifetime of following others' ideas for your life or living up to their expectations hurts the Real Self.

Passion and Intimacy

I met Lin, a 23-year-old actor from Hollywood, after a yoga class. We later met for coffee in Washington Square Park.

"Two nights with the same body rolling over me is too much. I need variety," she offered.

"When was the last time you dated a guy for more than two nights," I asked.

"A few months ago. One night, after a week of dating, we had really good sex. I then saw him shifting around uncomfortably. I could see he wanted to go. So I told him, 'You can go if you want.' When he said, he would, I screamed at him for using me. He then said he only wanted to leave because he felt I wanted him to leave. We talked about it for a few minutes. I then invited him back to bed. But after that, I felt grossed out."

"Maybe you were scared he was going to reject you after you had great intimate sex, so you wanted to reject him first," I offered.

"Never thought it about it that way, but, yeah, it makes sense."

"So, with all these two-night stands, are you not lonely?"

"I'm never lonely. I'm self-sufficient."

"Self-sufficiency is a dead give away for being shit scared of intimacy, lonely and aching for company," I thought, but said nothing.

After a pause, she continued, "I hate people coming close to me. I feel like they are going to dig into me like a cat."

She made her fingers into cat claws and pulled her face with such disgust that it was hard to believe she was talking about one of humanity's prize possessions: intimacy.

"If I sleep with someone," she continued, "I want to leave and not feel pressure to sleep with him again the next night. People who expect more than one night of fun are clawing their fingers into me."

"But what will happen if you want to sleep with him after one night and he refuses to see you again," I asked.

"Well, that won't happen. People like me," she said.

Later we spoke about her acting career.

"I can be so intimate in front of the camera. There, I can say my lines with passion and intimacy. I can cry. I can be so intimate, so passionate. But I have never been able to say the same lines in real life with the same conviction. I can't."

"How is the camera helping you to be more intimate, you think?"

"Camera brings passion. It's never hurt me, only supported me."

"What about feeling safe in front of a camera?" I prodded.

"Yeah. That's true. I feel safe in front of a camera."

I could not help think of Lin when I heard that Farah Fawcett, upon learning that she had terminal cancer, hired a filmmaker to document her struggles. In the face of life's most honest moment, she asked for a camera to be her intimate support. She could trust the camera to be there for her.

Lin and Farah, like so many celebrities and politicians addicted to the camera, struggled with intimacy. Forced to seek their sense of self in the eyes of the world, they could not bring their own self to a relationship. During intimacy, you need a real "I," not adoring eyes. You need to share your Real Self, not demand to be center stage. You need to be seen, not photographed. Life with millions of eyes on you, but no intimate eyes refueling you will ultimately lead to self-destruction.

Fame and Self-Care

I see Dr. Masterson every Tuesday at 10:20. I typically take the 6 train from Astor Place to 51st Street and from there I have a ten-minute walk to 54th street and Irving Place. The journey takes me approximately half an hour from door to door. This half hour is rich in experiences. Anthony, our friendly doorman, greets me with his Spanish accent; parking attendants drive customers' BMWs and Mercedes Benzes as if the parking garage is a Formula One track; Broadway is crowded with NYU students with long resumes and short skirts; frustrated bankers curse taxi drivers for not stopping to drive their large egos to Wall Street; an Asian man arranges fresh fruits in front of K-Mart; hawkers push *AM News* and *Metro*, free newspapers, up your nostrils; the subway is filled with songs of an old black man singing for a buck or two; the train ride is shared with mannequins pretending to be people, hoping the day at work will be over before it begins; NYPD cops wait for 911 calls at the 17th precinct; restaurants prepare for the lunch hour rush in Midtown—their "Grand Opening" banner still hanging after a year; businessmen with wedding rings stare after youthful breasts marching down Third Avenue; the Starbucks on First Avenue reminds me of hours staring into empty cups of coffee, not sure what to do with my time or my life; rich women take their "children" on leashes for a pooh on the pavement; the squeaky door announcing Dr. Masterson waiting for me.

I know many people who would love to make this half-hour journey every week. But on most Tuesdays, I go to therapy on autopilot. While my body walks to my appointment, I watch videos inside my mind: videos of me being interviewed on television, of me receiving an Academy Award, a Pulitzer, a Nobel Prize, of me having fun with famous stars. With Julia unavailable—I at least was conscious enough to know that she is finally out of the picture—I started to daydream about kissing Charlotte Johansson's full lips, or having great conversation over red wine with the sophisticated Natalie Portman or going for a run with Charlize Theron and her dogs on the beach in California or painting with Rachel McAdams in Canada.

I am wasting the life I have by daydreaming about another. I do this because intimate sessions with Dr. Masterson leave me riddled with demons. I prefer living another life to facing my own past.

Living in the moment, grabbing the power of the now, smelling the roses is impossible if we are focused on the future, the famous and the fairy tales. I am a workaholic. From morning to night, I work. Whether it is acting or writing, medicine or politics, my drive for fame has caused me to neglect the most important person in my life: myself. When my attempts to be famous are thwarted by life, I need a lot of booze to calm myself down. Long unforgiving hours at the office or working toward perfection and fame, the stress of failure and the booze to sooth my demons are hard on the body, mind and soul. An obsession with fame is treacherous.

A famous actor is in one of my aerobics classes. She always arrives late, leaves early, hiding behind sunglasses. On the surface, she has made it. But her life seems to revolve around avoiding contact with strangers. Fame forced her to abandon one of our humanity's most important abilities: freedom to explore. Life becomes very structured and limited in the constant struggle to avoid strangers or paparazzi.

Maureen Dowd, columnist for *The New York Times*, wrote an article discussing Bill Clinton's revelation in his autobiography that he had a relationship with Monica Lewinsky because, as President, he could. She then wrote that President Bush, after the September 11th terrorist attacks, went after Saddam Hussein just because he could. She argued that the two most powerful men in the world followed their alpha instincts and their sense of "who's gonna stop me" and did whatever they wanted.

A television psychotherapist frequently attacks his guests as if they were young schoolchildren, ostensibly in the name of helping them. On *American Idol*, a well-paid and famous judge feels he is justified in saying to a passionate man after a gutsy, but not wonderful performance, "Go home, close the door and sing in the dark room."

A famous athlete thought murder was justified when he could not win back his wife. Enron CEO Jeffrey Skilling, popular in Washington and on Wall Street, committed a white collar crime of enormous proportions.

Famous religious leaders and politicians over the centuries have led their loyal followers to death or to give their life's savings to a cause that only benefited the leader.

Fame makes us feel that we are above other people. Even above the law. The cost of our grandiosity on our own lives is high. But the cost on others and the community that trusts the famous with their faith, future and lives, is even higher.

The Craving for Fame

I once had a steamy love affair with Hollywood celebrity Julia Roberts. We had a perfect relationship. She was funny, sexy and caring. She was my "Pretty Woman." At a time when I was struggling to find joy while studying medicine, Julia's million-dollar smile never ceased to encourage me. I often thought about her, us, our children, our pretty life together; a life without old age or death, a life with perfect love, smiles, bodies and children.

There was only one problem. I had met Julia only in the movies. She was a two-dimensional figure whom I had taken from the big screen and molded into perfect three-dimensional fantasy to caress in the lonely sulci of my brain. I also fell in love with her at a time when at least a billion other men were daydreaming about her. I had no concrete plans of ever coming to the United States. Even if I wanted to visit my beloved Julia, I faced a lack of money, a

Green Card and a US medical license. An absurd fantasy by a man who would, months later, place first in his final year of medical school.

A year ago, I came close to meeting Julia. Jan, a friend who helps organize the Tony Awards ceremony, invited me as her guest. I was excited: Julia was one of the presenters. She ended up sitting seven rows from me and I could not keep my eyes off her. She is still as beautiful as she was in my dreams, when I tried to escape my loneliness while studying how to deliver babies, interpreting an ECG or treat TB meningitis. A few times, those long legs I know so well carried her smile a few feet away from where I was sitting. But you know the real story: my "Pretty Woman" is now another man's real woman and his children's real mother.

Painfully alone one Sunday afternoon, I walked around like a zombie in the busy streets of Manhattan. I felt as if I was a space walker whose cord to the mother ship had come untethered and I was falling into the abyss. "Maybe life in Cape Town, South Africa will be better," I argued. Immediately claustrophobia set in. Thomas Wolfe clearly stated that one never can go back home. "No, maybe I should move to Ladybrand and farm while I practice medicine in the town. Maybe then I will find a sense of belonging." I imagined living in that small rural town in the Free State, a province in South Africa on par with the American Midwest. I saw the main road of the small town. All the shops are closed. On any Sunday afternoon, potholes are the only company. The only sound is the panting of the stray dogs laying in the shade. I imagined this scenario repeating itself Sunday after Sunday for the next 40 years. Panic gripped my ribs. A life lived in the middle of nowhere? An insignificant life! One life to live, and no impact made. Zero. A life lived as an ordinary nobody?

My imagination counterattacked with another fantasy: "If I stay in New York, I will make it to Broadway, to Hollywood. I will be the man at the Tonys, the man at the Oscars. People in my apartment building will look at me differently. They will say, "Wow.""

To understand what triggered the surge in my need to be famous, let's revisit each of these episodes. When I was recovering from a heartbreak, I wanted to become President of South Africa; when I felt empty and passionless studying for my final medical examinations, I had an affair with Julia Roberts; when visions of an ordinary and insignificant life caused a panic attack, I dreamed of Broadway and Hollywood success; and when I am forced to live without my mask in front of Dr. Masterson, I use fantasies as a way of escaping the inevitable.

My fantasies of fame—already significantly above average at its baseline—surged during moments when I felt helpless about finding passion in my career, intimate love and a supportive social network.

Studies support the link between the desire for fame and psychological struggles. Researchers found that people who daydream frequently about or feel that they require fame experienced social exclusion, rejection or neglect in childhood or believe that they would only be loved if they achieved fame and role-model status.

A study showed that those who so need the approval of others have significantly higher levels of distress than those who are interested in self-acceptance and friendship. Many also have an acute sense of mortality and existential angst. Fame addicts are tortured by inner demons and a fragile Real Self.

Totally Helpless

Everyone feels helpless sometimes. Part of the beauty of living a full life is knowing when and how to trust others in areas where one does not have expertise or during moments when fate temporarily renders us emotionally or physically helpless. After all, to trust non-family members is one of a few criteria that separates us from animals. These moments also put perspective on life: We realize we are not in total control of our lives or totally independent. Healthy people know that sometimes they will need to accept help; other times they will need to give help; and sometimes they can easily walk alone.

But for those of us obsessed with fame, helplessness is a metastatic cancer of the soul. Dr. Masterson writes, "Although specific incidents can trigger it, it is not caused by specific incidents, but persists like a gloomy backdrop to life, casting a pall over most activities and life situations. Unlike a healthy man or woman who says, 'Well, this is one of those situations at which I'm not very good,' the false self says, 'You are totally helpless and good for nothing.'"

During moments when my fantasies of fame reach their highest, I feel I am ordinary, a failure, a nobody. Without fame, I feel that nobody will respect me. I'm a useless, hopeless, helpless child. Only fame seems to be able to counter my fears of imminent death.

The Link

We know that at birth we are absolutely helpless. We need a primary caretaker to look after our physical and psychological needs. If she does not, our brain tells us that we have been abandoned and that we will soon die. We scream as if our lives depended upon it. A good primary caretaker creates a fantasy bubble for her child. The strongest tool in her arsenal: caring, understanding and adoring eyes. During the Separation Phase, a good primary caretaker minimizes the adoring eyes and gives support for activities that develop a strong self. An eye celebrating our unique self in the external world becomes our budding "I" inside our mind. Only when our Real Self becomes strong enough to maintain our self-esteem based on what we do and our ability to overcome obstacles, do we stop caring about seeing adoring eyes in the world.

Fame addicts do not develop a caring confident "I" inside their right brain. With the Real Self, we remain programmed to seek adoring eyes to assuage the life-and-death helplessness raging inside them. We want to live in a fantasy bubble, because reality is too painful and frightening. We want to be connected with the primary caretaker's adoring eyes.

In their search, fame addicts often seek careers in which adoring eyes—substitutes for that of the primary caretaker—congregate to listen to those on center stage. It is no surprise that many fame addicts are drawn to careers as politicians, actors, singers, religious leaders, self-help gurus and professional public speakers.

Twitter now gives the famous the illusion that they are constantly watched by adoring people. They want to know that other people are really interested in their thoughts, where they are right now, how many eggs they ordered and where they will be going next. They finally have many someones who care about their every single move.

The link between acting and close links with primary caretakers became clear to me when I learned that at the Oscars, the words *mother, mom, ma* were used significantly more than *father, dad, parents* in actors' acceptance speeches.

Many fame addicts today are becoming famous for having a lot of children or adopting children from all over the world. The drive: To recreate adoring eyes from children, to keep living in the fantasy of a perfect mother-and-child bubble. They are recreating a childhood fantasy. They want to be the mothers they are still addicted to.

As for the link between politicians and their need for a mother's adoring eyes: In *First Mothers*, Bonnie Angelo, a longtime correspondent for *Time* magazine, studied 11 presidents and their mothers. Angelo started with the story of FDR's mother because she believe his presidency marked "the beginning of contemporary America and the modern presidency, the prize that now can be won only by men of supreme self-assurance who are willing to withstand the He distrusted adults for what they did to him—his father often beat him—or what they did not do to him—he never felt loved for who he was if he did not perform perfectly.

grinding process and microscopic examination."

Her research suggested that it is mothers who turn sons into presidents. Angelo writes that it was these "indomitable American women" who were driven to see their sons succeed.

One of the century's most loved orators, Bill Clinton, is renowned for making everyone in the crowd feel as if he is talking to them individually. His charm and energy make people feel wonderful about themselves. Clinton, who was raised by a mother who adored him and even had a shrine in her home dedicated to his achievements, recreates the fantasy bubble wherever he goes.

Case Study: Thriller

As this book goes to press, the world is in mourning for Michael Jackson. Commentators argue that he was the most famous person ever to have walked this earth. Unprecedented fame did very little for Michael. To the contrary, fame turned him from a loved pop star to a man with strange eccentricities.

The first signs of trouble started after Michael's worldwide hit, *Thriller*, made him a legend. His next few albums did extremely well, but never reached the record-breaking success of *Thriller*. Michael bought a ranch and called it Neverland. He wanted to be the boy who never grew up.

The boy who Michael showed the world was the boy who wanted to eradicate all signs of his true identity, who hid behind scarves and sunglasses, a boy who wanted to destroy his face, who wanted to shop without a care, who wanted to give to other boys love, care, bed times stories and lullabies.

When he was asked about his life, Michael said that the song "Childhood" was the most autobiographical song he ever wrote. The video shows Michael crouching like a lost child in a forest and singing in a fragile voice, "Before you judge me, try hard to love me. The painful youth I've had." He sings about how he tries to compensate for the childhood he never had and how he searched for the wonder of youth.

Like most fame addicts, Michael had two versions of himself: the perfect, famous, good, talented boy admired for his achievements and the ugly, rejected, helpless boy never loved for who he really was as a child. His talent and fame allowed him to believe the perfect version of himself. The scrutiny of millions of fans combined with the diminishing—though still outstanding—sales of his follow-up albums triggered Michael's image of himself as helpless, ugly and hurt. He started to attack his inner child, while giving other boys the love he himself craved as a youngster. Michael, like so many fame addicts, could perform and entertain adults, but he could not intimately connect with them.

He hoped fame would save him; but in the end, fame also treated him with disrespect and lack of understanding just as he experienced in childhood. But, due to our reptilian brain's call for more and more, fame as a crutch became fame as a drug. Once the drug pusher was unable to provide more and more, he turned on himself.

All the fame in the world could not heal the self-hatred Michael had inside him that stemmed from a childhood in which he was never supported for the helpless child we all once were. All the fame and cries for attention could never sooth the loneliness Michael experienced every day, a loneliness he rarely mentioned to others. All the fame cannot make up for the company of a healthy Real Self, which the best of humanity talk to every day.

Entourage

Here in New York, star spotting is a favorite sport and the cause of fantastic conversation around the coffee machine at work. Shows like *Entourage* are popular. Many people live vicariously through the famous to satisfy their needs for fame. This group typically knows that there is very little chance for them to make it in real life and the closest they may ever get is to be *associated* with stars. Life revolves around being part of a star's entourage or just being close to him or her in public. Hopefully, something will rub off.

Others are addicted to the popular magazines that tell about their favorite stars' every diarrhea or acne episode. They love to be the first person at the coffee pot in the office to reveal the latest gossip about a star or a politician.

When a gossip magazine editor was asked why the masses are so obsessed with celebrities, she said, "Because they see celebrities as part of their family!"

At first I laughed at the statement. As if Brad Pitt and Angelina Jolie's babies are really on par with my own nieces and nephews being born!

But then it clicked. She was halfway right: People obsessed with celebrities see celebrities as extensions of themselves.

Recall how a baby in her fantasy bubble experiences all people, toys and objects as extensions of her own body and grandiose will? People obsessed with celebrities are still little kids who believe that reading about the famous makes them famous too, that if they know the most recent gossip, they are part of the "in" crowd. They are people lacking a Real Self and therefore a full life; they need to fill the emptiness with all the details of a star who climbed out of her car without a panty.

But I admit it. I still get a rush of pleasure from reading popular magazines. I still have many moments when I dream about my moment on the red carpet, of making my Oscar speech, of being the center of others' worlds. Just like a drug addict, I am having trouble shaking my addiction. Knowing that an addiction with fame is foolish has not helped me to curb it. The only cure has been to strengthen my Real Self, my inner "I," to wean me from adoring eyes. But in a culture that has made our celebrities into gods, I sometimes feel like an alcoholic forced to work in a bar.

Section III
Obsessed with Success

Chapter 12

The Patient: Our Culture

Our culture is hurting. Not everyone notices what is going on. If you ask people you respect what is wrong with the world today, they may say, "Something is off" or "Something just doesn't feel right. We seem to have lost our way."

These descriptions are not very specific. For the ignorant, these complaints may sound like a bit of paranoia. But, as I know from medical practice, you have a gut feeling that helps you take "serious" complaints from a hypochondriac with a tired smile, but "non-specific" complaints from a person with character with serious attention. I also know that non-specific symptoms can be the first signs of a lethal disease, such as cancer.

In practice, I became energized when patients complained of multiple non-specific and unrelated symptoms. I enjoyed helping the patient make sense of his complaints and treating his disease early and effectively. Medical doctors employ two ways of thinking to make a diagnosis. First, we compare all the patient's signs and symptoms to the healthy range. We only know a patient has a fever if we know that 105 degrees is much higher than the normal body temperature of 98 or that a liver is enlarged because we know what a healthy liver feels like. Once we have identified a whole list of abnormal signs and symptoms, the real fun begins: We start mixing and matching the data into groups that fit the criteria of known diseases. The purpose is to take the unknown and fit it into the known. For example, a fever with a large liver can be a viral infection, lymphoma or heart failure due to pneumonia in someone with a heart lesion.

The final step is to confirm the initial differential diagnosis with blood tests, urine analysis, X-rays and other appropriate diagnostic tests. Only when a diagnosis has been confirmed do we know what has caused the disease. Then we design a treatment regime to bring the patient back to health and help him to avoid future diseases.

Instead of normal anatomy and physiology, I will be comparing the symptoms and signs of our culture against a list of criteria I compiled from research into the six human values, capacities of the Real Self and the functions of a normal human brain.

Human Value: Temperance

The best of humanity know that temperance is at the core of what separates us from animals. The best of humanity can delay their need for instant gratification and action. They can manage their negative emotions, especially uncontrolled outbursts of anger. They can manage their ego, but they know how to express pride in their accomplishments.

By controlling their animal instincts, the best of humanity commit to long-term goals. They know that we can enjoy what life has to offer, including pleasure and admiration, as long as we do not sacrifice our passion, intimacy and self-care activities for these rewards. To them, selfless cooperation within the community beats being dominated by unbridled selfishness.

Cash is King

Our culture is obsessed with money. This is in no way a new phenomenon. Walt Whitman argued in "Democratic Vistas" that America has an "extreme business energy," and an "almost maniacal appetite for wealth." The upside is success never seen before; the downside is a vulgar preoccupation with money, as expressed by David Brooks from *The New York Times*. But there is a difference with America's obsession with money today than that of a century ago.

Frank Rich discusses how we try to get rich quickly by recklessly gambling our money on the market. Instead of investing in new products that will benefit many people in the long term, we focus on short term gains by buying and selling products that are not tangible, products manufactured by "slicing and dicing of debt." Up until recently, everyone was in it for a buck. Of people who graduated from Harvard in 2007, 58 percent of the men and 43 percent of the women became finance and consulting associates as their entry career. Money, not making a difference or learning more about themselves, has been the main drive for young adults entering the workforce. Even half the engineers graduating from the University of Pennsylvania went to work on Wall Street! These numbers reflect the trend seen at many other top universities. Many of America's best and brightest followed the money.

But lacking a high-paying job has not stopped other Americans. Many used their savings or took out collateral against their homes to have cash in hand to join in the fun. The personal savings rate, as a share of disposable income, fell from 5.7 percent in early 1995 to nearly zero in 2007. The net equity extractions from United States homes tripled over this period. As a result, in 2007, people had debt worth 130 percent of their disposable income compared to 90 percent a decade earlier.

Credit card companies jumped in on the fun and began targeting students filled with age-appropriate fantasies that life will turn out well. The result: More than half of college students own four or more credit cards by their senior year.

Flush with cash and credit, people spent. In 2007, consumer spending was 72 percent of gross domestic product, a historic high in the world. We did not stop to consider that future-mindedness is a key criterion that separates us from animals. To steal from Barack Obama, we borrowed to spend, we did not save to invest in the future. All that we as a nation have cared about is immediate pleasure, preferably in copious amounts.

One night, a woman, a multimillionaire, told me, "My life seems to consist only of flying to one place or another to seek pleasure."

Pleasure of Food

Children today see 7600 commercials a year encouraging them to eat fast food, candy and sugary cereal. The result is that a third of children today are either overweight (17 percent) or obese (17 percent) for following the cultural call for instant gratification. "They're surrounded by [cultural] circumstances where the default behavior is one of encouraging obesity," said Dr. Marlene Schwartz of Yale University.

At the same time, the media bombards children with models, actors and celebrities like Paris Hilton, Nicole Richie and Lindsay Lohan. Not surprising then that 46 percent of teenage girls and 26 percent of boys are dissatisfied with their appearance. Ashamed by their weight, kids are left with two options: Ignore it by eating more or become obsessed with losing weight.

A 2006 University of Minnesota study showed that 57 percent of girls and 33 percent of boys use cigarettes, fasting or skipping meals to lose weight. The use of diet pills by teenagers has doubled over the past five years; in 2008 5000 adolescents underwent liposuction.

Talk about mixed messages—our culture is saying to our youth: "Eat like a pig, just so long as you stay skinny as a Paris!"

Pleasure of Sex

In Manhattan, every year a few executives find themselves stiff with embarrassment for having business dinners at high-end strip clubs. With a half naked woman pouring $1000 bottles of champagne, the bill quickly explodes. When the executive goes back to work and tries to claim expenses for the dinner, the naked truth often leaves him jobless. For others, a barrage of pornography in magazines and videos provides a quick release. But it is the Internet that made porn available at the click of a mouse.

Porn generates $12 billion in annual revenue in the United States, a sum comparable to the combined revenues of all professional football, baseball and basketball franchises. 40 million people use the Internet for sexual gratification, generating $1.2 billion annually. For a country based on puritan values, this is a lot of porn.

Our desire for sex goes beyond fantasy. Maggie Scarf, author of *Intimate Partners*, writes, "Most experts do consider the 'educated guess' that at the present time some 50 to 65 percent of husbands and 45 to 55 percent of wives become extramaritally involved by the age of 40 to be a relatively sound and reasonable one." When researchers ask people directly about their affairs, 22 percent of married men and 14 percent of married women admitted to having had a sexual affair at least once during their married lives. But married women below 40 are catching up.

Television and Videogame Pleasure

We all love our television. And plenty of us love videogames as well. But neither one are good for us in excess quantities. Research shows that our brain activity is lower when watching TV than when we sleep. Videogames stimulate the reptilian brain in the same way that cocaine does. Both television and videogames are a lot like a big bag of Halloween sweets for the brain.

Most of watch much more television than we think. We underestimate the amount we spend in front of the television by almost 25 percent. On average, American adults are exposed to five hours and nine minutes of TV each day. Of this time, 61 minutes consist of TV ads and promotions, moments when cunning advertisers manipulate our non-conscious minds.

The impact on our children is huge, with an average child watching three hours of television a day. 32 percent of children between the ages of two and seven and 65 percent of eight to 18 year olds have television sets in their rooms. According to the Committee on Public Education of the American Academy of Pediatrics, "Younger children cannot discriminate between what they see and what is real. Research has shown that television has primary health effects on violence and aggressive behavior, sexuality, academic performance, body concept and self-image, nutrition, dieting and obesity, and substance use and abuse patterns." Another longitudinal study found among teens a positive correlation between watching television and consuming alcohol.

Our obsession with the screen is hurting our youth.

Chemical Pleasure

"Americans have an insatiable demand for drugs," Hilary Clinton said on her recent visit to Mexico. This is not only causing a lot of problems on the US-Mexico border, but in our communities. 45 percent of us know someone with a substance abuse problem. Even more disturbing is the increasing use of alcohol and other drugs among young people. Over the past five years, drug use among eighth graders increased by 150 percent. By the time they graduate, 50 percent of all high school students will have used alcohol and drugs. The average age of using hard drugs has also dropped significantly. But at least they're not shocking their parents: 50 percent of baby-boomer parents expect that their teenagers will try drugs, while 40 percent believe "they have little influence over teenagers' decisions about whether to smoke, drink or use illegal drugs."

Ego Pleasure

"The Cultural Revolution swept away much of the old Chinese culture. It was followed by the wave of commercialism and materialism. Dignity is now defined by money and French and Italian luxury goods," David Brooks wrote in *The New York Times* about the life and times of Edward Tian, a determined Chinese man who, from a humble background, achieved significant success in the United States and then later in China. Brooks could have been writing about thousands of people I know or have observed here in America and all over the world.

We have become our possessions and our money. We are museum objects to be admired. In order to provoke envy in the hearts and minds of our neighbors, we buy everything that is bigger: a bigger house, a bigger diamond, a bigger wine cellar, a bigger car, bigger barbeques.

Our culture encourages the display of our masks of success. We give a lot of airtime to people like Madonna and Donald Trump who flaunt their talents and possessions without a blush of shame. We love the spectacle and the spectacular.

The Internet is supporting those of us constantly in search of admiring eyes. Instead of doing, feeling and learning about ourselves, we record our actions and then put them on Facebook or YouTube to be admired by the unseen masses. Or we cannot wait to rush our guests to our closest computer to show them the time we were interviewed on CNN or when we sang for a friend on YouTube. We are using our images and words on the Internet as the golden calf to be worshipped. Our self-esteem is based on what others see, whether it is on the Internet, the degrees on our walls, the skinniness of our wives, the luxury cars of our husbands or the size of our homes. What we have counts more than who we are.

There was a time when the American culture was focused on individualism. This may have partly been the cause for America's incredible success and power as a nation. But today, researchers like James Masterson and Christopher Lasch say, "healthy individualism" has been replaced by "pathological self-centeredness." As a result we are dealing with a culture where "realistic, adaptive social standards" based on our human legacy have been replaced by a culture of "exclusive, obsessive self-gratification."

Pleasure of Instant Action

Our culture is fast, very fast: Fast food, instant Internet access, fast computers, fast cars, fast trains, fast jets, fast frozen dinners and fast conversations. We hate waiting, even for our coffee in the morning. Everything must happen now, preferably with little to no effort. Our culture is caught on a hamster wheel that is turning so fast that most of us cannot jump off. Or worse, we don't want to jump off.

When our bodies tell us we are tired, that we need rest from our hectic lives, we decide otherwise. We drink caffeinated energy drinks that help us to keep going in order to party in cities that never sleep or to watch television that never stops or to simply keep working.

With its focus on short-term gains, stock exchanges all over the world have become casinos and the most important characters in modern society. It is ironic that we are humans because we have the ability of future-mindedness, but we give an institution focused on the short-term all our power and respect.

In our culture, role models snort cocaine, only to be given bigger contracts by fashion magazines. Politicians are caught lying, only to be offered millions for their story or offered a role on prime television. A probable murderer was paid a lot of money to write a book on how he would have murdered his wife.

Our culture rewards those who show no control over their instincts. Compare this to studies that show the healthiest communities in America are places where parents reprimand the misconduct of children from other families.

Human Value: Humanity and Love

The best of humanity know we are humans because we can and must relate to others, especially through non-verbal right-brain-to-right-brain communication. So they know how to express themselves fully and authentically in intimate relationships. They see other people's best interests as being as important as their own. They have a never-ending and respectful appetite to understand how others differ from themselves. An acting teacher once said, "The difference between a great actor and a very good actor is not technique, but the ability to understand the human condition." This is at center of our humanity.

Hating Love

"We have a longing to be free of longing," Christopher Lasch wrote. Our culture does not want to rely on people close to us. So we do not: 25 percent of people say they have no one to talk to about painful events. Overall, Americans moved from three intimate relationships per person to two over the last few decades. We rely on self-sufficiency and technology to get us through the tough days. We believe our "friends" who make us feel "in" and our work are more important than our family and community.

As for love, the only true romance is real romance. Perfect idealized love is fashionable, intimate but imperfect love is out. So we approach our marriages like we approach the stock market. If the stock is not hot anymore, call the broker. There is sure to be another one he can recommend.

We do not talk to one another around dinner tables. Two-thirds of Americans do not eat around a table together. Of the remaining third, half eat dinner together with the television set on. Our culture does not realize that time together without distractions at the end of the day is important fuel for the Real Self and our happiness.

At work, profit counts more than people. We treat people like objects, replacing them whenever we feel like it or throwing them out in the street so we can keep Wall Street happy. Many bosses on top of the dollar factories feel they can scream at us without any repercussions. After all, they are star earners, so why reprimand them?

Alone, but not wanting to admit it, we turn to technology for escape and a bit of love. On average, we are exposed to 8.5 hours of television, computers, cell phones, GPS devices, PDAs and other screen technology every day.

"I just do not understand it. We live in an age where we have all the tools to connect with people, but we never connect," a twenty-something woman complained to me.

"People are constantly saying, 'I first need to check my Blackberry,' but then never get back to you. Or people think it is fine to call a half hour before a social appointment and cancel," another chimed in.

Our frenetic pace of work and study combined with hours in front of screens make us very lonely people. Persistent lack of human contact has led many high school students to hug everyone they know, whether they are friends or not. This phenomenon has forced schools to ban hugging or put in place a three-second rule.

"Maybe it is because all these kids do is text and go on Facebook so they don't have human contact anymore," a mother speculated to *The New York Times*.

We also have designed a game of building people up to see how quickly we can break them down. We love making our heroes zeros. We love to hear how others self-destruct or were caught drinking and driving. The Germans use the term schadenfreude: other people's traumas bring us joy. Ask Britney Spears, Mel Gibson and other celebrities we just love to hate and hate to love.

We gossip, or watch movies about gossip, or read magazines that are filled with nothing but gossip. We support talent shows like *American Idol*, where judges are paid a lot of money to make fun of fellow humans performing before millions of viewers. Regardless of whether they are doing it for fame or because singing is their passion, they have guts. We sit at home and laugh with the judges, because we are ashamed at ourselves for not going out there and doing the same.

Human Value: Courage

The best of humanity embody physical valor on battlefields or during traumatic events such as September 11, 2001. They show moral valor to fight for what is right or to stand up and confess to mistakes. They stick to commitments and relationships that are good for them or their community. They pursue their goals while remaining flexible, realistic and positive. They get the job done without hurting people. But most importantly, they have the guts to remain true to themselves.

Cheats

Our leaders have created a moral vacuum. Bill Clinton thought nothing of telling the world under oath that he had no sexual relations with Monica Lewinsky. George W. Bush refused to admit publicly that there was no conclusive evidence of weapons of mass destruction in Iraq. Wall Street leaders told the world that they had no clue that their companies were in so much danger, claims disputed strongly by insiders. We lie, believe that others believe our lies and then are surprised if they lie.

Not surprisingly then that 90 percent of 25,000 high school students have admitted to cheating on school work or examinations. Another study shows that rates of cheating have quadrupled over the last few decades. In a culture where finishing first means being the best, the ends justify the means.

Spineless

A 28-year-old lawyer is living the life that many admire: Billionaires fly her to ski resorts all over the world, major news channels have interviewed her, she is invited to fancy parties. She seems to have it all. Still, she confessed, "I know I do not have the courage to face physical hardship."

On the surface, today's youth seem to be confident and capable. But, a lot of the courage is based on a fantasy. After a lifetime of being the center of attention in their households and getting whatever they wanted, many lack true courage, the courage needed in the face of scarcity and danger. Not surprisingly, some parents have noticed with dismay that their children react with frustration and anger when life slaps them and informs them that we all have limited abilities and means.

This lack of courage is daily evidenced by how many of us shy away from committing to meaningful relationships at work and home. We live in a culture that wants to keep our options open. We believe there will always be a better tomorrow. Everything can be "upgraded," stocks sold overnight, spouses changed as the wind blows. We commit to nothing for too long. So 50 percent of first marriages and 65 percent of second marriages end up in divorce. Management slashes employees without thinking of the cost on their lives or their families. Lust in bed and flexible labor markets drive the decisions, not moral courage to do what is right by other people.

But where we lack the most courage is in being OK with who we are. It takes psychological valor to live life with honesty, humility and integrity. It takes courage to say, "I am good enough for who I am. I do not need a mask of success to fit in with others. Nor do I need to flaunt my accomplishments."

Human Value: Justice

The best of humanity care more about being kind and caring than being "in." They can give group goals as much importance as their own. They know we are human to help one another, not to stand on top of one another. They have respect for their fellow humans, but only follow those who deserve to lead. They are focused on fighting for freedom and equality for all. They know how to lead people to just and humane goals by focusing on both the task and the people. They know that the best way to lead is to make the person next to them look like a star. The best of us also know that justice is only possible if we do not withhold respect, rewards and power from groups other than the privileged few.

Money Matters

Over the last 30 years, the top ten percent of all Americans moved from earning 33 percent of all reported income to 48.5 percent. The gains went mostly to the top one percent, whose average annual income in 2005 was $1.1 million. The average incomes for those in the bottom 90 percent barely changed.

Studies show that an increase in IQ can help erase poverty and inequality. Richard Nisbett, a professor of psychology at the University of Michigan, in his book, *Intelligence and How to Get It*, advises parents to encourage effort, not success; praise curiosity; minimize reprimands; and teach kids temperance. But in households where parents struggle to keep food on the table, there is often not enough time to give this type of nurturing. We are ensuring that the poor remain so, trapped in their struggles.

For many people living in Brooklyn, Queens, the Bronx and Staten Island, earning $200,000 or more per year would make them feel rich. But 40 percent of all people living in Manhattan believe that earning $500,000 per year would make them wealthy—an amount that rich people most likely would agree with. When asked "Does seeing other people with money make you feel poor?" the group that was most likely to say "yes" was the group that earned $200,000 or more per year! The author of the article, James Traub, concluded: "To earn $200,000 in New York's most rarefied precincts is to be made aware on a daily basis how modest is your place on the city's socioeconomic ladder."

We are creating a permanent hierarchy of those who have tons, those who have, and those who have not, robbing the latter from living up to their full potential and achieving a good quality of life.

Colorblind

Race still plays a role in our culture. Hundreds of thousands of online tests done over the last decade found that three-quarters of whites have a non-conscious pro-white/anti-black bias. This bias is present in white children from the age six onwards. Of all races, black people are less likely to show bias. When they do, half show pro-black and half show pro-white biases. Some of us are so worried about being seen as racist that we pretend to ignore difference. But white people who affect colorblindness come across as more prejudiced than people who acknowledge differences. Researchers find that the only way we can improve our non-conscious biases is to help people recognize the faces of people of different ethnicities. When we see the unique individuality of people who are of different backgrounds than we are, we forget about stereotypes. To deny that many of us are still discriminating on race is to deny truth. To deny our differences while our non-conscious mind keeps us reacting to it results in prejudice. Many people of color still find this a daily reality in the United States and elsewhere. Today, being Latino/a or Middle Eastern can be a significant liability in certain places.

Old versus Young

Historically, cultures have treated their elders with respect. They were constantly sought for their life wisdom, which gave older people meaning and a sense of purpose when they stopped being able to physically provide for the family. They kept on living through their children.

Today, with a growing faith in the wisdom of technology, we have no more use for the wisdom of the old. We call them old-fashioned and out of touch with what really counts. Some believe that a fear of becoming obsolete, like an old IBM computer gathering dust in the basement, is driving our obsession to stay young.

In return, we have created a holy altar for children. Many homes seem to revolve around their smallest inhabitants, who just cannot do anything wrong. Children are not taught boundaries or to be considerate of other people, whether they are other children or adults. From the time they are a few weeks old, parents walk their babies in strollers as if they are royalty on the pavements of New York. Everyone needs to give way: The prince is on his way to the park.

They must have all the toys and sweets the neighbors have or we are made to feel we are terrible parents. Parents permit everything their children do and defend their misconduct at school. They allow their teenagers to drink or go clubbing when they want. Children are dictating their parents' behaviors. Being seen as hip or their kids' buddy seems to be more important than being a guiding parent. There is a middle way between the "children should be seen and not heard" of previous generations to "children should be seen, heard and given everything they want" of today.

Being "In"

Britain's Got Talent delivered another surprise hit in Susan Boyle. When Susan walked on stage, everybody could see that she was not young, skinny, wealthy, pretty or dressed in fashionable clothes. When she stated her dreams of becoming a professional singer, people laughed and rolled their eyes. Just before she started to sing, Susan smiled, as if to herself. She knew what was coming. Her voice delivered.

Afterwards, Amanda, one of the judges, had the honesty to say, "Everybody was against you. We were all being very cynical. That was the biggest wake-up call ever."

Because Susan did not fit today's criteria of what is "in," people were expecting her to fail.

At St. Paul's University, a group of women were kicked out of their sorority for not being "cool" enough. Read: They were not attractive and hip enough. An overachiever friend, upon seeing two overweight and unattractive lovers kissing passionately, said, "Oh, it is wonderful that they found love." Her subtext: They are so ugly, but at least they have one another. In Hollywood, great actors are not invited for auditions because they are not skinny, young or attractive enough. Here on the East Coast, it is the elite degrees and money that separate the super humans from the failures.

We have come a long way in addressing many prejudices based on religion, race and sex. On all these criteria, a lot of work is still left to be done. But we have replaced these prejudices with others.

Human Value: Wisdom and Knowledge

The best of humanity live a life focused on building self-esteem based on self-knowledge, self-expression and self-actualization. They also respect their emotions, imaginations and the power of language. Experiences, emotions and craft are as much, if not more, valued than book knowledge, IQ and showmanship. The best of humanity constantly challenge their beliefs and non-conscious habits and creatively replace them with new beliefs that help them live more authentically. They hate that which is false in them. They love learning new skills and gaining knowledge not only for the sake of expanding their expertise, but because learning new tasks helps them learn more about themselves. They seek new and uncertain experiences. They embrace failures. An increase in consciousness, seeing the bigger picture and in understanding the complexity of life drives their behavior. As their knowledge of self and life increases, the best become sadder, wiser, more humane and more powerful. But they continue to see the humor in their lives.

Self Knowledge versus Knowledge

I have not heard a single parent say, "I am worried that my son is not making enough effort to understand himself." But I know many parents who make their children worry about what pre-K school they should get into so they can do well in order to go to their next school of choice to then go to an elite university of choice to go to a job of choice to go to a gravestone of choice. Within this linear path, all that is important is stars on foreheads, number of distinctions, GPAs and money made at work. Failure or bad grades are met with frowns. But, as we learned earlier, if we do something for the reward, we do not experience flow easily. Without flow, there is no self-growth or increase in self-knowledge.

When reporters asked a large group of employers about their biggest concern for the new generation of Americans, they mentioned reading and writing abilities. In Britain, researchers called in American specialists to help them figure out why is there such an increase in language problems among youn children. Publishers tell us that people do not read that much anymore. When they read, they use the Internet where they can quickly skim important points. Teachers complain that many children lack the ability to connect their emotions to words and words to their emotions.

Rene Descartes may have originated the distrust of emotions, but our obsession with the power of technology has undermined our emotions, the oldest and wisest computer we have. As Bill Gates said, "It's all about IQ. You win with IQ." But Einstein had a different idea, "The most beautiful thing we can experience is the mysterious. It is the source of all true art and all science. He to whom this emotion is a stranger, who can no longer pause to wonder and stand rapt in awe, is as good as dead: his eyes are closed." He also said that imagination is more powerful than knowledge.

Parents and schools are obsessed with certification, not education. If they were, our culture would emphasize emotions, language, imagination, critical thinking and self-knowledge more than standardized testing. After all, due to our information boom, even what we study at elite universities is quickly obsolete.

Conscious Will versus the Herd

Our society is based on the belief that every man and woman has a conscious will to evaluate all data and act with full awareness of intent and potential consequence. I have shown in earlier chapters that this is not the case. In the Millgram experiment, two-thirds of people are prepared to shock a "student" to death just because a professor told them it is in the "students'" best interest. This study was replicated all over the world with the same outcome.

David Brooks wrote in *The New York Times* about the Wall Street debacle: "To me, the most interesting factor is the way instant communications lead to unconscious conformity. You'd think that with thousands of ideas flowing at light speed around the world, you'd get a diversity of viewpoints and expectations that would balance one another out. Instead, global communications seem to have led people in the financial subculture to adopt homogenous viewpoints. They made the same one-way bets at the same time."

The idea of people behaving as part of a group without an identity has been discussed for decades. German philosopher Martin Heidegger called people without a conscious will "Das Mann," Friedrich Nietzsche used the term "herd animals" and Danish philosopher Soren Kierkegaard talked of the "crowd people." The idea of the people getting lost in the masses has always been a problem. Today, with Facebook, Twitter and constant access to mobile devices, the prevalence of the herd is much more problematic. All over the world, people forsake their own cultures and customs to join a global way of thinking and doing. As an example, watch the conformity in clothes, music and video culture among members of generation Y all over the world. Being part of the masses is in, individuality is out. Peer pressure is in, self-reflection is out.

The daily newspapers are becoming an extinct species. Every day one reads of another newspaper company folding or going exclusively online. For news, more and more people go to the Internet. But herein lies the problem: People are creating what an MIT academic called "The Daily Me," an online source of information that we use to understand the world. But we only read what we want to read, and what we want to read is often blogs and reports that support our views of the world. We avoid news or facts that frustrate us.

Nicholas Kristof of *The New York Times* writes, "The danger is that this self-selected 'news' acts as a narcotic, lulling us into a self-confident stupor through which we will perceive in blacks and whites a world that typically unfolds in grays."

Professor Haidt, author of *The Happiness Hypothesis,* countered by saying that it is not The Daily Me that is the cause for our narrow views. Even before the Internet, people confronted with information counter to their own intuitive feelings did not change their minds. Knowledge does not make people more open to new ideas. So what does? Prof. Haidt tells us that only when we become friendly with others with opposing views will we consider their point of view. He neatly tells us that to open someone's mind you must go through his heart.

His point is valid. The only problem is that good communication and debate between people seems to be waning. We communicate through technology rather than face-to-face. Is there a difference between reading a book and reading an email from another person whose eyes and heart are out of sight?

There are other reasons to think we are becoming narrower in our knowledge. Books titled *True Enough: Learning to Live in a Post-Fact Society* and *The Big Sort: Why the Clustering of Like-Minded America is Tearing Us Apart* support the idea that we are becoming smarter in knowledge that defends our views and that help similar minded people in communities all think and act alike.

"Democracy, at its best, rests on a foundation of mutual respect among co-equal citizens willing to take the time for serious debate. After all, even on the momentous issues that divide us, there is usually the possibility that the other side has a good argument," Stephen L. Carter, Yale law professor, wrote. But then he discusses how we will only take 150 words out of a 2,300 word speech to form a bumper sticker-like slogan with which we can "paint our opponents as monsters." Once smeared as monsters, he says, who cares what they really have to say? Democracy needs dialogue more than it needs bumper stickers.

Whether through our Daily Me's, bumper sticker slogans or following the herd on the Internet, we become less likely to challenge our worldview. The result is that we remain less conscious of ourselves and the world, making us ideal targets for more herd behavior.

Fantasy versus Reality

I met a woman at a Yale Alumni meeting in Manhattan. During the cheese and wine, she told us how she encouraged her son to see the movie *The Pursuit of Happyness* so he can learn how much people struggle to reach their goals. In the movie, based on a true story, the protagonist fails in every endeavor, despite hard work, friendly smiles and noble intentions. He loses his wife, his home, all his friends and every cent in the bank. But the man had the courage to prevail. In the last five minutes of the movie, we learn that the protagonist succeeded in achieving his dreams in real life.

No doubt the movie is painful to watch if you believe happiness is your right, a gift from the government or your parents. But I nearly burst out laughing when the woman told us that her son did not last half an hour before he ran out of the room. Today's children watch movie after movie filled with life's most gruesome horrors where blood and body parts fly from beginning to end without even blinking. But a movie about the realistic struggles for happiness sends them running for cover.

And it's not only the young who react negatively to the prospect of watching a struggle. A 40-year-old American friend said of the movie, "I heard it's a downer. No thanks." Another man, about to become a father, said, "I want to go to movies to escape. I do not want to be reminded of life."

The need for our culture to escape into fantasy is evident in the increase of use and purchase of videos. The movies we love also say a lot: Romantic comedies win, serious drama loses. Movies that distort the truth—a prostitute marries a rich investment banker or a knocked-up mother finds true love—scream against all the hardships that prostitutes and many knocked-up mothers face, but they are adored nonetheless. Movies that glorify violence, revenge and retribution are box-office hits.

Like with chocolate, alcohol or comfort food, enjoying escape movies in moderation is part of living in our culture. But we seem to use media and entertainment to create a view of life that is fantasy. So we come to believe that when we experience sorrow, loss, aging or death, life is unfair or someone else is to be blamed. We believe work must be easy and without suffering or struggle. We believe nature can be harnessed through technology. We believe aging can be stopped through by a scalpel or a skin product. We believe that if we say "40 is the new 30," it must be true. Our culture believes in perfection, pampering and predictability, while the wise believe in long term planning, imperfection and struggle. We use a lot of denial to keep reality from slipping into our fantasy.

Human Value: Transcendence

The best of humanity know they deserve appropriate entitlements, pleasure and mastery as they strive to fulfill their potential. They give themselves the time, permission and mental space to experience flow in our work, love and day-to-day activities. They are grateful for what they have and for the good in their lives. They can forgive and forget others for their past mistakes and control their impulse to be vindictive. They realize that forgiveness is as much a gift to ourselves as it is to those we forgive.

They realize that all the money in the world means nothing if they do not find meaning and purpose in life or see its daily miracles. They outgrow childish habits, but treasure the childlike qualities of play and wonder. They maintain a sense of humor about themselves and life. They experience themselves as an entity constant across space and time. They know they are the same confident, unique person, whether they have wrinkled eyes, a bald head or sagging boobs. They know they belong to something greater than their own lives: to Life, God or the collective human conscious.

Me, Myself, I

"Do not ask what your country can do for you, but ask what you can do for your country," John F. Kennedy famously said. Anton Rupert, a famous South African business magnate and my father's last employer, had his version, "A person of character gives more than he takes."

To experience transcendence, we need to experience interaction from deep inside ourselves with something outside our skin. Transcendence is a dynamic interaction between ourselves and all of life, a to and fro flow of energy, attention and appreciation.

Our self-centered culture is more focused on what we can get than give. Our drive to enjoy pleasure and admiration is more important than selfless contributions to life. But selfishness sabotages transcendence. Without transcendent experiences, there is no chance at finding meaning and purpose in life.

Puppy Attention

In my apartment building, I often see puppies in the elevator. To see young innocent life fumbling over its own feet is a wonderful sight. But what always amazes me is how little focus these puppies have. They rush toward you, then toward a shoe, then sniff the floor, then sit down for no reason. It is only after a few months of life and conditioning that they become a typical home pet.

Our culture reminds me of a restless puppy. We cannot keep our focus for long on a single task. We can listen to music, surf television channels with a remote control and send a friend an email all at the same time. Research shows that we are so good at multitasking that we can fit 27 hours of activity into a 16-hour day. We are puppies with a remote control in our hands.

"There is time enough for everything in the course of the day, if you do but one thing at once, but there is not time enough in the year, if you will do two things at a time," Lord Chesterfield wrote. To him, focused attention was the hallmark of a genius, whereas the "hurry, bustle and agitation are the never-failing symptoms of a weak and frivolous mind."

Isaac Newton believed all his discoveries were not due to talent, but to "patient attention."

The psychologist William James wrote that focused attention is a hallmark of a mature mind whereas the "extreme mobility of the attention" in children "makes the child seem to belong less to himself than to every object which happens to catch his notice." He believed that it is our human ability to repeatedly focus the wandering mind that "is the very root of judgment, character and will." His predictions were proven right: Researchers like Csikszentmihalyi today have shown that only those who can focus their attention on a task for long periods of time that can experience flow. Without attention, there is no flow, and no psychological growth.

We are a culture of multitaskers: We use technology to do, see and hear as much, as fast and as often as possible all at the same time. And multitasking is increasing: In 1999, we only spent 16 percent of media time simultaneously using several different technologies, such as television, the Internet, video games, text messages, telephones and e-mail; in 2005, we spent 26 percent of our media time multi-tasking. But do not think it is only the young; people from their 20s up to their early 50s multitask for essentially the same amount of time.

Research shows that if we complete each task separately and avoid multitasking, we will do more hours of work than we would otherwise. At first blush, this sounds wonderful. We are so much more productive than any other generation. But when we are constantly distracted by e-mail and phone calls, our IQ can actually diminish. We also start exhibiting symptoms of attention deficit disorder.

Brain scans show that it is our human brain that helps us with multitasking. But when we answer a call or an email, it takes our human brain 25 minutes to focus back on the original task. It takes the brain a lot of time and energy to task-switch. A tired human brain can focus less on important tasks and is more susceptible to cave in under our animal brain needs. Frequent task-switching also increases stress hormones, which have a significant effect on our health and short-term memory.

Russell Poldrack, a psychology professor at the University of California, Los Angeles, writes, "We have to be aware that there is a cost to the way that our society is changing, that humans are not built to work this way. We're really built to focus. And when we sort of force ourselves to multitask, we're driving ourselves to perhaps be less efficient in the long run even though it sometimes feels like we're being more efficient." Christine Rosen of the New Atlantis believes that multitasking is giving rise to a generation "of great technical facility and intelligence but of extreme impatience, unsatisfied with slowness and uncomfortable with silence" and as a result "their culture may gain in information, but it will surely weaken in wisdom." Other researchers claim multitasking is giving birth to a nation that isn't "going to do well in the long run" and will posses "very quick but very shallow thinking."

Quick and shallow focus is an unbridgeable obstacle for transcendence.

Culture is Sick

Our culture is not living up to our human values. We are off the charts of what is acceptable for our humanity. Vaclav Havel, playwright-turned-prisoner-turned-President of the Czech Republic-turned one of the foremost thinkers on humanity, agrees with the diagnosis. He wrote,

Whenever I reflect on the problems of today's world, whether they concern the economy, society, culture, security, ecology or civilization in general, I always end up confronting the moral question: what action is responsible or acceptable? The moral order, our conscience and human rights—these are the most important issues at the beginning of the third millennium.

We must return again and again to the roots of human existence and consider our prospects in centuries to come. We must analyze everything open-mindedly, soberly, unideologically and unobsessively, and project our knowledge into practical policies.

Either we will achieve an awareness of our place in the living and life-giving organism of our planet, or we will face the threat that our evolutionary journey may be set back thousands or even millions of years. That is why we must see this issue as a challenge to behave responsibly and not as a harbinger of the end of the world.

The end of the world has been anticipated many times and has never come, of course. And it won't come this time either. We need not fear for our planet. It was here before us and most likely will be here after us. But that doesn't mean that the human race is not at serious risk. As a result of our endeavors and our irresponsibility our climate might leave no place for us. If we drag our feet, the scope for decision-making—and hence for our individual freedom—could be considerably reduced.

Our patient is very sick. He may have a moral cancer that has metastasized throughout his whole body preventing it from functioning the way it was designed. But what is wrong?

Diagnosis

To figure out what is wrong, we need to highlight the main symptoms and signs found in our examinations. The following jumped out at me: instant gratification, ego, vanity, greed, pleasure seeking, admiration, fantasy bubble, escape from reality, objects, fear of intimacy, hierarchy, herd mentality, selfishness, self-centeredness, emotional illiteracy, lack of attention, lack of self, no conscious will, romantic love obsession, "me, me, me."

If we ask a professor of humanities what she thinks is going on, she will see the sins discussed in Dante's *Inferno*.

If we ask a theologian, he will see strong signs of the seven deadly sins.

If we ask an evolutionary psychologist, he will see signs pointing to an animal brain consciousness. But, he will add, this problem is even more dire. Animals consume what they can until they are full. They are also often too tired to go after more than what they need. Animal greed is checked by limited energy. With our ability to share jobs, cooperate and use tools, we have excess energy after our stomachs are full. So our culture is using human abilities to chase animal needs without our brain being able to tell us, "Enough is enough."

With my interest in child development, I see one umbrella concept: A toddler stuck in his grandiose fantasy bubble.

However you want to diagnose the problem, we can agree: We are not following goals essential to our humanity. We are reverting back to a consciousness that befits an animal or a one-year-old child. We are moving away from what is important to the Real Self. Our human soul is suffering.

Cause of the Regression

To find a cure, we must first find the cause of the problem. This brings us to the question: What has happened over the last 50 years that has brought such a drastic weakening of the Real Self? The increase in our reliance on technology jumps to mind.

A few points of evidence support this cause: Technology is helping to create a herd mentality through the Internet. We are replacing intimate or face-face communication with screen communications. Multitasking is decreasing our ability to concentrate, which is preventing us from experiencing flow and growing the Real Self. We are using technology, such a Facebook, to give purpose and meaning to our lives, instead of finding purpose in Real Self activities. Technology helps us to maintain our very narrow window of life through the Daily Me online newspapers. Technology, especially the media, is used relentlessly to stimulate our animal brains and its instincts, while telling us that we are only good if we are beautiful, an elite graduate, rich, famous or romantically in love. Since we all still need positive feedback from the environment, technology is helping us to focus on the false self, not the Real Self. Parents, instead of spending intimate time with children, throw them in front of television sets to keep them quiet. Children are robbed from caring eyes to strengthen their Real Selves. Or parents, unwilling to change their lifestyles after having children or addicted to their mobile devices, do not give their children proper or adequate attention.

With all its positive effects on our lives, we have to admit that technology used as it is today is changing our human souls and Real Selves into robots. But technology, systems or structures are never the real causes of problems, in and of themselves. After all, if we see how social networking sites and Twitter helped to organize an uprising in Iran and keeping the world informed of the conflict, we can conclude that technology can be beneficial for people who oppose power and its media. Technology can also help lonely people find others online and keep them engaged with life. Technology is neither friend or foe. It is how it is being used by those in power.

The key question is: Who is using the technology to encourage us to move toward a more primitive consciousness? Who are the leaders who prefer a herd culture to a culture of conscious will, courage and care for all people, animals and the planet? Why are they chasing these goals? And why are most people following?

Chapter 13

Portrait of a Success Addict

We are the golden boys and girls. Our academic résumés are filled with distinctions and stellar extracurricular accomplishments from the best colleges and universities that we could afford to attend or worked our butts off to get into. Our bank balances enable our luxury homes, imported cars and travels around the world. We are powerful in politics, business and religion. Some of our members are part of the Superclass that rules the world. Our faces are on the cover of popular magazines. We are known and in the know. The Social Darwinists are right: The best of humanity have made it to the top.

There is only one problem. Moments of failure, loneliness or broken relationships turn our golden smiles into coal. For a few seconds, before we distract our hurting selves, we are forced to admit that our success has not filled the gaping hole in our self-esteem, calmed our screams for meaning, brought us real love or filled our lives with a sense of belonging.

Success has not brought us happiness.

Without our masks of success, we feel alone, abandoned and adrift. We know there is only one cure: more success. Success is our Band-Aid, our bottle of whiskey, our cocaine. We are addicted to success.

I never considered that one could be addicted to success. I assumed that everyone was born with the same drive and subscribed to the same definition of success. The only difference between those who succeeded and those who did not was that the latter lacked either talent or perseverance. Why else would one compromise and *only* be a teacher or an accountant? Why else would one not excel in college? Why else would one not have the biggest house, most beautiful spouse and perfect children? Life belongs to the talented, the hard working and the deserving. Life belongs to those of us on top of the human pyramid. Or so I thought.

A few years ago, my struggle with my addiction became unbearable. One day, exhausted from the day-to-day fight for inner peace, I told Dr. Masterson that I had made some calculations and concluded that I must be one of the most damaged patients he had ever treated. He looked at me and said without any judgment, "You are so focused on being the best that even suffering the most is important to you."

It was only then, after many years of therapy, that I finally realized that we Success Addicts may rule the world, receive a lot of admiration and enjoy many privileges, but we are not mentally healthy. We see ourselves, and are even seen by others, as the best of humanity, but we are in the bottom 20th percentile when it comes to our HQ—humane quotient. We lack the six human values that the best of humanity embody so effortlessly.

Grandiosity versus Temperance

My first year as a strategic management consultant was humiliating. I felt insulted by the entry-level work I was asked to do. Searching for facts in the library, conducting telephone interviews with doctors, spending hours on useless presentation documents—all of these tasks were beneath me. I knew that switching careers meant I had to start at the bottom of the ladder, but I also felt I deserved better.

If you had asked me then to describe my character, I would have answered, "I am kind, good, humble, moral and hard working. I want to do good in life and to others. I want to make the world a better place." But my conscious mind was hiding my non-conscious beliefs, beliefs I could not acknowledge. Today I realize that the central non-conscious belief that guided my every decision was: I am special. My life was spent trying desperately to prove this to myself and everybody else.

Unlike us overachievers, the best of humanity have a sense of pride in who they are and what they have accomplished. This healthy form of pride makes them feel confident and unique, while allowing them to see others as equals and keep their best interests in mind. When they achieve their goals or receive admiration, they may have moments where their healthy sense of pride is overshadowed by their animal brain. For a while, they too can feel extra special. But a little voice soon goes off in their heads: "Despite my accomplishments, I know that I am no more entitled than others. We are all doing the best we can in this life." They go into self-care mode in order to slowly deflate themselves, land softly on mother earth and become equal with all again. They can temper their egos. They can remain humble, whether they just made a billion or lost a trillion.

Success Addicts cannot temper our grandiose egos and it's not often that we try. As Dr. Masterson writes, we are motivated by the continuous need for "supplies" to feed our grandiose views of ourselves. We are constantly looking to people in our environment as well as the environment itself—our clothes, cars, homes and offices to mirror our "exaggerated sense of importance and perfection." We are constantly scanning everything and everybody for hints of admiration. We are success addicts and we need admiration as much as we need oxygen.

Not all Success Addicts search for admiration in the same way.

Alphas love to be the center of attention. They will do anything—speak loudly, brag, charm, tell jokes, gossip, drop names, wear Fort Knox on their fingers—to feel everyone's attention on them. If they succeed, they scream from the top of the Empire State Building, "I am God." When they fail, they blame someone else.

The other group, the People Pleasers, including me, do not like to be so openly vain. After all, pride is one of the seven deadly sins. We are polite and well-behaved people who know our place, or so we think. We establish relationships with other people, gurus, groups, friends, partners or institutions that we can believe are special and perfect. Onto these people or institutions, we project godlike qualities of omnipotence and omniscience. We live to impress everyone in this group. We desperately want their recognition (read: admiration). When we get it, we bask in the glow.

When we receive admiration, regardless of its source, we start losing our fragile hold on reality. We start to believe that we know everything there is to know. People should heed our advice, for we are in the know. We are never wrong.

We also start to feel that we are bigger than life. We need to own possessions that fit our self-image. The Alphas in particular go overboard. They build palaces, buy massive diamonds, own large yachts and hire pilots. We do not think of this as excessive. For us, this is precisely what we have always deserved. It is high time the world treat us like royalty.

Some of us even decide it is time to play a larger role on a bigger stage and rescue the world from itself. So we aim for the ultimate jobs: presidents and prime ministers. So business people like Donald Trump and Ross Perot, actors like Ronald Reagan or sports team owners like George W. Bush suddenly believe they know how to run a country. Not only do they believe they can, but they are convinced their countries need them.

Michael Maccoby, psychoanalyst, anthropologist, executive coach and former lecturer at Harvard, has done extensive research into the behaviors of CEOs. At a company where he coached the CEO, a vice-president told him about a joke floating around: What is the difference between Larry and God? God doesn't think he is Larry.

When we are filled with hot air, we can easily forget our family, employees and shareholders. We have the power to make and break. Breaking a few hearts or rules is nothing compared to the importance of the goals we are chasing.

Contempt, Envy, Schadenfreude versus Temperance

Over coffee, I excitedly told an Alpha about a design I was working on for a project.

"Oh, that's so cheesy!" she said.

"You can't say that. I've thought a lot about the design," I countered.

"I can say what I want to say. I say things as they are. I'm just honest, you know," she said.

Success Addicts, especially Alpha types, have perfected the craft of breaking others down. We love to be critical of everyone except ourselves. We flatter ourselves by telling those we hurt, "I am only being honest. I do not lie." But we are lying. We are critical of others so that they can feel like worms in our company, admire us for our insights, and respect us for having the guts to tell the truth. We criticize to feel special.

Some of us will tell people to their faces that we respect their work, but behind their backs we are the first ones to stab them. We cannot take it that there are other people who may be better than us or deserve any form of success. After all, if they are succeeding, then we must be failing. So break them down, ridicule them, laugh at them, undermine them.

We are also envious of other people's success. We know that most people hate to feel envy, but we don't mind. We don't care that brain research shows that envy activates the same area of the brain as food and drink. Who cares that envy is something that even monkeys display to make sure they get what others have and maintain status in the group. Why temper an emotion that can be so painful for us success addicts when it also brings so much joy when our enemies fall on their faces. Who cares if Richard Smith, an author who has written about envy writes, "If you're an envious person, you have a hard time appreciating a lot of the good things that are out there, because you're too busy worrying about how they reflect on the self."

Envy, schadenfreude (the pleasure of seeing someone fall from grace) and contempt are brothers in our arsenal to inflate our grandiose balloon with the illusion that we are humanity's most important people.

Instant Gratification versus Temperance

I am lying at the swimming pool listening to the conversation of many of my fellow New Yorkers:

"We were at Gold Bar last night. $400 for table service. We were plastered," a man tells his friends.

"He is attractive. A friend introduced us. He came home with me," a woman tells a friend over the phone.

"Oh, man, I got smashed. I drank Gatorade with a Red Bull this morning to wake up," says another man in his late twenties as he brags about his night on the town.

We are thankful that we live in a time when humans have made so many products designed to bring us pleasure. So we buy the best chocolates, food and wines. We believe our palates are sensitive, but in reality we only have a greedy animal brain. Sometimes we cannot stop ourselves from finishing a whole bag of potato crisps or chocolates. Even a bottle of wine cannot remain half-empty in the fridge. For our delight, we will consume whatever we can get to give us a kick of pleasure. For some of us, illegal drugs are a must. Without them, life soon becomes boring. Deep down, we are selfish. It is all about "me, me, me" and "now, now, now." Many of us are part of the champagne and cocaine club found hovering about places where bottles of vodka cost no less than $450. Expensive vodka tastes much better than cheap vodka, even if it is the same type of vodka. One of our most famous members is Bill Clinton. He is an instant gratification prince. He is unable to walk pass delicious food or a willing woman.

We also love the pleasure of making money. But we cannot wait years for a reward. Constructing a cathedral over the course of a lifetime or two belonged to the Renaissance. We need to see our rewards this very second, or at least by the end of the quarter. So we take our elite degrees to work as investment bankers and management consultants. The huge salaries fit our huge self-images. Why would we want to do something that would bring us joy or help others if we can make money to buy things that will show the world how wonderful we truly are? With our money, we invest in the stock market, with its lure of short-term rewards. Or we take out mortgages on our homes so we can satisfy our pleasures. Our lives are perfect. Nothing will go wrong. The stock market, like our careers, will only balloon.

We care about our communities, especially when they are composed of people like us, people who are well-educated, drive around in luxury cars and have children who attend Poly Prep, the Dalton School, Princeton or Yale. We love to be admired for our work on the school's PTA. For the rest, especially the poor, we hope that they will get off their lazy bums and start climbing the ladder. This isn't selfish, you understand, just realistic.

Earlier on, I discussed how I went through a period of avoiding anything that could be considered a sin of the flesh: no sex, no alcohol, no meat, no swearing. I felt like an angel for my superhuman abilities to control my animal instincts. The problem was that I was motivated by a need to feel in control of my life. I was also unable to experience any form of pleasure. Even moderate amounts of pleasure or admiration brought on severe attacks of guilt.

People Pleasers can be either party animals or tetotalers, sinners or saints. And some regularly alternate between the two. During phases of being holier-than-thou, we make up for our craving for pleasures by preaching abstinence and becoming examples of goodness. We do not realize that our attempts to be the best examples of morality are only a mask for the shot of natural cocaine we enjoy for thinking we have greater self control than everyone else.

Immediate Action versus Temperance

Alphas believe that when employees make two spelling mistakes in a 100-page document, contempt and rage are deserved. As an executive coach to many Alphas, I tried to help them understand that the intensity and immediacy of their reactions were not justified. Some would look at me as if I was still in diapers. When I was lucky. A few reacted like rattlesnakes.

The temper tantrums of top leaders are legendary. Michael Maccoby writes that leaders such as Martha Stewart, Bill Gates and Steve Jobs are known for their temper tantrums. " [Gates and Jobs] are known for fits of anger and incredibly rude, even sadistic insults, almost always aimed at the stupidity of other people in relation to their own brilliance." He explains that the Alphas scream at others when they do not feel people are supporting them in their grandiose visions or heroics; when they are confronted with the truth, but they do not want to hear it; or when they feel people are preventing them from being rewarded for their work. Maccoby described how Jim Wolfenson, then president of the World Bank, had screamed at his subordinates, saying that it was their fault that he has not received the Nobel Peace Prize.

These examples come from corporate America. But I have witnessed the same tantrums among surgeons in the operating room, actors I've directed, parents of friends and coaches of rugby teams.

Unlike Alphas, People Pleasers tend not to attack others when they become frustrated with life. Instead, we attack ourselves. When I feel my special status is threatened, the demons in my head go off: "You dumb idiot. You are so stupid. You deserve to be slapped." Or we take it out on objects.

There was a time when Stephan, one of my oldest friends, refused to play golf with me. This was because, during almost every game, there would come a moment when I would throw my club farther than the ball had gone, and Stephan had had enough of my tantrums. The reason for my rage was that I felt that I had to be Tiger Woods, even if I only played five times a year. My golf clubs were a perfect release for my bottled up anger against myself.

Energizer Bunnies versus Temperance

Like all Success Addicts, I lived for my work; I did not work to support my quality of life. I believed that to not move forward was to fall behind. But for Success Addicts, moving forward is filled with restless energy and perfectionism, not a mindful consideration for worthwhile goals. Everything is a priority. Our perpetual sense of urgency to complete tasks and our unreasonable expectations of ourselves often leave us mentally and physically exhausted. Or we live by surviving at near burnout levels.

"A work and travel schedule that would exhaust the average person is an elixir," Dr. Masterson writes about us. What a compliment!

Our strong work ethic, the workaholic's favorite defense, helps us to get to the top. The hours that we spend at work show the world that nobody else is as committed to the business or cause as we are. Working long hours results in bragging rights when all the success addicts get together for a beer on Friday nights.

An Alpha friend tells me how he will not sleep more than five hours a night for weeks, before crashing and sleeping away a whole Saturday. He has almost no control over his biorythms. Even as a high-earning adult, he is still the little boy who never wanted to go to bed, who could never switch off.

Over the years, I have seen how other Success Addicts become restless while listening to speeches or presentations. They grab their mobile devices or fidget as if they have ADD. Another Success Addict complains, "I have so much energy, I don't know what to do with it. Maybe I will do a marathon. I am going crazy."

Regardless of our sleep patterns, all Success Addicts are energizer bunnies who cannot sit still for too long before we need to find something "productive" to do during our waking hours. Or we need to go out and play hard to reward ourselves for all the hard work we did throughout the week. We are unable to manage our energy and take care of our needs. We prefer to burn out or burn those around us rather than treat ourselves and others with respect.

We think we are pretty wonderful for working so hard; researchers of the brain suspect we have an immature right human brain that keeps us restless and hyperactive.

Fear As Fuel versus Temperance

At Yale, I was terrified of professors calling on me in class. Their questions were like prison floodlights. "I must know everything about economics. After all, I was first in my medical school class," I believed. My fear also tackled me on the sports fields. Despite playing state-level rugby, I played every game with my heart pumping fear into my legs. Fear of failure prevented me from taking risks or having fun.

As president of the Student Council of the University of Stellenbosch, I met many key South African political leaders, including Presidents PW Botha, FW de Klerk and Thabo Mbeki. I met Mr. Mbeki during his exile, almost a decade before he succeeded Nelson Mandela as the second president of the new South Africa. I also met a number of very impressive South African student leaders and one them stood out more than all the others. John had the charm, knowledge, intellect, physical attractiveness, oratory skills, perseverance and political sense that all leaders dream of having. He was the picture of confidence, if not arrogance. He was also a perfect example of an Alpha. Years later, I met him on a flight from South Africa to New York. My first thought was: "Oh, no! This is the last person I want to spend 20 hours with." But during the flight, I learned that life had scraped a few layers off his face. He told me that he wants to write an autobiography.

"I already have a title for my book," he said. "It's only one word: FEAR."

For some, our inability to temper our irrational fear leads to paranoia. We are often convinced that people are gossiping behind our backs. Or we feel that someone is out to get us. Henry Ford built elaborate escape tunnels at his home; Rockefeller loved secret codes "flavored with paranoia" and warned people to "be careful, be very careful" of friends visiting employees at work; and Bill Clinton often complained, "Why is everyone being mean to me?"

Jonny Wilkinson is a star rugby player. At age 28, he has the record for the most points scored through dropped goals in a test. As England's bachelor of the year, Sports Personality of the Year and World Cup winner, he has it everything except peace of mind. He told a journalist, "The sheer fear of failure destroyed everything that could have been good about [rugby]. He spoke about his insomnia before games and his fears of making mistakes that would cause his team to lose. After a win, he could not celebrate victory either. "I'd lie in bed analysing all the things I felt I'd done wrong. It was an addiction."

Dr. Masterson writes that a Success Addict "living with a death threat, or what is perceived as a death threat, hanging over his head leads a fearful life in which every move to express himself, to allow for his Real Self to emerge, is accompanied by the need to look over his shoulder in fear and panic."

We are unable to temper irrational fears that are pumping from our animal brain.

Self-Sufficiency versus Humanity and Love

As a medical doctor, I faced a few situations in which I had no clue about how to treat a patient. But rather than have the humility to say to my patients, to another doctor or, God forbid, to myself that I did not know what to do, I muddled my way through. I did not have the guts to say, "I don't know."

Success Addicts hate asking people for help. Whether we have to move apartments, need a lift or directions to the nearest gas station, we would rather waste time and energy than ask for help. Special and powerful people don't rely on others. So we tell ourselves that we are self-sufficient, thank you very much.

As an executive coach, my clients often complained about not receiving support from their bosses or reports. The more I explained that radiating a sense of self-sufficiency deters people from supporting them, the more they acted with superiority. They knew they needed to ask, but their non-conscious mind refused to let them reach out.

Researchers studied the behavior of 21 different groups and their leaders. Specifically, they zoned in on the leaders' underlying motives, their leadership styles and the impact leaders have on work climates. When leaders were mostly driven by achievement, did not listen to others and accomplished tasks by leading by example and personal heroics or doing all the work themselves, their teams' morale suffered. Going it alone does not help those we love or work with.

The best of humanity realize that self-sufficiency screams against the most basic foundation of humanity. There is a lot of joy and happiness in helping others and in being helped. That is what makes us human.

Self-Centeredness versus Humanity and Love

I dated another Success Addict for a few months. For a while, life was wonderful. But eventually someone had to do the dishes, clean the bathroom and buy groceries. I was convinced that my girlfriend was slacking off big time. As my frustration grew, I decided to talk to her about it. It turned out that she also felt frustrated and thought that I was not doing anything in the apartment. She also felt she did 80 percent of the chores. Since we both struggled with self centeredness, we both felt that the little we did was the equal of running a marathon.

I read of another executive coach whose client prayed to God every day before work. When the coach asked him how much time he spent talking to God versus listening, he answered, "Of course, I am always talking." Why do we need to listen if we know we have all the answers? Even if it is to God.

I have a reputation of being a great listener. People Pleasers listen a lot, but we listen not out of care, but because we believe we know the answers or we have to be good citizens. We cannot say "no." We need to help everyone, otherwise we are not good and perfect anymore. We also listen to be admired by others. Listening is a an efficent way to receive affirmation, to hear others say, "Oh, he is so caring." Listening was more about myself, my ego and my sense of being special, rather than truly listening to the other person or telling them honestly, "Now is not a good time."

According to Maccoby, the only time Success Addicts really listen are when we want something or when we believe our grandiosity is threatened. Only our survival instinct reminds us that we have ears.

Success Addicts also believe that giving advice to others or critiquing them is the best way to show others, especial those beneath us, that we care for them. The fact that we spend our precious time with them to talk about their lives means we really care. The Alphas among us do not realize that all people occasionally need a kind word or a sympathetic ear to keep them going.

If a boss comes to work with an ingrown toenail, Success Addicts will assume his frowns mean that we did something wrong. If a date suddenly has dust in the eye, we will assume he or she winked at us. If the train is late, we are convinced that God or fate has it in for us that day. Since life revolves around us, everything happens in order to make us feel great or terrible.

Objectification versus Humanity and Love

"He is a ray of sunshine in the class," my kindergarten teacher wrote in my quarterly school report. Later, when I was in grade three, a friend told his mother, "Pierre is like Jesus; everyone likes him." Through hard work and good acting, I maintained my "ray of sunshine" reputation among my family, friends, colleagues and strangers. At university, during a student government election, I earned the most votes in the university's history. In general practice, patients complimented my bedside manner. I was popular, perceptive and positive toward others, or so I thought.

"Children, in our society, are treated as non-persons quite often and so are servants. We feel, perhaps consciously, perhaps unconsciously, that before these non-persons, no mask is necessary. We cannot worry about hurting the feelings of a non-person. How can he have feelings to hurt? This attitude is usually seen as a class-orientated thing. A class in society will apply it to the class beneath; higher-status people will apply it to lower-status people. The boss may not bother to mask in front of his employee, nor the lady in front of her maid any more than a father will mask in front of his child."

With a shock, I realized that Julius Fast's description explained exactly how I treated people who I deemed not as special as me.

Our relationships always have a hidden agenda. We may appear friendly and sincere, but behind our masks of charm and caring, there is only one need: We want our grandiosity reinforced. We can manipulate others so well, becuase we know how we can be manipulated. We know how to make others, especially those in power, feel like a million dollars so they can make us feel like a billion dollars.

If you work for or love Success Addicts, on a non-conscious level, you are nothing more to us than a book when we need information, a body when we need sex, a wallet when we need a new designer-label skirt, a pretty child when we need admiration for our parenting, a chef when we need food. Oh, we will charm you, tell you we love you and need you, "you're the best!" People are less valuable than profit, product or praise from clients.

Because we see people as objects to help us reach our goals, we do not have a lot of interest in who they are, what they are feeling or their dreams and desires. Just as you never stop to consider your computer's feelings as you do your taxes or type an e-mail. But there is a point in every relationship when our view of our objects changes. Maccoby writes that when Success Addicts realize that our objects are imperfect or when we realize that the object actually has a mind of its own, we become cold or distrustful. We like our computers to remain computers.

An Extra Arm versus Humanity and Love

Recall how I dropped my girlfriend's hand when we encountered a group of strangers walking around a fake lake? Success Addicts believe that everyone and everything in our immediate environments—spouses, children, friends, partners, cars, dogs or homes—are an extension of us, an additional arm to our bodies.

Now if you had asked me whether Sonja was part of my body, I would have said, "Listen, I know physics, I can see that Sonja is separate from me." But again, it is not the logic of our conscious mind that counts, but the illusions of our non-conscious mind. To my brain, it was clear as daylight: Sonja is an extension of me. Holding her hand in public was like telling the world: "She is me!"

Psychologist Marian Solomon writes about Success Addicts: "Sometimes all it takes is for the wife to be late to a dinner party and now he's yelling at her, 'How could you do this to me?' [He] has no acknowledgement that this is a separate person, with [her] own needs and thoughts and desires. Just getting a patient to see that can make a difference in a relationship."

Since we are perfect and upbeat, we expect everyone else to be as well. We do not believe in bad hair days. When our partners fail to be perfect, our masks crack. We either give them a cold shoulder or scream at their betrayal. No wonder so many Success Addicts marry or work with other Success Addicts. Only another Success Addict wants to play the game "Let's Be Perfect 24 Hours Per Day."

We also expect our partners in work and love to be 100 percent compliant to our needs—even those needs that we have only thought about but never expressed. Our perfect partners should just know what we want when we want it. After all, an arm does not need specific orders to do what we think. We think and the arm moves. Similarly, we demand partners to drop everything to satisfy our needs when our mind makes a need conscious. Why ask if you can get it automatically?

Our need for perfection and compliance leads to many moments of conflict, which we hate. Perfect people in perfect relationships do not have conflict. Where loving couples use conflict to increase their understanding of one another and become more intimate, Success Addicts either suppress it to maintain the pretense of perfection or even small arguments escalate into World War III.

Jealousy versus Humanity and Love

We are also extremely jealous. A bit of jealousy is fairly common at the beginning of many relationships. The mentally healthy know how to sooth their jealousy or make requests from their lovers to minimize their fear of rejection. Success Addicts are eaten alive with jealousy. We know that when a lover or partner leaves us, we will feel as if someone had torn off one of our arms without anesthetics. We also know the ghost pains of such an amputation linger for years.

But it is not only the enormous pain of unrequited or rejected love that makes us jealous. Despite all our talents, Success Addicts are hopeless at judging whom we can trust in love and work. We often trust those who charm us, but who then end up using us only for their goals and grandiose needs. They do not care who we are and what we feel, only what they can get from us. This enrages us to a point of homicidal or suicidal proportions. Be we do not realize that what was done to us is exactly what we do to others. No wonder so many Success Addicts say, "People cannot be trusted." We don't know how.

Fear of Failure versus Courage

Meredith is an up-and-coming young professional at a prestigious Manhattan law firm. Thanks to her drive, she was promoted and now works closely with a senior partner who, from her description, sounds contemptuous. Within the first ten minutes of our date, Meredith told me that her boss often tells other senior partners that she is smarter than them all.

"They may know more than I do in their field of expertise, but when it comes to the ability to see the bigger picture, I am smarter," the twenty-something said. She talked about her own anger outbursts with her employees. "I have no empathy for people who make mistakes or miss deadlines. If I don't miss deadlines, why should I care why they do? You deliver, or you quit. No excuses."

On the surface, Meredith is courageous, confident, competent and poised to conquer the dragons at work.

"So," I said, "how strongly is a fear of failure playing into your life?"

For a second my unexpected question pricked Meredith's balloon. "In everything I do," she said with an embarrassed smile. Then she started to backtrack. "What I mean is that I set myself unrealistic and unattainable goals. The chances of failure are therefore high. So it is normal to have this fear."

I knew what Meredith meant. I too have always come across as brave to others for my high aspirations. But I had set myself unrealistic goals not only to impress others if I succeeded, but also to have excuses if I failed. I feared failure in simple tasks more than failure while attempting the impossible. Learning how to dance salsa, playing a game of leisurely golf or accepting the imperfections of a date left me more exposed and vulnerable than interviewing for the Rhodes

Scholarship or aiming for a *cum laude* in my final year of medical school. I knew that if I failed, people would still say, "Wow, you are brave for having tried."

Lies versus Courage

"I did not have sexual relations with Monica Lewinsky," Bill Clinton said under oath. "Americans do not torture," George W. said to the world. Michael Maccoby writes about how both Bill Gates and Steve Jobs have claimed to have products that don't exist; how Ronald Reagan truly believed he was in World War II; and how one of his clients would tell audiences one thing and his employees another. Success Addicts lie, or as we will put it, exaggerate the truth to get the job done. To quote one of Maccoby's clients, "You tell people what they want to hear, never the truth. You do not charm with the truth."

Maureen Dowd of *The New York Times*, and arguably the journalist with the most insight into the lives of Success Addicts writes, "For some reason, super-strivers have a need to sell what is secretly weakest about themselves, as if they yearn for unmasking. Edwards's decency and concern for the weak in society—except for his own wife. Bill Clinton's intellect and love of community—except for his stupidity and destructiveness about Monica. Bush the Younger's jocular, I'm-in-charge self-confidence—except for turning over his presidency, as no president ever has, to his Veep. Eliot Spitzer's crusade for truth, justice and the American way—except at home."

Telling lies and feeling guilty about it is one thing. But Success Addicts, especially Alphas, tell lies and believe them. Not only that, we expect time to go back so history can be rewritten to fit our story. Of course Hilary was under sniper fire in Bosnia. Of course, Bill never even met Monica. People are just quoting the wrong history book.

There is a painful lie I often tell: Often, when People Pleasers say, "yes, I will do it," they really want to say "no, I have no time, I'm not interested." I struggle to stand up for myself. Throughout my life, powerful teachers and bosses played with me as if I was a yo-yo. When those in power say, "Jump!" I never dreamed of saying "No!" Nor do we Success Addicts ask why, how high or when. We just assume we must put everything aside—our hobbies, families, friends or vacations—so that we can break the world record for high jumping yesterday. We have no boundaries.

"Of all the things my father did, it was the lies that make me hate him more than anything," a friend confessed. "He told my mother he loved her, showed his care, pretended to be the perfect father, spoke to the world about good relationships and then it came out he cheated on her for years." Success

Addicts do not hesitate to lie to their children. They want to be seen as perfect parents. The truth often spoils a fantastic story. So we tell them we love them all the same, but we favor the smart, sensitive or the attractive. We tell them that they can do what they want with their lives, but manipulate them to consider careers where money will flow into their bank accounts and our community's admiration into our grandiose bubble. We tell them they can marry who they want, but show our strong preferences for the ones with good degrees and family names. We tell them we love them for who they are, but we really love them for how special and wanted they make us feel.

But even worse than this are the lies we Success Addicts tell ourselves. We believe we are special and that everything we do must be perfect, on time and grand. We work hard and sacrifice the one life we have to maintain our mask of success. We do not have the psychological courage to live authentically and humbly among other humans.

Fair Weather Partners versus Courage

The sister of a top investment banker gives the following warning to her brother's girlfriends: "Trust me, he will never cheat on you, but he may drop you tomorrow."

A zebra does not change its stripes. Nor does a Success Addict change the pinstripes on her banker suit when she leaves her office at the end of the day to care for her "loved" ones. Many Success Addicts treat people like they treat hot stocks.

Success Addicts are also notorious for our inability to commit to people or causes if there is no immediate admiration to be found. When we do commit, we often run at the first sign of trouble in our partner, whether from a normal conflict, a physical disease, financial difficulty or aging. We may be the best doctor, mother or banker in the world, but in personal relationships, we are the worst caretakers. After all, aren't our partners or children supposed to look after us? Are they not the ones who need to praise us? Are they not the ones who must be perfect and bring us admiration from our envious competitors?

Perfectionism versus Courage

Remember Sam, the CEO from San Francisco, whose rigidity and unrealistic expectations filled his employees with fear? As part of my initial assessment, I asked him to state five of his most painful and most memorable experiences as a child, as an adolescent and as an adult. Tearfully, he told me how wonderful his mother was. "She was perfect. I was her special child. She even said so to me one day. I still miss her."

When I asked how his perfectionism helps or hurts him, he answered, "My perfectionism allowed me to achieve the grades I did at Stanford. My perfectionism caused our firm to be built on strong internal processes and procedures. My perfectionism allowed our firm to reach the level of client satisfaction we have today. Our clients love us. For over fifteen years, we have never given them any documents with mistakes. Not one."

Interviews with his employees revealed that when they made mistakes, Sam would change into a parental figure, scolding them for not performing as expected. Like almost all perfectionists, Sam expected his subordinates, some of them recently out of school, to be as "perfect" as he is today after 20 years in the business. To him, a mistake means his subordinates are trying to insult him. He then attacks them as if they are little kids who have just walked into the house with muddy shoes.

One complaint I heard from many of my Alpha clients is that their employees do not work hard enough. One client said, "Tom, Dan and Sanjay are the only people who care for this company. The rest I cannot take anymore. They are lazy and not committed to the firm." When I interviewed these "lazy" employees, I heard that they all worked extra hours, weekends and on holidays. But because they are not prepared to work around the clock, they are not worthy of their leader's respect. Because they want a family life, they do not want the company to succeed.

Success Addicts are slave drivers. We set unrealistic goals for ourselves, goals that make a normal life impossible, then we demand those we work with or love to live up to our grandiose dreams. Like all addicts, we not only destroy our lives with unrealistic expectations, but we also often destroy those we lead at work or love at home.

Alphas almost always struggle to create a positive team morale. A client used to scream at his employees when they made small mistakes but said nothing when they did well. My client did exactly the opposite of what is expected from healthy humans: He doubled the pain of his employees and halved their happiness.

When I tried to coach him on giving more compliments to his reports for their work, he reacted like a cobra. "I will never do it. Compliments are a form of manipulation."

Since Success Addicts often use compliments as a way of manipulating people, we assume that when other people give us compliments, they are trying to manipulate us. Success Addicts are unrealistic, caustic and perfectionistic not only at work, but also at home. They expect their spouses, children and friends to be equally perfect. They demand a lot and they give little. Everyone needs to deliver to maintain the bubble of perfection and grandiosity, or you will be sent to the dog box, if you are lucky.

Success Addicts lack the human value of courage, especially moral and psychological courage. We do not have the guts to be ourselves, to lead others with a realistic, flexible and positive attitude. We don't stick to long-term relationships that are important to us. Short-term pleasure and admiration is too important.

Masters of the Universe versus Justice

Recently, I watched an Alpha treating a waiter as if he were the scum of the earth. Never a please, never a thank you. His cold orders left me feeling embarrassed to be sitting next to him.

After barking his food and drink order, the CEO asked another dinner companion, "How do you define yourself?"

"What do you mean?" the confused man asked.

"Well, if you had asked me the same question, I would've said, 'By God and by my family.'"

I nearly burst out laughing. How can you define yourself by God and then treat waiters with such disrespect? I also knew that the chances of him being a good family man are almost zero. An hour later I saw the man trying to chat up the only single woman at the table. Months later, I heard that he had lost both his family and his job. Everybody was fed up with his need to be the powerful one.

We need to be special, the best, the powerful. Our lives depend on this position. It follows that Success Addicts cannot believe in an egalitarian society. Hierarchy must exist and we must be on top of the heap, whether at home, at work or in a restaurant.

Thirsty For Power versus Justice

"Tom knows he is paying us much more than the market, so he thinks he can scream at us and ridicule us. We will not leave him. We are like modern day slaves," a Success Addict complained.

Power has always been an important character in the human story. In my Organizational Behavior class at Yale, I learned that power is the ability to get things done the way one wants them to be done. I also learned that there are many sources of power. Referent power, the strongest power source, is where people admire and respect you and want to be like you. Famous people have referent power. Informational power is having information people need. This is a close cousin of expert power, which is to have knowledge or skill that others need and do not possess on their own. Legitimate power is the right to influence others due to your structural standing in the system. Here we are dealing with power that comes from positions, such as CEO, president, judge, priest. Reward, the final power, is when you can give people something they want for doing what you want them to. Money is today's most powerful form of reward power. Whatever the source, be sure that we Success Addicts will buzz around it like bees around honey. We need a lot of external sources of power to combat our lack of inner power. So Success Addicts stream to Wall Street for money, Washington for structural power and Hollywood for fame. But power is nothing if you cannot exercise it.

Success Addicts in power love to ridicule their employees, partners or children. When someone makes a suggestion, Success Addicts like Bill Gates love to say, "This is the stupidist thing I have ever seen." When employees present their work, they interrupt the presenter to say they know the answer and do not want their time wasted. To allow an employee to take pride in her work is not as important as feeling omnipotent. We are control freaks, unable to trust that anyone can do as good of a job as we can. By micromanaging, we are telling the rank and file, "You are not capable, only I know how to please the client."

Success Addicts who stay at home to raise their children—surely no caretaker could be trusted to raise our perfect kids—become helicopter parents, with their children serving as stand-ins for employees. They think they are being good parents when they enroll their children in language, music, art and athletic classes when they are still toddlers. But this is not about care. Caring parents set their children free to discover life. Helicopter parents wants their children to know how important they are in their lives. Without mom's micromanagement, the children are nothing.

Finally, like King Lear, Success Addicts love to pit employees, children, lovers and waiters against one another to bid for their attention. So they encourage competition within their teams, not cooperation. They love to create an atmosphere of gossip, a cut-throat culture and favoritism. Within chaos, the one with the most power rules supreme.

When we do not have the power, we become abnormally sensitive to those who do. In the company of a distressed boss, parent, spouse or client, we become little children. We have the feeling that a boss or parent is constantly watching everything we do, whether they are continents away or a floor away. Without being in the room, they know when we make a mistake. Even if they are dead, they still make us feel like guilty kids if we kiss someone in public or let our hair loose at a party. We are paranoid about those more powerful than us.

Being "In" versus Justice

Upon meeting a person, my mind automatically and non-consciously boxes him or her based on two criteria: "Is this person 'in'?" and "Does this person like me?"

The "in-crowd" consists of the powerful (parents, teachers, bosses, clients, senior partners and professors), the admired (the bold and beautiful, the rich and famous, the sexy and smart) and the romantic (girlfriends). When my mind assesses whether someone likes me, it really wants to know "Does the person think I am special?" or more specifically "Does this person admire me?"

If you were part of the in-crowd and you liked me, you were my new best friend. I immediately trusted you and would do anything for you. If you were part of the in-crowd, but you did not like me, my mind would scream, "Charm, charm, charm." I would become highly sensitive to your opinion. I would work hard to change your attitude toward me. If you were not part of the in-crowd, but liked me, I would talk to you and say everything to make you feel good about yourself, while scanning the room for someone more important. Once spotted, I would leave you with a fake smile, feeling special for having spent time with a non-person. Finally, if you were not part of the in-crowd and did not like me, I would block you out of my reality. You are a non-person and not worthy of my time or attention.

Dr. Masterson also explains that in the company of a Success Addict, even the mentally healthy experience the pressure to feel either more than they are or less than they are. We are so good at manipulating people that we even succeed in making them feel in or out, even if they normally wouldn't care. The reason we are so obsessed with being "in": We want to surround ourselves with "the right people who will appreciate and advertise [our] best qualities, announcing to the world that [we are] unique, special, adored, perfect and right."

What is "in" is almost always what society admires. If white male is in, we want to be "in" with white males. If black, gay, woman, child, white male, Middle Eastern or poor are out, they are out. Today, the bold and beautiful, rich and famous, smart and sassy are in. The rest simply don't count. Success Addicts have few qualms about discriminating against those who aren't "in."

During a recent reunion dinner at Paarl Boys High, the high school I attended in South Africa, I ran into Paul, an old classmate whom I had not seen for 25 years. Paul and I were in the same class for five years and played rugby together. But at the reunion, I saw Paul for the first time as a man filled with passion and love for his wife and family, a man who could have been a loyal and fun high school friend. He wasn't. At the time, Paul did not fit my criteria for being "in." Despite all our interactions at school, he was invisible to me. I shudder to think of how many hundreds of people I did not see because they were not "in."

As a student leader, I had the opportunity to meet with President PW Botha, leader of the National Party, during some of the toughest moments of apartheid. He was arrogant, paranoid and instilled fear in many. He had contempt for people who did not think like he did. No wonder he was called the "Oud Krokodil"—Old Crocodile. Still, no matter what he did, he was convinced that God was on his side.

All Success Addicts carry within us contempt for those who dare to take away our admiration. Being indifferent or of no use to us can easily turn you into the object of scorn. We do not realize that the contempt we have for ethnic minorities, women, poor people, children or other groups come from the barrelfuls of contempt that we have for ourselves.

Success Addicts are incapable of embodying the human value of justice, despite the fact that many of us are lawyers, judges or leaders of organizations that that fight for justice and equality. Our search for power takes us anywhere there is a power vacuum.

Baboonish versus Wisdom and Knowledge

For most of my life, I thought that I was very wise for my age. I felt like I was an adult, responsible and serious, from the day I left the birth channel. Even in my mid-twenties, I thought I was pretty mature for my age. I recall saying a few times that I felt so comfortable with myself and what I knew about life. Today, I realize I was nothing more than a baboon.

Once, on a visit to the family farm in the Overberg, an area close to Cape Town, my uncle once told us that to catch a baboon, you cut a hole in a pumpkin large enough for a baboon to put his hand through, but too small for him to take his hand out when his fist is filled with pumpkin seeds. A baboon, when stuck to the pumpkin, is too dumb to realize that dropping the seeds will free him. So he clings to the seeds, focused only on the prospect of a full belly. But bliss never comes; the baboon either dies from starvation or is killed by farmers.

I heard this story and thought; "Stupid baboon. Just let go!" But I too had my hands filled with the seeds of success that my meritocratic society and my parents admired. Instead of realizing that my obsession with elite education, beauty, fame, romantic love, parent pleasing and people pleasing would never bring me happiness, I grabbed for more. So I was stuck with a pumpkin for a job, for a love, for a life. I may have thought I was wise, but in reality I did not learn from any of my experiences. Despite earning distinctions at school, I was not wise enough to let go of the hubris I lived with since childhood. I was not becoming more mature . I was working harder and harder to avoid growing up and taking my position as an adult at the table of life.

When Jack Welsch, admired former CEO of GE, was asked about his tragic flaw, he answered, "That's something I've never thought about. I don't think much about myself." Success Addicts are notorious for have no ability to reflect on our behaviour. We do not have a lot of self-knowledge. After all, we are perfect, so why waste important time thinking about failures and shortcomings. We are happy, we had happy childhoods and our parents were perfect. So what is there to reflect on? Others cannot stop talking about our pasts. We had it so rough, we had to work so hard, but look how great I am, for I escaped all of that.

Emotionally Dumb versus Wisdom and Knowledge

Once on vacation, three friends and I boarded a plane to go deep-sea fishing near an island off the coast of Mozambique. Due to rough waters, we never saw a sailfish. But that didn't prevent us from island hopping for a few sundowners every evening. One night, with daylight fading fast, our captain anxiously pleaded with us to leave the bar so that he would have enough light to steer us safely back home. The older fishermen in our party, drunk and overly arrogant, ignored the captain. The brandy and coke kept flowing. When we finally left, the night was pitch black. Soon we were lost. No one had a clue where we were. The drunken men shouted, "We know what we are doing." We were charging full throttle either toward the vast sea or the rocks off the mainland. The survival hormones on the boat reached code red levels. Everyone on the boat started to shout. I did not say a word. As usual, I was Dr. Cool.

After radioing back to the island, they shot up a flare and we arrived home safely. That night, one of the arrogant fishermen came up to me and complimented me on being so composed. I took the compliment seriously.

Today I know that to feel nothing in the face of a life threatening situation is not normal. My happy exterior was hiding an emotional life filled with stormier currents than the seas surrounding our island. In fact, I can count on my hands and feet the number of times that I have allowed myself to be sad, afraid or angry in public. For a man of 40, this number is astoundingly small. I believed only the weak cave in to sadness, fear or anger. We hate emotions because we believe we cannot control them, we think only the weak show emotions and we believe they confuse our cold reasoning. But you either feel emotions or you don't. There is no a la carte menu for emotions.

Alphas do feel a lot of rage, though. Dr. Masterson writes that Success Addicts "use life's ordinary frustrations as a target upon which is projected a deep inner rage." He explains that this deep inner rage originated "from painful childhood experiences that may not be easily recalled because they are too solidly defended against."

Smart overachievers can be very dumb when it comes to understanding the cause, intensity and effect of their rage at people "inferior" to them. They are not conscious enough to know that rage comes from the past, not the present. We can be the smartest people in the world, but if we cannot feel, label and manage our emotions, we will become smarter in our fields, but remain dumb as a two year old to life's wisdom.

The Tortured Thinkers versus Wisdom and Knowledge

While in corporate America, a friend set me up with one of his best friends. "Oh, you'll like her. She is a modern dancer," he said.

I was excited. I envisioned her beautiful toned dancer's body. But then a slight panic struck me. I knew nothing about modern dancing. She will think I am a complete loser, I thought. So that night I searched for a bookstore to find a book on modern dance to read before my date.

I never wanted to be caught in a situation where I did not know something. I was a bookworm not because I loved knowledge and wisdom, but because I hated feeling like stupid when I had no book knowledge about the topic of conversation around a dinner table. Success Addicts are often voracious readers. Our apartments are filled with books. On the surface, we seem to have a lot of knowledge. We may even fit the definition of an intellectual, someone who likes to stretch the mind.

"Unemotional and analytical in their cognitive style, alphas are eager to learn about business, technology and 'things' but have little or no natural curiosity about people or feelings. They rely on exhaustive data to reach business conclusions, but often make snap judgments about other people, which they hold on to tenaciously," the *Harvard Business Review* reports.

A person who gains knowledge without feelings can never comprehend the human condition and gain wisdom. Wisdom lies in our gut-feeling, not in the number of books we have read, how much we have impressed others about what we know or how often we have asked existential questions.

Self-Help Gurus versus Wisdom and Knowledge

One Sunday I followed my gut to brunch at City Bakery. As I sat there, completely dumbfounded that I had walked so far for no obvious reason, I suddenly heard two middle-aged women talking. One was saying to the other, "That's exactly it. If you tell yourself you are bad with directions, you will always be bad. But if you stop saying this, then maybe you can find out if you really are!" My interest piqued. I was sitting next to two self-help addicts, one clearly playing the role of self-help guru.

I listened. They were taking some self-help course in the city. Each one had gone to every self-help course on earth, taken the advanced courses, sharing their inner lives with the masses, crying with them, stating their intentions to them and believing that all this would make their lives better. They still sounded very confused.

I could not look at the guru directly because she was sitting next to me. But her tone of voice had a metallic quality as she gave advice. She was loud. She overpowered the conversation and interrupted her "disciple" without knowing it. The "self-help guru" was approaching the sun with waxed wings. She knew it all, had read it all and attended every landmark conference in the world. Her "disciple" eagerly listened to every word. It is not only a little knowledge that can be dangerous. A lot of self-help knowledge can be dangerous too. It lulls us into believing we know how to live life.

I recalled many situations where I too was Mr. Know it All or "Professor Peanuts," as my mother once called me. Like the guru, I too happily gave my advice to the masses. I still do, but today I know it is a sign I am having a bad day; what I really am saying is, "Please give me a hug."

Too often, self-help gurus on television or around the dinner table are hurt children seeking admiration for what they know about life. But what they do with their lives often shows they are experts in knowledge, but they lack in wisdom.

Hating Feedback versus Wisdom and Knowledge

Success Addicts are caught in a tough predicament. On the one side, we want to hear feedback from other people. We want to hear how we can become the best in our fields. We also need to hear positive comments to keep our balloons filled with hot air. But we have a problem. We hate to hear negative feedback. After all, a major goal in our lives is to deny any weakness in ourselves. So we are overly sensitive to any comment that goes against our knowledge that we are perfect and the best. When we hear criticism, we feel betrayed and we shoot the messenger. After Michael Maccoby gave a CEO critical feedback, he responded, "You know I can fire you." If we don't fire the messenger, we give them the "I have done so much for you and this is what I get in return" guilt trip. Or we just ignore the feedback and pretend it never happened.

If the evidence is too strong and persistent, we will blame the world or other people. We did nothing wrong. We never will blame ourselves first. If that tactic fails, we, like so many discredited CEOs of the last decade have done, justify our behaviours by telling the world we truly only did what we did for the benefit and good for our employees, customers, shareholders and loved ones. We are not to be blamed. We are just misunderstood.

A coach writes how Success Addicts believe that everyone else gets defensive when we give them feedback, whereas we simply speak the truth. We can dish, but we cannot receive.

Neverland versus Wisdom and Knowledge

Success Addicts experience life as our oyster. Everything we want is ours to take; we are the center of the universe. We are wonderful and the world is wonderful. We are guaranteed unlimited power, beauty, ideal love, fame and intellectual success. Rules don't count, nor do other people's needs. We are God's gift to the world.

We obviously do not live on planet earth. We live in a fantasyland. Our sense of self is not based on reality, but on a grandiose fantasy. We live, as Dr. Masterson puts it, not "to cope or adapt to reality but to reinforce grandiosity." When we receive success, we blow up with false pride and vanity and believe that we are God. So we start to isolate ourselves from our best friends, advisers or loved ones, especially those who care for us enough to tell us the truth. But truth is a word in the dictionary, not part of our fantasy. Only our views count and if you don't agree, then you are wrong. In the process, we often destroy relationships, businesses and countries. Or, we surround ourselves with people who will say yes no matter what and who will offer constant praise.

Success Addicts, with our black or white, in or out, for us or against us view of the world, combined with our disregard for emotions and self-reflection, are not the wisest in the class. We may be smart and know a lot about many things, but we do not have the knowledge that will make us wise, happy and valuable contributors to the rest of humanity.

Take and Take versus Transcendence

Being special, we believe the world owes us something. So we take more than we give. When we give, we often give to receive. Even those of us pretending to be selfless enjoy the praise of being kind and caring more than the joy of actually giving. But transcendence only happens when we can be in an active and equal give-and-take with others and with life. Inner shouts of "me, me, me" scream against the prerequisite for transcendence that is "be, be, be."

Success Addicts have created the New York minute of pleasure and admiration seeking at the cost of the eternal minute focused on play and wonder. To have is more important than to lose ourselves in our activities, moments where time disappears, where we become part of something bigger than our lives, something eternal and more permanent than the goals we are chasing. Being in the rat race, we also struggle to enjoy the simple pleasures of life. We cannot enjoy wine, food, art or music without knowing everything about it. We need to be connoisseurs, not ordinary people just having fun with friends around a dinner table.

Forbidden Passion versus Transcendence

At home, being special meant that I worked hard to be my parents' perfect little boy. I made sure that I was up and dressed for school on time; seen, but not heard in the company of adults; never upset with tears or tantrums; and the best in all activities I took part in. Where normal children used their childhoods to explore themselves, especially their passions and emotions, including helplessness, fear or sadness, I used my childhood to please my parents.

At school, being special meant I had to be the teacher's favorite, her A student. I had to be an old soul and a perfect example for other kids to follow. I was never a boy who played pranks and learned through fun and mistakes.

Our beliefs that we are special prevent Success Addicts from discovering our passions. Instead, it makes us obsessed with our rewards. Our beliefs command us to do and be what others admire, not who we are and want to become. Without passion and needing admiration from others, we become part of the herd. We become ordinary and yet, ordinariness is what fear most. Without passion, we struggle to find meaning and purpose.

We are always forced to compare ourselves to the nearest competitor. We cannot be special if we do not prove ourselves to be so every moment of the day. Even though we know there always will be someone smarter, prettier and richer than us, we must keep comparing ourselves against others. This makes us extremely ungrateful for what we have and have accomplished. Life remains a battle one day after the other.

Our drive to be the best in everything we do or know, everything we eat, our abuse of time and energy and our cries for "me, me, me" prevent us from enjoying the moment, from enjoying transcendence. No wonder so many Success Addicts believe there is no higher power.

Diagnosis

Success Addicts do not measure up to our human legacy. We lack the core human values that humanity has been built upon. We do not care that much about others or the planet. We care about keeping our grandiose bubbles filled with pleasure, admiration and all sorts of objects, such as people, diamonds and palaces that make us feel perfect, special and famous. It is through this bubble that we observe ourselves, people and life. We are not in touch with reality. We cannot truly feel the plight of the disadvantaged or appreciate the struggle of the planet. All that has ever and will ever count is maintaining the bubble. Our lives depend on it, or so we believe. We may possess all the power in the world, but we do not possess a healthy Real Self. But what is not clear so far is why we defend our bubble as if our lives depend upon it. It is often in love that we Success Addicts show our real colours.

Chapter 14

Success Addicts and Love

A few years ago, I went to listen to an author read from his book at a local bar. On my way out, I spotted a pretty woman sitting alone, staring deeply into her vodka and soda. Seeing no signs of either friends or boyfriend, I sat next to her, ordered a beer and gave her an interested look. She gave me a quick smile, before peering back into her vodka.

"Tough day?" I asked.

"No! I'm not drowning my sorrows! I went for a walk and ended up here. It's my neighborhood bar. I just live around the corner," she replied.

We were off. The dirty martinis began to flow. We laughed, joked, talked about life's struggles and made a pact that if the conversation got too heavy for more than five minutes we would be required to down our drinks. We touched one another's arms, then upper thighs, then a quick kiss. Olives were seductively placed in glistening mouths, tongues stretching far out, an invitation to a night of carnal bliss. At some point, our masks dropped and Erin—that was her name—began to cry softly.

"Now I know what love at first sight is. This. Even if I never see you again—I know," she said, wiping away her tears with the bar napkins.

A few minutes later, she was back in form and the magical evening continued. On our way to her apartment, we joked with other pedestrians, held hands, danced in the streets and touched each other. Erin's body was a perfect ten—I later learned that she, while at college, was a sports fashion model. She still could be. We promised to meet up the next night.

"There is a God," I sang. I finally met a New Yorker I could see as both a friend and a lover.

Eighteen hours later, and I was preparing for our first date. I was a bit perplexed that Erin reacted like a viper when I wondered where we should go for dinner: "Why don't you figure that out and call me back!" she ordered. I rationalized that she was excited, keen on having a romantic night, a night she had dreamed of during many lonely hours. I did not want to disappoint. So I searched for a restaurant, showered, shaved, tried on three shirts, worried whether I should tuck the shirt in or let it hang loose. I finally settled on letting it hang loose. But as I entered the restaurant, I tucked it back in.

I saw her from a distance. I walked to the stairs, excited, waiting for that moment of reconnection. She walked toward me, her face taut, her smile false and her ballerina body battle ready. She stretched out her hand to greet me; I felt as if I was at a business meeting. Her hand was cold. I tensed. "Maybe it's nerves, maybe she's just shy after her tears last night, maybe it all will be fine as soon as we have a drink." It wasn't. Amidst all the laughter in Chelsea, we looked like a bored, unhappily married couple. The food arrived. Erin had ordered a large bowl of pasta filled with cream and butter.

"Well, my mother says there's nothing better than a big bowl of pasta for PMS. Complex carbs work!"

I responded carefully, "So you mean you are going to eat the whole plate?"

"It will be better for everyone if I do."

Soon she had to run to the bathroom; then she had to make a few business calls; then she had to rush off to a party that she forgot she was invited to—all this while I still had food on my plate and wine in my glass. Then came the goodbye.

"Well, we're walking in separate directions," she declared, making sure I would not walk her home. "So see you soon." I could not help but think how those same lips had promised me heaps of joy the night before, each time I placed a vodka-drenched olive into her seductive mouth.

"Feel better," I ended the evening, the dream and my fantasy that life is fair—again.

I walked home and laughed out loud. Another $140 meal wasted. $140 that my writer's wallet could not afford. Love makes us blind; loneliness makes us dumb.

The Search for Authenticity

Filled with martinis and loneliness, Erin and I connected deeply and intimately. Or we thought we had. But where normal people would have felt excitement, fun and anxiety at such a fast connection, the two of us freaked out. I turned into a little schoolboy, unsure of how to dress and impress. Erin's non-conscious mind made her body a fortress. Filled with anxiety, she crushed the seeds of what could have been an intimate relationship.

Not all intimate relationships begin with an intimate connection. Some start with lust, friendship or romantic love. But regardless of how they begin, there comes a point when a relationship needs to move from pleasure and fantasy toward intimacy, if it's going to last. Having a strong Real Self is essential for the relationship to move forward.

A strong Real Self allows the best of humanity to enjoy self-expression, self-revelation, autonomy and independence, all important for long-term, intimate relationships. They also know how to take care of their partners. The best partners, without any prerequisites, frequently acknowledge, approve and support their partners' Real Self. They view their partners' interests as being as important as their own, not out of neediness, but out of genuine interest and care. They also know that everyone, even those they love, have strengths and weaknesses, good days and bad days, dreams and fears. To them, the wholeness of the partner is more important than the mask of perfection or adoration. They seek authenticity, not fantasy.

People with healthy Real Selves know how to deal with the anxiety and even the moments of jealousy that are common in the first few months of even healthy relationships. They know what to ask for from partners in order to build mutual trust. The best of humanity know life is not always a walk in the park. They know how to share themselves with others regardless of fortune, failure, fair weather or fumbles. They enjoy sharing themselves with one another emotionally, intellectually and sexually. They expect conflicts to arise, but know they can deal with them in a way that will ultimately bring them closer. They know that when they are alone, their partners are still with them, even only in thought. Being alone does not bring on anxiety attacks.

It is clear: An intimate relationship is to the Real Self what running a marathon is to our leg muscles—a tough, enjoyable and strengthening workout. But herein lies the rub for us Success Addicts with our fragile Real Selves. Dr. Masterson writes that being addicted to success is synonymous with having difficult intimate relationships. Often during moments of intimacy, we revert to grandiosity, entitlement, aggression, jokes or intellectualization. We desperately reach for our masks at moments that demand us to be ourselves.

The Triad

But lacking a strong Real Self does not explain all of our negative behaviors surrounding intimacy. After all, if someone without legs is asked to run a marathon, he would probably politely decline and say he cannot. Erin and I treated intimacy as if we were entering a battleground. Instead of fighting courageously, we deserted, fear written all over our faces. For us, the prospect of intimacy felt as if zombies were rising from their graves and pounding at our doors. This is the sad irony of being a Success Addict: We can climb Mount Everest, reach the gilded chairs of Wall Street or sit in the White House, but when it comes to intimacy, we are cowards.

In the world of executive coaching, there is a saying: After a breakthrough comes a breakdown. This describes how people, after pushing themselves into new psychological territory, often have emotional hangovers. They will go from hero to zero in seconds. Dr. Masterson calls this the *Disorder of the Self Triad*. Every time people who struggle with their Real Selves begin to activate them, they feel awful. We start to hate other people, life or ourselves. In order to escape this feeling, we call in the defenses. First, we are forced to drop what we are doing immediately. Code Red it is called. Secondly, we search for psychological supplies. In the case of Success Addicts, we search for any source of admiration. Self-activation deflates our balloon of grandiosity and forces us to face our fragile Real Selves and our inner demons. We are forced to pump that balloon up as quickly as we can. Without the balloon, we will experience the wrath of six terrifying demons hidden in the dark caves of our non-conscious mind.

Demon 1: Depression

I grew up in a country of rugby, barbeque and sunshine, a place where chicken is regarded as being a vegetable. When Afrikaners have dark moods, we tend to take a hot bath, drink a few beers or kick the dog. Anyone who admits to being depressed is seen as a weakling. Who cannot get going when the going gets tough? If you see a shrink, you must be certifiably crazy.

But everybody has depressive moments. "I just feel sad"; "I'm gloomy"; "I have the blahs, " mentally healthy people say. They acknowledge these experiences and deal with them. They exercise, go for a meal, shop, read, turn on the television for a show or two, talk to a friend or hold hands with a spouse. They know bad days, like good days, will pass. Dr. Masterson writes, "It is the mark of maturity that we can get through periods of depression either on our own or with the help of someone who understands us and has our best interest at heart."

Behind our masks of success and contempt, Success Addicts struggle with depression. Depression has many medical definitions, but to me, the best one comes from understanding its opposite. As Alice Miller puts it, it is not gaiety or absence of pain, but *vitality*, the freedom to experience spontaneous feelings. Depression is saying no to our inner self and to life by blocking all our feelings, emotions, sensations and our impulses to stand up for our authentic needs. Depression is saying no to emotions that will help us to understand ourselves and our lives. Depression is locking ourselves in a psychological prison and giving our keys to people whose admiration we seek, people whom we believe to be cool, calm, and collected.

Like a child, my first line of defense against depression was denial. "Perfect people do not have bad days," I told myself. When I struggled, all I could say was: "Life is boring"; "I'm numb"; or "I have no feelings in me."

But the body never lies. If you see how Success Addicts move like stickmen or with the calculation of a ballerina, if you see how we speak with affected speech or a monotone voice, if you see how little time we have to take in the moment, if you closely look into our glassy eyes, you can see all the signs of a body fighting depression, a body void of vitality. But we will always tell you, for we believe the lie ourselves, that we are the happiest people in the world. The top of the world must be happy after all. People must envy what we have, and happiness is another gold medal that those beneath us so desperately crave.

After many years of therapy, after the layers and layers of defenses against the demons have been thinned, I finally am facing the magnitude of my hidden depression. Despite our success and our can-do attitudes, Success Addicts possess levels of despair and sadness that would overpower even the mental healthy. No wonder suicide is such a common way out for us Success Addicts.

Demon 2: Rage

I used to believe that anger was the greatest of all sins. I can recall the five times I lost my temper in the first 30 years of my life. Good boys don't become angry, I thought.

Today I know that anger is a healthy emotion, one that ensures emotional and physical survival. Appropriately expressed, anger allows us to fight for our rights and defend our lives. Anger is the check and balance of all good relationships. When both parties in a relationship know that the other party will become angry if he or she feels trampled upon, they will remain respectful. Anger is our inner police chief; it forces others to treat us with decency and respect. But like all good chiefs, its presence is often sufficient to deter infringements. The French refer to non-destructive anger as "anger of life." They know that anger used well drives us to reach for our goals and live boldly.

Therapy exposed the real reasons why I was so prim and proper. For most of my life, I believed that expressing my anger would mean immediate rejection from caretakers. Anger equaled abandonment. But that did not mean I never felt anger. I suppressed it in my non-conscious to the point where it was like a ton of dynamite forced into a tiny barrel. Later in life, I feared that any outburst of anger would ignite the dynamite. I feared my own power and rage. So, instead of using my anger appropriately, I turned my anger onto myself. People Pleasers are often self-haters.

Alphas are different though. They don't have a problem expressing their anger. They are often seen as walking time bombs, creating fear among employees and loved ones. They love the fact that they are feared. They project their demon onto everyone around them. Everyone is to blame when life is unfair, except Alphas. So they relieve the rage they bottled up in the past by finding someone in the present to blame for their pain.

Demon 3: Fear

I mentioned my irrational fear when I resigned from corporate America. Fear, the third demon, helps animals to survive. Fear helps us to protect ourselves when faced with an oncoming car or a stranger in a dark alley. In these situations, ignoring fear will cause harm or death. Courage is the ability to do something, despite fear.

Irrational fears with no substantiating evidence is called anxiety and Success Addicts, as well as many other people, are riddled with it. We fear failure, uncertainty, intimacy, spontaneity, rejection, death, life, ourselves. We fear people, even those who we view as our inferiors or loved ones—people who would never cause us physical harm. Some Success Addicts have so much fear that they can be diagnosed with posttraumatic stress disorder, a condition common among people who have witnessed or experienced unbearable trauma. Success Addicts may have a golden smile, but below that smile many of us are as traumatized as a victim of war, but for no discernable reason.

Demon 4: Guilt and Shame

At the beginning of the book, I told about how a television crew interviewed me once during my participation in the annual Halloween parade. I felt like a lost deer as I imagined the whole world watching me dressed in a stupid monk uniform. At the time, I thought my feelings arose from being a responsible and mature adult caught in an uncharacteristic moment of juvenilia. But now I know that it was my demons that were telling me, "This is not what responsible citizens do. You are supposed to be a man of status. A doctor." For three hours, instead of being filled with life, joy and exuberance for being part of such a wonderful parade on a beautiful autumn night, I was overcome by another demon: guilt.

Guilt is a newer emotion than rage, fear and sadness, one that humans developed in order to ensure that we do unto others as we would have them do unto us. But Success Addicts experience guilt for all the wrong reasons. We feel guilty for following our own authentic goals, for marrying the partners we want to marry, for living instead of performing. Guilt ensures that we will remain good little boys and girls. Guilt also tells us that if we do what we are told, we will be safe and secure. If not, we will be rejected.

A close ally to guilt is shame. Researchers believe that shame is an emotion we share with all mammals—look at your dog after he has peed on the carpet—where guilt is a higher order human emotion. Shame is the pain for experiencing a drop in status and it has played as big a part in my life as any other emotion. Shame is what I feel when I make a mistake, which proves I'm not perfect. Shame is what I feel for wanting to be true to myself. Shame is what I feel for being a man with animal desires that need to be met in moderation.

I once mentioned to Dr. Masterson that shame should have been included in his list of the six Demons. He acknowledged the fact. Since guilt and shame have the same impact I have grouped them together.

Demon 5: Helplessness

"I just don't know what to do. How do I break into acting? How do I meet the right woman? How do I make money? I'm at a complete loss." I have uttered variations on these themes more times in therapy than I could ever count and far more often than I have said, "I know I will be fine!" Helplessness is the fifth demon.

All people are more or less helpless at any given point in life. Part of the beauty of living a full life is being able to trust others in areas where we do not have expertise or during moments when fate temporarily renders us emotionally or physically helpless. After all, to trust non-family members is one of a few criteria that separate us from animals. These moments also give us perspective on life: We realize we are not in total control of our lives, but neither are we totally dependant.

Dr. Masterson writes, "Although specific incidents can trigger it, it is not caused by specific incidents, but persists like a gloomy backdrop to life, casting a spell over most activities and life situations. Unlike a healthy man or woman who says, 'Well, this is one of those situations at which I'm not very good,' the false self says, 'You are totally helpless and good for nothing.'"

"Totally helpless and good for nothing." I know those lyrics.

Demon 6: Worthlessness

During a rough patch earlier this year, I dreamed of being in a crowded place with many friends and acquaintances. As I mingled, the distinct smell of feces followed me wherever I went. Later in the dream, I removed my shirt. On my back, a gaping wound oozed fecal matter from deep inside me. During a session with Dr. Masterson, I emotionally connected with the dream and I was forced to face a painful truth: Under my golden smile, I possessed no self worth.

None of my accomplishments changed this feeling. I have told friends, "I wish I could take my résumé, eat it and vomit it out. Everything on my résumé is not worth the paper it is printed on. Everything I did was to impress other people. How could one value such a résumé?"

Eugene O'Neill was a Success Addict. A documentary on his life revealed that O'Neill had the habit of constantly looking at himself in every mirror he could find. One day, a friend, noticing that he was again staring at himself in the mirror, exclaimed, "You are one of the most conceited men I know!"

"No," O'Neill replied, "I'm just trying to make sure I'm still here."

O'Neill had a black hole at the center of his being that sucked in all his accomplishments. At the end of his life, Eugene O'Neill, a winner of the Nobel Prize for Literature and four Pulitzers—an accomplishment not equaled by any other American writer since—still loathed himself.

When worthlessness, the sixth and last demon, strikes, a Success Addict feels as if everything he or she has ever accomplished is meaningless. We are incapable of remembering any personal strength or success. We are convinced our lives are empty or a collection of our mistakes and rejections.

We fear our demons more than death, so we spend a lot of time avoiding them. We work hard and sacrifice a lot. When success and admiration are absent, we fantasize, use drugs, drink ourselves into oblivion, watch mindless television, shop endlessly, think until we are intellectual zombies, throw the cat out the window or beat our children. When all that fails, we consider suicide. "Maybe death will kill our demons," we hope.

Due to our lack of Real Self and the six demons in our right human brain ready to torture us every time we try to love another person intimately, Success Addicts are forced to love people with the other areas of our brain: primate brain with its fantasy love, mammalian brain with its need for romantic love and the lustful reptilian brain.

Primate Love: Perfect Love

Our criteria for love are daunting. We deserve a person who adores and admires us at all times. We need him or her to be perfectly compliant to our needs; she needs to know what I want when I want it, before I say a word, and deliver instantly. We need our partners to be perfect all the time, too. After all, if they are perfect, everyone else will believe we are perfect for being such a perfect couple. So God forbid that we or our partners have food in our teeth or the same dress as another woman at a party. When our partners are perfect, we feel validated: "If this perfect person adores me, then I too must be pretty perfect." For us, love is not about sharing, but about convincing ourselves and everyone else that we are worthy of the love of an attractive, intelligent, successful person.

We also have a list of what we do not want. Some of us, especially People Pleasers, do not want too much conflict, lust or sex in a relationship. Things need to be clean, orderly and pious. Some of us, especially the Alphas, do not even like our partners to follow their own passions. Time spent on their passions is time spent not adoring us. How dare they! We deserve to be admired after working so hard and achieving so much.

Fantasy Hollywood Love

In my play *Anton*, I wrote an imaginary scene in which Anton Chekhov, the eminent playwright, was having a conflict with his wife, Olga, the Julia Roberts of the Moscow Art Theatre.

Olga, feeling neglected by the commitment-phobic Chekhov, complains to him, "If only I knew that you needed me, that you trust me."

"I do trust you. From the first time I saw you on stage —Playing Tsaritsa Irina…" Anton begins to reply, before Olga interrupts him.

"You were touched by my nobility, my voice. Touch me. I am Olga, your wife. I'm sorry to inform you, but Tsaritsa Irina died when the make-up came off."

The first category of fantasy love is Hollywood Love. My daydreams of marrying Julia Roberts were pure fantasy fabricated after watching *Pretty Woman*. I was in love with Vivian Ward, not Julia Roberts. Who knows how she is in real life and whether we would have two words to say one another? Not only is my beloved a character in a movie, in real life she is untouchable. I have never met her in a class; we have no mutual friends; and I don't have the first idea of how to get a hold of her. At the time of my crush, I was living in South Africa and I was a struggling medical student. The whole affair was concocted in my brain. Yet, for a while, I did experience a lot of pleasure as I daydreamed about those long legs and perfect smile. Today, Allie Hamilton, Rachel McAdams' character in *The Notebook,* is my fantasy of love when I feel a bit lonely.

Popular magazines are popular partly because so many of us are struggling to find real love in our lives. Daydreaming about George Clooney, Natalie Portman, Charlize Theron or Clive Owen helps to fill those lonely minutes. We cannot wait to find out more about our fantasy lovers on the Internet, Twitter or television shows—sure beats listening to our boring partners. Many eternal bachelors and spinsters, terrorized by their demons, waste their lives dreaming the improbable.

Weekend Love

On the surface, Anton and Olga's marriage seemed to be the best the world has ever seen. Their love letters are filled with poetry and sappy remarks. In reality, they could not stand to live with one another for more than six weeks at a time. Both would become depressed. Only time apart, with the magic of fantasy mixed with longing, kept their marriage going. Soon post carriages were carrying long letters, beautifully written by two artists more in love with love than with their spouses. Based on these letters, most Chekhov fans still believe Anton and Olga had the great love of the twentieth century.

I call the second type of fantasy the Weekend Love. In these relationships, there are two real people in love, who talk to one another by phone or send emails. But the relationship is built around non-consciously planning not to be at home too much or with the lover for too long. As soon as conflict or intimacy becomes a reality, it is time to run. Classic examples are long-distance relationships, marriages with workaholics, relationships with consultants who travel five days a week or marriages where the partners live in different towns. The key to these types of relationships is "I don't want to be lonely, but I don't want to be too close."

Another example of a Weekend Love is being madly in love with someone who is in a committed relationship. You daydream about him or her. You know he is the one. But what you don't know is the reason you are so attracted to him or her is that they are safe. After all, they are married. They will never intrude onto your fear of intimacy. Unfortunately, many people only realize their lover has commitment issues after they leave a spouse; suddenly the ardent lover is running for cover. The focus on intimacy, the lack of trust (after all she left her husband, why will she not leave me!) and the guilt sabotage almost every relationship that begins with deceit. Research shows that very few affairs that break up a marriage ever result in happy marriages.

Blaming the Other Love

A friend recently told me how she spent seven years with a man she loved. From day one, the man told her that he did not want children, nor did he want to marry again. She consciously believed that he would change. But, at 37, she confronted him with her need for marriage and children. He stuck to his story. My friend was devastated. "All these years wasted on him," she said. Later I asked her, "Don't you think you were living in a fantasy that he would change? Aren't you the one afraid of commitment? Did you not stay with him, non-consciously knowing he would never propose or want kids?"

She bravely admitted that there was truth in my questions. She herself fears intimacy, lived with a man with an equal fear of commitment, fantasizing that both of them would one day wake up and have the perfect marriage.

I'll call the third category Blaming the Other. In these situations, people marry or love people with whom they spend a lot of time. But these relationships are often based on self-deception.

One frequently hears people, especially wives, complaining that their spouses are not romantic enough, not intimate enough. Some may even go further and call their spouses "weak," or "spineless" or "cold and aloof." Men complain too. They often say that they are not getting enough sex, but what they really mean is intimacy.

It is easy to blame someone else for faults that we ourselves possess. These complainers would be the first to run if a real man or woman approached them with a bag full of romance and intimacy.

But Blaming the Other can have darker tones. Many people are in physically or emotionally abusive relationships, or in relationships lubricated with tons of booze. People then say, "I want to give him or her my intimate love. But he does not want to return it. In fact, he hits me. Or she humiliates me. All my attempts are in vain." These people blame their partners for not giving them what they deserve. The truth is that they "enjoy" the presence of another person to avoid their unbearable loneliness, but they also enjoy having an excuse not to seek intimacy.

Loving the Weak

"Do you know Albert Camus?" Mary asked. "He wrote *The Stranger*. In the story, there is a man named Salamano who has a dog. Throughout the story he abuses his dog, but it is clear that he needs the dog to not feel lonely. When the dog disappears, Salamano was filled with compassion for the dog. When the dog did not come back, he was destroyed. I know I am like that. I use men like that. I can blame them when I feel bad about life. The problem then lies in the outside world. They are my problem."

Mary, unable to find positive romance, seeks romantic partners on whom she can project her inner demons. She then lives in the fantasy that she is perfect, that the men in her life are the cause of all her loneliness, suffering and imperfections. "Men deserves to be castrated," her mind screams to distract her from her inner reality.

"My partner is a very successful lawyer. A really powerful man. Our relationship was great. So, to please him, I decided to become more powerful myself. I successfully ran for the presidency of a not-for-profit. I won. I could not wait to tell him. When I told him, his face dropped. Our relationship only went downhill from there. I still don't know what I did wrong," a friend complained.

She had made error 101 in dating an Alpa male. If he is powerful and you play the role of the weakling, don't improve yourself. Your job is to make us feel powerful, not to become powerful yourself. Your time should be devoted to us, not to your passions. After all, there is only 24 hours in the day. We need all your attention, all the time. Your job is to be weak, so stick to your job description.

We've all seen these relationships and it's always clear who is in charge. Sometimes the power difference is based on age, money, emotions or status. Typically, the one partner has a very low self-esteem. Their fragile Real Self tells them they don't deserve better. So they go for men or women who overpower them, if not humiliate them, which with their image of themselves. They are worms, and worms are supposed to be tramped upon. Abusive relationships stop the Real Self from screaming for more.

Power hungry people enjoy manipulating. For them, it's second nature. Their grandiose balloons are filled with self-admiration for their conquests. Treating another person like dirt makes them feel like God. Contempt for self and others, even loved ones, is often the other side of the grandiose coin.

With Michael Jackson's death, the world is again analyzing his obsession with young boys. Even in an interview, Michael defended his actions by saying that there is nothing wrong with tucking boys in at night, telling them stories and singing them songs. Michael, in desperate need of intimate love, was expressing love in the way that he wished adults had when he was young. To Michael's mind, his care for the boys was love. From our minds, he was loving people who were weak and vulnerable. He was using innocent children to create a perfect fantasy love.

Michael is not alone in his fantasies. It happens everywhere. It is surprising to see how many parents use their children as a fantasy love, an escape from their own hurt childhoods and from their inner loneliness and lack of romance. Mother's love or father's love often hides stronger undertones, which can confuse and hurt a child. In too many cases, mother and fathers cross physical and sexual boundaries. After all, incest, like murder, is a cross-cultural phenomenon. Some people are not able to resist this fundamental social taboo.

Prince and Princess Love

You only have to read the wedding section of *The New York Times* to understand the final category of fantasy love: The Prince/Princess Fantasy Love. "Tom, son of Professor So-and-So, a senior consultant at McKinsey, married Ann, daughter of Mary and John Smith, both doctors at Memorial, yesterday on Nantucket. Ann is a vice-president at Goldman Sachs."

Yesterday's prince and princess are today's popular, perfect, pampered, polite, professionals parading their pedigrees at every place of pomp and pinot. Many of our beloved actors fall into this category. The princes of Hollywood are men like Zac Efron, Matthew McConaughey and George Clooney. As a dreamer put it to me the other day, "These men are loved by your younger sister, your mother and even your grandmother. All of them can relate to them." As for princesses, Natalie Portman is my ideal: regal, sophisticated, brainy and beautiful.

Away from the screen, princes and princesses often struggle to be emotionally and sexually spontaneous. Many are extremely sexy and seductive. Many princesses wear short skirts and show their perfect abs or dance as if they had just taken a course in pole dancing. Which many have. Pole dancing is the new Pilates. But in private, a seductive attitude often disappears as the clothes come off. Prince and princess are not Marlon Brando and Marilyn Monroe. We have sex like we have a Sunday afternoon picnic: very polite, very boring and nothing like the romance and glamour that others imagine.

So we get a bit bored after a while. Playing "Perfect for 24 Hours a Day" can be exhausting, but we fear that we will be lonely if we separate. Some of us have very low self-esteems. We feel that nobody will want us if we end our relationships. So we persist, "You know, for the sake of the children." This also enables us to blame our partners for our unhappiness. "I am perfect and regal, but my partner…What a mess!" Projecting our pain onto him or her helps us to survive and even to get some admiration for it.

But our anger at life and ourselves does not go away, so we start to take our frustration out on our partners. We don't do it in the open—heaven forbid that we have raised voices in our perfect homes! But subtle emotional stabs are just fine. We can manipulate and demean just as easily with perfect smiles on our faces.

John Gottman spent 30 years videotaping and analyzing couples during conflicts as well as during normal moments. He found that couples that suppress emotions eventually do let them out, but not in full force. There are microseconds where their sadness and anger shows before they hide again. Overall, where great couples have five minutes of positive affect between one another versus one moment of negative affect, the prince and princess have slightly more negative than positive affects. They often shut down the person trying to communicate with them by saying through their body language, "Can't you see that I am reading?"

"Many nights my wife and I kiss one another goodnight. We say, 'I love you' to one another. But when I turn around to sleep, I feel I want to cry. I feel there's an ocean between us that we will never be able to sail across," a prince confessed with tears in his eyes.

Mammalian Love: Romantic Love

I have heard it a million times from Success Addicts, especially Alphas: I cannot live without the chemistry of romantic love. Most Success Addicts are addicted to it and the signs and symptoms of romantic love tell us why: euphoria, high energy, focused attention, drive and goal-orientated behaviors. Romantic love makes us feel we are the center of the universe. It proves to us what we all know. We feel rewarded for our hard work and sacrifice. We enjoy the sense of reunion that romantic love brings. We feel whole. We need our mammalian brain pumping us with admiration.

One of the main reasons for the high divorce rate among Success Addicts is our addiction to romantic love. We love the chemicals. If they are gone, it is time to search for a new source. But, as mentioned in an earlier chapter, chemical romantic love will not last long for Success Addicts. Without a Real Self to discover novelty in our partners, we will run at the first sign of boredom, empty bank account, sagging boobs or gray hair. Like a child, we are addicted to perfect, unconditional love.

Reptilian Brain: Lust and Bartering

Sara, a Success Addict who earns more than $200,000 a year, walked into my office and in a near panic asked me if I could help her with a personal problem. I immediately dropped everything to help my colleague in distress. "So," she said, "I'm going out on a date with John. I booked two restaurants. One is very expensive and I've always wanted to go there. The other is cozier, more romantic. I am not sure which one I should go for. You're a guy, what do you think?"

Relieved that she had not just been diagnosed with untreatable cancer, I asked her how long she had known this guy. After learning their dating history, I answered, "Why don't you take him to the romantic restaurant and offer to pay for the meal. After all, he spent a fortune on you during the first three dates."

"I am a lady!" she said in disgust. "I still like to be wined and dined when someone courts me."

When I expressed my shock that this highly educated, sophisticated, liberal woman still believes in princes with white horses, she replied, "Here in Manhattan the saying is: A woman needs to eat."

My colleague was convinced that it was her right to have a man pay for what she wanted to eat, wherever she wanted to eat, at whatever price—all in the name of courtship. She still believed in princes and princesses, while fighting loneliness as she enters her late forties.

Born into a wealthy family, Marie married her first love after graduating from college. Months after her wedding, she found herself becoming a shopping maniac. But nothing her husband bought her was good enough. She needed larger diamonds, a seafront condo, a more expensive car and more fashionable clothes. She bought and bought and bought. When her husband stopped being the object of chemical romantic love, he had to become the object of all her instant gratification needs. A year later she realized how unhappy she was in her marriage. After her divorce, her need for luxury goods settled down.

To date in Manhattan is a nightmare. Despite the supply of literally millions of single people, only a few seem to meet the loves of their lives. But the Internet has changed the landscape forever. In the United States, Internet dating has become close to a one billion dollar industry. Online, a heterosexual man finds himself in a paradise as he views photo after photo and decides who is beautiful enough for a first date. But how does a money-obsessed woman find out if her potential dates have money? When a man contacts a woman for a date, the want-to-be trophy wife kindly offers to make the dinner reservations. She then books a table at one of the most expensive restaurants in Manhattan. If the man agrees, she knows she is "in the money." If he refuses, she knows without leaving her computer that this person is "just not right for me."

Success Addicts are obsessed with the bold and the beautiful marrying, or the rich and the famous kissing or the prince and princess riding in carriages to their wedding. We believe in love based on beauty and power, whether money, fame or political power, as the pinnacle of humanity. The truth: At its most basic, it is our reptilian brain giving us an excuse not to seek intimacy. For Success Addicts, going for gold is easier than sharing a vulnerable state of mind. But our sex lives are not much better.

Golden Smiles, Sexual Cries

"I am cursed. I only have orgasms with men I do not love! I had five orgasms with my boyfriend of five years," a Success Addict complained to me. She is lucky. Many overachieving women I know have never had orgasms while having sex. I've also stopped being surprised by how many Success Addicts enjoy having sexual attention lavished upon them, but when it is their turn to return the favor, they claim fatigue or perform favors as if they were accomplishing a tedious household chore.

"I need to stay in control to the extent that I feel detached from myself, watching myself perform," a CEO told Michael Maccoby during analysis.

"When I have sex with a woman, it's important that she climaxes or else I feel like I'm a lousy lover. In fact, I'm always more concerned about her response than I am about my own satisfaction because her enjoyment is a measure of my performance, and I'm never happy with one woman for very long if I'm not at my peak sexually. Then when I finish with one, I have to go after another," a Success Addict told Dr. Masterson.

A former owner of an impotence clinic in South Africa told me that his patient list read like the who's who of affluent Johannesburg men. I have no doubt that the success of Viagra and other impotence drugs is an indication of the magnitude of psychologically induced erectile dysfunction here in America. After all, only a minority of men have impotency issues because of actual physical conditions. The rest are struggling psychologically.

Men and women obsessed with being the best outside the bedroom often fail inside the bedroom. When your self-esteem depends on how much money you have in your pocket, how beautifully you are dressed or how your diamond glitters in the sun, what happens when you need to take off your real and psychological clothes? What happens if you need to look deeply into another person's eyes during moments of intimacy and you non-consciously know they will see the worthlessness, anger and depression that lurk deep in your soul? What happens if you are surrounded by a grandiose bubble that only takes and never gives? A bubble that robs you from feeling the body of another person fully and intimately?

You cannot relax. You cannot stop seeing sex as a competition for admiration or selfish gratification. You cannot reach orgasm or you reach it too quickly to end the struggle.

Good sex is play, not a contest. Good sex is having a focus both on our own joy and the joy of the other. Good sex is giving and taking care and touching. Good sex is allowing our bodies to lead, not a chance for our egos and minds to compete. Herein lies the dilemma for Success Addicts. Sex does not bring happiness, it wakens our demons. We are forced to be selfish or doormats, to control our feelings and impulses.

No wonder so many success-obsessed people only have sex with those they do not love or only love those they can't have sex with. To have sex with a loved one is impossible. To put it another way, Success Addicts can lust, they can mate, they can mate when in love, but they cannot make love with those they love. In today's hypersexualized world, our fears are thorns in our grandiose bubbles.

What to do? Many Success Addicts, especially People Pleasers, numb their sex drive. For the longest time, I lived a nearly celibate life. During those years, I thought that I was pretty awesome for being so far above those who give in to such animalistic pleasures. Had I been raised a Puritan, I would have been one of the men preaching about the sins of the flesh. In the process, I would have gained admiration for a pure life that was really built on fear of sexuality.

Many Success Addicts take the path of least resistance and choose as their partners people who also struggle with intimacy. It can be a relief to know that your partner is not going to want sex every night, or every week. But this does not mean that we will not complain about our lack of sex and intimacy. Many Success Addicts complain that their husbands are not romantic enough or that their wives do not give us enough sex. The truth is, had they to meet a healthy person with a high need for sexual intimacy, Success Addicts would run for their lives.

Many Success Addicts, single or married, men or women, become one-night-stand specialists. In these relationships, only sex matters. Emotions and intimacy are left at the door next to the Prada or Churchill shoes. On the surface, these sexual relationships serve as a source of admiration for having scored or a place to release bottled-up sexual lust. Our grandiose bubbles enjoy these sexual encounters. Dr. Masterson writes that many Success Addicts see their multiple sex partners as an "idealized oasis of warmth, comfort and nourishment" and "a fantasy of a healing metamorphosis." Success Addicts sleep around hoping that someone will finally make them whole. Some of us also sexually act out to avoid the screaming demons inside of us. Focusing on another is easier than listening to all of the shouting in our heads.

Safe sexual experimentation and fooling around while being respectful of another person's emotions and health is an important part of life for many adolescents and young adults. Through safe early sexual experiences, we learn more about our sexual identity, our sexual preferences and what type of partner evokes our affection in and out of the bedroom. But when mature adults are still sexually acting out, it can be a sign that we are running away, not moving toward.

Those of us who are admired for having it all and who think we are the best of humanity often cannot enjoy the most basic of human pleasures. Our need for success makes us perfect failures in bed. We are the most eligible men and women in town, but we are either bad in bed or bad at fidelity. We are also not very good at taking care of the emotional needs of our families.

Success Addicts and Family Life

A friend told me how his boss called him on the Friday evening of a Thanksgiving weekend to question the assumptions he had made in a financial model he built. The reason for this nitpicking? Two days with the family was driving him up the wall. He was lonely in the company of his loved ones and tortured by his inner demons. He had to keep busy until he could make love to his computer screen when the markets opened on Monday morning. Then he would finally feel connected again.

Joe Gibbs, the coach of the Redskins, mentioned in a *New York Times* article how he tried to be home to tuck his two children into bed. One night he leaned over to kiss the younger of his two sons, Coy, and was startled to see that he had facial hair. "I went, 'Oh my gosh, this guy's got a beard and he weighs 200 pounds,'" Gibbs said during a teleconference. The 66-year-old Gibbs hinted that those lost moments with his children—and now his grandchildren—haunted him more than any defeat. "I always worry about them and my relationship with them," he said.

A life lived for success, whether money, NFL trophies or awards, haunts people when old age or sickness squashes the excitement of the chase. Then, when one needs nurturing relationships to make our final days on earth full of joy and camaraderie, many Success Addicts will find that no one is waiting at home for them.

All this, and when you ask Success Addicts about the most important thing in our lives, we will always say "family." Our grandiose bubble distorts the fact that we are workaholics who don't have a lot of time for anyone else. We make it our mission to believe the lies we tell about our perfect partners, perfecting parents, perfect families.

Isolation

Whether popular or powerful, in a crowd or alone, single or married, Success Addicts are tortured by humanity's worst punishment: loneliness. Our loneliness is not the sadness or yearning that the mentally healthy occasionally experience. Our loneliness is an excruciating physical pain: a knife in our chest, a bayonet in our eyes.

I hid from my loneliness by being a workaholic. I also searched every room I entered and every event I attended for the woman who would transform my unbearable longing for a partner into intimate love. But despite knowing that a love that cures often kills, I still wish for magic.

Alcohol too has been a dear friend in my fight. Often after a disappointing date, I would barhop my way home to numb the longing. On these occasions, I would just sit and stare at my drink, finish and order another. And another. I had to numb myself. I too have had many one-night stands. But sex with hundreds of partners cannot heal broken hearts.

I also search for company in cliques of friends. But in groups, I've always felt as if I have to be "on." People exhaust me. Like many other Success Addicts, I reached a point where I believed that being painfully lonely was better than being pained by betrayal, abuse or the constant need to please. Like Heath Ledger's character in *Brokeback Mountain*, Orson Welles in *Citizen Kane* and Daniel Day Lewis in *There Will be Blood*, I withdrew from life when success failed to keep me company.

Loneliness makes me feel as if I am not worthy to be loved.

In *Long Day's Journey into Night*, Eugene O'Neil wrote: "It was a great mistake, my being born a man, I would have been much more successful as a seagull or a fish. As it is, I will always be a stranger who never feels at home, who does not really want and is not really wanted, who can never belong, who must always be a little in love with death!"

This is the monologue I use for my acting auditions.

Whether we are married or single, have lots of sex or no sex, spend time with the family or live alone, Success Addicts never really feel we belong. To belong, we must first belong to ourselves. Without a healthy Real Self, this is impossible.

Success Addicts Defined

From our discussion so far, we can conclude that Success Addicts live to fill their grandiose bubbles. Nothing and no one else matters. We need a buffer around us to protect us from the world. We lack a healthy Real Self to interact fully, vulnerably and fairly with people and the world. Finally, and most painfully, merely trying to live up to our passions and humanity triggers six vicious demons that force us to run back into our grandiose bubble. We are not Success Addicts because we want to be. We are Success Addicts, because, according to our warped minds, we are dead if we do not pump admiration into our bubble. This need destroys almost any chance of finding real, intimate love.

Chapter 15

People Pleasers, Self-Haters

I mentioned before that when I was in grade three, one of my (misguided) little friends told his mother that I was like Jesus. Now, in many people's minds, Jesus was pretty, perfect and popular.

My people pleasing skills ensured that I was voted headboy of all the schools I attended and I garnered the most votes in a student government election at university. I was also able to anticipate any conflicts my actions or words might have. When I say something, I watch people's eyes for signs of doubt or disagreement and effortlessly adapt my argument until I see that my point of view fits with that of the rest of the group. I was popular, polite, political and pleasing, so people responded to me.

It was a child who finally saw through my mask. Visiting friends in South Africa, I was in overdrive, laughing loud, talking fast and breathing shallow. After another forced laugh to show how happy and confident I was, a five-year-old asked, "Mommy, why is Uncle Pierre laughing so loud and strangely."

When I was at Yale, I took a class called Team and Interpersonal Effectiveness, in which groups had to come up with a team name based on what people saw in each other. After a few warm-up comments, Ginger said, "Pierre, you seem to hide behind something. There is a dark side to you that you never show."

To hide the truth, I smiled even more broadly. "I don't know what you mean."

We ended up naming our team "The Dark Side of the Moon."

Portrait of Princes and Princesses

We, the princes, are polite, perfect and play by the rules. We are professionals or Ph.D.s. We go to work in pinstripe suits, but wear Polo shirts on weekends. We plan our lives and have a precise timetable of when we will make senior partner at a firm with a Park Avenue address or when we will be accepted into a private club, with all its privileges to wine and dine with the popular and powerful in the city. At home, our main task is to pamper our princesses. When they become pregnant, we say at parties, "We are pregnant" because we are so PC. When children are born, we love to play with them—until their need to wrestle or be read to makes us rush for our PDAs. The pleasure and purpose of playing papa has an expiration date and, in the long run, making partner means more.

We, the princesses, are popular and perfect in appearance. Jackie O. is our perfect role model. We wear pearls and love purchasing multiple pairs of shoes. We love to preach our self-help knowledge gained by reading books like *The Celestine Prophecy*. We also enjoy poetry, especially Sylvia Plath, and photography. We dream of living in a palace, so we make our homes as spotless and picture perfect as MOMA. We are planners of weddings, charity events, conferences and blind dates for our friends. After marriage, some of us want to become permanent vacationers. Some of us resign from high-pressure jobs and sit on the non-governing boards of non-profit organizations. As parents, we are professional students. We know the latest programs that can help get our precious babies into Princeton. We become powerful members of the PTA. On weekends, we passionately read popular magazines while we go for pedicures. We like to gossip and pull others down. We abhor three things: to poop and pee if another person can hear us; to use public transport; and to perform sexual favors. Our dream: perfect, polite, performing and pleasant little princes and princesses that will bring our parenting skills a lot of praise.

People Pleasers do not please because we are altruistic. We please to be admired. We need the admiration, the compliments, the sense of being in the right crowd and being good. Parents of People Pleasers receive significant admiration from society for being such wonderful parents to have nurtured such well-behaved children who are so friendly, so kind, so nice. Pleasing others stimulates the admiration needs of our mammalian brains, for both child and parent. We please so our grandiose bubbles can be filled with admiration. But under our mask of happiness, perfection and goodness, there are secrets can't even admit to ourselves.

Pagliacci

At boarding school in Paarl, a small town an hour away from Cape Town, my eldest brother, Etienne, and I were neighbors in one of the residence halls. Every morning, as the wake-up bell ordered me to face another day of tradition, discipline and suffocating neckties, I played the following Roy Orbison song:

Crying over you
Crying over you
Yes, now you're gone
And from this moment on
I'll be crying, crying, crying, crying,
Crying, crying, over you!

Back home on vacation, I continued my cheery early morning ritual. Then Etienne burst through my door, "It's you! We've been trying for months to find the guy who plays such morbid music first thing in the morning!" I smiled sheepishly. To me, it seemed perfectly normal to listen to depressing music upon waking.

Later in life, I upgraded from Roy Orbison and "Crying" to Placido Domingo and *Pagliacci*. In one of my favorite arias, Pagliacci sings:

"You're a clown. Put on your costume and powder your face.…Turn into jest your anguish and your sorrow, into a grimace your sobs and your grief. Laugh, clown, at your broken love, laugh at the pain that poisons your heart."

I understood *Pagliacci* long before I read the translation—I was an expert at powdering my face to hide my inner demons. Ironically, a year ago, my singing teacher, Jonathan Hart, one day out of nowhere, and without knowing anything about my love for *Pagliacci*, said, "There is something in your voice that wants me to teach you an opera aria. It is called "Vesti la gubba." Jonathan's right brain picked up the Pagliacci pain in mine without us saying a word.

Music, like language, is a collection of abstract symbols that we use to translate our non-conscious feelings into consciousness to express who we are and to help us make sense of our lives. Language is specific, but music is more honest. My choice of music showed that behind my mask of happiness and my beliefs of being a happy, perfect child, a lot of sadness, longing, grief and depression were bottled up.

There are Pagliaccis all over the world. One example is a CEO of a global company who always answers the question "How are you?" by saying *terrific*, *wonderful* or *never been better*. But while coaching him, I could see how he strained his facial muscles to maintain his smile. On the rare occasions that he let his smile drop, his eyes gave me chills. Interviews with his employees showed that he was an ineffective leader. This CEO's golden smile took him to the top of his career where he spent more time fighting his demons than running a company. He, like so many others who smile their way into politics, power and the pulpit, have no choice. Dealing with our demons comes first.

When pollsters ask random people in the United States how happy they are, 80 percent indicate an above-average level of happiness. But when scientists objectively assess people's happiness, they find that only 30 percent of Americans are happy; it may even be closer to 15 percent. At least 50 percent of people seem to live with a mask of happiness. But doing so comes at a great personal cost. At the end of the opera, Pagliacci kills his wife.

Smiley Mask

As a medical student, I loved studying rare diseases and syndromes. Ordinary medical situations bored me. One day, during a pediatric oral exam, my professor pounded me with questions on what advice I would give mothers on breastfeeding and bottle feeding. But this was a topic I never even considered studying. After all, this was something a nurse would know, I reasoned.

During the oral exam, I was at a loss for answers. All I did for ten minutes was laugh loudly and smile. On my way out of the office, a friend, waiting his turn to be grilled, asked me, "What were you two drinking in there? You sounded like you were at a bar!"

Smiles and laughter have little to do with happiness and confidence. We learn to smile as two-month-old babies and to use our smiles socially by three months. By four months, we can laugh. Laughing and smiling are our most primitive forms of communicating with the world and our earliest defenses against maternal rejection. What sane mother—despite nights without sleep—would reject a smiling baby? Later, our smiles and laughter signal to other children that we are friendly, well intentioned and fun. These signals encourage them to play with us; play then teaches us the social skills essential for living a full life. Smiles and laughter as social signals continue throughout our lives. Researchers found that 80-90 percent of laughter is not in response to wit or funny situations, but comes after seemingly banal statements, such as "I know" or "I'll see you guys later." Most people, particularly women, laugh more when they speak than when they listen. People use laughter as language.

Laughter also signals the status hierarchy in a group. In a research study, scientists randomly selected people and assigned them the roles of either "boss" or "underling," and then observed how the participants reacted to a boring joke that would put normal people to sleep. When the "boss" delivered the joke either in person or by videotape, those assigned as "underlings" laughed much more than when those same people played the "boss." We laugh to signal our respect. What is fascinating is that we do not laugh as a conscious strategy to manipulate our superiors; "underlings" laughed when they watched the "boss" telling the joke by videotape—he wasn't even in the room. The study suggests that we laugh more when we believe that we are not able to determine our own fate. Our false laughs and smiles say to others, "I acknowledge that you are my superior. I want to please you. Don't hurt me." This is similar to an insecure dog that lies down on its back in submission to a more powerful dog to avoid a fight. Like the mask of success, the mask of happiness hides the demon.

Today I know those "happy" loud laughs during my medical exams, a laugh that I repeated a thousand times a day with family, friends or even strangers, were not belly laughs of happiness, but fake laughs born of embarrassment, insecurity and shame.

Red Light

As I sat down to write about how I used to blush at the most inopportune moments, I started to wonder what metaphor I could use for blushing. Something that's red and shining... The first idea that popped up: the red light outside a prostitute's window. I immediately wanted to discard the image. But then I thought: How appropriate!

Darwin said that blushing is "the most peculiar and most human of all expressions." And, he could have added, the most embarrassing. At first blush, the science suggests that blushing is a positive expression. When participants are put through tests in which college seniors tease and rip into freshman, the frequency of blushing predicted whether people would grow to like one another by the end of the study. Blushing helps friendships to form. Why? It shows that people care.

Dacher Keltner, psychologist from the University of California at Berkley, tells us that blushing is a way "to repair daily betrayals and transgressions quickly."

Charles Darwin had another opinion: Blushing is the result of knowing what other people think about us.

My tendency to blush quickly earlier in my life pointed to my constant wondering of what others thought of me and my anxieties about perpetrating social transgressions by accident. I was walking on eggshells all the time, always taking other people's needs in account before my own.

I was prostituting my fragile Real Self to make others happy and pleased with my conduct. They counted, not me. The only difference between the old me and a prostitute: She gets money and I get admiration. Blushing as a red light is an apt metaphor.

Debilitating Fear

During an experiment, participants had to prepare a small speech on a well-known topic and present it to a panel of judges while their cortisol levels were tested. As they walked through the doors, a surprise awaited. Numerous cameras were pointed at them. The judges, dressed in white lab coats, stared rigidly and silently ahead. The room itself was set up like an interrogation room.

Male A presented his work. He seemed in complete control. He smiled and focused on the task in front of him. All this, while the judges never betrayed a facial expression. At the end, he thanked everyone and left.

Then Male B entered. He was visibly distraught. He choked, sweated, forgot his speech and continuously licked his dry lips. For a long time, he just stood there, like a little boy about to burst into tears.

Afterwards, the cortisol levels revealed that the people pleasing Male A had drastically higher levels of cortisol. Despite a cool exterior, his interior was in a state of unhealthy fear. Male B, despite his poor performance, had less cortisol. Excess levels of cortisol over long periods have been linked to numerous diseases.

Dr. Masterson writes that a Success Addict "living with a death threat, or what is perceived as a death threat, hanging over his head leads a fearful life in which every move to express himself, to allow for his real self to emerge, is accompanied by the need to look over his shoulder in fear and panic." The fear that Success Addicts deal with does not arise from actual events in the real world, but comes from past events.

"If you do not do what is expected of you, if you do not please those in charge, you will be rejected. You will lose all support from those who 'care' for you. Alone, you will not be able to cope. You better do what you are told to do," our demons tell us.

"Comply, and you receive rewards. If you do not comply, you are killed," Dr. Masterson writes. He also discusses how the commercial success of both *The Godfather* and *The Sopranos* show that many of us understand the rules of the game.

But living without a Real Self adds more fear in the moment. Life and events are so random that to live without an ability to make one's own decisions escalates fear.

Pleasing Kills Passion

For most of my life I had no idea who I was and what I wanted to do. The idea of following a career that I was passionate about did not really cross my mind. I had an idea of what a successful life was and how to obtain it, at almost any cost. Even when I realized I needed passion in my life, I was unable to find what I was looking for.

People Pleasers lack many abilities essential to finding and then following our passions. We are too self-conscious and self-centered to do any activities just for the sake of doing them. We cannot experience flow because we are too focused on performing for others. Without experiencing flow, we cannot experience the urge to scream to the skies: "This is the real me!"

Even if we do find our passion, we struggle to follow it. We have a belief that emotions are too messy for our perfect lives. Stripped from anger and its capacity to drive us to do what we want in life, we often become victims of other people's ideas of what we should do. We cannot fend for ourselves if we cannot allow ourselves to defend our choices.

Stripped from our emotions, we are forced to rely exclusively on thinking to get us to our goals. But thought without the benefit of emotions tends to not be helpful in the rapids of life. We need to feel in order to make sense of our lives and to make even the most basic decisions. We need all our emotions to make us proactive in our passion. Instead, we react to life and other people's will.

We also hate asking for help from others. We do not trust other people to care about us and our passions. We need to be self-sufficient. But complete self-sufficiency kills the reason we became human in the first place: to cooperate so we can help one another survive and live up to our full potential.

Embracing failure is one of the key tools in finding our passion and living up to our full potential. We need to know that we are okay even if we fall flat on our faces. But People Pleasers need to be perfect all the time. Even small mistakes take on a life-or-death quality. We are petrified of seeming ordinary, stupid, unattractive, boring or a failure. So we live our lives trying to escape our fears, rather than developing our strengths and our weaknesses.

If one constantly worries about others' opinions, we cannot act authentically and realistically in the face of our problems. We can only use past experiences, past commands. The result is that many Success Addicts are completely unable to live fully. When the authors of the Harvard Business Review wrote the article, *Teaching Smart People to Learn*, their findings should have been that many smart people, especially management consultants, make decisions based on past information and guidelines passed on by their parents, elite business schools and powerful partners. Like good little boys and girls, we can follow instructions perfectly. Just don't tell us to think outside the box or to learn from criticism. Adapting to unique situations was not the focus of childhood; obedience to the laws in our family homes was.

No wonder Michael Maccoby found that we People Pleasers are lacking an inner compass to direct us. We are constantly asking, "Is this the appropriate answer? Am I doing okay? Is this working?"

The late Dr. McClelland, celebrated researcher on human motivation and leadership, found that People Pleasers are terrible leaders. So focused on making sure that everyone is happy, these leaders seldom give strong directions nor do they hold subordinates appropriately accountable. The result? People pleasing leadership styles cause the lowest team morale, even lower than task-orientated Alpha bosses. But all the while they consciously and non-consciously believe they must be doing well. After all, everyone loves them.

A senior partner at a prominent management consulting firm acknowledged his love for hiring People Pleasers. Our anxiety to perform and please others translates well into the management consulting model where pleasing the client is the final goal. But what he failed to address was that People Pleasers may please, be smart and analytical, but we lack the Real Self capacities to be wise, predict the future or be adequate leaders. We can analyze the past, but we fail to see the future. Management consultants are paid extremely well to advise CEOs. One has to wonder if we really add any value.

Hating People

Parties should be fun. That is the whole idea. But by the end of most parties I have been to, my mind is racing: "I can't force my smile anymore. They're going to see my smile is fake. Why did I say that stupid thing in front of this politically correct crowd? What was I thinking! Damn it. If they do not turn the music down, I will explode. Why is the music so loud? Pinch yourself to stay calm. Breathe. Drink. This pinot is made from water. Four glasses and still no buzz. Maybe I need a whiskey. When are the first people going to leave? I can't leave first. What will John and Sarah think? I am sure they'll think I didn't like the party. That will be no good. I will feel terribly if they think that. No, I must stay. Must get another drink. I am exhausted from being nice. I wish I could be home now, listening to some opera, far away from the madding crowd."

If that was how I felt at a party, imagine my inner dialogue during client meetings. People Pleaser *magna cum laude*. I had to impress clients, my boss and my colleagues. Impromptu comments in such meetings left me feeling as if I was a small deer caught in the headlights of a Hummer. After a client meeting, I typically felt as if an atom bomb had exploded in my brain. I would turn into a little boy eager to hear from my superiors that I had done well and that I did not mess up too badly. I so desperately wanted to hear that I had added value.

Now imagine me on a first date with a woman. After one hour and one glass of wine with me, healthy women would leave with a saccharine overdose. My sweet smile and honey-coated comments probably seemed insincere and over-the-top to the well-balanced women in my dating pool.

"Mary told me the other day that I am one of her best friends," a People Pleasing friend said to me with a smile as large as an alley cat's. To her, the idea that someone liked her and wanted to be friends was inconceivable. I know Mary. I value my friend's talents and personality much more than Mary does. But from my friend's perspective, she is not good enough to have Mary as a friend. We People Pleasers worry constantly that our friends and family do not like us. We may be popular, but we typically only have a few real friends who have been cultivated over many years. In our friendships, we work hard. We are the givers, the listeners. Most of the time, we never receive what we put into our friendships. We feel we must please or give, otherwise our friends will leave us. The friendship will be destroyed. We also go along with the flow. To say "no" when we do not want to go to a certain movie or restaurant is beyond us. We would rather say "yes" and try to rationalize that movie will be good to see. We are slaves to our friends' needs. Even our friendships are a struggle. Despite our popularity, secretly, we confess we would like to be more confident socially.

Pleasing Partners

We are petrified of love. Even if our partners tell us a thousand times a day that they love us, we are convinced we will be rejected. We just do not believe them. We are also passive in relationships; we are scared to rock the boat. We become dependent on our partners, concerned where they are and whether they will come back. We can be a bit obsessive about their whereabouts. We know pleasing works with parents and bosses. Surely it will work for lovers. But pleasing means that we never show others who we really are. Nobody really cares about our true emotions and needs. So, good people who are potential partners run for the hills. They do not want to be in a television show the rest of their lives. They seek real people, not phonies, even if we are princes and princesses. When something goes wrong, we blame ourselves for everything. We are a walking apology who guards our emotions as if they were top secret. But deep down, despite our pretenses, we are filled with an unbearable longing for real love. We desperately want to be who we are and have someone support our Real Selves. Our demons, however, do not agree.

My life as a people pleaser made me popular and extremely lonely at the same time. When I found myself, for the millionth time, sitting down alone for brunch next to couples holding hands and groups of friends drinking bloody marys, I felt sadness bunching up in my throat. I wanted to cry out in utter hopelessness. But, like I have done for over 40 years of my life, I had to brace myself, cut off all feelings below my clavicles. There is no other way to survive this intense loneliness.

A friend sent me the following email: "I just spoke with John. His wife is expecting. You are now my last friend who is not married or who does not have a child."

I wrote him a return email: "Thanks for reminding me on this painfully lonely Sunday that I am completely incapable of love."

But I did not send it to him. After all, he wouldn't understand. Who does? They all think I am just picky. Or gay.

The truth is that I am a recovering People Pleaser who cannot please people or lovers anymore without hating myself. Loneliness is a better option than selling your soul to others.

The self-imposed law that kills all our relationships is: "Thou shalt never ever cry in front of another human being." Some of us believe we are physically incapable of crying, as if our tear ducts had been surgically removed. But if being vulnerable in front of our intimate partners is the essence of all great relationships, what are the chances of us truly finding real love? Very slim. We must avoid vulnerability and tears at all cost. Maybe we know that if we start crying, we will never stop. Underneath our charming smiles lies a great lake of tears.

Pleasing Power

Everyone in power is God or Lucifer. They know everything we do and will destroy us if we make one single mistake. So we are obsessed with pleasing our parents, spouses, bosses and clients. To these people, we struggle to say "no" when we need to, whether it is to an invitation for a dinner we don't want to attend, or "no" to an abusive partner, or "no" to a boss expecting us to chronically work overtime.

We also believe anger aimed at this group, even if deserved, is a sin punishable by death. I can recall with exact detail the five times I got angry in my first 30 years of life. The amount of times I vented my frustration against the power of being: once. I believed that good citizens do not become angry. Power is always right. They are God. So turn the other cheek.

Dr. Masterson says that Success Addicts "express our anger and risk losing the love of others or we deny the anger in order to remain in the helpless state of dependency and hold onto others. As panic grows, patients report that it feels like facing death or actually being killed."

People Pleasers have no anger to protect themselves against abuse by those in power and feel guilty for expressing their wishes. These two handicaps often make us lapdogs that cling to our boss' every command. We need their security and approval.

Our paralysis in the presence of those in power can border on the absurd. We believe non-consciously that our bosses, parents or partners know exactly what we did and when we did it. If we kiss someone in public, our parents in Oregon will know about it that very second. They will frown on us showing emotion in public. When we steal an hour of work to watch the World Cup, our bosses will know exactly what we did. We better walk back and start apologizing the minute we walk past reception.

I know many People Pleasers from all over the world who live far away from their hometowns. They are constantly wondering whether they should return home. On the one side, they miss their families and friends. People pleasers are usually very tight with their families. But the tightness is not a healthy love. If you live to please parents, you are conditioned to sell your souls, whether you are 20 or a hundred years old. People Pleasers, lacking a Real Self, do not wise up over the years. We stay who we are: people afraid of others.

Going back home feels like walking into a prison. Even after decades of living away from home, we fear we have to be the same good, perfect people we had to be as children. We fear becoming prisoners of our parents' prohibitions and paralyzed by our need to be perfect. Even if we tell ourselves, "This time I will stand up for my rights," we walk off the airplane and in seconds become a Pleaser again. Our non-conscious habits beat our conscious mind 6-0, 6-0 every time.

So we live far away from our parents, but we never feel settled where we live. We feel guilty for not taking care of family and friends back home, but we treasure our freedom from pleasing, even if it means being alone. When we go back, we feel useful, but we live in a psychological prison. We are damned if we do, damned if we don't.

Fearing People

We know that our interpersonal relationships are essential for our humanity. We became human because of or in order to trust non-family members and to connect intimately. When researchers set out to look at how people relate to one another, they found that humans who struggle with relationships have at least one of two characteristics. The first is a high level of anxiety. Highly anxious people tend to worry that people will leave them. They wonder if they are good enough, whether their behavior will be acceptable, whether people really care for them or whether they have done enough to make sure the other person is happy. The second characteristic is avoiding intimacy. People who have an intense need to be self-sufficient, who hate depending on others or showing their emotions are people who need to control their relationships. Researchers found that secure, mentally healthy people score low on both anxiety and avoidance. People who identify strongly as caretakers do not avoid intimate relationships, but when they are in them, they tend to cling. They drastically need to be in a relationship, but they never stop worrying. Alphas typically do not worry about their partners leaving them. After all, who would leave God? But they do avoid intimacy. But we People Pleasers score high on both anxiety and avoidance. We are filled with fear of rejection and fear of engulfment. The researchers categorized us as The Fearful.

People Pleaser fear people and avoid relating to them on precisely the levels that make us human so I never allowed others to truly see me for who I am. I was liked by many, but loved by very few. How can someone love you if they are only offered a fixed smile and edited speech? Love is sharing emotions, imperfections and spontaneous laughter, not the version of yourself that your non-conscious mind tells you to project.

Pleasers and Self Care

I met a beautiful bright barrister from London. She exhibited all of the mannerisms of a classic people pleaser, the perpetual smile included. I noticed her abstaining from alcohol in a nightclub where booze flowed like a tsunami.

"Why are you not drinking?" I asked.

"I'm in AA," she said.

"Oh," I replied, not knowing what to say.

"No problem," Sarah said. "I never felt good about myself. Never. Barrister, no barrister. When it came time to marry, I married my best drinking buddy. Just someone who I could come home to at night and who could help me drown my loneliness and sorrow. Well, we became good drinking buddies. Too good. My health was starting to suffer. I asked for a divorce. I'm fighting back."

People Pleasers love the bottle or drugs. Chemicals allow us to forget about our painful self-consciousness. We can relax and forget when we are drunk or high. We can be free from our fears. But we often wake up the next morning riddled with guilt for having had such a good time.

Another People Pleaser, a New Yorker, told me how he swallowed any tablets he could find the day after he asked his wife for a divorce. "I asked for the divorce. I wanted to be alone, because I felt so lonely in our relationship. But after the divorce, I did not want to be alone. I felt guilty. Sad. And the nightmares! Unbearable. I wanted it all to end. I woke up the next day and thought I was dead."

People Pleasers are often burdened by medical illnesses. Working and living with high levels of cortisol in our bodies causes many problems. I am convinced that many diseases, from Diabetes Mellitus Type II, back pain, peptic ulcers, asthma and other autoimmune diseases are the result of the body turning on itself. The mind is not independent from the body. Self-hate become body-hate.

The research done by Dr. John Sarno, professor of Rehabilitation Medicine at the New York University School of Medicine, informed me that my mind caused my chronic back pain. He believes that back pain helps me to avoid my non-conscious rage, sadness and pain from pouring out into my consciousness. My back pain is an emotional plug. His research shows that 94 percent of the 104 back-pain patients he treated had an abnormally high drive to be perfect and good. Ah, our People Pleasers so desperately want to be good.

"I can be sad or happy whenever anything makes me sad or happy; I don't have to look cheerful for someone else, and I don't have to suppress my distress or anxiety to fit other people's needs. I can be angry and no one will die or get a headache because of it. I can rage when you hurt me, without losing you," a patient told Alice Miller after successful therapy.

Feeling all our emotions and then managing and making sense of them gives us vitality and wisdom. Emotion care is at the centre of a good life. But when we please others, we often have to cut off our own emotions and needs. No wonder so many People Pleasers consider suicide.

A Culture of People Pleasing

I was fortunate to attend a workshop for actors conducted by Oriza Hirata, one of Japan's leading playwrights and directors. During the workshop at the Japanese Society in New York, Mr. Hirata explained the challenge of training Japanese actors to make strong individual choices during rehearsals and performances. For example, just asking "What fruit do you like?" to a group of actors creates some confusion. No one steps forward to say, "I love oranges." Mr. Hirata explained that in Japan people are more concerned with consensus-building than decision-making.

I have spent a lot of my life as a People Pleaser building consensus. "Can't we all just agree to love one another?" is the motto of People Pleasers throughout the world.

I have a favorite Japanese restaurant that I frequent almost once a week. Often sitting alone, I would observe the behavior of the Japanese waiters and chefs. Based on Mr. Hirata's comments and these observations, I, while running the risk of making a gross generalization, want to suggest that if the Japanese are the best People Pleasers in the world, then Japanese women are the best People Pleasers in the galaxy.

A study of the quality of life of Japanese women gives a perfect window into the lives of People Pleasers throughout the world. Research shows that in a country where 23 percent of women—based on medical criteria—are overweight, 52 percent of Japanese women claim to be overweight; only 20 percent of Japanese women are satisfied with their overall beauty (which includes physical attractiveness, body weight and shape); only 16 percent of Japanese women seem to be happy with their romantic relationships; only 12 percent of Japanese girls agree that everyone ought to marry. Finally, Japanese women have among the highest suicide rates for women in the developed world at 14 per 100,000. A life of people pleasing is a life of self-hate.

But Japan is not the only country struggling with an epidemic of people pleasing. In *The New York Times*, the editors bemoaned the unusually high suicide rate among Latinas, a group that soon will comprise the majority of mothers in the United States. The editors mentioned one of the main reasons: In a highly machismo culture, one that is dictated by men, women are expected to serve the family's needs first and their own needs last. They are forced to please everyone before they please themselves. Life starts to seem like an endless labor camp and suicide provides the only key to freedom.

Back in my home country of South Africa, white boys have traditionally been raised with reprimands such as "boys don't cry" when you are sad, "don't be a sissy" if you are afraid or "be a gentleman" when you are angry. We also had to be perfect Christians by the end of our first year. This outright denial of our emotional lives combined with an unusually harsh strictness and beatings both in homes and schools have led to many of us becoming either arrogant racists or spineless People Pleasers. The result? The suicide rate among white South African men is among the highest in the world.

People Pleasing Prohibited

The best of humanity know how to say "yes" and "no" without being selfish or hurting others. They know they have the right to stand up for their needs and passions, even against those in power. They know they have the right to identify their own unique individuality, wishes, dreams and goals and then be assertive in expressing them autonomously. Because of a strong Real Self, they know life can be lived fully without feeling anxious or preoccupied with other people's desires.

People Pleasers do not believe we have the right to be our authentic selves. We need to please to survive. But a life of pleasing others is a life of hurting and hating ourselves. As a result, our life is filled with excessive cortisol, drugs and alcohol and even suicide. All this, while parents and society commend these good citizens. Maybe it is time society started frowning upon parents who have these well-behaved angels for children. Children should have personality, guts, confidence and respect for others. Why live if you have to put your soul second to someone else?

Chapter 16

From Success to Sex, Drugs and Suicide

Pump the Pleasure Balloon

Many of us Success Addicts are skilled at using alcohol to medicate the working week. Stop by any bar in Lower Manhattan after the closing bell of the New York Stock Exchange and see Success Addicts on parade, escaping their day by diving head first into the nearest martini. Those of us who head home often walk straight toward the liquor cabinet.

Alcohol directly stimulates the pleasure centers in our animal brain. Alcohol brings instant gratification for people who equate instant gratification, especially if we have worked hard, above health and even life.

Success Addicts are riddled with stress. We often have jobs that demand perfection and bosses who punish without mercy. We constantly fear being rejected by the "in" group or fear that we are not doing enough to be the center of attention. These jobs and fears would stress out even the best of humanity who possess soothing whispers from their Real Selves. Success Addicts, saddled with tons of stress, do not have the ability to sooth ourselves naturally. So we grab for the bottle for support. For some, the bottle is not enough. We watch excessive porn, have lap dances, use drugs, enjoy one night stands, dance in clubs until sunrise, eat copious amounts of expensive food, watch mindless television. Our culture is filled with activities that bring us artificial pleasure and help us to deal with life's stresses. In the natural world, pleasure does indeed equate to survival. But the confused minds of success addicts can't tell the difference.

Inflating the Grandiose Balloon

One day I stumbled upon a writer in Bryant Park, doing a public reading of his latest book. I had read his earlier book, which was about how he had fought alcohol addiction after it nearly destroyed his life. Days later someone told me that this man had said to an interviewer, "I don't know if I would still be sober if I was not famous." His addiction to cigarettes, coffee and fame kept him sober. Another alcohol addict confessed: "When I drink, I am in control. It is all about me. My needs, my wants. It is all about me."

Fame and alcohol are brothers in our non-conscious mind. Both make us feel special and stoke our bubble of grandiosity.

John, a thirty-something Wall Street investment banker told me, "Cocaine makes you feel confident. You think clearly. You feel you can do anything." This feeling of grandiosity is what all Success Addicts strive for. It is our daily goal. When we need an extra shot of grandiosity, we reach for cocaine or alcohol. Cocaine, in the presence of the "champagne and cocaine club" elite; $450 bottles of booze at clubs with selective, serious and snotty bouncers; sexy waitresses in skimpy clothes serving our every need; and potential lovers falling over our wallets or our beautiful bodies—these are the things that fill our bubbles with grandiosity.

There is one thing that is as good as a one-night stand: the moment when you know you have booked the job. There is a rush of endorphins when you succeeded in convincing someone to come home with you. The more attractive she is, the higher the rush of grandiosity. Then there are men and women who love to watch themselves perform during sex. They love their way of making love. They love the sounds of a partner's orgasm. Cries of delight means we have performed well and are great in bed. Sex in the city, or anywhere, is indeed another great source of grandiosity. Some Success-Addicts love to pretend they are having a fun time in bed. One told me, "I am a screamer. The sex ain't that great, but I know it makes John feel good." Sex is another tool to seek or give admiration to our success addicted partners.

Some do not even need others to feel great about their sex lives: "I love watching myself in the mirror while I masturbate. I love my own body. I think the man within me is in love with my female body," a Success Addict confessed. Another Success Addict also confessed to a similar obsession with masturbating in front of the mirror. Like Narcissus, they love the mirror as much as they love themselves.

A bubble filled with alcohol, drugs and sexual admiration helps us to believe that we are indeed king or queen of the hill and unconditional love does exist.

A Real Self Substitute

"My life is so numb. I just need something to bring some excitement to my day. I know cocaine is not good for me. But, if I don't have cocaine, what do I have?" an overachiever asked.

"I use cocaine, because it makes me feel free. I can be who I want to be. I am not my parents' perfect little girl anymore. I am me. Until I go home, at least," a friend told me.

Elvis Presley started taking drugs shortly after his mother died. His ex-wife, Priscilla, would later tell Larry King that he used drugs because he had lost direction in his life.

Six months after he married Nicole Kidman, the country music star Keith Urban booked himself into the Betty Ford clinic.

He told *People*, "Because I've been playing since I was six, there was a big part of me that thought it was a trick…. I just got onstage and played, and everybody claps, so my identity was wrapped up in it and my self-esteem was built a large part on audience reaction."

When asked when he realized he had a problem with alcohol and drugs, he said, "It was a slow process. [After I first got to Nashville in 1992] it was how I dealt with a lot of loneliness. I wasn't used to rejection. I wasn't used to loneliness. It just seemed like nothing [my band and I] did was connecting or happening and it was very frustrating."

Later he added, "I was so confused….It was my diversion, my way of numbing myself to rejection and loneliness and confusion."

Sitting in a coffee shop, I heard two NYU graduate students in psychology talking about addictions. So I asked them if there is any research pointing to emotional reasons why people become addicted.

"Emotional pain and confusion, interpersonal conflict and peer pressure are the main reasons why addicts relapse," one said.

Where the best of humanity have a healthy Real Self to give them autonomy over their lives, passion and purpose for living and advice during tough times, Success Addicts often rely on a chemical substitute.

Numbing Our Demons

A while ago, I began dating a woman and within one week, I twice felt convinced that she was about to reject me. To my own surprise, the only thing I could think of to deal with my angst was to light a cigarette. At that point, I seldom smoked at all.

When I told Dr. Masterson of my cravings, he said, "You seem to need to sooth your anxieties."

I understood. When I started to date Jane, my Real Self was brought into play. I had to deal with a woman in my life. But as soon as I activated my Real

Self, my demons emerged, especially my fear of rejection. Cigarettes, known to numb our emotions, helped me not to feel my demons, which are composed of emotional memories. Smoking also helped me to feel that I was not alone. As a chain-smoking lonely Success Addict told me, "Cigarettes are my best friend. They never leave me."

Keith Urban did not speak about what triggered his return to booze. But when he asked how it felt to be on the road, away from Nicole Kidman, he responded, "It's hard. But I've learned to really be grateful for the pain too because it tells me I'm in love. It tells me that I'm without someone, that there's something missing—my partner, my friend, my lover, my wife, my everything. She's missing. So yeah, I used to get really sort of weighed down by those sorts of thoughts. Now I go, well God, it just means I'm alive and I've got a heart that's beating and I'm vulnerable. It's okay."

Love for us Success Addicts is a double-edged sword. When we meet someone we care for, we feel vulnerable and lonely and fear rejection. Away from our lovers, we feel alone. We are jealous because we imagine that they will reject us as we felt rejected in childhood. We are convinced that they will cheat on us. We cannot even recall their love in our minds. We need to see them to know that they exist and are there for us. Away from our partners, our demons haunt us too. We are damned if we are close to people, and we are damned if they go away. Fortunately, alcohol, cigarettes and other drugs numb our demon-riddled minds.

One Sunday, I had another major breakthrough in my acting. I was able to be in the center of a group of actors and be completely emotionally free. I went from rage to laughter to bawling tears when I heard a song with the lyrics: "I have so much love to give." After another lonely Sunday in the Big Apple, I could completely identify with the song.

This free flow of self-expression taunted every demon I have.

But by then, I expected them. The next morning I gave my best in my NIA dancing class, sat for a few hours in my favorite coffee shop and went to the park to enjoy the late autumn leaves. Back in my apartment, I kept saying to myself: "Take care of yourself." To distract myself from an increasing sense of desperation, I started to clean my apartment. After only five minutes, I was overcome by fatigue. Sleep was my only salvation. Halfway between sleeping and waking, I had this weird daydream. I imagined I had a needle filled with cocaine that I injected it into a vein. I felt I was floating on a cloud of peace and joy. I was living a life without demons. I should also explain that I have never used illegal drugs and have never had any interest in doing so—my daydream wasn't based on any physical memory.

JoAnne explained how she, just before her boyfriend left her for an indefinite period of time, started to do line after line. "I don't know why. I just had to."

A lover saying goodbye to go on a trip can trigger our fears that they will leave us forever. Our demons convince us they will never return. Cocaine helped Jo to numb the demons and make her feel in control of her life, at least for a few hours.

Destroy the Self

Recall the incident in an acting class when my teacher exploded into rage, how I tried to take care of my unquiet mind, but instead I ended up stumbling from bar to bar? The next day, after I told Dr. Masterson about my night, he said, "Sounds like you wanted to wipe out your self."

Success Addicts often give in to our demons and use cigarettes, alcohol or drugs to hurt ourselves even more. Just as parents, teachers, coaches and religious leaders punish us for not toeing the line—their line—our demons take over the role of torturer and punish ourselves when we do something good and authentic. "You're not supposed to" or "you are such a disappointment" the voices of the past attack. We hate that part of ourselves that wants to become mature and follow our own passions, connect intimately with others and take care of ourselves. Wiping ourselves out with alcohol or drugs seems the only way out. We want destroy that part of us that wants become "the authentic me."

Addictions

My last job in England was as a doctor at private hospital. During my last week, I worked with an addiction specialist who tried to wean addicts off their drugs by putting them under anesthetics for a day. I recall a couple coming in, excited to try this new way of ridding them of their addictions. A few hours after they were awakened from their sleep, the nurse called me to the ward. As I walked in, I saw the man preparing drugs for use. Despite their high standing in society and their educations, both addicts were helpless even in the face of drastic medical intervention.

Andy Reid, coach of the Philadelphia Eagles, has had to face the tragedy of having two of his sons, Garrett and Britt, caught in the maelstrom of drug addiction. Each faced prison for up to 23 months. When Judge Steven O'Neill publicly called the Reids' household "more or less like a drug emporium," people were outraged. Some say he was too harsh. Others stated that, as a disease, addiction has nothing to do with parenting.

But Judge O'Neil seems to know something about addiction. *The New York Times* reported his actions and comments one Friday as he checked the progress of 15 of the 72 addicts whose recovery he is overseeing in drug court. He praised a man clean for two months after using drugs for half his life. "I think that's pretty incredible," O'Neill said. To another man who was in jail for a parole violation, he said, "You don't make choices in your life. Crack makes all your choices."

"Being an addict means that you admit you're powerless over your addiction and take it one day at a time," he said.

The Judge is right on both accounts. Addictions come from lacking a healthy Real Self and having demons. A healthy Real Self is a function of nature, nurture and culture. So parenting plays an important role in addictions. He is also right that when we are addicted, we are never free. We become more and more powerless over our learned habit. Our animal brain becomes even more voracious in its needs. Chronic abuse both physically and psychologically weakens the Real Self, already weakened since birth. That is why some addicts reach a point of no return. Their habits have given their animal brain too strong of an advantage. The Real Self has been destroyed.

During a directing class, a fellow student directed J.P. Miller's play, *The Days of Wine and Roses*. It tells the story of two people falling in love with one another because of their mutual love of booze. The heart wrenching play portrays the power of the addicted non-conscious mind over conscious will. Toward the end of the play, the husband asks the wife to give up booze. But she responds that without booze, life looks as dirty as the Hudson River. Addictions are a chronic attempt to numb our demons, our painful non-conscious demons that contaminate the filter through which we view life. Unless addicts work through their demons and develop a healthy Real Self, they will always need a shot of something to feel that they have hope for a future.

Dr. Masterson writes,

Hours are spent 'acting out' in order to avoid the abandonment depression. They have learned to engage in a long string of pathologic activities that function like a kind of armor to protect against the emptiness, helplessness and depression that would otherwise consume them. Avoiding the abandonment depression in these self-destructive ways is their 'fix.' Their entire day is given to it. It's their 'business.'

Some people's false self will actually lure them into drugs, alcohol or abusive behaviors. Others sink into passivity or dead-end activities, such as excessive daydreaming, mindless shopping, overeating or unfulfilling sexual liaisons. Some will cling to people, familiar places or objects such as furniture, clothing, art or daily schedules and routines that do little to further the meaningful activities they are ostensibly engaged in. Their primary purpose is to avoid the fear associated with independence and self-expression—fear of the abandonment depression.

Addictions of all kinds serve to support the fragile Real Self, maintain our fantasy bubble and numb the demons that are always ready to enter our created reality and creating chaos in our lives.

Murder of the Real Self

During the last decade that I have spent in therapy, I have thought about ending my life thousands of times. There were days when all I could think of was death. I would wake up in the morning and lie in bed until noon, preoccupied with fantasies of suicide. I could not go on. I felt completely powerless to find a newlife. I knew that in order to have a life, I had to love life, and to love life, I had to have a life. But I had nothing. On most days, drinking coffee was the only activity that gave me pleasure.

First-year university students leave home and their parents, often for the first time. For many, life can become bleak without their mothers present to tell them what to do or to buffer the every up and down of campus life. The self-activation required during the first year—making new friends, dealing with career choices, dating intimately—can bring out the demons. The struggle in a new place easily can mirror the struggle within as the present and past collide to cloud the future. For some, suicide seems the only way out. A rigorous study showed that 55 percent of first-years students at a respectable university had at least one suicidal thought during their first year.

Johannes Kerkorrel was one of our most talented Afrikaner singer-songwriters. As a young man, he was brave enough to take on the Afrikaner establishment with his songs of revolt against apartheid and Afrikaner narrow-mindedness. Years after the birth of the new South Africa, Johannes was found hanging from a tree close to my parents' home. Afrikaners reacted like Americans did when Elvis died.

Koos Kombuis, a friend and fellow artist, wrote an open letter to his dead friend asking him why he killed himself at a time he seemed happiest.

Depressed people killing themselves when they start to enjoy life is a common phenomenon. The self-activation it takes to self-express, self-care and self-share also triggers demons. Without therapy, the Real Self stands no chance. The demons that caused the depression may ultimately cause suicide.

In the newspaper, I read of a young overachiever in the Midwest who was caught by the police for driving his mother's car while still underage. In response to his minor infringement, he shot himself.

When I have tried to strengthen my Real Self over the last year, I was bombarded with suicidal thoughts. When first-year students need to activate their Real Selves to make a life for themselves away from home, 55 percent of them thought of suicide. When Johannes Kerkorrel started to strengthen his Real Self and feel happy, he killed himself. When a young overachiever needed his Real Self to deal with his deflated bubble of perfection, he killed himself. Suicide is murder of the Real Self. Suicide is letting our demons have their way.

Six Murderers

Facing night after night of loneliness, feeling hopeless that I will ever find intimate love or a job that will pay the bills that won't break my spirit, I am peppered by thoughts such as, "If I am going to die in 40 years, why not now? 40 divided by eternity is zero anyway."

My demons make me feel that I am worthless, that nothing exists within me, that nothing was worth living for. I would imagine dying, being cremated and then my ashes flushes down my own toilet.

Dr. Masterson writes,

At the darkest level of depression, a person can despair of ever recovering her real self, and thoughts of suicide are not uncommon. When one is brought low enough repeatedly, or for an extended period of time, it becomes increasingly harder to imagine oneself happy again or able to push through life with the strength and confidence with which the reasonably healthy go about their daily living. At this point a person can teeter on the brink of despair, give up, and consider taking her own life. If the separations they experience in their external lives are painful enough to reinforce their feelings and fear of abandonment, some will commit suicide.

America was shocked by the news that Owen Wilson had attempted suicide by cutting his wrists. Here you have one of Hollywood's success stories: a nice guy from a close family with many friends, the lover of some of Hollywood's most beautiful women and in high demand as an actor. Wilson is living the American super dream. He had everything, yet he nearly ended his life. There have been plenty of rumors as to the cause. From the reports, it seems that Wilson, like so many of Hollywood's leading men, has commitment issues, arguably stemming from a fragile Real Self.

On a Sunday afternoon, I experienced again that awful feeling of a relationship being on the rocks. Two messages that I sent by text and voicemail were not returned. I started to imagine my date sleeping over with another guy the night before. Into my consciousness drifted my memory of my patient who had killed himself by soaking himself with gasoline and lightening a match. I recalled the agony of his girlfriend running in screaming "Why? Why? Why?" I morbidly reflected that at least his girlfriend had loved him.

I also recalled how, when I told Dr. Masterson of a friend who attempted suicide, he immediately asked, "Did her boyfriend leave her?"

These reflections informed me that I was fighting another attack of suicidal thoughts. "I'm not worthy of love. I'm worthless. So why live?"

I clung to Keith Urban's quote: "It's hard. But I've learned to really be grateful for the pain too because it tells me I'm in love." All the self-care activities barely worked.

Our desperate need for intimacy is always engaged in battle with our fear of intimacy and the demons it evokes. It often feels like the battle will never be won. All that remains is the tearing loneliness, emptiness and unbearable longing to feel whole. Suicide seems to be a trusting and safe lover.

Earlier this year, I had another attack of the blahs.

"I feel completely hopeless. I've worked so hard for so long. But where is my payoff? Where is my break? I owe my brother a bank's worth of money, I've no one in New York City I can call a close friend, I've been burned by at least ten women in the last three months. There is just no hope. All I can do is to drink until the end of the year and then jump on January 1. That's all that's floating in my mind. Life is useless. All my efforts are useless."

"You must make sure you connect this feeling with the past. It is not the present. You must realize that it happened to you before," Dr. Masterson said. "You must realize that there is another aspect in play at the moment. You have worked hard at self-expression, but now it seems the voices are telling you that you were wrong to have tried for it seems nothing has changed. But it has."

"You mean they are saying, 'I told you so, I told you so!'"

"Exactly," he answered.

I wanted to kill my Real Self for wanting to mature. Feelings of guilt made me feel as if I was doing something so terrible that I was not worthy of existing.

I am not supposed to do what I want to be doing. I am not supposed to live my life. So I needed to be punished.

All this, while both of my parents are extremely supportive of my life as a writer. But for our brains, what counts is past experiences, not present realities. We are our memories and during tough moments, we are our demons.

There have been times when I wanted to kill myself to spite my family and the world. I would imagine everyone standing next to the grave, what they would say and what they would think. I would feel angry at the way I was forced to live my life and rage for having to be the people pleasing prince of South Africa.

Some nights, panic grips me, making me feel as if the entire building was bending to shake me out of my bed and onto the streets 35 floors below. I feel as if my body takes over my conscious will and I become a puppet, with invisible hands directing me to a window or to the edge of a cliff.

It is clear: Activation of the Real Self triggers the six demons either separately, but more often as a pack, devouring the fragile Real Self. At one point, especially when events in real life start to mimic the horror fantasy of the non-conscious mind, murder of the Real Self seems to be the only solution. At least then, we believe, we are guaranteed that demons will never attack again.

But consciously, I know that my family would do anything and everything for me today—and they have. Research shows that for every person who commits suicide, six people close to them will never recover from the trauma. Every suicide destroys a minimum of seven lives. But all this does not matter when the demons take charge. The past is the present. The non-conscious mind becomes the world's best lawyer and tries to convince you to end it all.

In his book *The Emotional Life of Nations*, Claude DeMause goes one step further. He believes that war is a nation's way of dealing with our collective guilt for self-expression, self-share or self-care. After periods of success and prosperity, we need to cleanse our collective soul. Nations also feel the need to commit suicide by sending our own into battle as sacrificial lambs on the altar of life. We have sinned. We are sorry.

Facing Suicide

Dr. Masterson has often had to remind me that my current feelings of wanting to kill myself were born in my first few years of life. "It is a fantasy to think that killing yourself will solve problems," he says.

Suicide is not the way out; finding a good therapist or a trusted friend is. And in moments of existential despair, the best advice I was given is: "Keep moving." Just don't sit still and say "To be or not to be." Get out. Ride a bike. Go for a walk. Go and drink in a bar. Physical activity and people, even strangers, short-circuit the terrible movie that is playing in our heads at those times. I also remind myself that, according to a friend, most survivors of suicide attempts say that the moment they jumped, they wished they had not. All minds want to live. It is in our genes. Only a tortured mind caught in a fantasy believes that killing oneself is the only way out. At least until you jump.

In the United States, 30,000 people every year feel forced to kill themselves rather than to seek passion and intimacy. This is ten times the number of people who died in the attacks of September 11, 2001. 50-70 percent of all people at least once in their lives think about suicide. Still, suicide and suicide ideation are condemned, more or less, in every society in the world. Instead of making it easy for people with suicidal ideas to talk about their angst, society hushes all conversations about the most important question of all: to be or not to be? Counterintuitively, in the search for life's meaning, life often seems to be meaningless. When we seek passion and love, the non-conscious demons of the past attack us and we lose all sense of reality; the past is the present, and the present is unbearable and meaningless.

But our parents are not to be blamed. These demons are not the product of one generation, but are passed from generation to generation over thousands of years by those who share our DNA. While blaming our parents is both misguided and fruitless, we *can* start demanding that our societies accept struggles with suicide as a cancer of the soul, not as a way out for weak, spineless people. We are hurt people, not sinners.

America has come a long way. But many people still avoid the issue. As one American woman told me after I told her about my suicidal ideations, "I just want to smack you in the face for having those thoughts." There is no doubt that her reaction shows that the same ideas are percolating in her non-conscious mind. South Africa and many other countries with very high suicide rates still have archaic beliefs about suicide. The world needs to shift its attitudes toward suicide. Too many people are dying.

Real Murder

It was in acting class that I first thought of murder as another form of suicide. While doing *Hamlet*, I had to stab Polonius behind the curtain. Failing to have any emotional reaction from this, my acting teacher, Carol Fox Prescott, said, "Think of murder as a suicide."

A mass murder-suicide by Robert Hawkins rocked America in December

2007. In a suicide letter to his family he wrote, "I never meant to hurt you all so much....I just can't be a burden to you all....I can't take this meaningless existence anymore....I've been a constant disappointment....Just remember the good times we had together....I love you mommy. I love you daddy."

This letter suggests that Robert Hawkins lacked a healthy Real Self; he was tortured by the demons that made him feel as if his life was meaningless and that he was fundamentally bad. He projected his demons and pain onto the world.

A few years ago, I woke up to the news that in my neighborhood, Greenwich Village, a filmmaker, who suffered a string of professional and personal failures, had shot a worker at a pizza restaurant. Why? The worker had "offended" him a few days before. I believe the worker's comment was the final event that ripped off the filmmaker's mask of success. Overwhelmed by his demons, murder seemed to be the only way out. The event left four people dead.

Capote is a movie depicting events in the life of Truman Capote, the famed author who investigated two murderers for his book *In Cold Blood*. This book invented the genre of literary nonfiction and made Capote a legend.

When they broke into a Midwestern farmhouse, one of the murderers had little intention to kill. In fact, he made sure that everyone in the house was unhurt and prevented his friend from doing any harm. But when he saw the hatred the father of the house had for him, he snapped. The looks had triggered the demons of his past. Suddenly the man of the house represented everyone who had humiliated him in his life. He wanted revenge. The man's demons killed a good family.

Truman Capote later confessed that he somehow felt he knew the murderer, that they were raised in similar households. The only difference was that the murderer had walked out the backdoor while Capote had walked out the front door. The realization that he too could have been a murderer given the right circumstances forced Capote into an even deeper addiction to alcohol, from which he died years later.

The Way Forward

The world spends billions of dollars fighting drug smuggling and prostitution, incarcerating criminals and maintaining people on death row. The cost of suicide and addiction are astronomical. Would this money not be better spent on ensuring that all children leave their childhoods with a healthy Real Self? Then people would not need the comfort of an empty bottle, a syringe in their arms or the need for revenge. They would find solace from this hard and sometimes unforgiving life in the arms of someone who really cares, wake up in the morning excited to chase their unique dreams and contribute to society.

Many parents of suicide victims, drug addicts, overdose victims, criminals and murderers feel guilty for their children's anguish and self-destructive behavior.

In the chapter "Blaming our Parents," I make the case that no parent can be held responsible for the mistakes of their children. A mother and father can only give the intimate love to their children that they received from their parents, who only gave what was given to them. If we keep tracing the line of blame from generation to generation we will realize that we all are part of the ongoing human struggle. Life on earth was never perfect, especially not family life.

That is why we have tears to mourn: to mourn the lack of love we received in childhood or in the present, to mourn the pain our mothers received as little girls, to mourn a son addicted to drugs, to mourn the suicide of a daughter, to mourn a son killing another human, to mourn our nation's involvement in wars.

As humans, all we can hope is that our tears will wash away the notions of sinners and saints, prisoners and popes, good and evil, blame and judgment. Let's hope our tears can clean the slate of callous judgment.

Then, with the power of modern science, let's rethink the way we deal with addicts, criminals, suicidal patients, murderers, prostitutes. Let's stop seeing them as people who need to be punished, but people with broken hearts filled with demons to be rehabilitated. Let's seize the opportunity science has given us to improve the lives of all people and make sure that it does not matter whether they leave their homes through the front door or the back door, but that they leave their homes with a healthy Real Self.

Chapter 17

Perfect Parents, Clueless Children

I met Mandy, a beautiful actress from the West Coast at a Broadway play. At intermission, I asked her and a friend out for dinner. During the dinner conversation, Mandy told us about how, shortly after college, she had married a man she had only known for a year. She was madly in love, but the wedding cake was still fresh on the dining room table when her knight in shining armor removed his guard. He became obnoxious and selfish, suppressed her wish to act and became physically abusive.

"Why I married him, I don't know. But trust me, I will never marry a man like that again."

"Tell me about your mother. Do you get along with her?"

Mandy gave me a perfect Duchenne smile.

"Oh yes. My mother is perfect. We're best of friends."

If primary caretakers, in her case her mother, teach us how to love, why did the perfect daughter of a perfect mother end up so clueless about love or about believing she deserves better?

Attachment Styles

In the mid-1980s, Main and Goldwyn designed an 18-question questionnaire, called the Adult Attachment Interview (AAI) to evaluate an adult's attitude toward relationships.

Some sample questions from the AAI are:

1. I'd like you to choose five adjectives that reflect your childhood relationship with your mother. This might take some time, and then I'm going to ask you why you chose them. (Repeated for father.)
2. To which parent did you feel closest and why? Why isn't there this feeling with the other parent?
3. When you were upset as a child, what would you do?

4. What is the first time you remember being separated from your parents? How did you and they respond?

The key is that all relationships are assessed, not only the history of parental relationships.

Main and Goldwyn then took the data and judged it by four criteria designed by Grice that assesses ideal rational discourse. Was a person's response truthful with ample evidence for what was said (quality)? Was it succinct and yet complete (quantity)? Was it relevant to the topic at hand (relevance)? Was it clear and orderly (manner)?

Based on the data, they were able to group participants into four categories. Researchers found that mentally healthy people value all intimate relationships, remember the good and the bad aspects of their relationships with detail and objectivity and can continue to appreciate the other person regardless of how they are feeling. They do not see parents as perfect or failures. They see them for who they are.

During the interview, Success Addicts, also called dismissive adults, "normalize and give positive descriptions of his or her parents (i.e., excellent, very normal mother), but these categorizations are essentially unsupported, or are contradicted by specific incidents. Negative experiences are said to have little or no effect. The transcripts of these individuals are short, and also show a lack of memory—so they are denying any negativity and are pseudo-positive in their orientation to their past and their history."

This group tends to be less comfortable depending on others and being intimate. Dismissive adults tend to have extremely brief stories. Many don't recall memories of childhood to avoid reliving painful experiences. Those with painful experiences either deny them or rationalize them by claiming that those experiences "made me stronger, more independent and the person I am today." In short, these people have almost no memory of childhood and believe their primary caretakers were perfect. In short, Success Addicts are saying, "My parents were perfect; but, sorry, I can't remember how perfect they were."

Believing in perfect parents is a lie that those of us with fragile Real Selves need to keep telling ourselves over and over again. Our work, passion, love and self-care activities may border on the brink of self-destruction, but we will take the belief that our primary caretaker was perfect to the grave.

Perfect Partner

Joan is an extremely successful woman in her forties who lives in San

Francisco. Every night is filled with expensive wine, dinner dates, movies and youthful revelry. She is also painfully alone and perplexed at her inability to find the right man. "I am looking for someone with as much humor as I have. Someone who can make me laugh. He does not need to be rich." To me, Joan's sense of humor is more akin to humiliating sarcasm than true humor. Nor have I seen her fall for a man who was not tall, dark and handsome and who made a gazzilion dollars a day.

But on all levels, Joan is in a very serious relationship. For every event in her day, rather than calling her husband or boyfriend, she calls her mom. Her "perfect" mom is her surrogate husband. To me it also seems that Joan is her mom's surrogate husband, despite her own husband still being alive. One night, after a glass of wine, she confessed that her parents do not have a perfect marriage. That is all she said. "Their marriage is not perfect." But the confession that something about her mom was imperfect left her in tears. The next morning she called me, filled with shame for revealing this tidbit of information. She is 45 and a professional consultant to CEOs, but admitting to one imperfection about her mother turned her into a sobbing child.

Why is this woman with a perfect mother still single? Why is she still tied to her perfect mother's coattails as a 45-year-old woman? Why is she still seeking Prince Charming rather than fulfilling herself?

Perfectly Clueless

Elvis Presley is still an icon today, almost 35 years after his death. In an interview on CNN, Larry King asked Priscilla Presley, "His relationship with [his mother] was extraordinary, right?

"Oh my gosh, yes," Priscilla answered.

Larry pressed, "I mean, it was really tight."

"Yes, they were very tight. You know, they…he depended on her for her… you know, her ideas, her opinions. He babied her. She watched out after him. It was a very unique, extraordinary relationship and a lot of love there."

Priscilla and Elvis met in Germany while he was stationed there after he joined the army and shortly after the death of his mother. Priscilla, at the age of 14, was the only person the then vulnerable Elvis could confide in. They got married two years later. Years later, she would confess that Elvis had already begun to use drugs in Germany.

In a 2003 interview, Larry King asked Priscilla, "What bothered him? What did he…what troubled him?

"What troubled him? You know, I think Elvis lost sight of his purpose in life, believe it or not. He never really understood why all the adoration. He never really understood where, I think, he wanted to go. I know he wanted to be a great actor, but he honestly couldn't understand where it was all going. And he had to keep motivated and it was, you know, keeping him motivated, keeping him focused was very difficult."

The perfect son with the perfect love from a perfect mother lost direction and his sense of self after her death. Should perfect mothers not leave behind resilient children able to face life after their own death? Children with the right kind of love, and lots of it, do not die of overdose, the ultimate form of self-hate. Nor are children supposed to baby their parents.

Perfect Presidents

George W. Bush, at a Boy Scout jamboree in 2005, said the following, "… one of the most valuable lessons I've learned—listen to your mother. I didn't have much choice—Mom always has a way of speaking her mind. When I paid attention, I benefited."

But by all accounts Barbara Bush instilled fear in her children and would "let rip if she's got something on her mind." According to an uncle, "letting rip" included slaps and hits.

While studies show that boys with such mothers have a higher risk of becoming wild, alcoholic or antisocial, Bush ignored these negative memories.

Bill Clinton had a very close relationship with his mother. A friend said, "I know Bill showed more affection toward his mom than any of us showed toward our moms. You could tell they were close and drew on each other and they both loved to be around people."

Both US presidents, who both brought significant scandal onto the White House, seemed to have had perfect mothers. But would perfect mothers not nurture ethical courageous sons and daughters?

Beauty and the Beast

Marc is one of the most talented people I know. Give him a calculator or a musical instrument or an essay to write, and he will succeed. He's lived all over the world. In a moment of self-revelation, he admitted that he was not living the life that he would like to. He is confused and his relationships with women are chaotic. "But," he said, "my mother and I are good friends. Really good friends. That at least makes the struggle worthwhile." When I asked about his father, he paused, "Well, my dad is not a man who can talk. He's very reserved.

He's an introvert. She married the wrong guy."

Perfect mothers or perfect fathers always seem to be married to assholes or yawns leaving their children feeling sorry for their perfect parent.

Lets examine this logic. A stranger knocks on your door at this very moment. You open the door. She tells you. "Hey. I want to tell you that I am perfect, or near perfect. I also want to tell you that I married a man who never gave me the love I wanted or who always was away or who drank too much or always worked till late at night or was emotionally unavailable."

Interested in the statement, you ask, "Did you marry him out of free will, or were you forced to marry him?"

"I married him out of free will, off course. But trust me, I'm perfect."

Will you believe that person that she is perfect? Off course not! How on earth can someone be perfect if they could not even make a "good enough" decision about whom to marry? Not what car to buy. Not what pedicure to have, but who to spend the rest of her or his life with, who to make the father or mother of her or his children.

Perfect Foil

Time voted her one of the world's hundred most important people. She is one of Hollywood's hottest actors and an ambassador for the plight of many children all over the world. Her past is filled with many painful break ups, self-cutting, father-hating and her body mutilated with excessive tattoos, signs of enormous self-hatred. When a CNN interviewer asked her about her mother and whether they ever had any arguments, Angelina Jolie answered, "We never once had a fight."

Is it possible for two mature confident people to live fully and intimately for almost 30 years without any conflict? Will a perfect mother cause her child to destroy her body with tattoos and self-cutting?

Perfect versus Good

A while ago, I went to an expensive restaurant near Union Square for lunch. Even writers need to treat themselves after a few days of productive writing. I sat down and ordered my meal. I was treasuring my time with myself in the lap of luxury. I felt content. The next moment my bliss was interrupted by a two-year-old throwing a tantrum. Great! My luck! The mother smiled apologetically. I smiled back. Or rather, I faked a smile back.

The businesspeople at the restaurant were less kind, as they shot dirty looks. 30 seconds later and the Terrible Two again shook the restaurant to its foundation. I am a medical doctor and actor, but even with this combined expertise on physiognomy and vocal projection, I still don't know how it is possible that such a small child can make such a loud noise. It seems physiological impossible.

Writing the book, and fully informed of what is going on between mother and child psychologically, I watch the mother dealing with the situation. The mother had kind lively caring eyes. She was well dressed, but not a fashion freak. She had womanly curves and seemed to move well in her body. She looked like a next-door mom. I made a bet to myself that this woman would deal well with the situation. She did. She did not scream or threaten or tell her child that she was embarrassing her in front of the stuck-up business crowd. She soothed the child. She lovingly held the child. She showed the child she was there for her. Two minutes later, the child was a happy camper. The mother tried to lie her down. Out again came the trumpet. The mother sighed tiredly. Again, she restrained herself from losing control. Imagine the self-control that took.

There is no doubt that she will occasionally lose it. No parent can exert this type of self-control time after time after time. Especially not parents who want to be perfect: the perfect parent, the perfect spouse, the perfect citizen. Being a parent is most probably the toughest and most complicated task in life. No ifs, ands or buts. To be a "good enough" parent is a miracle. To be a perfect parent: a fantasy.

Origins of Perfection

We know that during the first 13 months, all babies live in a bubble of fantasy created by their primary caretakers. Life is great, the baby the center of attention and the recipient of unbridled admiration and pleasure. We also know that a child, through his imagination, believes that his caretaker is an extension of himself. So when she is perfect in her care, he feels perfect about himself. A "good-enough" parent is a *really good* parent, but certainly not perfect, because she is human too. There are many moments when she cannot be there with a bottle, to soothe fears, to admire.

During these moments, a child panics. He experiences the world as frightening and abandoning—remnants of our innate drives. At these times, he experiences his caregiver as the cause of pain. He has no way of rationalizing that his parents have rarely failed him in the past and will certainly return. To the child, you are either there or you are not.

So what can a child do when he feels helpless and in danger because his mother is not there?

All children are capable of splitting their experiences of the world and of their parents into two parts. The one part is the experience of mother being perfect and the child being perfect. The other is the experience of the mother as uncaring, if not wicked, and of the child feeling himself to be the scum of the earth. Obviously all children prefer to live with the fantasy of mother and child being perfect. The other experiences are sent to the non-conscious.

To understand this concept even better, remember that a year-old child has two DVDs of memories in his mind: the Heaven and the Hell DVD. Imagine the bubble to be a big Imax theater with a huge white screen. The child's non-conscious mind tries to play the Heaven DVD, in which he feels perfect, his mother is perfect and life his oyster. He avoids the Hell DVD with footage of the worst of times. Life is all about escaping reality.

A good-enough parent knows that her child cannot spend his life in the Imax theater. She slowly deflates his bubble and makes him emerge from the controlled environment. The more the child experiences himself as capable outside the bubble, the less he needs to split his experiences of his mother and the world in two. Around the age of three or four, with the Real Self stronger, the child starts to become his own editor and combines the two DVDs. The new DVD, called the Reality DVD, presents his parents in a more realistic light: both good and bad, supportive but in need of support. In the Reality DVD, he sees himself and other people in the world similarly. Ordinary, but unique individuals who can deal with what life throws at them, sometimes with aplomb, often with failure and tears.

Dr. Masterson writes, "Mothers of normal children teach them about the realities of life by introducing them to frustrating experiences in carefully measured doses that gradually dispel the notion that the fused 'grandiose child-omnipotent mother' entity can go on forever. They deflate their children's feelings of grandeur and bring them back to earth."

Perfect Child, Perfect Mother

Success Addicts never reach this stage. Arrested in development and struggling with a fragile Real Self, we cannot face the reality of the world. We only have the Heaven DVD or the Hell DVD to watch. We cling to the view that we and our mothers are perfect. We ban the Hell DVD to the Siberia of our mind. We know that if the Hell DVD plays, we will feel worthless and as if we are about to die.

Dr. Masterson writes that the Success Addict "will go through life relating to people as parts—either positive or negative—rather than as whole entities. He will be unable to maintain consistent commitments in relationships when he is frustrated or angry; and he will have difficulty evoking the image of the loved one when the person is not physically present. He will never fully realize that his parents are complete individuals who have positive and negative attributes. He will continue to think of them as two separate entities, one benevolent, the other wicked."

It is only after therapy that we can appreciate the lie.

A patient described to Alice Miller how she used to believe her mother was perfect, affectionate, warm-hearted, discussed her own struggle with life and worked hard for her children. But after she experienced her demons in therapy, she recalled how "cold, petty, obsessive, easily offended, but hard to please she was." The perfect mother was a shield to hide from her demons.

When one meets people who truly believe that their parents are *perfect*, it probably indicates that they do not possess a healthy Real Self and rather than living in reality, exist in their own grandiose bubbles. They will likely have intimacy issues for the rest of their lives because you cannot be intimate if you cannot see another as a complete person. They also surely have a Hell DVD hidden in their psyches containing all the painful moments in their childhoods. You can know that when the Hell DVD is triggered, it will project a world filled with people who are wicked and of the Success Addict being bad, yet still the central figure in the movie.

Lacking a healthy Real Self, life and the world caused the beautiful Midwestern actress to project Prince Charming onto a man who was closer to the Wicked Witch; Sam, the perfectionist CEO, to feel like a hurt child when his employees did not live up to his expectations; Bush and Clinton to feel justified in acting unethically; and Elvis to project his Hell DVD onto his life and feel lost. The emotional umbilical chord was never cut. Mother and child still felt like one.

A life lived in a bubble pleasing a perfect parent without the aid of a healthy Real Self is indeed a clueless life. But it also can be a dangerous life.

Transference at Work

I have often been disappointed by bosses, teachers and leaders. I would join a group, figure out who the leader was, and make him the focus of my attention and care. I would be nice and polite, bend over backwards to please him and make him feel perfect. But at one point, I would always feel betrayed. The teacher would either abuse my trust or I would realize that I had the wrong expectations of the teacher.

In a *Harvard Business Review* article on the power of transference, Michael Maccoby showed how in work and politics, we tend to transfer images of our parents onto authority figures. Typically, people who transfer their fathers onto their bosses revert to the mentality of a five-year-old in their presence: "Father knows best," they say. They expect their bosses to give assignments, rewards, constructive criticism and approval. If the boss does not abuse this transference, it can lead to good outcomes. Maccoby discussed how employees call Francis Ford Coppola "Papa" or "Godfather" and Steven Spielberg "Rabbi" and "Teacher." If the boss or leader abuses this transference, we see companies and countries led astray by egomaniacal leaders. Followers often trust the wrong person for the wrong reasons.

Success Addicts often transfer a maternal image onto their supervisors. We can have the same adoration and respect for our bosses that we had for our mothers as children. We feel that our bosses have the same power to reject us and cause our deaths as if we were helpless infants. So we feel guilty if we cause her suffering, Maccoby writes, because "guilt is the fear that the mother will cut off her life-giving nurturance." We also expect our bosses to exhibit the empathy, care and compassion we expect from a mother. So when we transfer our irrational image of a perfect mother onto a boss or leader, we become like children. This position is treacherous. At best, good bosses cannot live up to our expectations; at worst, manipulative supervisors can wreak emotional havoc on us by abusing our infantile trust in them. When we finally wise up, we realize that we have wasted years trying to please people who in no way have earned our respect.

On a national level, we can see how politicians use our need for empathy, care and direction during moments of crisis. Many people revert to a childlike state and want others to hold their hands when the going gets tough. Throughout history, we see that when the right leader appears, this maternal or paternal transference can boost morale and lead to success. We also can look at Nazi Germany to see how an economic depression allowed otherwise rational Germans to follow Hitler.

From Hollywood to Hell

He was confident and skilled and he knew it. A prominent surgeon in our community led my last ward round of my final surgical rotation at medical school. I remember how he explained his surgical approach to different abdominal hernias. Later, I was shocked to learn that, after his wife filed for divorce, this top surgeon drank rat poison. He didn't die, but his vocal cords were permanently destroyed.

I live close to Washington Square, the home of New York University. A year ago a young NYU woman, after a quarrel and break-up with her boyfriend, turned around, ran to the window and threw herself to her death.

I ran into an acquaintance one day in the Village. He was pale from emotional pain. He started to tell me how he had met his wife, fell in love and they enjoyed a perfect time together. But the day they got married, she turned into an obsessive, castrating and controlling person. She also became pregnant. After many months in therapy, he decided to leave his wife and child. "But it was as if my departure triggered something. She became even worse. She forbade me from seeing my son. I had to beg money from family to pay lawyers to get two hours a week visiting rights. When I am there, she treats me like dirt. She does not trust me with my own son."

Those of us obsessed with romantic love project our perfect mother image onto our potential partners. When the person returns our approaches, our brains pump us full of chemicals. We start jumping on Oprah's couch or driving down red carpets on our motorcycles. Life is exactly the way it was when we were at our happiest as a child.

So people in love are not in love with a real person. We are in love with an image of perfection that we have created in our brains. We are seeing a movie projected onto another human and memories of a perfect caretaker who never existed.

Sustaining this type of relationship requires a tenacious denial of reality. We work hard to avoid noise and sunlight from entering the cinema complex in our brain. We want to believe the movie we are watching is real. "My life depends upon it!" the hurt child within us screams.

But, like in the movies, the lights do go up after a few hours. We are forced to confront the reality of other people in the cinema coughing and sneezing, the lines at the bathrooms while our bladders are about to burst, the unbearable honking of irritable cabdrivers. Reality does find its way into our lives. It is only a question of when.

When people spend a lot of time together, they start seeing flaws that do not fit the constructed reality of the Heaven DVD. Some of us immediately cut and run. The thought of going through the same pain of the past is too much. These are people I call the "very hot to very cold in a few days" lovers.

Others set about trying to change their partners to become the perfect lovers they want them to be. The start telling their beloved how to behave, how to dress, how to make sure their teeth are cleaned before they leave the bathroom. They demand perfection—at least as they see it.

People in relationships that are based solely on romantic love often have a schizophrenic experience of love: perfect or rejecting; hot or cold; black or white; beautiful or ugly. For those in the claws of the Cupid, nothing is ordinary.

If reality keeps interrupting the Heaven DVD, we become unable to maintain the lie that we, our partners or our relationships are perfect. So our brain goes for the Hell DVD. Within a short period of time, our concoction of perfect love is transformed into a rejecting demon. Suddenly Cinderella or Prince Charming has become the Stepmother or the Devil who will hurt us. Retaliation is called for. The relationship turns ugly. Eventually one person decides to move away. Often both parties are filled with hurt, anger and a sense of deep betrayal. "Where did it all go wrong? What did I do?" they ask. They did nothing wrong. Reality just burst the fantasy bubble in their minds.

When a beloved decides to leave another, the Heaven DVD is immediately replaced with the Hell DVD. A lover experiences painful rejection, a tearing of her heart. Her sense of being one is ripped into two pieces. The pain is unbearable. The hurt child starts screaming in his created reality, "Do whatever it takes to become whole again!"

Sometimes lovers start stalking the rejecting lover to force a reunion. They are convinced that they need to have the lover back again or they will die. To them stalking is the only way to bring back what is rightfully theirs.

When the lover continues his or her dismissal, the Hell DVD informs him that the demons are about to humiliate, beat or kill. The hurt child now may scream, "Humiliate, beat or kill the demon before it kills you!" But killing the demon in our fantasies translates to killing a real person.

A few of us hear the same command to kill, but we feel helpless to defend ourselves against the homicidal demons. We are left with only two options: Endure unbearable pain and humiliation or numb it with drugs, alcohol or suicide.

The surgeon and NYU student chose suicide over a life without a partner. The castrating wife, stalking husbands or murdering partners chose emotional and physical violence to attack the partner onto which an evil maternal image was transferred.

A life spent believing in perfect parents is a life of pain, confusion and broken love. We are seeing life through a bubble of perfection so we trust the wrong people, avoid danger when real and expect life to be what it never can be.

The Lie that Destroys

Despite our mask of success and conscious beliefs that we are the best of humanity, Success Addicts are hurting. We may think that the world is our oyster, but life is a daily challenge for us. When we face moments that demand spontaneous and wise action, we lack a compass to help us. We dread encountering situations that healthy people take joy or interest in: searching for hobbies and interests during adolescence, sexual experimentation, going to college, finding a job, changing careers, making friends, being ourselves, doing what we love, interacting intimately with a spouse, child or friend, saying "no" when we want to, being creative and dealing with conflict constructively. Mentally healthy people typically look forward to raising children and encountering new phases of life. They have a realistic view of death, both their own and their loved ones. We cannot be truly happy because self-expression, self-care and self-share trigger massive attacks of our demons. The demons of Success Addicts force us to survive our lives rather than experiencing them. Instead, we focus on inflating our bubbles. The chaos of our non-conscious minds makes many of us addicts of one sort or another.

This, and we believe that at least one of our parents was perfect. It is this illusion that keeps us children despite all our success. It is this illusion that is destroying our lives. This begs the question: If we know that happy parents nurture happy children, can we blame our parents making us Success Addicts?

Section IV
Becoming a Success Addict

Chapter 18

On Blaming Parents

Happy parents nurture happy babies. But within that one sentence we see the three main variables important to the mental health of a child: What type of nurturing do they use? Who are these parents? Who is this baby?

Nurturing Styles

Some people believe that there was a time when perfect parenting was the status quo. Life on earth was great. Then we humans somehow screwed it all up and today families are falling apart like no other time in history. The truth is that parenting has been evolving from an almost animalistic view of raising babies to the kinder, gentler rearing methods of today.

In his book *The Emotional Life of Nations*, Lloyd deMause discusses six modes of child rearing in Western nations, which are still found today, even in the most advanced countries. DeMause states that five book-length historical studies and numerous academic articles in the *Journal of Psychohistory* support his models. What follows is a discussion of deMause's research on the different models for parenting and how each evolved over time. The time periods indicated refer to when researchers found the very earliest evidence of the new mode of parenting and represent only a minority of the population, rather than the dominant mode of parenting at any given time.

The Early Infanticidal Mode took place during early civilization when humans organized themselves into bands and tribes. "Survival of the fittest" was the main approach to life. The goal was to have as many children as possible, provide them with minimal care and selfishly hope that at least a few survived to look after parents later in life. Fathers typically were too immature to act as caregivers and emotionally and physically absent. Children were seen mostly as objects or commodities and were often sacrificed. The results were very high infanticide rates, incest, body mutilation, child rape, tortures and emotional or physical abandonment by parents. Prepubertal marriages of girls were common.

The Late Infanticidal mode took place from chiefdom to early states during antiquity. Various institutionalized schemes for care by others become popular, such as adoption, wet nursing, fosterage and the use of the children of others as slaves. As society became increasingly complex, young children were not overtly rejected as much by mothers, and fathers became more involved with the instruction of older children. Genocidal slaughter and the routine enslavement of women and children were still common. Child sacrifice was still present in early states.

The Abandoning Mode lasted from the beginning of the first century of the common era to the late eleventh century. The goal of parenting was to eradicate all evil within the child. During this period, Christians began Europe's two-millennia-long struggle against infanticide. Still, children were thought to be born full of evil and so were beaten early and severely. Many children were abandoned to monasteries, wet nurses and to the rich to work as servants or apprentices. Routine pedophilia of boys and girls continued.

The Ambivalent mode started at the beginning of the twelfth century. The goal was to shape children into moral beings whose inherent sins could be forgiven. Children were beaten severely, but parents started to love children who were well behaved. Parents still hated them during their "evil" moments—hence the ambivalent mode. This period showed the first movement toward a child's independent rights, child instruction manuals, outlawing of child rape, institutionalized schooling and pediatric medicine.

The Intrusive Mode started during the Renaissance, at the beginning in the sixteenth century. The goal of parenting was to make children "obedient," to control their minds, their insides, their emotions and their lives. Parents started to bring up infants themselves rather than sending them elsewhere or at least had a wet nurse at home. Parents gave children attention if they were able. The child was nursed by his or her mother, not swaddled, not given regular enemas, but toilet trained early, prayed with, but not played with, hit, but not battered, punished for masturbation, but not raped, taught and made to obey with guilt and threats as often as physical means of punishment. As a result, arranged marriages declined, as did spousal battery, and real married love and companionship began. The seeds for the religious, scientific, political and economic revolutions of the Renaissance were shown.

During the Socializing Mode, which started at the beginning of the eighteenth century and is still the most accepted mode of parenting in America and Europe, the goal of child rearing was to assume the parent's role and goals in the society they were born into. With industrialization, mothers were able to move away from previous modes of parenting and focus on their own instinctual desires. Mothers started to employ childcare. Even fathers began to play with their children. Parents started to decrease the number of children, in order to give them more care and personal attention. Children began to be controlled by spanking and psychological manipulation. The result is that fewer people cling to authoritarian figures. This was a major contributing force to the building of the modern industrialized world and its new values of nationalism and democracy.

The Helping Mode started at the beginning of mid-twentieth century. The goal: to help children reach their own goals at each stage of life, rather than being socialized into the parents' goals. In this mode, both mother and father are equally involved with the child from infancy. Children are bathed in love, not showered with blows; they are also apologized to. Children raised in this fashion are much more empathic toward others, which led to an overall increase in happiness levels.

Cultures all over the world differ in how they nurture their young. Then, within cultures, people may still be stuck in primitive parenting modes. When parents cannot escape their own communities and cultures, a repetition of the dominant mode of parenting will take place. In the process, the sins of the fathers and mothers are passed on while everyone believes they are doing what is right by society.

In apartheid South Africa, I believe that most of us were raised with a mixture of the Intrusive and Socializing modes. My parents—merely complying with the cultural norms of the day—did what was most likely done to them, which was the accepted practice of the day.

Here in America, and increasingly in Europe and South Africa, the culture has created an interesting spin on the Socialization Mode. I call it "My Friend" Mode. Parents are not raising their children to assume their roles in life, they raise them to be their friends and objects of admiration. Even though, on the surface, children seem to be more cared for than ever, the reality is that many are being psychologically used. Children are not raised to follow their unique goals, but to please their parents' need for instant gratification and admiration.

Nurturing and Knowledge

Every month, dozens of books are released on child rearing. The research is overwhelming and often contradictory. "Never let your baby cry," one group says. "Babies must learn to sooth themselves," says the other group. "Let them cry. It is good for them."

Based on my own research, I have my own set of nurturing principles that I believe is essential. But who says it is the truth? And even if it is the truth, can I blame parents who have been raising their children as best as they can, without the support of science? Can I blame parents who did not have the luxury of living in a time when research in positive psychology, attachment theory, neuroscience and clinical psychiatry are starting to support each other's findings? Can you blame a child for putting his finger into an electric outlet if he didn't know better? Of course not.

Nurturing and Fate

You can have the best parents and a baby born with perfect genes. You can live in a culture that supports the Helping mode of nurturing. But then fate strikes. A child gets seriously ill and is hospitalized for months, isolated from his parents. A mother dies in childbirth or before the child is three years of age. A father dies or leaves, causing enormous stress on a mother with a young family. Famine and hunger can prevent the right nutrients from supporting a child's neurological development. Children can become victims of child abuse, forever throwing him or her into a maelstrom of betrayal, fear and rage. Fate, despite a parent's best intentions, knowledge and care can cause significant psychological and physical trauma.

In my own entry into the world, I was a difficult delivery at a time when there were minimal observation monitors compared to today. Is it possible that the surge of cortisol I experienced during a difficult delivery sensitized my developing brain and made me more of a clinging baby? Absolutely.

Happy Parents

March 28, 2006. I am reading *The New York Times* Op-Ed section. In bold, the letters read: "In Asia, female lives come cheap." The article discusses the life of Aisha Parveen, who was kidnapped at fourteen and spent six years in a harem before being rescued by a man whom she would marry. The perfect Hollywood story. Except now the courts want to charge her with adultery and send her back to her "owner" where she most likely will be killed. Her family wants to kill her for dishonoring their family name. Her husband and savior, Mohamed Akram, is facing pressure from his family to divorce Parveen. Specifically, the husband of Mohamed's sister has threatened to divorce her and leave her on the streets with two children if Mohamed does not comply. Parveen is quoted as saying: "God should not give daughters to poor people. And if a daughter is born, God should grant her death." Please look at the date of the article. It is the year 2006.

An anomaly, we in the Western World would say, belonging to Asia. Wrong. It is not an anomaly. In India today, girls under the age of five are 50 percent more likely to die than boys , who are seen as a blessings. Because of this strongly held view, in some countries, such as India and China, ultrasounds are often used to detect the fetus's sex, which often results in selective abortions, also known as eugenics. In certain parts of the world, girls are simply not valued. The fact that some of these girls will grow up to become mothers to the future generation of children is frightening.

This preferential treatment of boys is not only taking place only in Asia. It is still a part of our Western culture, and if not present today, carved into our emotional DNA. Today the difference in treatment does not lead to the physical death, but since a child experiences lack of full support as abandonment, one can only conclude that preferential treatment of boys harms the emotional lives of girls and women.

Sexual discrimination against women is still rampant all over the world. How can we expect a mother to raise her child with a healthy Real Self if we value men more than women? If mothers are supposed to transfer their passions in life to their children, how can they when many cultures around the world still place archaic restrictions on women's right to self-express politically, professionally, creatively and sexually?

Alice Miller discusses how emotional, physical and sexual trauma can rob a woman of her instincts and the pleasure of taking care of another. A disrespected woman will pass on her disrespect to her children. Her son will learn to idealize her, but will treat other women with disrespect. Her daughter will continue the chain of disrespect by obeying men, but taking out her childhood pain on her chidren. Where women's emotional, political, sexual and physical rights are not recognized, everyone suffers.

As for men, society encourages us to leave our emotions in childhood. We are taught to be cool, calm and collected. But research shows that we are better spouses, fathers and leaders if we have more access to all our emotions and can express them appropriately.

Over the centuries, society has robbed women of their political and sexual power and rights. It has stripped men of their emotional power. We need to work toward full emotional, physical and sexual liberation for all sexes to help us raise healthier children. Or to put it into Jungian speak, we need to encourage all men to develop their anima, that side of their personality that wants to be caring, vulnerable and intuitive. We need to encourage women to develop their animus, their rational, assertive, analytical and functional abilities. Together, we must aim for a society that celebrates both the anima and animus.

When and where I was born, women were oppressed from living out their true potential. You either became a nurse or a teacher. And you had to be a virgin until you got married. Men were raised to be tough rugby players who never to shed a tear. Can I blame my parents for living in a culture that had little respect for their full humanity?

Modern Culture

Our culture's obsession with pleasure and admiration influences the care that parents give to their children. We think it is fine to leave our babies with the grandparents so that we can fly to exotic destinations for ten days. We do not realize that this sudden separation bursts the much need fantasy bubble that every child needs to incubate a healthy Real Self. We think we should lose our pregnancy fat within two weeks instead of enjoying our bodies and their response to our newborns. We think eating dinner in front of the television is a good way of parenting our children. We are encouraged to believe that we should buy our children whatever they want, whether it is the latest computer game or the biggest cheeseburger. Our modern culture is making us lonelier. So we start using our children as friends. We become obsessed with their lives so we do not have to worry about our own loneliness. We also need to perform as parents: We need to get our children into the best schools and universities. Elite education will make everything right. When our neighbors say *wow* to our children's big cars and homes, we know we were good parents. All that counts is doing, doing, doing.

Parents and Past Traumas

I have asked friends who tell me that they will not raise their children the way their parents raised them to take a piece of paper and write down ten things your parents did that you hated the most. Then have children. And when they leave for university, ask them to write down the ten things they hated about their parents. I bet you nine out of ten will be exactly the same.

So when parents come from drug or alcohol addicted homes they will bring their scars. When they come from verbally abusive homes, they will erupt with the same rage, whether verbally or non-verbally. We are a collection of memories and habits, even in parenting. We parent with our non-conscious minds, not our conscious minds. We naturally do what was done to us. How would we know better?

We know that a baby at the age of one year gazes into his mother's eyes to discover himself. During this time, a lot of the mother's experiences are downloaded to the right brain of the baby. What happens if a mother's brain is filled with painful trauma? Without lifting a hand, a hurt mother will hurt the developing Real Self.

Can we blame hurt parents who try their conscious best but hand over non-conscious demons to their children?

We often hear about mothers being extremely cruel to their children. We are filled with amazement: How can geese protect their young, but humans can put babies in a microwave, lock them up like dogs, burn them with cigarettes or sexually abuse them?

Earlier we saw that memory is what guides us in our behavior. Instinct works, but memory is more powerful. But what happens of the memory is faulty? What happens if a mother, trying to care for her child, is non-consciously reminded of all the abuse that she received in life? What happens if she projects her hurt onto her baby? She hurts him or her. Can we blame parents if their own childhoods may have been riddled with all forms of abuse? If most of us do not possess conscious will, especially not over our demons and traumas, can we blame our parents?

Baby and Genes

In a study in which 442 white male New Zealanders were followed from their births in 1972, researchers found that abused boys with a low activity MAOA gene were twice as likely to engage in unacceptable and even violent crimes than abused boys with a high activity MAOA gene. The gene seemed to protect children from being scarred for life. This study supports other studies done in the United States and Britain, which show that some children are more resilient than others after abuse and neglect because of genetic differences.

Dr. Masterson writes, "Is it possible that there is a gene that acts in the personality disorders just as the gene in the above study did? If the gene is high, it protects the child exposed to maternal lack of support from becoming prone to a personality disorder; if it is too low, a personality disorder could develop— thus the etiology is a combination of environment and genetics. The frontier of research now focuses on find the genetic factor."

We are living in an age where we hope that genetics will replace God, but it is becoming clear that behavioral genetics is not the answer to everything.

Research shows that childhood trauma can create survival genes in some and not in others. It is clear that the nature versus nurture debate is over. Both impact one another. This interaction combined with cultural influence make us who we are and how we respond.

Whether a small or a significant role, the issue of nature forces me to ask: Can I blame my parents if I had a genetic predisposition to have a disorder of the Self? Can a hemophilia patient blame his parent for giving him the wrong genetic make-up?

Blaming Parents

I have struggled with life and love more than I care to admit, even more than I have shared in these pages. My life forward will always remain a steep hill in many aspects, especially in love. I am slowly coming to accept that I have a chronic condition of the soul. I will never reach the level of living that the best of humanity have. I must manage my demons like a person with diabetes must manage his glucose level. But like managing diabetes, this is not the end of the world. It is a matter of living my life more realistically, mindfully and healthfully.

At first blush, I have all the right in the world to blame my parents for the life I have. But I can never blame my father or mother for what they did or didn't do. Both did what was done to them. Both tried to do as best as they could. Both followed the example of other Afrikaner families around them. They tried their conscious best. A difficult delivery or a genetic predisposition would have helped to create a perfect storm.

In the end, we can only judge a person if he or she was conscious when harming or withholding care from a child with a budding Real Self. The rest is out of our control. Always has been, always will be. That is why it is call the human struggle and not the human Sunday afternoon walk in the park.

Chapter 19

Parenting a Success Addict

The best of humanity live their lives armed with healthy Real Selves, which allow them to enjoy passion, intimacy and self-care activities on a daily basis. These activities further strengthen the Real Self, which is rewarded with the feeling of happiness. These happy moments become happy memories, which form a happy filter through which the best of humanity views life. Their happy filter allows them to see life as fundamentally positive and good, regardless of fame or fortune. A stronger Real Self and a happier filter allow the best to push their limits in following their passions, in their intimate relationships and in the way they care for themselves. This positive cycle allows them to expand their potential. A few even actualize their full potential.

They were lucky. Nature, nurture, fate and culture smiled upon them in their earlier years. They had primary caretakers who allowed them to successfully move through the three phases (Safety Bubble, Grandiose Bubble and Becoming Human) necessary to form a healthy Real Self. Both parents taught them to interact with their culture and community to ensure that both individual and group needs are respected. Self-expression, intimacy, self-care and community care come almost naturally to them.

But for many, if not most of us, something went wrong on the path to a full and happy life. The earlier our Real Self development was arrested, the more disastrous the consequences for living a life in reality and happiness.

Safety Bubble Arrest I: The Loner

When parents are emotionally unavailable from birth, either because they are depressed or dispassionate, the child thinks, "My parents do not care for me. I must avoid them. If they do not love me, maybe I am not worthy of love. If I have no needs, then no one can ever hurt me again. So I will just take what I can get and shut up."

From the outside, these children look like the perfect babies. They never cry, never ask for anything or have bad moods. They seem self-reliant, even "little adults." But throughout life, they will know deep inside, "Nobody is there for me. Nobody cares. If I try to be intimate with others, I will be hurt. I will go it alone."

The Lonely struggle with a low sense of self and extreme fear of people. They do not care about admiration, or keeping up with the Joneses, or being taken care of. Their daily goal is to keep a distance from all people so that they will feel neither controlled nor isolated by people. The Lonely keep under the social radar, enjoy back office work and avoid social gatherings. Many are very creative. During conflict, the Lonely retreat into their shells.

Safety Bubble Arrest II: The Caretaker

When the primary caretaker is inconsistent in her care by being hot the one day and cold the next, or too self-centered, the child thinks, "My mommy is not there for me all the time. I am in serious danger. I have to cling to her when she is around, otherwise I am done. If she is like that to me, what does that say about me? That I am good, then bad, then good, then bad. She confuses me. I need a constant caretaker. Big time. Nobody is here now, but boy, if somebody comes close, I will grab hold of him or her forever."

Just like a baby in the Safety Bubble phase, Caretakers are still plagued by an excessive fear of rejection. Their early childhood experiences did not give them the non-conscious muscle memory to know that people do care for them and will not leave them to die. The single most important goal for the Caretaker is to find someone who will take care of them personally and professionally. To achieve that goal, they will often act incompetent, passively or obey whatever their caretakers tell them to do as long as they are taken care of. Many have a mask of taking care of others to ensure that others will take care of them in return. During conflict, Caretakers may react with uncontrollable rage. To them, conflict means rejection and rejection means death.

In addition to being taken care of, Caretakers, like babies, often make pleasure, especially bodily pleasures, a high priority. Sex, food, alcohol and music can be a daily distraction from a feeling of not belonging.

Since their Real Self was arrested early in development, Caretakers struggle with an extremely fragile Real Self. They do not care about society's definition of success. Many feel too inferior to seek admiration or to even attempt to keep up with the Joneses. Caretakers often act out the exact opposite of what society defines as success. Black clothes, excessive tattoos and body piercing are the hallmark of the anti-society group.

Grandiose Bubble Arrest: The Success Addict

Unlike the Caretakers and Loners, Success Addicts passed the first nine months. But from nine months until the present, we have enjoyed the fantasy bubble of grandiosity created by a primary caretaker. With the intense gazing into our primary caregiver's eyes, the grandiosity gets even stronger. We feel we are the masters of the universe. We see everyone as objects made to serve our every need. People are extra limbs that bring admiration and pleasure to us. And the coolest thing: We don't even have to ask. Everyone's eyes shine admiration into our brains. Our mothers dote and adore. They tell us we are special and wonderful. We are allowed to do and have whatever we want. And we expect to get it right this very instant.

Good primary caretakers, at 13 months, gradually and caringly start to frustrate the grandiose bubble. They start to tell their children about acceptable human behavior and enforce discipline without crushing their children. At the same time, they start supporting Real Self activities. They encourage exploration of the world and separation from them. They encourage interaction with other people. Their mind, body and soul say, "Find your wings. I will be there for you." As the Real Self strengthens, the need for living in a fantasy bubble decreases. At one point, the healthy child does not need the fantasy or their primary caretakers' brains to function. They now have separated emotionally, mentally and physically from their primary caretakers. Inside their minds, they have a healthy Real Self, a creative space to construct reality, and the foundations of skills to follow our human values.

There are many reasons why a primary caretaker may fail to help his or her child through the separation process.

Three Main Causes

I see three categories of primary caretakers who are unable to nurture a child to have a healthy Real Self. The first is parents with an average Real Self who focus their nurturing to raise model children and who use child raising techniques found within their culture that scream against their instincts. I will call them the Model Parents. The second group are primary caretakers with fragile Real Selves who go through the motions of parenting without a thought of their child's Real Self. After all, you don't know what you don't know. I call them the Clueless Parents. The final category are the Hurt-Child Parents.

These are parents who suffered significant emotional, physical or sexual trauma as children. Some may be surprised to see emotional trauma as part of sexual trauma. Research is clear that chronic emotional trauma damages our brains, especially during the early years when most brain development takes place.

Model Parent: Culture knows best

When I practiced medicine in Canada, I once treated a premature baby who suffered many complications after birth. After almost a month in the ICU, she went home. I specifically and frequently told the parents to avoid all cow's milk and only to give her special formula. Ten days later the mother came to me and confessed that, because of pressure from her community, she had started the child on cow's milk so she could gain weight. I had to be harsh. I told her: "You either listen to the specialist and you child has a chance or you listen to your community and the child will die. Your choice."

Our cultures play a vital role in how parents raise their children. Some thinkers believe that the reason Britain was so successful as a nation during Industrialization was not only the job opportunities that industry brought, but also because many families moved away from their communities and raised their children without interference from the communities in which they were raised. They could allow their instincts to dictate what they wanted to do without meddling grandparents and neighbors.

Over the last hundred years, we have been inundated with advice about what is "best" for babies and their mothers. In the middle of the last century, parents were told that babies should be separated from their mothers at birth so that moms could rest. But we now know that, after a natural childbirth, mothers are immediately flooded with hormones to ensure healthy mother-child bonding. It is essential for newborns to stay *with* their mothers. Then we were told that bottle feeding is better than breast feeding, even though nature has found breast feeding to be the best answer for millennia. Later still, we were told that parents should ignore their child's cries in order to not raise a "spoiled" child. We believed nature was a joker; it gave babies such a piercing cry just to annoy parents. Now we are told that we must put babies on a strict schedule for feeding and sleeping. We believe we can train our babies from birth to conform to our schedules, like we program a DVR.

As a gross generalization, my Afrikaner culture is not very kind to young children. We still believe that children should be perfect by the time they turn two. During the apartheid years, when I was born, the expectations of our Calvinistic leaders were even more stringent. It was acceptable—and expected—

that parents would scream at their children and even beat them when they misbehaved. This was also true at school. My most vivid memories of school may indeed be the many times I was caned for even the most minor infractions. We definitely learned what *not* to do wherever we went. Unfortunately, we were not equally praised for what we did right nor was positive reinforcement used to create positive habits. In hindsight, during the apartheid years, there was little difference between how you trained a dog and how you raised your child. Screams, shouts and orders to ensure perfect obedience. No wonder so many atrocities took place under apartheid.

I have no doubt that one can look at the countries that have committed the biggest offenses against their own people or to humanity and also find a culture that disrespected their children. Contempt for children shapes a culture that has contempt for others, especially those more vulnerable or different from its ruling class.

Model Parent: Material Rewards

Today, many countries face the opposite problem. Children are little gods who ought never to be disciplined, but rewarded for everything they do. Children are objects of status: Babies and toddlers are dressed as if they were models parading for luxury brands. They are called "our star" if others adore their dancing, singing or acting numbers. They are called "my prince" or "my princess" for being cute and attractive.

More than ever, parents reward their children who are pretty, smart, perfect and charming. Parents love the admiration that their perfect children elicit from others. So they keep reinforcing the behavior that brings compliments. They do not focus on compliments that point to hard work, kindness or enjoyment, but on compliments that show how special and perfect their children are.

Parents also overwhelm their children with all sorts of pleasures: theme parks, fast food, sweets, videogames, television, soda and potato chips, the latest toys. Many parents believe that providing excessive pleasure makes them good parents. But rewarding children with excess admiration and pleasure keeps them stuck in a fantasy that life is lived for these rewards alone.

Many parents bribe their children with rewards so that they will play with Baby Einstein, Kumon or the million other tools that "experts" say will ensure a child's entrée into an Ivy League school and into the best jobs on Wall Street. They do not realize that allowing a child to play and discover his own interests and hobbies offers the best opportunities for happiness and success. After all, Einstein, Copernicus, Michelangelo and all of the geniuses over the last two thousand years had none of these aids to play with. Self-made toys and imagination went a long way.

Model Parent: What Will the Neighbors Say?

Many parents are very concerned about what others will say regarding the moral behavior of their children. Teaching morality is important, but when it comes from overly sensitive parents who are constantly afraid that they or their children will offend others, then morality lessons can quickly kill the pleasure that children find in exploring all their senses, emotions and fantasies. Children quickly learn that there is good, bad, right and wrong long before they have time to discover all they have within themselves. So for the rest of their lives, they will judge themselves, or parts of themselves, as bad and never to be seen. Often it is the parts of us that fuel the Real Self that were too scary for our parents to face.

A close cousin to What the Neighbors Will Think is the belief that children must always be busy with activities that adults see as being sensible, educational or productive. Alice Miller talks of a patient who discovered later in life that whenever she began, through her imaginative play, to have a true sense of herself, her parents would ask her to do something "more sensible." This meant that she had to achieve something that they could be proud of. But to the child, this meant that she had to avoid the magic of her inner world, which was starting to open up. Such commands, especially to a sensitive child, will scar her imagination for life.

Clueless Parent: Emotionally Handicapped

Some people assume that, if a person is a woman, she must be naturally nurturing and possess emotional intelligence. But we know that, like most generalizations, this is not true—just as not all men enjoy hunting, violent sports or going to strip clubs. Mothers or fathers with a fragile Real Self are clueless about their own emotional lives and cannot teach their children about their emotions. Some people are emotionally cold, depressed and dispassionate. Or they are emotionally warm at times, then cold and absent. They are not consistent in their emotions, and not consistent in their emotional care. Parents with fragile selves are terrible at managing conflict. They either explode like an atom bomb or they become as cold as the North Pole before global warming. Misunderstandings and conflicts with their children are often treated in similar fashion. Non-existent, inconsistent or avoided conflict-repair with a baby leads to significant despair in the child. These parents have one thing in common: They are unable to act as the emotional buffer between the child and the external world. They do not calm the inborn fears of a child; they may even add to them. If they cannot calm down the child's fears, then they also cannot teach a child emotional intelligence.

Clueless Parent: Sensorial Blockage

Throughout the centuries, a woman's body has been admired for its capacity to be tender, soft, caring and nurturing. Women were celebrated for having huggable bodies and women felt proud of their capacity to give life. So they lived in their bodies and for their bodies. They loved to eat and make food. They loved creating a home.

Today, women are forced to see their bodies as trophies to be shaped for their bikinis for the summer in the Hamptons. They need to go from "baby to body" in a few weeks. How they look after childbirth almost seems as important as how great they are at nurturing the child. But toned skinny bodies are not necessarily huggable bodies or filled with vitality from feeling all emotions and sensations in the moment. A body shaped to impress may not be a body shaped to enjoy or give touch, one of the most important building blocks of the developing Real Self.

Clueless Parent: Everything Goes

A while ago, I visited a family's farm in South Africa with Mary, my girlfriend at the time. One day we decided to go horseback riding. We had one problem: Mary could not for all the tea in China take charge of her horse. She did not want to pull the reigns or give the horse a kick to get it to moving. So we were stuck with the horse going where it wanted to go and Mary going along for the ride. Some people, especially those with weak Real Selves, believe that one should never reprimand or take charge of animals or children. After all, they are so sweet and innocent. "I will hurt my child or my best friend's feelings if I say 'no,'" they think. Or even worse: "My child will not like me if I reprimand him."

I recently was told of a mother who was unable to socialize her child out of fear of being "too cruel" to him. As a six year old, the child, by other people's accounts, was spoiled rotten. His mother still thought he was the next President of the United States. One night the child came in and asked for a favor. Both parents said no. The child, not used to this two-letter word, went to the kitchen and came back with the kitchen knife. He was ready to kill his parents.

Add to this our culture's belief that parents should be friends with their children and we have a recipe for disaster. If parents do not frustrate their child's sense of entitlement, need for admiration and instant gratification, who will? Without appropriate controls of our mammalian brains, the fantasy bubble will never be frustrated and the Real Self will never develop fully. A too-kind-and-caring primary caretaker may win the battle, but she will lose the war. These parents will nurture a child who will struggle with moderating his needs for admiration and pleasure. As a result, activities that bring happiness will always play second fiddle to instant gratification, grandiose egos and immediate action. It is often this type of nurturing that leads to Alpha personalities. They are still stuck in a bubble where they are allowed to receive whatever they want. They never learned that there are other people in the bubble or how to control their need for pleasure and admiration.

Clueless Parent: Passionless

The importance of encouraging a child to find his own interests through self-exploration is crucial for a successful resolution to this phase. In order to do this well, parents need to be happy and intimate with each other, filled with their own passions in life and able to deal with separation, loss and aloneness. Good parents must have an above average Real Self.

We've already seen that many people do not have passions in their lives. They survive life, but they do not live it. Many will tell you that being a mother or father is their passion. This is a recipe for disaster. How can parents through example, word and non-conscious right brain communications encourage their child to seek passion if they do not have one themselves? Besides, if your child is your passion, you probably want to keep him very close to you and not let him move away, just as passionate musicians avoid playing football for fear of breaking their fingers. Many parents cannot encourage their children to find passion because they can't begin to imagine what that feels like.

Clueless Parents: Loveless

Data tell us that many primary caretakers are unhappily married, lonely and lack romance. For them to give up the best relationship of their lives is almost impossible. They want to cling to the child as much and for as long as possible, often to their graves. A life without their child clinging to them, calling them all the time and taking care of their loneliness is inconceivable. In the process, they limit the child severely in his exploration of the world, and by so doing, squash the child's developing Real Self. The child learns: Being there for my parents is good. Being there for myself is bad.

The child then learns, "My mommy does not allow me to play, to discover the world, to figure out who I am and what I want to do. I will have to listen to her, otherwise I will be dead. But, boy, I hate it that she is so intrusive, so over me. The only way I can survive is to withdraw emotionally from her. I cannot tell my mother 'no' either. She will not like that. I'll play the game, but I won't love her. I won't love anyone ever again. I will rebel against her restrictions."

For the rest of his life, this child will believe he cannot be himself and follow his passion and be loved at the same time. He needs to comply with other people's wishes or he will be abandoned. But since he cannot trust others to be there for him, he avoids people, especially when they need him. He needs freedom, not people, and definitely not their neediness. To him, people are selfish, people are hell.

Clinging parents often are easily spotted even when their children start going to school. Sometimes called "helicopter parents" for their propensity to hover over their children 24 hours a day, they are prone to life-long hyper parenting. They believe they are good parents. They are always to be seen at sport games and PTA meetings, but in reality, they are taking care of their own fears of being abandoned. They are psychologically abusing their own children to fill the hole in their soul. The cost of this on their own children's sense of self-expression is huge and will forever harm them, even when they enter adulthood.

But these helicopter parents do not—more correctly, cannot—stop their helicopter parenting even when their children leave home. They never can accept the idea that their sons or daughters are now adults focused on dealing with life and not there to be their friends, slaves, therapists and marriage counselors. To achieve this, they become highly skilled at emotional blackmail. You will often hear them say, "I'm so lonely. You never have time for me anymore! I may be dead tomorrow."

They constantly call and need every day to bond with their children otherwise they feel neglected. These parents, whether in early childhood or late in life, live to keep the emotional chord intact, the child dependent upon them, and will do anything and everything to make sure they remain the center of their child's attention.

Clueless Parent: Stressed

We live in a time where, in most families, both parents work. At the same time, stress at the workplace has significantly increased. There is no more job security, the economy looks like a roller coaster, jobs are outsourced, we spend more time communicating with an impersonal computer than with people who care about our careers and families. Technology has also increased employer expectations—we are expected to do 27 hours worth of work in the 16 hours that we are awake. Television shows and advertisements also promise more happiness and success if only we can buy more of this or that product. Stress is part of our daily lives. Even more so for those of us struggling with a fragile Real Self. For us, there is always a crisis about to happen. Within such a frame of mind, positive caretaking is almost impossible. A stressed mother or father at the end of the day does not sooth a child's inner fears and does not help to build a healthy Real Self.

Some parents feel the best way to deal with their stress is to go away for ten-day vacations to exotic places. "We have not had a vacation together for years. Time for us to connect again and recharge our batteries to look after the children." On the surface this argument is plausible. Parents need to focus on their marriage as much as on their children. But leaving a baby within the first eighteen months for such a long time will burst his safety or grandiose bubble, leaving him with scars on his Real Self.

Clueless Parent: Avoiding Eyes

Judith had just had her second son. Sitting around a table, she held her nine-month-old as we talked about research on child development. I watched as the son kept staring at his mother, but she kept avoiding his eyes.

"So, Pierre, you must tell me what we must do to make sure we do not make mistakes with the children. Any tips?" Judith asked.

"For one, staring into a child's eyes is extremely important. They feel security in your eyes. They learn about themselves through your eyes."

"No wonder Jack wants to look in my eyes all the time. I often feel like saying to him, 'Stop looking at me.' It somehow scares me!"

She then looked at Jack for a brief second and he cooed with pleasure.

"I guess you're right," she said.

I do understand Judith's reluctance to look deep in her son's eyes. Before therapy, I too hated the penetrating eyes of a baby. I felt as if babies put me on the spot; they somehow knew my secret—that I was living a fake life to cover an emptiness and lack of self worth. One can only nurture a child's Real Self if you have an average or healthy Real Self that will allow you to open up to your child so that she can use your brain as a bypass brain to discover her own mind.

Hurt-Child Parent: Babies as Objects

"I only *began to be fond* of him when I could go back to work and only saw him when I came home, as *a distraction and toy*, so to speak. But quite honestly, a little dog would have done just well. Now that he is gradually getting bigger and I see that I can train him and that he is devoted to me and trusts me, I am beginning to develop tender feelings for him and am glad that he is there," a patient told Alice Miller.

This reminded me of comments I have heard so often from Success Addicts: "I do not like children when they are babies. I am not very good with them. But I love them when they start to have a bit of a personality."

To them, personality means when children can take orders and stop being a nuisance. This stands in stark contrast to healthy parents who find the time with their babies as some of the most rewarding experiences in their lives. But when a mother or father were never nurtured with love, tenderness and care, even if they were upset or scared, they struggled to be caring parents themselves.

An equally destructive attitude is having children to fill one's loneliness, to cover one's lack of passion in work, to save a loveless marriage, to deal with depression. Sometimes such a caretaker can look as if he or she is the best, most passionate and most caring parent in the world. But it is the wrong type of love. There is no framework in which the child can learn about his own feelings or needs. Life revolves around being what mom or dad wants him to be. His Real Self can never develop, because he needs to be his parent's substitute self.

Some parents use their children as objects of happiness. They are there to be the equilibrium to the parents' enormous non-conscious sadness. So everyone in the house must play the game, "Lets be happy all the time." At no given moment should people discuss problems. No arguments is allowed. Any signs of non-happiness triggers the parents' rage or resentment for being used as a happy object when she was a child. Adults who were happy objects as children struggle to deal with people, including their own children, who have emotional problems.

Many children are used as objects of success. Their children must be the talk of the town. Achievement and success are all that matters. At the same time, these Success Addicts do not want their own children to outperform them. So they often say, "Do not let it go to your head. Imagine what it took for us to get you through school. You need to show us more respect." Achieve, but do not take confidence from your success. We do not like you being confident. You may leave us then.

The final, and maybe most common use of children by an abused parent, is to blame the child for all the abuse that the parent was subjected to as a child. As one patient said in an inner dialogue to her parents: "I have used him again as a scapegoat to protect you." Abused children will grow up to abuse their own children rather than accept that their parents were not only imperfect, but also abusive.

Children used as objects cannot develop a Real Self. They will take on the role given to them by a parent until the end of time, never questioning whether being happy all the time really makes sense.

Hurt-Child Parent: Avoiding Eyes

I have known Sam, a close friend, for years. I know many of his ups and downs in life and that he is struggling in many ways, whether direction in work or personal intimacy. A few years ago, I happened to meet his mother at a function. I was glad to see her and we chatted away. But I felt myself holding my breath. I was laughing a lot. And I wondered why? Then I looked into her eyes. Despite her smile and kind words, I felt as if cold pieces of glass were staring at me. In that instant, I knew exactly what my friend was struggling with. Those eyes staring at him as a child must have increased his fear of life, not soothed it nor lead to the development of a healthy Real Self.

When parents were abused, they carry their painful and frightening trauma non-consciously in their right brain. When a baby stares deep into his primary caretaker's eyes and their right brains connect, the baby will experience his parent's hidden trauma. This will cause him fear or make him avoid her eyes. Without his mother's eyes mirroring his own sense of self to him, the Real Self is never discovered.

If you want to understand the cause of your pain in life and have empathy for your parents' childhood pains, just look deep into their eyes. It may be worth more than ten years in therapy with a wrong therapist.

A woman on her deathbed told Alice Miller that only in death was she able to enjoy the love and care her children gave her throughout her life. But because her father abused her, she only sought the pleasure of love when it was connected with pain and rage. She so desperately wanted to accept the love and understanding of her children, but she ended up spending most of her life seeking sexual pleasure with men who abused her physically and emotionally.

She sadly confessed, "And now, I can see it, but it is too late."

Many other parents avoid their children's eyes by numbing their souls with alcohol, long hours at the office or travelling for long periods.

Hurt-Child Parent: Rage, Contempt and Guilt

The terrible twos are, at best, highly unpleasant for everybody involved. Good enough parenting uses this period to show a child how to sooth his fears and how to deal with conflict with others. For parents unable to deal with conflict, this phase brings out their worst. Without sensing the fear behind the child's behavior, they believe that the child is filled with evil, to be screamed at and beaten. One can imagine how a child, frightened by his own inner fears, now must deal with the love of his life treating him no better than the dog. When a primary caretaker frequently attacks a child during this period, they start focusing on avoiding the attacks rather than exploring the world and their interest. Life revolves around avoiding his parents' wrath, rather than discovering the Real Self. Parents, especially primary caretakers, with short tempers often nurture People Pleasers. They learn that keeping the person in power happy is the most important goal in life. "People are not there to decrease my fear of rejection. They add to it. Life alone is better than life with others. People cannot be trusted to make me happy," their non-conscious mind argues.

"With them she had constantly felt that excessive demands were being made upon her, that she was a prisoner and that the babies were taking advantage of her, that she was a prisoner and that the babies were taking advantage of her and exploiting her," Alice Miller wrote about a patient.

To some parents, babies represent what happened to them. The babies become their abusive parents. Rage is justly called for. After all, raging at a smaller and weaker person is a perfect remedy for the helplessness of one's own childhood. But people out of touch with their childhood pain have no idea how their behavior is impacting their children. If a person does not want to feel humiliation, how can she have empathy for the humiliation of another human being, especially one's own child.

There are parents who try to escape the cycle of abuse. They genuinely try to love a child unconditionally in the first few years of life. But then they are overcome with guilt. When a mother is treated as a toy, a pet, as a non-person, she will feel guilty for treating her own child like a person who needs respect. Her inner demons will scream that she is misbehaving, stepping out of the family line. Guilt may force her to treat her baby as she was treated: as an object.

Hurt-Child Parent: Ego

Primary caretakers with grandiose egos to cover their childhood abuse negatively influence their children in a number of ways. Many Success Addicts hate being pestered by a needy child. They dislike anyone wanting anything from them. They are the center of attention, not anyone else. Not even children can dethrone them. So a nagging child is like construction workers drilling holes in the road at six in the morning. The parent pushes the child away, rather than embracing him at his most vulnerable.

Success Addicts also want to be admired for being great parents. They want perfect adorable princes and princesses, not exuberant, self-directed, occasional cranky children. After all, a clinging, cranky child is a disgrace, a nuisance and a bad reflection on their parenting. They discipline them harshly until the obstinacies are beaten out of them or they push their children to perform in the world away from them long before they are ready to do so. A child pushed to explore the world before they are ready thinks, "My parents want me to leave, but I am not ready. I am afraid. If I don't do what they say, I will be rejected too. Maybe if I stay happy, my parents will spend time with me. Maybe if I am a good child, they will support me."

This child will grow up constantly afraid of their parents and other people who may push him away if he does what he wants to do. So, he develops a compliant, pleasant and cheerful personality so that people won't leave him. But below the mask of niceness, the child thinks that nobody is there for him when he really needs them. He learns to hate longing for others. He learns self-sufficiency is the key to a pain-free world.

Finally, children learn by imitation. They see how the rewards and respect go to the person in the house with the biggest ego. They learn to imitate the one in the home with all the power. Success addicted parents often have favorite children who they encourage to succeed in life so they can feel great about their own parenting skills. Their favorite children's success is their success. This excessive doting by a powerful parent adds to a child's sense of specialness.

Hurt-Child Parent: Vampire

"My brother is a cocaine addict. For years, my mother knew it, but did nothing. She just kept giving him pocket money. Then he nearly died from an overdose. We got him to the best rehab we could afford. He did well. He came out and was ready to take on life again. To leave home. My mother went crazy. Against everyone's orders, she started to give him pocket money again, to emotionally manipulate him. My own mother was willing to have my brother be a cocaine addict so that he doesn't leave home. She wanted to control his purse strings. She knew she could then control him. She is his mother! My mother. How does one understand that!" Petra asked me with tears flowing freely.

There are mothers and fathers in the world who were cruelly treated in their youth. As children, they had to survive by clinging to the illusion that their parents were wonderful and there was good that came from their trauma. But the pain did not go away. Frightened and hurt children did not change into happy innocent children through fantasy or faith. Within them, they carry the contempt they experienced like a poison dagger.

When they finally have a helpless child in possession, they use him to deal with the trauma of their childhood. They transfer the abusive father or mother's power onto themselves. And they transfer the weak, bad, rejected children that they were made to feel onto their own young ones. Their children are beaten and abused in the same way that they were beaten and abused. Onto another child, they transfer the idealized images of their parents. They use their children as an object of unconditional love. Their children finally make them feel whole, secure and wanted. The devoted, undivided love from their children is all that counts. They will protect this right, this love, this escape with the poison dagger hidden in their scarred souls. Parents humiliated as children will seek children that will value them constantly.

Mothers and fathers with severe traumas easily become vampires that will suck their children dry in order to get what they need to not feel the pain of their own past. They will cut their children from friends, family or romantic interests that they see as threats to her supreme rule over them. The mother or father needs the son or daughter like oxygen. So, like Petra's mother, they will stop at nothing. They have destroyed any signs of a Real Self in their children from their earliest years, rendering them spineless and unable to escape the emotional blackmail. Some find the only way out is escape through drugs, alcohol, endless work or suicide. Others will leave their hometowns and go as far as they can. Or they will marry and become vampires to their own children, continuing the abusive cycle.

Some escape. They will emotionally disinherit their parents and try a life away from the trauma. We may stand on the sideline and applaud these people. And we should. No one can be emotional food to anyone. But herein lies the sad truth about life: Those who were the most hurt among us often turn out to be the most abusive parents who then end their lives alone with children who never want to come and visit. All this, and these parents honestly believe that they have done nothing wrong. They were not conscious that they were reenacting their own abuse on their own children.

Life is not fair. Often, it is extremely cruel.

Dysfunctional Families

"When I go home, I just give it over to Jesus and fight with my older brother for the remote control as we have done since we were six," a 30-year-old Success Addict told me of how she regresses to a child whenever she goes back home.

We can be the CEO of Goldman Sachs, but when we are with our parents and siblings, we will behave as if we were three. The only difference is in the toys we play with.

"My parents complain about one another all the time. They have been threatening to divorce for 50 years. They love getting us wound up. When I bring a guest home, then suddenly they love one another. You could swear that we're the happiest family on the East Coast. Until the friend leaves and then I am finally seeing the light. But not my siblings!" a 50-year-old Success Addict told me.

Perfect happy families are often very imperfect and covered in non-conscious lies.

Families are not only the histories of the parents and siblings. It is a character in its own right, a character with substantial power. It carries with it the weapon of habit. When we come from a dysfunctional family, we do not only need to deal with the dominant parent. We need to deal with everyone in the family. They all will react. We humans do not like our comfort zones to be upset. We hate change, even if the status quo is smothering everyone. "The devil you know is better than the devil you don't," the non-conscious mind of the family tells us.

Dysfunctional families continue the assault on the Real Self for years after a person has left the first three years of life.

Living Without a Real Self

Without a Real Self, we do not have the mental capacity or non-conscious memories to maintain self-esteem and a sense of being good-enough, especially during moments of ambiguity, conflict or intimacy. Lacking a Real Self forces us to live life feeling utterly worthless. There is nothing inside us that can dispute that horrible truth. Without a Real Self, none of our accomplishments are caught in our created space within the Real Self. This is why some Success Addicts, despite all their achievements and the admiration of others, have many moments of feeling worthless. Their successes fall through the "net of a fragmented Real Self" like sardines through a net for tuna fish.

To cover our worthlessness, we, like a baby, cling to our inflated grandiose self. Some of us exaggerate our accomplishments. Some of us surround ourselves only with other "special" people, people like ourselves. We are often envious of other people's performances or believe others are envious of our performances. We project onto the world that we are the masters and mistresses of the universe. Really, we feel lower than an ant. We will lie to God or anyone else not to face the fact that behind the mask of our success, we believe ourselves to be enormous failures.

Since we were used to having a source of safety, pleasure and admiration that made us feel special and whole, we live our lives seeking that one person who will make us feel safe and whole again. I have walked into every class, outing, bar or meeting dreaming that I will finally meet someone who will connect with my fragmented self and miraculously make me whole again. The fact that no one can make me whole is something I have known for years. This does not prevent me from fantasizing. Without the fantasy, my life is filled with an unbearable longing, a longing that has the physical sensation of a blunt fish knife ripping at my chest. Why then let go of fantasies of youthful, innocent, perfect love if it keeps such excruciating pain away from my conscious brain and my fantasies of a perfect childhood?

Other Success Addicts do find spouses or work for bosses onto whom they transfer all the power and fantasies they have of their primary caretaker. For a while, they feel reunited with a person who makes them whole. But love that cures, kills, as we know by now.

Without a healthy Real Self, we are also often overwhelmed with fear. In particular, we fear failure. To our non-conscious minds, failure means we lose our special status and that we will be rejected as worthless rats. We fear failure almost as much as death.

Lacking a healthy Real Self, we struggle to create a realistic reality of our primary caretakers. We remain caught in seeing ourselves, other people and the world through our two DVDs, the Heaven or Hell DVDs. We never have a place in our brain where we can go to deal with ambiguity or uncertainty. So our lives are dichromatic: black or white, shit or gold, hell or heaven.

We do not have a strong separation between our inner world and the outside world, so we often confuse fantasy with reality. What happens in our inner world becomes our reality and vice versa. We opt for fantasy over reality. Reality, with its ambiguity, death, sickness or unfairness, scares us. We do not have a Real Self to successfully deal with the imperfect.

Without separation and a creative space, we also have trouble learning how to understand our emotions, label them and manage them. Our language abilities will always be void of emotional or sensorial content. Compared to the best of humanity, most of life takes place in our non-conscious minds. We experience very little of the abundance of life. We are too scared to sit still and enjoy the moment. Things need to be done to keep the bubble from bursting. We also do not trust our emotions and feelings, for we cannot control them. Without feelings, life is numb and depressing.

Without a healthy Real Self, we struggle to find our passion, enjoy intimate relationships or take care of ourselves. We cannot strengthen our Real Self. As a result, we lack the engine that allows us to do those activities that bring us the emotion happiness. Without non-conscious happy memories, our filters of life fail to make us feel happy and in control of our futures.

Without a healthy Real Self, we struggle to have empathy for others or to mature and become wise through our experiences. We fail to live up to the six human values treasured by communities all over the world. We may be the most powerful group in the world, but we are some of the most hurt people, struggling with the human consciousness found in one year old child.

Stuck in a Bubble

To maintain our Grandiose Bubble, Success Addicts need to feel special and admired every second of the day. So we work hard to amass wealth, education, beauty, fame, perfect admiring love or compliments for our good behavior. We live for that $10 million in the bank, the presidency of the United States or a major corporation, the Olympic gold medal, an Academy Award, a cover photo in *Vanity Fair,* or membership in the Academy of Sciences. We are perfectionists in at least one area of life, if not in all. We would prefer to have our toenails pulled out without anesthetics to failure, or worse, admitting to failure in public. Failure means we are not worthy of admiration. When reality become too much, we enjoy fantasies of unlimited success, power, brilliance, beauty or ideal love.

Donald Davidoff, a Harvard University neuropsychologist, was interviewed on a number of executives who faked suicides in order to escape the consequences of fraud they committed during the recent financial bubble. But, he says, they were not running because they feared being arrested. They ran because they feared the loss of their wealth and power that would result in a loss of self and a "dissolution of their personality." They ran away from a burst of their grandiose bubble.

Some addicts, especially the Alphas, can be pleasure addicts. You name it, they will consume it if it gives them a buzz. Alcohol, shopping, eating, drugs, gossiping and porn all make us feel we are the kings and queens at the table of excess.

There are other problems to life in a bubble. We believe we are at the center of the world and that everything revolves around us. When dust causes a pretty woman to close an eye-lid, we know she winked at us. When people talk in hush voices and laugh, we know they said something bad about us.

Within this bubble, all people are objects to bring to us what we want when we want it. In fact, just like our primary caretakers, they need to know what we want even before we say it. Like a child, we need perfect attunement to our unexpressed needs.

Demons

From the day we are born, we are hardwired to seek unconditional love, to attach to an individual, to form a Real Self and expand to our full potential. Whether you believe in God or evolution, we can agree on this. This need is as strong as our need to eat and breathe.

So what happens if primary caretakers do not give us the emotional care we need to develop a Real Self? Our response is as if we were attacked or left to starve. Our bodies respond with homicidal rage. Not anger, but rage for the person who did not support us. But expressing this rage is disastrous for a child. First, rage may cause the parents to withhold the only bit of attachment the child has. Secondly, a child believes that he and his primary caretaker are one. Recall that when a good-enough parent gives her child his bottle just as he starts to feel hungry, the child believes he magically, through his need, created the response. So what happens if he starts having homicidal rage against his mother? He fears his wishes may destroy the object that brings him his milk. He must suppress the rage into the non-conscious and only does what he knows will give him the most attention from his parents. How does he do this? By splitting his experiences of his parents into two. He creates a DVD of Hell and a DVD of Heaven.

But rage is not the only emotion the child feels. We are also bombarded with fear. Without proper nurturing, we never outgrow the massive fear of rejection that accompanies all babies into the world. We never feel completely safe. Now we also need to deal with life's uncertainty and ambiguity without a protective mother or a Real Self. Life seems scary. All this, and many of us had a primary caretaker that screamed, slapped or made sarcastic comments as we struggled to express our needs, passions or fears. Overwhelmed with fear, our lives revolve on controlling our behavior in order to avoid punishment or rejection.

We developed the emotion of sadness to help us deal with loss of an idealized form of life. Humans have tears so we can gather support around us. Crying is good for us, whether baby, banker or believer. So when we lose the care we expected, our bodies react with intense sadness. Babies cry, but their attempts to connect with their parents are sometimes seen as "fussy" or "colicky." We are ignored, screamed at or a nanny is called in to take the crying baby away. Our emotional needs are made to feel unwelcome; so are we. To survive, we are forced to swallow our tears, to numb our pain, to smile while our hearts feel as if they are ripped out of our chests.

But since our desires and wishes to individuate and follow our own dreams never stop, we are constantly in a state of guilt and shame. We want to please our parents, but we also want to please ourselves. The constant punishment, verbal or physical, for not doing what our parents want fills us with guilt.

If happiness is the ultimate motivation for humans to connect with others, the pain of loneliness and regret is the stick to make sure we live up to our human legacy of intimacy. Children who did not receive proper emotional care have a difficult time relating intimately to others. So not only can we not engage in intimacy without a strong Real Self, we fear it. But a life without intimacy is an empty and lonely life.

A child is born helpless. When we do not have someone to sooth our helplessness or to nurture a healthy Real Self, we always will remain helpless. Add to the enormous feelings of helplessness we experience when we want to explore the world and ourselves but we are constantly oppressed by a clinging or rejecting parent, we can understand why so many of us, beneath our masks of competence, struggle with an suffocating sense of helplessness.

I have just described the six demons found in the right prefrontal cortex of Success Addicts instead of a Real Self. Neuroscientist Alan Schore states that the emotional interactions, or lack thereof, that occur during the first two years of life form a template that determines all future neurological and psychological functioning.

Every time we try to self-express, be intimate or take care of ourselves, these six demons, either in a pack or alone, attack our non-conscious mind. Unable to deal with this, we search for more admiration to heal the bubble.

Then we act out by drinking, using drugs or sleeping around. Some of us seek attention by throwing tantrums. We blame our spouses, children or employees for our failures. When we scream at them, we do not have to face the truth: Our non-conscious mind is not perfect or special, but filled with terrifying demons. Others attack their fragile Real Self as the cause of all the pain. We then non-consciously try to wipe ourselves out with excessive drinking, by directing our own antibodies against normal tissue or we become convinced that only a self-inflicted bullet will end the attacks. We rather die that let go of our fantasy bubble. Life without it is unbearable pain.

The Culture Hurdle

There is one more personality type that is shaped by inadequate nurturing in the early years. Many people leave their first few years with a strong enough Real Self. However, their Real Self can often be oppressed by strict parents who expect their children to behave according to every little rule within the community. Culture is placed above individuality.

The Conscientious don't care so much about winning admiration. To them, doing things the right *way* is more important than doing the right thing to succeed. And the right way is what their leaders and parents (especially fathers) say is right. Guilt is the major driver of their behavior. This group works hard to achieve the American Dream: the house, the car, the kids, the good schools, the whole deal. After all, that is what our culture says is the right thing to do. To them, puritanical behavior is more important than self-expression, intimacy and self-care. As a result, many struggle with phobias and anxiety disorders. Their right brains are fighting their rigid and righteous left brain.

Long Lonely Days and Nights

In *Long Day's Journey into Night*, Eugene O'Neil attributed the following dialogue to his mother as she discussed her son Jamie, an Alpha success addict: "But I suppose life has made him like that, and he can't help it. None of us can help the things life has done to us. They're done before you realize it, and once they're done they make you do other things until at last everything comes between you and what you'd like to be, and you've lost your true self forever."

I am sitting in Washington Square when I suddenly see hundreds of bubbles floating in the air. A man was selling a bubble machine. I watched a few bubbles as they float on a cool summer's day. They go where the breeze takes them. They are fragile. Any contact with another person or with the ground causes them to burst. Life as a bubble, like life in a bubble, is precarious and void of substance. Every day our non-conscious mind fears the moment the bubble will burst.

Where the best of humanity live a life chasing happiness, I have lived a life working every second to maintain a fantasy bubble and to deal with enormous fear of what will happen if the bubble finally bursts.

Section IV

On Becoming Humane and Happy

Chapter 20

Treatment for Individuals

Do you feel you lack purpose in life? Do you feel lonely and empty? Do you feel you can be happier? If your answer is yes, reflect on the following questions: Do you have a number of intimate relationships with people you can cry in front of? Do you have or did you ever have a hobby that made you passionate or excited? Do you use language well? Do you trust a number of people outside of your family, people who do not end up hurting you? Do you have true empathy for others, not just sensitivity to their feelings? Do you recover quickly from failures? Do you deal with uncertainty and risk? Do you deal well with loneliness? Do you see conflict as a positive part of living with others? Do you have people in your life who truly support you for who you are and what you want to achieve regardless of whether it brings money or admiration?

If you answer "yes" to most of the above, you probably have an above average Real Self. I am convinced that people with above average Real Selves can cure themselves. The first task would be to avoid the success-obsessed influences found in our culture. Cut out of your day people, television shows and magazines that celebrate the animal goals of our existence.

Then learn how to ignore your parents' advice, your friends' taunts, your professor's "wisdom" or your spouse's anxieties. No one can help you find out what you like. If anything, people we approach are often those who non-consciously fear that we will outperform them or leave them. Their advice will often reflect their own non-conscious fears and dreams. Unconditional love and objective advice, especially from those close to us, are fantasies.

Then go out and do. Life's answers do not come from thinking, dreaming or talking, but they do come from doing, feeling and reflecting. Do as many different activities as you imagine you may enjoy until you finally find something that makes you say, "This is who I am!"

Once you follow your passions, you will start to strengthen your own Real Self. The more you strengthen your Real Self, the more you can follow our human legacy, find meaning and increase your intimacy with those you love.

Speaking of love, seek someone who loves you for who you are and for what you do, whether you make a billion or just enough to pay the bills. Seek someone whose passion you can support as if it is your own. Go out and meet millions of people until you can say, "This woman is both my best friend and a great sex partner. We can fight well. We see life in the same way. I want to get to know her until end of time. And I want her to achieve the best in her passions."

As for work, aim to have at least one of the following three in your daily grind: First, do something that makes you excited and brings flow. Secondly, work with people you like. Don't settle for working with people who stress you out. People can be toxic and cause your Real Self to move off-line. Find people who celebrate all our human values and work for them. Having friends at work is one of life's most precious gifts and a great tool to enhance happiness. Thirdly, do work that you feel has a good cause.

Finally, be prepared to feel resistance to all the above. Activating the Real Self is a challenge for everyone, even the healthiest of us. Demons will come up. The demons destroy some of us, but for others they are more like a stone in the shoe. So make sure you surround yourself with people who will pick you up when you fall and will cheer for you when you are in the arena of life bleeding and sweating as you expand your potential and expose your vulnerabilities. Make sure you have people in your life who will celebrate your victories as if they are their own. But just as important, support another person's Real Self. This can be some of the most energizing and confidence building activities that humans can do.

In short, self-express, self-share and self-care in a community of people who have shunned the success-obsessed aspects of our culture for a culture based on our human values.

Disorder of the Self

If your answers to the previous list of questions are mostly "no," then you have a fragile Real Self. A struggling Real Self can only be cured through psychoanalytic psychotherapy.

For years, people with fragile Real Selves were seen as incurable. Dr. Masterson's research over 30 years has found a way into the complex and confusing world of those with disorders of the Real Self. What follows is a brief description of his approach. This is important, because people often waste decades and thousands of dollars going to therapists who are unable to help themselves, let alone a client.

The Masterson Approach is based on three major goals: frustrate the mask, confront the demons and build a healthy Real Self.

The first task of the therapist is to frustrate the grandiose mask of the patient by not falling for his tricks and by avoiding any form of admiration. This, combined with the intimacy of a therapist's office, will throw all the attention on the patient's hurting self. The patient will work hard to charm or please or try to get on the same page as the therapist, who becomes the primary caretaker. Like they always have done, Success Addicts try to please or impress. A good therapist will not give in, but will remain focused only on the Real Self. The demons will start pouring out until they fill the creative space in the brain. Suddenly, all reality will shift. The "witch" image is now at play. Patients then either attack the therapist or start attacking themselves. Often at this point, either the therapist starts running or the patient. But a good therapist will continue with the same approach to allow the patient to face the demons.

Once this happens, the therapist reflects the patient's emotions back to him to teach him the language of emotions and to teach him how the triad of the self works (self-care, self-share and self-expression lead to demons and vulnerability that lead to defenses and the need for admiration). Over thousands of repetitions in the therapist's office, the patient will come to realize how extremely dependant he is on others for personal value and how extremely sensitive he is to other people's opinions.

Every time a demon is felt and expressed to a therapist, the impact of the demon on a patient's life becomes less and less. The reason is that the "feeling and then talking cure" (as opposed to the traditional "talking cure") takes the demon from the non-conscious implicit memory where it was in charge and puts it in the conscious memory, the explicit memory, where the patient now controls it. With the demons weaker, the patient now has more space to realize that demons come from the past and cannot kill them. In the process, the patient is able to live in a more truthful version of reality. The process is aptly called containment—containing the impact of the demons on the patient's life.

The second part of the process is called adaptation. Here the key is to build implicit memory that supports the Real Self. Little work can be done on the Real Self if the demons are still in control. With the demons more controlled, the patient can now let go of past reunion behaviors and grieve for the loss of his perfect fantasies of his childhood. At the same time, he starts to commit to and practice Real Self activities and to choose people who support Real Self activities. He also learns how to adapt to life away from the strict rules handed down over years of avoiding the attacks of the demons.

My short version of the process may give the impression that a patient can be fixed in a short period of time. The reality is that the brain needs rewiring. Years of repeating the abovementioned process is so far the only way that we know of that can bring about a neurobiological change. Therein lies the hope of treating Success Addicts. Often, a patient only really sees the value after years of therapy, even though short-term improvements are often experienced after six months.

To find the right therapist is difficult. I had to endure the inadequacies of two therapists before I found Dr. Masterson. He was right for me because he believes that a therapist must show emotionally warm interest in patients' problems, hold the assumption that the person can cope, be neutral to patients' masks and need for admiration, but never be neutral to Real Self activities. He should sympathize with real life defeats, congratulate him on triumphs of Real Self, be emphatic that coping and adaptation are vital to emotional survival and willing to enter into a Real Self-to-Real Self communication.

A therapist must also have compassion and respect for the "heroism" for these "difficult patients" who are nothing other than adults stuck in their terrible twos and terrified by their inner demons. Like a good parent, a therapist does not "suggest, seduce, threaten, attack or torture" a patient to self activate. The therapist must be comfortable to "watch, wait, wonder and hold witness" to the rebirth of the Real Self in their offices over many years. She too allows for many moments of quiet separation from her patient while she offers an emotional presence. This leads to a self-focus in the presence of others. The therapist must also immediately repair moments of true misunderstanding between patient and therapist when a patient's Real Self activities were misunderstood by the therapist. As such, the therapist must be brave enough to say, "I'm sorry. I misunderstood you." This repair of conflict or misunderstanding shows the patient that differences and misunderstandings are solvable, non-destructive and can strengthen trust and understanding.

A good therapist is nothing other than a "good primary caretaker" who has her child's best interest and Real Self at heart. But like any good parent, a therapist cannot allow childish behavior, admiration-seeking and instant gratification. They need to frustrate it with skill and compassion. It is often here that many therapists fail. They either try to be their patient's mother, best friend or confidant or they attack the patient like an abusive parent. It follows that a therapist must be a real person with a strong sense of self.

Research is clear that a therapist's empathy and the right brain-to-right brain interaction between patient and therapist are the most crucial tools in all of therapy. A patient needs "someone with a mind that has his mind in mind," someone who understands and feels his Real Self needs and whose Real Self he can internalize. This right brain-to-right brain interaction, which takes place when reality is shared beyond words or gestures, is satisfying and usually encourages patients to seek more intimacy outside the office. In short, a therapist must be a person with the highest degree of human consciousness.

Analyzing Therapists

Every year thousands of people leave universities and colleges with MDs in psychiatry or masters in clinical psychology or social work, ready to treat others struggling with life's issues. But to almost all patients, the mental health of their therapists is not known. A degree from an elite school means nothing. If a person does not have a healthy Real Self, he or she cannot help another. The right brain-to-right brain communication will destroy any technique or good intent. You only can teach someone something you are an expert in. The same applies for human consciousness and the Real Self.

A specific case: I know a psychiatrist who is often viewed as one of New York's best in popular magazines. I know this man to be riddled with demons and struggling with a fragile self. Yet, somehow, he is the best in the city. Imagine the cost of an unsuspecting patient who comes to his office for years and pays him $225 per session. But the money and time wasted is nothing compared to patients' lives, which remain empty of self-expression, self-care and self-share.

For more information on how therapists themselves can be hurt children seeking treatment, I recommend reading *The Drama of the Gifted Child* in which Alice Miller discusses many of the concerns one should have when seeing a therapist.

The American Psychiatric Association and other relevant organizations owe it to patients to have all therapists evaluated for their mental health and the capacities of their Real Selves. The time when smart people can use patients to relieve their own demons and struggle by advising others must come to an end. We need therapists whom patients know are operating at the highest level of human consciousness.

ABCDEF of Success Addicts

One of the key goals of therapy is for patients to learn how their minds work so they can know what reality they are dealing with. My cheat sheet is still a work in progress. But here is a checklist I use to understand my behavior throughout the day. I call it the ABCDEF of my mind: A (Admiration), B

(Bubble), C (Contempt), D (Depression), E (Evil Demons) and F (Fantasy Love). When I am not present, my mind's default behavior is to seek Admiration. Admiration to my warped mind means that I am unconditionally loved by a perfect caretaker and that I am safe. Today I try to tell myself that admiration is not real love and that I do not have to work for real love. To be "average, unadmired but cared for" is better than "special, admired and self-sufficient."

When I experience Admiration, I feel I am the Master of my Bubble. The world revolves around me and I am entitled to respect.

When the world frustrates my need for admiration, I feel Contempt for myself. I try to avoid this feeling by seeking more admiration to heal the Bubble. If I fail, I resort to booze, daydreams or fantasies in order to pretend that I am in control. I also can I project the contempt I have for myself onto others. I suddenly feel that I am judging others by how they look or behave. Being contemptuous of others is my mind's way of trying to feel superior in the absence of admiration.

If neither Admiration nor Contempt heals the leak in my Bubble, I must cut off all emotions, sensations and needs. The result: Depression settles in. In the old days I used to say, "I feel numb" or I would just withdraw from the world feeling nothing.

After years of therapy, I can often, but not always, search for the feelings that are causing my Depression. I know I must face my childhood memories, I must face my Evil Demons, especially if they make me feel worthless, angry and helpless. The demons will not kill us. We must learn to feel them since we were not allowed to feel these so-called negative emotions in childhood. Only if we feel them and make them conscious are we set free from our past. Only when we feel our demons can we have empathy for the hurt child within and start to love ourselves. This is a start to loving another and moving away from the idea that of pretending to love.

On days when I prefer to be Depressed and not confront my Evil Demons, I want to keep clinging to the Fantasy that I am and was loved unconditionally. Those are the days when I revert to childlike belief in perfect childhoods, parents and egos. Today I try to tell myself that I can never do anything that will bring unconditional love. Unconditional love never happened. For many plausible reasons, we never were loved for who we were. We performed to find admiration and admiration was a substitute for real love. We must mourn the fantasy and give up hope that unconditional love exists in the world. It does not.

After 11 years of therapy, maps like these give me a fighting chance to bring order to my chaos. To bring order, you need to know where you are.

Play Therapy

Humans have a strong affinity for activities that don't seem to have immediate survival functions: We love to play. Since nature seems to function on the dogma that conservation of energy is important, we must assume that play is not frivolous, but extremely important.

Researchers are debating the role of play. Is it important? Why? What type of play? Do Internet games counts as play? There are many opposing views on these questions, but I believe that play is essential for the simple reason that if it were not, it would have disappeared from our brains. Play in childhood teaches us coordination, social and physical skills, among other things. Play, especially pretend play, helps a child to discover his inner world and develop his imagination. To Einstein, imagination was more important than knowledge. Play is essential for a child to help him discover his interests and hobbies that later will help him find his calling. Some researchers believe all kinds of play allow a child to become more flexible, to see more possibilities in situations he is in, and therefore, to adapt better to what life throw at him. Adaptation is indeed a powerful predictor of survival and personal fulfillment in life. Play researcher, Stuart Brown believes that without play "there's a sense of dullness, lassitude and pessimism, which doesn't work well in the world we live in."

But play also serves another function: A child can use play to express the pain of his childhood. Play may help him to deal with the emotions he is not allowed to show at home; emotions, which if suppressed, will become adult demons. Play can help him tell his story as he is making sense of his life. Play may indeed be a cry for help. The bully at the school is sending very clear messages to teachers: Help me. All is not well at home. I am not respected for who I am. Research suggests that play can indeed help to heal a brain destroyed by trauma. Play can cure.

But play is not only for children.

As much as I believe in therapy with a healthy therapist, so much do I believe a major goal of therapy should be to get people out and playing. I do not know where I would have been today if I did not discover acting, which after all is a form of pretend-play. In addition to acting, playing in my NIA dancing class with fellow dancers, playing with my body and breath in yoga and playing with my computer or pen while writing have helped me to heal. Of all my play activities, my weekly singing class with Jonathan Hart has helped me the most. Jonathan approaches singing not as an activity to reach certain notes, but as an activity to express your non-conscious mind and feelings. I leave class every time feeling full of life. I know my Real Self had a good workout session and had fun. And with fun, comes healing.

Today, I believe in the "talking, feeling and playing cure." All elements are essential for recovery from a past that ignored self-expression in these crucial areas of a child's development.

Chapter 21

Treatment For Our Culture

Our culture is sick and needs treatment. There are two main approaches to the problem: Changing the way we nurture our children and changing our materialistic culture.

Parenting is a sensitive issue and people believe that they have the right to parent their children the way they want to. On so many levels, no one can disagree. But now that we know that certain nurturing choices may lead to killing, addiction, mental illness, sexual abuse or inadequate egomaniacal leaders who destroy people through greed or war, can society really do nothing? Is there a difference from a government strongly advocating for all children to have small pox, measles and rubella vaccines to ensure that diseases from individuals do not turn into epidemics that kill millions? I have no doubt that a government not only has the right, but the obligation to act on behalf of newborn children to ensure the gift of humanity bubbling within them is unlocked by good-enough parenting.

What follows are my own ponderings on how to help parents to help their children. These are only suggestions, made with the hope that the best and brightest of policy makers take them into account.

I propose a program that evaluates mother and child at all the critical moments in the long path from embryo to young adult: during pregnancy, at birth, nine months, two years, four years and adolescence.

Dr. Sarah Berga from Emory University researched the impact of chronic stress on the body. When asked if she believes that chronic stress hurts the fetus, she answered, "I do believe stress on the mother may imprint the fetal genome forever. There is some pretty solid animal research, done by other researchers, and some highly suggestive human studies. Other researchers have shown that stress decreases thyroxine levels, which controls energy availability. The mother is the sole source of thyroxine for the fetus during the first trimester of pregnancy and the major source of thyroxine for the second two trimesters.

And thyroxine is absolutely vital for appropriate fetal brain development. I think doctors should tell women that if the maternal component is stressed, the fetal component will also be exposed to maternal stress hormones."

A stressed traumatized brain in the uterus may never be able to catch up. Our obligation to a child does not start the day he is born. It begins before, by ensuring that mothers are in control of their chronic stress, maybe even before they become pregnant.

Chronic stress in future mothers should be addressed on two levels, societal and individual. Dr. Berga defined chronic stress as the result of a person not being in harmony with herself and her culture. I will tweak it by saying chronic stress is the result of a person not enjoying self-expression, self-share and self-care. A government focusing on its children must first ensure that all social barriers that may prevent all its future mothers from self-expressing, self-sharing and self-caring are removed. After all, we know now that happy parents nurture happy babies. A society focused on its children must first and foremost focus on ensuring equal rights and freedoms, politically, intellectually, sexually, physically and emotionally. The battle for women's rights has come a long way, but it still has a long way to go.

On the individual level, I suggest that all parents, when they find out they are pregnant, be required to undergo tests to assess their level of stress, their attachment styles and their personality types. Prenatal care focusing solely on physical signs and symptoms is not sufficient.

If stress is found to be high, couples should be supported to help them take care of themselves and their children with care and sensitivity. A course in short-term cognitive behavioral therapy to remove stress at home or work would be helpful.

At nine months, all primary caretakers and their babies should be given the Strange Situation Test. This test can easily be done in a doctor's office and should become part of well-baby care. Insecure attachment between primary caretaker and child should result in significant support and care for both caretaker and child.

This test would also be a wonderful tool for professional parents who work full time. Even though studies have shown that children of parents who work full time are as mentally as healthy as children of stay-at-home parents, some children may need more, some may need less. Knowing that a test will show whether parents need to spend more or less time with their children will significantly alleviate many parents' anxieties about how they split their roles as spouse, employee, parent and friend.

At two years of age, at least two tests can be performed to ensure the child is developing control over his mammalian brain and building a healthy Real Self.

A study that assesses a child's ability to delay gratification—one of the most important foundations of humanity and often lacking among Success Addicts—will be important. Researchers designed a study in which they left a child with candy in a room and told him not eat it until the adult comes back. Some children could not control their need for instant gratification and ate the candy without permission. These children were more likely to struggle with numerous tasks than those with control. Such a test easily can be conducted on two-year-olds in any general practice office.

Verbal milestones may also be a sensitive indicator of the health of the Real Self. Children with speech delays and their primary caretakers may need evaluation to make sure that separation between caretaker and child have taken place.

At the age of five, children should be tested for their ability to mentalize. Specifically, the test previously discussed in which a child was asked where his friend would search for the chocolate bar, where the friend thought it was or where the child knew it was, can also be done to see if this milestone has been met.

Finally, if sexual abuse among girls and boys is as high as reported, especially among children under the age of seven, authorities should consider doing spot checks in schools by asking children directly about their sexual experiences. Sex abuse can undermine all the work done in shaping a healthy Real Self.

During their final year at high school, children should be evaluated for their ability to enjoy passions and hobbies, intimacy and the ability to take care of themselves emotionally and physically.

Again, these are suggestions that may make some people concerned about the rights of parents and the role of society. More research into what exactly the government can do is advised.

Screening Childcare Providers

With almost two-thirds of mothers working outside the house since 1980, childcare workers are essential to the mental health of future generations. Gail Collins from *The New York Times* wrote, "For child care workers, the average wage is $8.78 an hour. It's one of the worst-paying career tracks in the country. A preschool teacher with a postgraduate degree and years of experience can make $30,000 a year. You need certification in this country to be a butcher, a barber or a manicurist, but only 12 states require any training to take care of children. Only three require comprehensive background checks. In Iowa, there are 591 child care programs to every one inspector. California inspects child care centers once every five years."

She later quotes Linda Smith, the executive director of Naccrra, who said, "You have a work force that makes $8.78 an hour. They have no training. They have not been background checked, and we've put them in with children who don't have the verbal skills to even tell somebody that they're being treated badly. What is wrong with a country that thinks that's O.K.?"

I have often witnessed how frequently people with severe emotional issues become childcare providers. Often it is people who did not receive proper parenting who grow up wanting to parent others. But good intentions do not translate into good nurturing practices. During moments of conflict, when a child learns to deal with life, these childcare workers will revert to the style they received from their parents. In the process, a child is hurt.

Childcare workers need to receive better background checks than a potential CIA spy. They need to be screened for empathy and ability to mentalize. Fortunately, these skills are equally present in people regardless of income levels. But allowing a person into your nursery who brings her own demons will be disastrous for your child. Add to that the high rate of sexual abuse that children for generations have had to endure from babysitters. Yet many parents are more concerned about whom their tennis or golf coach is and how to make money to ensure they keep up with the Joneses than who the real person is behind the superficial smile and caring attitude toward their children.

Preventative Care

Van den Boom found that a three-month coaching intervention designed to enhance maternal sensitivity responsiveness for irritable six-month-olds and their mothers improved the quality of mother-infant interaction, infant exploration and infant attachment. At the end of the three months of training, mothers were more responsive, stimulating, visually attentive and controlling of their infant's behavior. Infants had higher scores on sociability, self-soothing capacity and exploration, and they cried less. At 12 months the infants who had received the intervention were more securely attached than those who had not received the intervention.

McFarland is a physician-psychohistorian who, after studies showed the strong link between child abuse and violence (both war and social violence), decided to design a program to end child abuse in his city of Boulder, Colorado. He designed an institution called the Community Parenting Centers with the purpose of reaching out to every new baby born and giving parents substantial support in nurturing their babies. His program included "parenting discussion groups, baby massage courses, single mothers assistance, advice on how to raise children without hitting them, how to foster independence, etc." Almost half of parents wanted to have such support at least once a week. McFarlane found that most people want to do good for their children and that "providing this help and hope for parents allowed their underlying affection to replace the abuse and neglect that comes from fear and despair." The program had success. Police and hospital data showed a significant drop in child abuse reports.

McFarlane calculated that a 0.001 percent increase in sales tax could fund every community in the world with a parenting center.

This is negligible if one takes into account what sociologists believe to be "the cost to society of career criminal behavior, drug use and high school dropouts for a single youth is $1.7 to $2.3 million." In addition, imagine the savings, both financial and emotional, if we can prevent future international conflicts caused by contemptuous leaders lacking a healthy Real Self.

Such a program will significantly help a society to reduce its social ills and to increase the level of happiness per capita. However, as we know by now, a culture focused on the mammalian brain goals of admiration and instant gratification will torpedo the health of the Real Self. We need to actively change the culture we live in. This will only happen if we demand that those in power work to create a culture in which our human legacy, not our animal legacy, is celebrated and rewarded.

Improving Literacy

"If there is one thing you wished all teachers did that would significantly improve literacy amongst children from all income levels, what would that be?" I asked Alice Miller, a literacy expert who trains teachers to improve literacy among children.

"I wish that all teachers would change their objective from 'covering the curriculum' to enabling children to find their own voices and discover their personal meaning from what they read, write and learn. In this way children will not only want to motivate themselves to read, write and learn, but will love doing it because it is rewarding, meaningful and personally fullfilling. With this wish, the lessons would be transformed into experiential workshops of discovery learning. The questions posed by the teachers would change from closed-ended ones with preferred right answers (e.g. who, what, when, where type questions) to open-ended questions that allow children to make personal connections to what they read, explore and write about what they want to write about, pose their own questions, and discover how they are transformed by what they read and how they express themselves. In addition, the curriculum would be presented so that it is project-based and meaningful, i.e. very relevant to the children. It would allow them to make meaningful contributions to the school community and the broader community. The assignments would allow children to express what they understand in a variety of ways—not just through language but through music, art, bodily movement, role plays, reflections, with lots and lots of student-student interaction. Co-operative Learning and Differentiated Instruction would be the teaching methods of choice, and there would be lots of interaction between the children and lots of fun. Children would feel accepted and included, have power to influence what they learn and how they learn it, and feel liked by their peers."

After reading this, I realized that Miller is suggesting that we should put the Real Self at the core of education, not in the back corner of the basement as we do today.

Changing our Culture

Our culture must change. We can do all the work to ensure that people have healthy Real Selves, but if the brain washing that is going on through the media, commercials and movies continues, the impact will be minimized.

We need to move away from money, beauty, fame, elite education and romantic love as the measurement of our worth and focus on self-expression, intimacy and self-care. We need to ensure that we move toward a culture that respects both the individual and the group. We need to move away from the selfishness found in our society and toward the selfless dedication to making the world a better place for everybody. We need to stop celebrating our animal brain instincts and needs, and focus on our human legacy and values.

For this to take place, we need to remove leaders who are struggling with demons and living in grandiose bubbles. We need to make sure the best and the most humane are accepted into the best schools and most powerful of jobs. We need to make sure that we pay those whose work serves humanity more than those who serve their own greed. We need to stop being brainwashed by the media, commercials and movies. We need to alter our schools to focus on the right brain instead of the left.

How?

That is the exciting part of starting the 21st century. No one knows, but there is a consensus worldwide that things need to change if we want to save the planet and our children's futures.

Epilogue

No Hollywood Ending

A few major events happened to me over the last month.

Dr. Masterson, the psychiatrist who supported my journey from a stuck and stuck-up medical doctor, confused Yale graduate student and lonely New Yorker to a man who knows what my passions are in life, had to retire from practice.

During our final session—neither of us knew that it would be our last—he uncharacteristically shared some of the sad moments in his life. He treated me like an equal. But for no simple reason: I finally felt his equal. Not in terms of success or knowledge, but in terms of being a man with a strong enough Real Self to treat others with respect and honesty. Gone was my need to see him as perfect, to put him on a pedestal and to please him so that he could admire me for my goodness, success and achievements. After 11 years of therapy, my non-conscious brain knew better: If I wanted warmth, care and respect, I had to be myself. Whether happy or sad, confident or helpless, full of life or sharing my suicidal thoughts, I had to express what I truly feel, not what I think he wanted to hear. After many years of depending on his Real Self to support mine, I was finally ready to leave the nest.

On my way out of the office that day, he said, "Enjoy your end of the book party tomorrow night. You worked hard for it. I'll be thinking of you tomorrow evening. You deserve a good time."

As always, he showed himself to be the best supporter of my passions I have ever had. But never once in 11 years did he give me advice or tell me what my passions should be. With rare exceptions, we never spoke about science or his legacy in the field of psychiatry, which by any comparison is enormous. All he ever mentioned about his work was his love for what he does. "I would still have a full practice if I was stronger," he mentioned to me a few weeks before the illness forced his retirement.

As for my passions, he never told me what to write, when to write, not even that I must write. He just kept to his motto: watch, wonder and wait for the Real Self to give birth to itself. He, like me, had no inkling that my passions would turn out to be acting, directing and writing. For 11 years, he would be there for me and my journey to discover my Real Self: on time; dressed in a tie and jacket; strict but empathetic; open and honest; supportive for my helplessness and confusion as well as my baby steps into self-expression.

When I received the call from Nancy, his assistant for many decades, that he would not practice again, I was weak from rigors and night-sweats from a streptococcal infection. But for some reason, the news did not throw me into a massive panic. "Maybe I am too weak to panic," I reasoned.

A few days later I was completing a children's story I had written for my only niece, Celeste. *Lulu, the Lioness* is the coming of age story of a little lion cub that had to leave her parents and her past to find the Great One. After many travails, she meets an old lion that tells her that he knows where to find the Great One. At first, Lulu is not impressed. But later she becomes fond of the old lion and, thanks to him, she discovers her passion for singing. She even meets and falls in love with a very average lion, a far less successful lion than Prince Ralph, who she was planning to marry. One day, she comes across the remains of the old lion. When she realizes that the old lion is dead, she does not panic or cry. Then, out of nowhere, she hears the old lion talking to her. After a while, she realizes that the voice is coming from inside her. She discovers that the old lion, the Great One and all other animals are inside of her, part of her.

I wrote to my brother Andre, "How ironic that, with the sudden departure of my shrink, I should finish this story. Now I also feel I have the old lion within me."

A View to the Future

During this period, I took a directing class with Karen Kohlaas, a founding member of the Atlantic Acting School. For my final scene, performed in public, I chose Arthur Miller's *A View From the Bridge.* I auditioned actors for the role, enjoyed the scene analysis, conducted rehearsals with novelty and a sense of play. The cast of five people wonderfully came together as an ensemble.

On Sunday, June 7, the day before our public performance, I called a rehearsal for 9 a.m. One cast member was nowhere to be found. Instead of panicking or getting angry, I kept saying to myself, "Happy accidents, happy accidents." I remained flexible to the new reality and asked the other cast members to talk about their wants for a scene. It soon became clear that one actor was stuck in her head. After a most riveting and vulnerable performance the day before, she had shrunk into her shell. She was intellectualizing her answers, not feeling them. Since I know this defense mechanism well, I was able to let her understand that I had no expectation for her to be emotionally where she was the day before. In many ways, I was telling her that as a director I will only watch, wonder and wait to see what her artist wants to show the world that day. She responded to the assurance.

At 11 a.m., I called another rehearsal. There was no one else in the room besides the five actors and me. For 20 minutes, I was in awe of the humanity they showed through their characters. They were all funny, impulsive, vulnerable and intimate. My body reacted with joy, with sadness, even with fear as I felt the drama inside the home of Eddie Carbone. I would have paid $500 for that seat that day. But the biggest victory of all was that I felt happy, so incredibly happy, for just being present in that moment.

Afterwards, I went to a coffee shop. As I reflected on the rehearsal, tears of joy hindered my vision. I did not mind that I was teary eyed in a very public place. Not bad for a man who thought he could not cry and that he had to be cool, calm and collected every day of his life. I also did not require any form of admiration from anyone: not the actors, critics or an audience. I finally felt I was good-enough not for who I am, but for what the actors and I had created, all while having so much fun. My feeling good-enough did not last, but it sure gave me a conscious and non-conscious memory that already is helping me to see the future as a bit more positive.

A Call to My Parents

A week ago, I called up my parents. "I want to ask you a favor. I want you two to sit down and tell me the three things you did to us as kids in our first three years in life that you felt was positive and what three things you would do differently," I said. I didn't have a single butterfly. Years ago, I had many sleepless nights before I told them that I was seeing a shrink. I felt I was betraying them by asking for professional help. Their initial reaction was not positive, to say the least.

Today, 11 years later, we talked about the past as if it was a rugby match we were analyzing. This did not change overnight. There was a long period of time when I broke off all communication with my parents. I had to find my voice and I knew that contact with the past would keep me stranded. No one understood the extreme measures I took. Everyone at one point tried to talk me out of my actions. Somehow I had the courage to persist.

Honor thy mother and father has haunted me for the longest time. I thought to honor them meant that I had to listen to their wishes, commands and advice. After all, they mean well. But today I know—to honor your parents is to become the most you can become. To honor your parents is to spread your wings and fly away. To honor your parents is to give yourself advice on what to do with your life.

Some parents will applaud, some will revolt, some will disown. But that is not our problem. It is theirs. It is not our duty to take care of our parents and live out their dreams for us. It is our duty to find our own dreams.

My battles with my parents led to the biggest reward of all: a caring relationship of mutual respect with my parents. Understanding my childhood brought a new way of seeing and appreciating those I call "mother" and "father." With my Hell and Heaven DVD edited, I see real people, not projected fantasies. Today, I love my parents more than ever before. I see their unique humanity, their pain, their dreams, their regrets. I laugh with pleasure when I hear their voices over the phone. I know time with them is limited and precious. Lately, I have found their voices richer, their laughs deeper and their enjoyment of life fuller. There are many reasons. But maybe the biggest gift we can give our parents is to oppose them and by doing so, free them from their own misperceptions of who they should be, what love and what the role of a parent is.

Even if this was not the outcome, I had no option but to stand up for who I am and what I wanted to become. If this had resulted in my parents rejecting me and refusing to speak to me ever again, I know the joy of living for my Real Self would have far exceeded the pain.

Life is too short to live it for one's parents.

Understanding Drama

Over the last month, my gut told me to reread Alice Miller's book *The Drama of the Gifted Child* before my book went to the printer. I opened my copy. On the title page, I read:

September 24, 1997: Dear Pierre, Just another tool for your lifelong journey(s). After reading this book (and it deserves more than just one reading) you will be a little bit closer to understanding yourself and those around you. What better gift could there be? Thank you for being almost as crazy as I am (and I mean that in the best way possible). All the best, always, Nikki.

A fellow Yale MBA graduate gave me the book almost 12 years ago. I recalled how I felt slightly angered by her comment that I was a bit crazy. "After all, I am perfect, ain't I? How dare she!" my conscious mind had screamed.

Nikki was wrong on two accounts. First, I turned out to be a bit crazier than she claimed to be herself. Secondly, reading the book did not help me understand me or the people around me. I recall reading the book twice after Nikki gave it to me. I understood the theory, but still it had no impact on my life. I first had to feel the demons of my past before I could feel the wisdom captured by the book. But the book did have one major effect: It help me realize I needed professional help.

Goodbye Therapy

For three and a half years, this book was my best friend, my lover, my baby, my pet, my everything. Therapy and writing this book stood between me and emotional disaster. Soon I will be without both. My logical mind informed me: "This is not good. You need continuity of something. Find a therapist who Dr. Masterson had trained." So I listened. But after I visited a therapist in his institute, I hesitated. I somehow felt I had enough of searching my non-conscious mind for answers. It was time to let go of the idea that I need to remember everything that had happened to me before I can live. I have put in my pound of sweat and tears, and now it is time to leave the psychological prison of the past and test my Real Self in the real adult world.

"There is no doubt I still have many, many dangerous demons that are still creating havoc in my love life. Maybe they always will block me from finding true love. I may have to make peace with that sad fact," I told myself with sadness, but not with despair.

But something interesting happened. The more I tried to make peace with not being perfect, but instead an ordinary, unique man in love with the theater who harbors a hurt child that needs special care, the more I began having hope that I may find real love. By accepting my childhood pain, I have hope that there may be a woman out there who will accept me for who I really am, a woman who will have fun with my Real Self, a woman who can sooth my hurt child.

In addition to *The Drama of the Gifted Child*, my gut suggested that I study an article that appeared in the *The New York Times Magazine* in February, 2008, simply titled, "Taking Play Seriously?" I suspect that my non-conscious wants me to write that we should change from a culture of success to a culture of play. But two studies caught my attention. My mind went, "Bingo!"

Two different researchers conducted two separate experiments on rats. In one study, they compared the brains of juvenile rats deprived from play with rats that had unlimited play time. They discovered that the prefrontal cortex of the play-deprived rats was more immature in their connections than those of the rats that played to their brain's content. (The prefrontal cortex of the rat is a tiny version of the more complex human brain.)

In another study, scientists damaged the right prefrontal cortex of rats and compared their behavior to rats that had surgery but no damage done to the brain. The result: The brain-damaged rats showed increased signs of hyperactivity. One should not be surprised: In humans, this brain gives us future-mindedness, focus and the ability to read social clues.

But then the researchers did something else: They allowed the brain-damaged rats to play one hour extra than the control group. The result: Playing for an extra hour a day allowed the damaged brain to recover!

I believe that those of us who became Success Addicts so early in our lives never fully developed our right human brain to its full potential. Like the rats deprived of play, we were deprived of playing the way we wanted to play. As a result, in addition to excess cortisol, our right human brain never fully developed. But here is the good news: extra play can help us heal our own brain.

This dovetailed with the advice Alice Miller gave in the Afterword of her book: We do not have to understand or discover all the traumas of the past in therapy. We too can discover much about ourselves by being in loving relationships or by doing what brings us happiness. Play can cure humans. But herein lies the trick: It only will heal if we have a strong enough Real Self to tell us our passions and allow us to play with abandon. We also need to feel the demons that prevent us from playing in order for us to know how to deal with them. Without the years of struggle under the competent, watchful and caring eye of Dr. Masterson, I never would have developed the real "I" inside my right human brain or the conscious map of how to deal with my demons. I believe that I am finally ready to take the real me into the real world to play.

Seeing the Past

I wish I could go back to my youth with the real me I know today. I wish I could go back to my grandmother's farm in Africa and hear the sound of Sotho voices in the kitchen and the smell of coffee and Matabele porridge. I wish I could go back and jump into the small swimming pool overlooking the Maluti mountains, feel the cold water burn my skin, jump out and lie on the warm cobbled stones baked by the African sun. I wish I could go back and take the time to truly taste the apricots and peaches from the orchard, or the ice cream made from milk that Charlie had retrieved from the cow at 5 a.m. I wish I could go back to all the servants on that farm and at our home and tell them what they meant to me. And thank them.

I wish I could go back and fall madly and silly in love every summer holiday at the beach. I wish I could go back and scream at those friends who betrayed me. I wish I could go back and be the one in the classroom making the most noise, not the one adhering to every single rule, or even worse, enforcing the rule as head prefect. I wish I could go back and appreciate the humanity of so many of my classmates that I never saw, blinded by my drive to be the best. I wish I could go back and learn to play the piano at an early age. I wish I could go back and give my childhood dog, FEPA, the food he always begged from me rather than pushing him away for invading my space. I wish I could go back and laugh deeply and often at the folly of being a careless child prone to many mistakes as I learn to love learning and failing. I wish I could go back and watch my brothers play rugby as little boys and cheer them on or play tennis with them and argue vehemently that the ball was out, when I knew it was in. I wish I could go back and be a normal horny teenager and chase every skirt I saw. I wish I could go back and on Saturday afternoons watch rugby with my father at Newlands and share his indignation at the referee. I wish I could go back and talk freely and passionately to my mother while eating her freshly baked cheese scones and drinking her Rooi Rose tea on a rainy winter's afternoon at Plettenberg Street 80 in Cape Town, my childhood home. Oh, if only I could go back. But I can't. It's over. Forever gone.

Still, I have found, that the stronger my Real Self is becoming, the easier I can appreciate all the good that has happened to me in the past. I even can enjoy the intimacy others offered to me at a time when I could not receive people's gracious gifts of vulnerability and care. I can go back and see the world with a Real Self much more attuned to the world and all its wonders. After all, time is a human brain concept. But our emotional and sensorial experiences encoded in our memories are not stuck in time. They live in us. They are us. With a strong Real Self, we can transport ourselves to a memory and relish the moments we missed. It is important to cherish what we can of past experiences; but it's even more important to focus on the here and now.

Today

Today, small things matter to me. The sound of the water complaining after a ferryboat disturbed its calm. The crooked teeth and joyful eyes of a three-year-old girl as she clumsily and fearfully skates in her Rangers outfit for the first time at Rockefeller Center. The late winter sun painting the white clouds with colors I can't even begin to describe. The sun stroking my face on an early spring afternoon. Beethoven's Ninth Symphony at Avery Fisher Hall, transforming my body with every sigh and every note. The oxtail gnocchi at my favorite Italian restaurant on Thompson Street. Five hours of a cheese and wine party with friends miraculously evaporating into one second of conversation. The flow of creative energy passing through me on stage. My body moving freely and joyfully to music in my NIA dancing class. The warm body of a passionate woman lying next to me in the mornings. My words of "I love you" to my parents and my brothers, not out of guilt or duty, but out of love for their unique humanity and for what they mean to me. Hearing "I love you" back. The joy in my parents' voices after a vacation in Paris. My brother Etienne making a birdie on the golf course. My brother Andre taking care of his children. My brother Francois with tears of farewell in his eyes. Ordinary moments. Ordinary moments I couldn't appreciate as an overachiever. Ordinary moments I lost while chasing success and admiration. Ordinary moments that are extraordinarily important in the new chapter of my life.

The Future

This is not a Hollywood ending, but it is the beginning of life in the real world. The future looms with its uncertainty. Will I live until I'm crooked with age, or die young now that I am finally starting to enjoy a full life? Will I be able to enjoy progressively more ordinary moments than the few I do now? Will I pursue my career as an actor, writer and director with courage, or give in as obstacles, both inner and outer, keep pushing me back into my shell? Will I overcome my fear of commitment and marry a sincere and mature woman, or will I continue to struggle with lonely Friday evenings, unavailable pretty princesses and fantasies of The Perfect Woman? Will I have the opportunity to love my own children, or will I look for the rest of my life at other people's children and wonder "what if?" Or, even worse, have children and fail in helping them to enjoy their uniqueness in love, in work and in play? Will I survive the moments when life pushes me to my limits? Moments natural to living a full life. Moments of failure. Moments of rejection. Moments of pain. Moments of loss. Moments of standing next to the graves of people I love and whom I never ever will see again. Moments of seeing my own approaching death. Moments when theory flies out the window, raw emotions rule and the real me is left alone to batter the onslaught. Will I then give in to homicidal rage, unethical behavior, alcohol or suicide? Or will I stand up and defend our human legacy of wisdom, love, temperance, transcendence, justice and courage?

With a stronger Real Self and a slight grip on reality, I have a shot. But there are no guarantees. It is life after all.

The real me. A life of reality. Two amazing gifts.

Acknowledgements

There are three people without whom this book would not have been possible.

Dr. James Masterson, to whom the book is dedicated, was my guide as I journeyed into my mind. But his contribution to my mental health started even before I was born. By following his passion for the human mind and for helping patients, Dr. Masterson became a pioneer researcher in the causes and treatment of people struggling with an impaired self. Before his contribution to the field, people like me had almost no chance at a full life. For 11 years as my therapist, his supportive and guiding hand helped me to crawl through the demons of my mind. He became a staunch supporter of my search for my passion. Not once did he tell me what I had to do. When I finally found my passions, he sometimes was the only one in the room cheering my doubtful self. But most important of all was knowing that he was on my side, especially on days when I felt that all of life is against me. Thanks to Dr. Masterson, I today have a shot at a full life. How do you thank someone for such a gift?

Over the last three years, my brother Andre paid my way as I followed my journey into my mind and into this book. There were days where my financial woes mimicked my psychological woes, days where my hold on life felt precarious. Then, out of nowhere, I would find money transferred into my bank account. Not once over the last three and a half years did he ever mention money to me, except to know if I needed more. But my gratitude goes beyond what the money allowed me to do. It was the faith he had in me that I would finish this book that filled my emotional vaults. Financial resources, faith and brotherly love go a long way on lonely tortured writing days. Baie dankie, Andre.

Through serendipity, I met Rebecca Wilson, my editor. A mutual friend described her as the best and smartest copy editor she had ever worked with. The friend was wrong: Rebecca turned out to be even better than that. Not only is she a magician with the English language, but her keen insight and interest in humanity and her willingness to challenge my theories strengthened the book considerably. But her contributions went beyond editing: She cared about the book and me. She was there when I had to bounce off ideas, whether it was on the title, subtitle, cover design or some days just needing to hear that a tough chapter turned out good-enough. You can see her wonderful fingerprints all over this book.

My parents, Pieter and Christy, my other two brothers, Etienne and Francois, my sisters-in-law, Ina-marie and Sylma, and my uncle Andre were of great support over the last few years. Their interest in the book, suggestions on titles, and reading of drafts all helped to keep my emotional fuel filled. And thank you for not once saying, "When are you going to get a proper job!"

A big thanks to all three of my brothers for wonderful vacations and golf games together. Thanks for always picking up the tab, for the smiles and for being such amazing siblings.

I had many people who had to struggle through earlier drafts, drafts that resembled the confusion of my searching mind. Thank you to Luc Marest, Michael Small, Simon Roberts, Martina Swart, Max, Brenda, Pablo and Maria Calo, Joanna Miller, Dennis and Eileen Heaphy.

Thank you to Christina Antonakos-Wallace for the perfect cover design for this book about the imperfections of humanity.

Thank you to my friends in South Africa who attended a speech I made on the topics covered in this book. To all who called on dark Sunday afternoons just to say hi, especially Stephan van Dijk. To all who directly or through their interest in my theories told me to keep going. To the people from 300 Mercer who always asked after my progress: Max, Frankie, Dino and Freddie. To all who came to my party to celebrate my last day of writing. To all the students I learned from in acting and singing classes. To all my acting, writing, singing and dancing teachers who taught me so much about humanity and the human mind.

Finally, I am grateful to all the researchers, artists, writers and thinkers whose passion for our humanity shaped my theories on life and the human mind. Your work fills the pages of the book. I just hope that I have done your work justice and have given you the credit you deserve.

Appendix

Appendix A

Science, Primary Caretakers and Children

As with many of medicine's most important findings, the role primary caretakers play in the mental health of their children was discovered by chance. In 1949, John Bowlby, a British psychiatrist and psychoanalyst, observed that infants, when forced to separate for a long period of time from their parents during hospitalization, went through a number of changes. The infants protested and showed signs of wishing a reunion with the primary caretaker. When their wish was frustrated, the infants experienced despair. When despair did not result in reunion, the infants detached from all relationships. Separation from the primary caretaker forever and negatively changed the relationship between parents and child.

Ainsworth took Bowlby's observations further and designed the "strange situation" test to assess the strength of a primary caretaker/child relationship. A caregiver and infant are placed in a room, a stranger enters, all three stay in the room, then the primary caretaker leaves, comes back and leaves again. Throughout the test, the infant's reactions are closely observed and documented based on an attachment rating system. A child's reaction shows how he copes with separation from and reunion with his caregiver.

Her research showed that there are four main types of attachment styles between a primary caretakers and child: secure, dismissive, resistant-ambivalent and disorganized. A happy secure primary caretaker/child relationship leads to a securely attached infant who misses his primary caretaker when she leaves for the first time. Upon return, he greets her actively, crawls to her immediately and requests to be held. After brief intimate contact, the child settles down and returns to play. When the primary caretaker leaves the second time, he cries, but upon reunion again settles down after a period. This child knows implicitly that his primary caretakers are there for him; he feels secure in their love.

Attachment Among Adults

So researchers asked the question: are the four relationships between a primary caretakers and children similar to those found among adults? In the mid-1980s, researchers designed an 18-question questionnaire, called the

Adult Attachment Interview (AAI) to evaluate an adult's attitude toward all relationships (family and non-family).

Some sample questions from the AAI are:

- I'd like you to choose five adjectives that reflect your childhood relationship with your parents. This might take some time, and then I'm going to ask you why you chose them.
- To which parent did you feel closest and why? Why isn't there this feeling with the other parent?
- When you were upset as a child, what would you do?
- What is the first time you remember being separated from your parents? How did you and they respond?

All the data was then judged by four criteria to assess ideal rational discourse: Was a person's response truthful with ample evidence for what was said (quality); was it succinct and yet complete (quantity); was it relevant to the topic at hand (relevance); was it clear and orderly (manner).

Based on the data, they were able to group participants into four categories: secure, dismissive, preoccupied and disorganized. Specifically, secure-attachment adults talked coherently, objectively and openly about past relationships, value all intimate relationships, remember the good and the bad of their relationships, remember it with detail and can continue to appreciate the other person regardless how they are feeling.

The way we relate to each other as adults shows similar patterns to those that exist between parents and baby.

Primary Caretakers and Our Adult Relationships

Researchers then asked: Does how we relate with our primary caretakers in the first few years in life determine how we relate to all people later in life? Is the man indeed still the boy?

Study after study shows that teachers and observers judge children with secure attachment styles to have higher self-esteem, to be more self-reliant and to be more flexible in the management of their impulses and feelings. In middle childhood and adolescence, those with histories of secure attachment carry forward patterns of effective emotional regulation. The reverse is true too. Insecure attachment histories (i.e. dismissive, ambivalent and disorganized) lead to "problem kids" at some or all of the major milestones that children face. Attachment theories made the clear link that how we relate to our primary caretaker in childhood becomes the predominant way in which we relate to all people in life, even to life itself. Specifically, secure infants become secure adults, avoidant infants become dismissive adults and resistant infants become preoccupied adults.

We see the world and other people through the mind of our primary caretakers.

Happy Primacy Caretakers, Happy Babies

Researcher then asked: Can one predict how a baby-turned-adult interacts with the world by assessing how a primary caretaker interacts with others even *before* the child is born? Do secure primary caretakers have secure babies who become secure adults?

In the early nineties, Peter Fonagy, a major child development researcher, using the AAI interview, assessed the attachment styles of 96 primary mothers before the birth of their children. 12 months after the births of their babies, he tested the babies using the "strange room" test. He found a 75 percent correspondence between the rating of the primary caretakers and the rating of the child.

Researchers also found a strong correlation between primary caretakers with an insecure attachment style and children diagnosed with failure to thrive, sleep disorders, behavior problems, developmental delays, conduct disorders, ADHD (to a lesser extent), borderline and dysthymic patients.

Unhappy parents have a high likelihood of having unhappy babies.

Appendix B

The National Institute of Child Health and Human Development used survey questions to determine positive caregiving among caretakers that is based on direct observations of caregiver behavior. Positive caregiving behaviors include:

- Showing a positive attitude—is the caregiver generally in good spirits and encouraging when interacting with the child? Is he or she helpful? Does the caregiver smile often at the child?
- Having positive physical contact—Does the caregiver hug the child, pat the child on the back, or hold the child's hand? Does the caregiver

comfort the child?

- Responding to vocalizations—Does the caregiver repeat the child's words, comment on what the child says or tries to say and answer the child's questions?
- Asking questions—Does the caregiver encourage the child to talk/communicate by asking questions that the child can answer easily, such as "yes" or "no" questions, or asking about a family member or toy?
- Talking in other ways—such as:
- Praising or encouraging—Does the caregiver respond to the child's positive actions with positive words, such as "You did it!" or "Well done!"?
- Teaching—Does the caregiver encourage the child to learn or have the child repeat learning phrases or items, such as saying the alphabet out loud, counting to 10, and naming shapes or objects? For older children, does the caregiver explain what words or names mean?
- Telling and singing—Does the caregiver tell stories, describe objects or events, or sing songs?
- Encouraging development—Does the caregiver help the child to stand up and walk? For infants, does the caregiver encourage "tummy time"—activities the child does when placed on his or her stomach while awake—to help neck and shoulder muscles get stronger and to encourage crawling? For older children, does the caregiver help finish puzzles, stack blocks or zip zippers?
- Advancing behavior—Does the caregiver encourage the child to smile, laugh and play with other children? Does the caregiver support sharing between the child and other children? Does the caregiver give examples of good behaviors?
- Reading—Does the caregiver read books and stories to the child? Does the caregiver let the child touch the book and turn the page? For older children, does the caregiver point to pictures and words on the page?

Eliminating negative interactions—Does the caregiver make sure to be positive, not negative, in the interactions with the child? Does the caregiver take a positive approach to interacting with the child, even in times of trouble? Does the caregiver make it a point to interact with the child and not ignore him or her?

Bibliography

Bibliography

Books

Albom, Mitch. Tuesday With Morrie (New York: Double Day, 1997)

Amen, Daniel G. Healing the Hardware of the Soul (New York: The Free Press, 2002)

Benson, Nigel C. Introducing Psychology (Cambridge, UK: Icon Books, 1999)

Csikszentmihalyi, Mihaly. Flow (New York: HarperCollins Publishers, 1990)

DeMause, Lloyd. The Emotional Life of Nations (New York: Other Press, 2002)

Fast, Julius. Body Language (New York: Pocket Books, 1970)

Flaherty, James. Coaching (Burlington, MA: Elsevier Science, 1999)

Gilbert, Daniel. Stumbling on Happiness (New York: Random House, 2006)

Gladwell, Malcoldm. Blink. (New York: Little, Brown and Company, 2005)

Gottman, John M. Marital Therapy: A Research-Based Approach. (Seattle: The Gottman Institute, 2004)

Greenberg, Leslie S. Emotion-Focused Therapy (Washington, D.C.:APA, 2002)

Haidt, Jonathan. The Happiness Hypothesis (New York: Basic Books, 2006)

Helen Fisher. Why we Love? (New York: Henry Holt and Company, 2004)

Maccoby, Michael. The Productive Narcissist (New York: Broadway Books, 2003)

Masterson, James. The Personality Disorders (Phoenix: Zeig, Tucker & Co., 2000)

Masterson, James. The Personality Disorders Through the Lens of Attachment Theory and the Neurobiologic Development of the Self (Phoenix: Zeig, Tucker & Co., 2000)

Masterson, James. The Search for the Real Self (New York: The Free Press, 1990)

Miller, Alice. The Drama of the Gifted Child (New York; Basic Books, 1997)

O'Neil, Eugene. Long Day's Journey into Night (New York: Yale University, 1989)

Rothkopf, David. SuperClass (New York: Farrar, Straus and Giroux, 2008)

Seligman, Martin E.P. Authentic Happiness (New York: The Free Press, 2002)

Website

Dubuc, Bruno, The Brain from Top to Bottom, www.thebrain.mcgill.ca

Articles

Aamodt, Sandra and Wang, Sam (2008). Tighten Your Belt, Strengthen Your Mind. The New York Times.

Allen, Eugenie (2006) Harvard or Bust. The New York Times

Allen, Jon G. (2003). Mentalizing. The Meninger Foundation.

Angier, Natalie (2009). In a Helpless Baby, the Roots of Our Social Glue. Harvard Business Review

Anthonissen, Kobus (2009) Massamense. Die Burger

Baldauf, Sarah (2007). Why Affluent, High-Achieving Teens Are Often Depressed. US News and World Report.

Belluck, Pam. (2009). Yes, Looks Do Matter. The New York Times.

Bergner, Daniel (2009). What is Female Desire? The New York Times Magazine

Blumenthal, Ralph. (2009). If Bernie Met Dante... The New York Times.

Brooks, David (2008) The Behavioral Revolution. The New York Times.

Brooks, David (2008). The Great Seduction. The New York Times.

Brooks, David (2008). The Luxurious Growth. The New York Times.

Brooks, David (2008). The Neural Buddhists. The New York Times.

Brooks, David (2009). An Economy of Faith and Trust. The New York Times.

Brooks, David (2009). Greed and Stupidity. The New York Times.

Brooks, David (2009). Harmony and The Dream. The New York Times.

Brooks, David (2009). I Dream Of Denver. The New York Times.

Brooks, David (2009). The Commercial Republic. The New York Times

Brooks, David (2009). The Empathy Issue. The New York Times.

Brooks, David (2009). The End of Philosophy. The New York Times.

Brophy, Gwenda (2008). 'You feel a city in your heart and soul' Financial Times

Carey, Benedict (2008). Making Sense of the Great Suicide Debate. The New York Times

Carey, Benedict (2009). After Abuse, Changes in the Brain. The New York Times

Carey, Benedict (2009). For the Brain, Remembering Is Like Reliving. The New York Times.

Carey, Benedict (2009). Hold Your Head Up. A Blush Just Show You Care. The New York Times.

Carey, Benedict. (2009). At the Bridge Table, Clues to a Lucid Old Age. The New York Times.

Carter, Stephen L. (2009). We're Not 'Cowards,' We're Just Loud. The New York Times.

Casey, Maura (2008). Digging Out Roots of Cheating in High School. The New York Times.

Cohen, Patricia (2008) Midlife Suicide Rises, Puzzling Researchers. The New York Times.

Conley, Dalton (2008). Rich Man's Burden. The New York Times

Coontz, Stephanie. (2009) Till Children Do Us Part. The New York Times.

Dolnick, Edward. (2009) Fish or Foul. The New York Times.

Doskoch, Peter (2008). The Winning Edge. PscyhologyToday.

Garner, Dwight. (2009). If You Think You're Good, You Should Think Again. The New York Times.

Gilbert, Daniel (2009). What You Don't Know Makes You Nervous. The New York Times.

Gladwell, Malcolm (2008). Late Bloomers. The New York Times.

Gordon, James (2009). For Gaza Psychologist, Hope Amid Despair. The New York Times.

Jay, Rickey (2009). Desperately Seeking Susan. The New York Times.

Kirn, Walter (2009). The Gentle Art of Getting Ahead. The Washington Post.

Kristof, Nicholas D. (2009). Humanity Even For Nonhumans. The New York Times.

Kristof, Nicholas D. (2009). Would You Slap Your Father? If So, You're a Liberal. The New York Times.

Leake, Jonathan (2009). Wealthy men give women more orgasms. The New York Times.

Lehrer, Jonah (2008). Decision Time. BBC News

Lohr, Steve (2009). Crème de la Career. The New York Times.

Ludeman, Kate and Erlandson, Eddie (2004). Coaching the Alpha Male. Harvard Business Review

Maccoby, Michael (2004). The Power of Transference. Harvard Business Review

Marantz Henig, Robin (2008). Taking Play Seriously. The New York Times Magazine.

Nussbaum, Emily (2007). Say Everything. New York Magazine.

Parker-Pope, Tara (2008). Colleges High Cost, Before You Even Apply. The New York Times.

Parker-Pope, Tara (2009). What Are Friends For? A Longer Life. The New York Times.

Rosen, Christine (2008). The Myth of Multitasking. The New York Times.

Senior, Jennifer (2008). The Loneliness Myth. New York Magazine.

Smith, Dinitia (2009). Slippery Hitching Posts: Upheaval in an Institution Based Stability. The New York Times.

Spreier, Scott, Fontaine, Mary and Malloy, Ruth (2006) Leadership Run Amok Harvard Business Review

Tierney, John (2009). Message in What We Buy, But Nobody's Listening. The New York Times.

Wang, Sam and Aamodt, Sandra (2008). Your Brain Lies to You. The New York Times.

Weingarten, Gene (2009). Violinist in the Metro. The Washington Post.

WolfShenk, Joshua (2009). What Makes Us Happy? The Atlantic.

Zimbardo, Philip (2007). When Good People Do Evil. Yale Alumni Magazine.

Printed in the United States
151100LV00001B/66/P

9 781615 843756